MW00806191

THEOCRITUS
SELECT POEMS

THEOCRITUS
SELECT POEMS

Edited with Introduction and Commentary by
Sir Kenneth J. Dover

Bolchazy-Carducci Publishers

(by arrangement with Macmillan Education Ltd.)

Introduction and Commentary
©K.J. Dover, 1971

1994
Printed in the United States of America

International Standard Book Number
0-86516-204-2

Bolchazy-Carducci Publishers

1000 Brown Street, Unit 101
Wauconda, IL 60084 USA

First published by Macmillan Education Ltd., 1971
Reprinted, with minor corrections, by permission of
Macmillan Education Ltd., 1985 and 1987.

Preface

THE scenes and events which Theokritos portrays are not as a rule complicated or obscure, nor are the sentiments which he expresses profound. The difficulties which his poems present to the learner arise from his dialect (strikingly unfamiliar, at first sight, to anyone whose acquaintance with Greek poetry is limited to Homer and Attic Tragedy), from his very large vocabulary (which includes many zoological and botanical names), from the wealth of literary allusion to archaic and classical poetry which his motifs and phrases offer, and (this fourth difficulty is closely related to the third) from our constantly recurring uncertainty about what we might call the 'emotional temperature' of any given passage. The purpose of my Introduction and Commentary is to help the learner (in the sixth form, at university, or later in life) to read Theokritos for the first time; that is to say, to help him to understand what the Greek *means*, not only in terms of translation from one language into another but also in terms of literary, mythological, ethical and sensory associations. I have not made, and I do not pretend to have made, a serious contribution to the study of Hellenistic poetry at the level to which the work of experts in that field has accustomed us. In particular, I am aware that in respect of the series of interesting and difficult stylistic problems with which

Theokritos presents us I have not gone very far below the surface.

In excluding certain poems I have been guided in part by aesthetic judgment, in part by the evidence for and against authenticity. These two criteria are for the most part in harmony with each other and have led me in the same direction as the majority of scholars; in the Epigrams, however, my purpose has been to present only material which in some significant respect differs from that of the major poems. I recommend a learner who does not have time to read all eighteen of the major poems on which I have commented to give priority to I, II, V, VII, XI and XV.

I have furnished my text with a brief apparatus criticus, in the belief that although the learner should not be swamped with textual problems of a comparatively trivial nature he should certainly be warned when the printed text before his eyes is significantly different from what the surviving manuscripts of the work actually say.

The name of Mr. A. S. F. Gow will not be found very often in my book. This is because I am so deeply indebted to his edition and commentary — as anyone must be who has written anything on Theokritos since 1950 — that adequate acknowledgment on passage after passage is hardly practicable; I must content myself with the general acknowledgment that his work is the base, wisely planned and lavishly stocked, without which I would not have ventured on this foray. I am deeply indebted to Professor Thomas Rosenmeyer for allowing me to read his book on pastoral poetry in advance of publication, and to

Mr. Malcolm Campbell, who read the Introduction and Commentary in draft and offered acute and helpful criticisms; all responsibility for errors of fact or judgment is mine.

St. Andrews   K. J. DOVER
December 1969

Contents

Bibliography

1. Fragments of Greek authors are cited (unless otherwise specified) from the following editions:

Aischylos: H. J. Mette (Berlin, 1959)

Alkaios: E. Lobel and D. L. Page, *Poetarum Lesbiorum Fragmenta* (Oxford, 1955)

Aristophanes: T. Kock, *Comicorum Atticorum Fragmenta* (Leipzig, 1880–1888); the numbering in the Oxford Classical Text is the same.

Bacchylides: B. Snell (Teubner edition)

Epicharmos: G. Kaibel, *Comicorum Graecorum Fragmenta* (Berlin, 1899)

Euripides: A. Nauck, *Tragicorum Graecorum Fragmenta* (ed. 2, Leipzig, 1889; reprinted with a supplement, 1964)

Hesiod: R. Merkelbach and M. L. West (Oxford, 1967)

Kallimachos: R. Pfeiffer (Oxford, 1949–1953)

Menander: A. Körte, revised by A. Thierfelder (Teubner edition)

Sappho: as for Alkaios

Sophokles: A. C. Pearson (Cambridge, 1917)

Sophron: as for Epicharmos

Pindar: B. Snell (Teubner edition)

When fragments (or anthology-items) of other authors are cited, the editions are indicated as follows:

CAF: Kock, *Comicorum Atticorum Fragmenta* (see above)

Coll. Alex.: J. U. Powell, *Collectanea Alexandrina* (Oxford, 1925)

D³: E. Diehl, revised by R. Beutler, *Anthologia Lyrica Graeca* (Teubner edition)

DK: H. Diels, revised by W. Kranz, *Die Fragmente der Vorsokratiker* (ed. 6, Berlin, 1951)

FGrHist: F. Jacoby, *Die Fragmente der griechischen Historiker* (Berlin and Leyden, 1923-)

GPh: A. S. F. Gow and D. L. Page, *The Greek Anthology: the Garland of Philip* (Cambridge, 1968)

HE: A. S. F. Gow and D. L. Page, *The Greek Anthology: Hellenistic Epigrams* (Cambridge, 1965)

PMG: D. L. Page, *Poetae Melici Graeci* (Oxford, 1962); I have followed the continuous numbering, also to be found in the margin of the same editor's *Lyrica Graeca Selecta* (Oxford Classical Text)

TGF: Nauck, *Tragicorum Graecorum Fragmenta* (see above)

2. The principal commentary on Theokritos is:

A. S. F. Gow, *Theocritus, edited with a translation and commentary*, 2 vols., Cambridge, 1950 (revised edition, 1952).

The same editor's *Bucolici Graeci* (Oxford Classical Text) includes, as well as Theokritos, the poems attributed to Moschos, Bion and a few others. See also his translation (with an introduction and some notes), *The Greek Bucolic Poets* (Cambridge, 1953).

Among earlier commentaries,

R. J. Cholmeley, *The Idylls of Theocritus* (ed. 2, London, 1919) contains a useful introduction and a scattering of interesting observations on individual passages, mixed with many dogmatically expressed eccentricities.

U. von Wilamowitz-Moellendorff, *Die Textgeschichte der griechischen Bukoliker* (Berlin, 1906) contains many interpretations of individual passages in the course of, and in addition to, discussion of the problem indicated by the title of the book.

3. The principal books about Theokritos are:

Ph. E. Legrand, *Étude sur Theocrite* (Paris, 1898; reprinted 1968)

E. Bignone, *Teocrito: studio critico* (Bari, 1934)

T. G. Rosenmeyer, *The Green Cabinet: Theocritus and the European Pastoral Lyric* (Berkeley and Los Angeles, 1969)

A fourth book,

Gilbert Lawall, *Theocritus' Coan Pastorals* (Washington, D.C., 1967) offers an interpretation of Poems I–VII as a self-contained collection designed as such by Theokritos.

Among dissertations published since Gow's commentary the two most important are:

M. Sanchez-Wildberger, *Theokrit-Interpretationen* (Zürich, 1955)

A. Köhnken, *Apollonios Rhodios und Theokrit* (Göttingen, 1965)

4. Three books which will be found useful as 'background' reading are:

R. Pfeiffer, *History of Classical Scholarship from the Beginnings to the End of the Hellenistic Age* (Oxford, 1968), notably Part Two, Chapters I–III

Sir William Tarn and G. T. Griffith, *Hellenistic Civilisation* (London, 1952)

T. B. L. Webster, *Hellenistic Poetry and Art* (London, 1964)

5. Reference will be made also to the following works in the Introduction and Commentary:

Denniston, *GP*: J. D. Denniston, *The Greek Particles* (ed. 2, Oxford, 1954)

*DGE*³: P. Cauer, revised by E. Schwyzer, *Dialectorum Graecarum Exempla Epigraphica Potiora* (Leipzig, 1923)

GVI: W. Peek, *Griechische Vers-Inschriften* (vol. i, Berlin, 1955)

IG: *Inscriptiones Graecae*

LSJ: the ninth edition of 'Liddell and Scott'

Introduction

A. Transmission

A1. The poems transmitted to us under the name of Theokritos are:

(*a*) Fourteen poems (I, III, IV, V, VI, VII, VIII, IX, X, XI, XIV, XX, XXI, XXVII) in hexameters (cf. **D1**) and in a predominantly Doric dialect (cf. **E4–10**) portraying rustic life (fishermen in XXI, herdsmen in the others); some of them (e.g. VII, XIV) are anchored to Theokritos's own time by contemporary references, others (e.g. XI) portray the mythical past, and the majority cannot be allotted decisively to the past or the present. Some (e.g. V) are essentially mimes, i.e. dialogue in dramatic form from first to last, with no narrative element to introduce or conclude them; some others (e.g. VI) are dramatic within a narrative framework.

(*b*) Two mimes, II (a soliloquy) and XV (a dialogue), with an urban setting; these two are in hexameters and in a predominantly Doric dialect.

(*c*) Poems about the heroic past (XIII, XVIII, XXII, XXIV, XXV, XXVI), of which XXII and XXV are in the epic dialect, the remainder in a Doric and epic mixture of which the ingredients vary from poem to poem; all are in hexameters. The end of XXIV is lost.

(*d*) XII, a personal poem addressed to a boy; hexameters and epic dialect.

(*e*) XVI, a poem obliquely addressed to Hieron II of Syracuse and asking for his patronage; hexameters; predominantly epic dialect, with Doric admixture.

(*f*) XVII, an enkomion on Ptolemy Philadelphos; hexameters, and dialect like that of XVI.

(g) XIX and XXIII; anecdotes, in hexameters, predominantly Doric.

(*h*) Four poems, XXVIII, XXIX and XXX and XXXI, which employ the dialect and metres of the Lesbian poets Sappho and Alkaios (XXXI is known only from a few half-lines in a fragmentary ancient copy).

(*i*) Epigrams. Nos. 1–22 are transmitted both in the *Palatine Anthology* and in the same manuscripts as groups (*a*)–(*h*); nos. 23–26 are preserved only in the *Anthology*, and no. 27 in the scholia on Theokritos. They are mostly, but not all, in Doric elegiacs.

(*j*) The *Syrinx*, a 'stunt' poem composed approximately in the shape of panpipes.

(*k*) Five lines quoted by Athenaios from a poem called *Berenike*, otherwise lost. A few allusions in writers of Roman and medieval date indicate the likelihood that some further poems ascribed to Theokritos in antiquity have been entirely lost.

A2. No manuscript which contains complete poems of Theokritos (with the exception of *Anthology* manuscripts containing the epigrams) is older than the end of the thirteenth century A.D.; in all, there are nearly 180 medieval manuscripts of Theokritos, the majority being of the fifteenth and sixteenth centuries. Poems I–XVII appear in most manuscripts, but XVIII–

XXX are confined to a minority. We now have also fragmentary ancient copies, ranging in date from the first century A.D. to the sixth (generically called 'papyri', though some of them are made of parchment, not of papyrus). The total fraction of the text surviving in these ancient fragments is very small, but they have cleared up some difficulties and have strikingly confirmed some conjectures made before their discovery. The scholia, explanatory notes written in the margins of some of the medieval manuscripts, also help us to decide what the poet actually wrote; they are ultimately derived — via a long process of condensation, accretion, omission and re-wording — from the work of scholars who commented on Theokritos from the first century B.C. onwards.[1]

A3. The present ordering and numbering of the poems goes back in essentials to the Renaissance. The order in ancient and medieval texts varies, but it tends to keep together the poems of group (a), to put I at the start and to put VII early. We do not know the order in which Theokritos wrote the poems or the order in which he would have liked us to read them.[2] The ancient and medieval texts and the scholia give titles to the poems, often two or more alternative titles to one poem, not all of which are appropriate. We do

---

[1] The symbol Σ will be used in the commentary in the sense 'composer of the scholion on the passage in question'.

[2] Lawall (cf. p. xiii) argues for the simultaneous publication of I–VII, in that order, by the poet himself, although II appears between I and III only in one portion of the medieval manuscript tradition.

not know which titles, if any, go back to the poet himself.

It has been customary since Roman times to call the poems of groups (a)–(h) εἰδύλλια, 'idylls'; why, is far from clear, and the word serves no useful purpose. There is no good reason to think that Theokritos himself used the word or even knew it.

B. Authenticity

B. There was a tendency throughout antiquity to ascribe to a famous poet works which had a generic resemblance to his but were in fact by lesser-known poets; the same tendency operated recklessly and notoriously in the ascription of speeches to orators (a fact of which ancient scholars were themselves well aware), and to a lesser extent in the ascription of essays and dialogues. It would be surprising if the Theokritean corpus were an exception to what is demonstrable in the case of so many authors, particularly since he created a genre in which others (notably Moschos and Bion) wrote in subsequent centuries. The poems which particularly come under suspicion are VIII, IX, XIX, XX, XXI, XXIII, XXV and XXVII. Indeed, the ascription of XXVII to Theokritos cannot be traced further back than the sixteenth century A.D.; nor that of XIX, XX, XXI and XXIII further than the fifteenth; nor that of XXV further than the fourteenth. VIII and IX, however, were regarded as Theokritean in ancient times, and suspicion of their authenticity (with which I fully sympathise) is modern; they give the impression of rather ill-judged parodies of Theokritos, and are probably the work of Hellenistic imitators. There are also various good reasons for doubting the authenticity of Epigrams 23–27.

C. Life of Theokritos

C.1 In XXVIII.16f., addressing his friend Nikias, Theokritos says, '. . . since you are from my own land; for your native city is that which Archias of Ephyre founded, the very marrow of Trinakria.' 'Ephyre' is Corinth, 'Trinakria' is Sicily, and the famous Corinthian colony in Sicily was Syracuse. Similarly in XI.7 the poet refers to the mythical Polyphemos as 'our Cyclops' ($K\dot{v}\kappa\lambda\omega\psi$ ó παρ' ἁμῖν), and later (XI. 47f.) portrays the Cyclops as living near Mt. Etna. These passages accord with the tradition that Theokritos was a Syracusan. Epigram 18, in honour of the fifth-century Syracusan poet Epicharmos, speaks of Syracuse in laudatory terms, and the two Greek women on XV are Syracusans living at Alexandria but exceedingly proud of their origin (XV.89ff.). Daphnis, the legendary hero of poem I, is treated as having lived in eastern Sicily (I.68f., 117f.), and Thyrsis, who sings of the death of Daphnis, is from Etna (I.65).

C2. Poem VII, which is related in the first person singular by a young poet ('Simichidas') and contains allusions to contemporary poets and poetry, is located on the island of Kos in the Dodecanese; local detail (1, 5ff., 10f., 130) is conspicuous. The setting of II is probably also Kos (cf. p. 96); and some details

appropriate to Kos appear to intrude into alien
scenes elsewhere (I.57, V.62 nn.), though it is only
fair to remark that Attic details also appear to intrude
(I.147, VII.71). The nature of VII is no doubt the
reason why one ancient biographical tradition
regarded Theokritos as a native of Kos. It has been
observed (by Miss Alice Lindsell, in *Greece and Rome*
vi [1936], 78ff.) that whenever Theokritos says any-
thing in his rustic poems about trees or plants (and he
mentions a great many) which happen not to be
uniformly distributed in the Mediterranean region
his allusions and descriptions suit the Aegean and not
Sicily. This is true even when the ostensible setting of
a poem is Sicilian or Italian, and it suggests that
however familiar he may have been with Sicilian
legends he drew all the visual detail either from the
Aegean countryside which he knew during the time
that he was writing the poems or from descriptive
passages in earlier and contemporary Greek poetry.

C3. Two of the poems, IV and V, are set in the south
of Italy, but there is no positive reason to suppose that
Theokritos was personally acquainted with that area,
and the poems offer some reason (apart from the
question of vegetation, mentioned above) to think that
he was not (cf. p. 121). With Alexandria the case is dif-
ferent. Poem XV, set in Alexandria, could certainly
have been written by someone who knew about the city
but had not been there. But in the days of Kallimachos
it would be surprising if an accomplished poet did not
go there, and there is no doubt that Theokritos hoped
for the patronage of Ptolemy Philadelphos; somewhat

fulsome references to the king are made in VII.93,
XIV.59ff., XV.46ff. and XV.94f., the last two at the
expense of realism in the dialogue. XVII is a eulogy
of Ptolemy — one might call it a hymn to him — and
as it contains no open or even covert request for
patronage it may be fair to infer that this patronage
had already been given when it was written.

C4. In XVII Ptolemy's mother Berenike is already
dead and deified (34ff., 121ff.), and Ptolemy, adopting
the practice of the pharaohs (not to mention Zeus and
Hera, the precedent naturally preferred by a Greek
poet) has married his sister Arsinoe (128ff.). We
know from Oriental sources that Ptolemy Philadel-
phos and Arsinoe were married by 274/3, possibly
some years earlier, and Arsinoe died in 270; we do
not know the date of Berenike's death, but at least we
can say that XVII is datable to the 270s. Poem XV
also refers to Ptolemy and Arsinoe and to the deifica-
tion of Berenike (22ff., 106f., 110f.), and therefore
has the same upper terminus as XVII. A third poem
which can be dated is XVI. This is an appeal for
patronage to Hieron II of Syracuse, who came to
power in 275/4, took the title of king in 269 and died
at an advanced age in 215. Since the poem says much
of what he will do and nothing of what he has done
(76ff., 98ff.), it should be dated early, perhaps as
early as 274. There is no precise evidence of date to be
gathered from any of the other poems; they are
consistent with the supposition that they were all
concentrated within the 270s and equally consistent
with the contrary supposition that they were written

over a longer period (Kallimachos's poetic career falls within the limits 295–245; the limits of Apollonios of Rhodes are not easily fixed, but seem to have been slightly later than those of Kallimachos). It is improbable that the ancient commentators were any better provided than we are with evidence for the dating of Theokritos's poems, and demonstrable that ancient commentators in general were less careful than we are in using what evidence they had. Σ says that Theokritos 'flourished' ($ἤκμαζε$) in the 124th Olympiad (summer 284–summer 280); the accession of Ptolemy Philadelphos fell within that Olympiad, and commentators could observe as well as we can the passages which link Theokritos to Ptolemy. Modern reconstructions of Theokritos's life which are founded on the assumption that poems of group (a) which closely resemble each other in-form and content were written at about the same time, and on the hypothesis that he studied botany on Kos in company with his friend Nikias (who became a doctor), are reasonable enough and may well be right; although they do not have the same .evidential value as the data which can be extracted from XV, XVI and XVII, they do not conflict with those data.[1]

D. Metre

D1. The metre of poems I–XXVII, with the exception of part of VIII, is the dactylic hexameter, of which the basic scheme is:

$$\underline{1}\,\cup\cup\ \underline{2}\,\cup\cup\ \underline{3}\,\cup\cup\ \underline{4}\,\cup\cup\ \underline{5}\,\cup\cup\ \underline{6}\,\cap$$

[1] On the general problem of literary chronology in the period 300–250 B.C. cf. T. B. L. Webster, *Wiener Studien* lxxvi (1963), 68ff.

Here (*a*) – means 'position occupied by a long syllable', i.e. by a syllable which

   (i) contains a long vowel or diphthong

or (ii) contains a short vowel separated from the vowel of the next syllable by more than one consonant-sound.

(*b*) ⏑ means 'position occupied by a short syllable', i.e. by a syllable which

   (i) contains a short vowel

and (ii) this vowel is separated from the vowel of the next syllable by only one consonant-sound or by none.

(*c*) ⌒ symbolizes the last position of a verse, which may be occupied by any kind of syllable.

D2. (*a*) Either the first long or the first short syllable of the third foot must be the last syllable of a word. This is represented symbolically as $\underline{3}: \overset{\smile\smile}{}$ and is called 'caesura'.

(*b*) The fourth foot is very commonly a dactyl (– ⏑⏑); its two short syllables belong both to the same word, and there is word-end (the 'bucolic diaeresis') between the fourth and fifth feet. This pattern is symbolized $\overset{4}{}$ ⏑⏑ : ; every one of the first thirteen verses of poem I follows this pattern and so do all but twenty of the 152 verses in the poem. If the fourth foot is a spondee (– –), its second syllable is part of the same word as the first syllable of the fifth foot: symbolically, ⌒⁵. This way of treating the fourth foot (foreshadowed in epic, but taken much further by the Hellenistic poets) is not consistently adopted in poems

XI and XV, and there are a few exceptions elsewhere (I.130, XII.24, XIII.59, XIV.23).

(c) The fifth foot is usually a dactyl, but occasionally a spondee; and when it is a spondee, the fifth and sixth feet together are almost always a single four-syllable word, e.g. I.38 μοχθίζοντι (an exception is XVI.56 περίσπλαγχνος Λαέρτης, i.e. $\cup \frac{4}{-} - \frac{5}{-} | - - -$).

(d) When the expressions 'word-end' and 'the same word' are used in speaking of Greek metre, it must be remembered that the Greeks did not regard word-end as falling between a word and a following 'postpositive' (e.g. γε, γάρ, ἄν, or enclitic pronouns) or between a 'prepositive' (e.g. καί, the article, prepositions) and the following word. Thus in I.6 χιμάρω δὲ καλὸν κρέας ($\cup\cup \frac{3}{-} \cup\cup \frac{4}{-} \cup\cup$) the caesura falls between δέ and καλόν, and in I.7 ὦ ποιμή, ντὸ τεὸν μέλος ($\frac{2}{-} - \frac{3}{-} \cup\cup \frac{4}{-} \cup\cup$) between ποιμήν and τό. Similarly, I.14 ἐγὼν ἐν τῷδε ($\cup \frac{4}{-} - \frac{5}{-} \cup$) is not an exception to the generalization given in (b) above. In speaking of prosody, however (D3), we mean by 'the end of a word' the point at which a letter-space is printed in a modern text.

D3. The general rules of prosody are essentially those familiar to us from epic.

(a) A long vowel or diphthong at the end of a word may be treated as a short syllable if the next word begins with a vowel. Thus I.31 καρπῷ ἕλιξ εἰλεῖται ἀγαλλομένα κροκόεντι is scanned $\frac{1}{-} \cup\cup \frac{2}{-} - \frac{3}{-} \cup\cup \frac{4}{-} \cup\cup \frac{5}{-} \cup\cup \frac{6}{-} \frown$, -πῷ and -ται both being treated as short. Cf. I.52 καλὰν πλέκει ($\cup\cup$) ἀκριδοθήκαν, I.63 οὔ τι πᾳ ($- \cup\cup$) εἰς Ἀΐδαν γε, I.72 τῆνον λύκοι ($\cup\cup$) ὠρύσαντο, I.152 μὴ ὁ τράγος ($\cup - \cup\cup$) ὔμμιν ἀναστῇι.

(*b*) The combination of β, γ, δ, θ, κ, π, τ, ϕ or χ with ρ, or of θ, κ, π, τ, ϕ or χ with λ, μ or ν is sometimes treated metrically as if it were a single consonant-sound, e.g. I.54 περὶ πλέγματι (‿‿ – ‿‿), I.113 νικῶ Δάφνιν (– – ‿‿); contrast I.20 ἐπὶ τὸ πλέον (‿‿ – ‿‿), 24 ποτὶ Χρόμιν (‿ – ‿‿), 101 Κύπρι θνατοῖσιν (– – – – ‿). Initial ῥ is sometimes treated as two consonant-sounds, e.g. I.125 λίπε ῥίον (‿ – ‿‿).

(*c*) At the end of a word, ᾰ (except in the word τά), ε and ο are normally elided when the following word begins with a vowel. The same is true of ι in certain words (e.g. ἀντί, ἐπί, ἐστί, ἔτι) and, rarely, of -αι in the verbal endings -μαι, -σαι, -ται, (e.g. II.40 ['30'] χὼς δινεῖθ' [= δινεῖται] ὅδε ῥόμβος).

(*d*) When καὶ or the article is followed by a vowel it commonly coalesces with that vowel to form a single syllable, e.g. I.82 κῆφα = καὶ ἔφα, 97 κεῖπε = καὶ εἶπε, 100 χὠ = καὶ ὁ, II.24 χὠς = καὶ ὡς, 25 κοὐδέ = καὶ οὐδέ: I.65 ὠξ = ὁ ἐξ, 80 ᾡπόλοι = οἱ αἰπόλοι, II.112 ὤστοργος = ὁ ἄστοργος, 67 τωὐβούλοιο = τῷ Εὐβούλοιο. This phenomenon ('crasis') is occasional with other words, e.g. II.54 ὠγώ = ὁ ἐγώ, and three syllables can be reduced to one, e.g. I.72 χὠκ = καὶ ὁ ἐκ, 109 χὤδωνις = καὶ ὁ Ἄδωνις.

(*e*) Certain other successions of vowels can be treated as single syllables without any modification of the way they are written; e.g. in VII,122 φρουρέωμες is scanned – – ‿, and in XI.81 ἢ εἰ is scanned as one long syllable.

D4. Sporadically we find the rules given under **D3**

(a), (c) and (e) ignored; a vowel at the end of a word may be treated ('hiatus') as if a consonant-sound intervened between it and the next vowel, and in similar circumstances a syllable consisting of a short vowel separated by only one consonant-sound from the initial vowel of the next word may be treated as if it were separated by more than one consonant-sound. Some of the examples are imitations of epic phrases, expecially phrases containing words which originally began with the sound (not written in the epic texts) w- ('digamma'), e.g. I.41 ἀνδρὶ ἐοικώς (– ⏑ ⏑ – –), II.51 μαινομένῳ ἴκελος (– ⏑ ⏑ – ⏑ ⏑ –); and anything which precedes the dative singular pronoun οἱ is treated in this way (as in Classical lyric). Apart from these, we find the phenomenon:

(a) At the mid-point of a foot, e.g.

XV.123 ὦ ἔβενος, ὦ χρυσός, ὦ ἐκ λευκῶ ἐλέφαντος ($\underline{1}$ ⏑ ⏑ $\underline{2}$ – $\underline{3}$ ⏑ ⏑ $\underline{4}$ – $\underline{5}$ ⏑ ⏑ $\underline{6}$ ⌢)

XVI.62 ἢ ὕδατι νίζειν ($\underline{1}$ ⏑ ⏑ $\underline{2}$ – $\underline{3}$)

X.30 ἁ αἲξ τὰν κύτισον, ὁ λύκος τὰν αἶγα διώκει ($\underline{1}$ – $\underline{2}$ ⏑ ⏑ $\underline{3}$ ⏑ ⏑ $\underline{4}$ – $\underline{5}$ ⏑ ⏑ $\underline{6}$ –)

I.75 πολλαὶ δὲ δαμάλαι ($\underline{1}$ – $\underline{2}$ ⏑ ⏑ $\underline{3}$)

I.86 βούτας μὲν ἐλέγευ ($\underline{1}$ – $\underline{2}$ ⏑ ⏑ $\underline{3}$)

I.115 ὦ λύκοι, ὦ θῶες, ὦ ἀν' ὤρεα φωλάδες ἄρκτοι ($\underline{1}$ ⏑ ⏑ $\underline{2}$ – $\underline{3}$ ⏑ ⏑ $\underline{4}$ ⏑ ⏑ $\underline{5}$ ⏑ ⏑ $\underline{6}$ –)

I.127 Μοῖσαι, ἴτε λήγετ' ἀοιδᾶς (– $\underline{4}$ ⏑ ⏑ $\underline{5}$ ⏑ ⏑ $\underline{6}$ –)

I.98 ὑπ' ἀργαλέω ἐλυγίχθης (⏑ $\underline{4}$ ⏑ ⏑ $\underline{5}$ ⏑ ⏑ $\underline{6}$ –)

(*b*) At the caesura after $\underline{3}$ ◡, e.g.

> VII.8   αἴγειροι πτελέαι τε ἐύσκιον ἄλσος
> ὕφαινον.

(*c*) At the bucolic diaeresis, e.g.

> I.67   καλὰ τέμπεα ἢ κατὰ Πίνδω (◡ ◡ $\underline{4}$ ◡ ◡
> $\underline{5}$ ◡ ◡ $\underline{6}$ –)

> II.83   τὸ δὲ κάλλος ἐτάκετο. οὐκέτι πομπᾶς
> (◡ ◡ $\underline{3}$ ◡ ◡ $\underline{4}$ ◡ ◡ $\underline{5}$ ◡ ◡ $\underline{6}$ –)

(*d*) In phrases taken from, or modelled on, phrases already existing in epic or archaic poetry, e.g.

> XVI.2   ὑμνεῖν ἀγαθῶν κλέα ἀνδρῶν (– $\underline{4}$ ◡ ◡
> $\underline{5}$ ◡ ◡ $\underline{6}$ –)

> XV.149   χαῖρε Ἄδων ἀγαπατέ ($\underline{1}$ ◡ ◡ $\underline{2}$ ◡ ◡
> $\underline{3}$ ◡)

D5. The metre used in most of the epigrams, and in part of VIII, is the elegiac couplet. This consists of a hexameter (as above) followed by a pentameter, of which the scheme is:

$$– ◡ ◡ – ◡ ◡ – \mid – ◡ ◡ – ◡ ◡ ◠$$

The upright stroke here symbolizes caesura. The prosodic practice of elegiacs does not differ from that of hexameters.

D6. Other metres will be explained in the notes on poem XXVIII and epigrams 17–21.

E. Dialect

E1. Any word taken from any Greek text must itself be, or must contain, elements which are either 'invariable' and of 'unlimited distribution' or 'variable' and of 'limited distribution'. Consider, for example, the words καὶ ἁ πίτυς, αἰπόλε, τῆνα in I.1. So far as our evidence goes, the word πίτυς was always and everywhere πίτυς, irrespective of period, region or literary genre; καὶ and αἰπόλε are very nearly invariable, but not quite, for a Theban in Theokritos's time would have written κή and ἠπόλε; ἁ appears elsewhere as ἡ and ἀ, and τῆνα appears as ἐκείνη, κείνη and κήνα, so that ἀ and τῆνα are forms which quite certainly have a limited distribution.

E2. The many thousands of Greek inscriptions which we possess enable us to plot, in terms of period and region, the distribution of any given word or element of a word; the further back we go in time (the earliest Greek inscriptions take us back to the eighth century B.C.) the more gaps and uncertainties there are; but by the time we come down to the latter part of the fourth century B.C. the evidence is abundant. Since the majority of inscriptions are state documents, we have to bear in mind the possibility that their language is sometimes archaic (like the language of the law in English); but the conclusions we draw from them are in general confirmed by a certain number of extremely informal inscriptions incised on pottery, walls or rock-faces, and by caricatures of dialect which we find in Aristophanes. We can therefore be reasonably confident that the inscriptions of (e.g.) Kos in the third century B.C. represent the language used by the Koans at that time.

E3. The language of any given place at any given

time is necessarily in process of change; some of its characteristic forms are yielding to the encroachment of alternative forms from other politically or culturally dominant places, and some of the 'unlimited distribution' forms which it shares with all the places in the same linguistic continuum are being replaced by peculiar local developments. Hence no language at any given place and time can be wholly consistent. Even in the archaic and classical periods we find plenty of inconsistency — for example, a Chian document of the sixth century B.C. has both δημαρχῶν and δημαρχέων, and an Athenian document of c. 420 B.C. uses both ἐλάττων and its older Attic synonym ὀλείζων — and from the late fourth century onwards inconsistency increases everywhere, since all regional dialects are under pressure from the (essentially Attic) Koine which was the official language of the Macedonian dynasties and emerged everywhere as standard literary Greek. Thus it is not surprising that we find in the third century αἰ and εἰ, τοὶ σύμμαχοι and οἱ σύμμαχοι, αἱρεύμενοι and ποιούμενοι, keeping close company in the same document.

E4. Certain Greek states regarded themselves as 'Ionians' (e.g. Athens, Chios), others as 'Aeolians' (e.g. Thebes, Mytilene), and others again as 'Dorians' (e.g. Corinth, Sparta). Colonies of such states naturally adopted the same classification as their mother-cities, so that Syracuse, for example, was Dorian, being a colony of Corinth. But three important facts should be remembered when this classification is applied to dialect:

(*a*) It is by no means exhaustive; it excludes, among others, the Arcadians, Cypriots, Eleans, Achaians, Phokians and Lokrians, none of whom regarded themselves as Ionian, Aeolian or Dorian.

(*b*) The Doric dialects — using the term in the sense 'the dialects spoken by the communities which called themselves Dorians' — do not exhibit one single phenomenon which, at any given date, is found in every Doric dialect but is not found in any other dialect. Most of the phenomena which are shared by most of the Doric dialects occur also in Elis, Achaia, Phokis and Lokris, and some of them occur in Boeotia too. The Doric dialects in fact form part of a larger group generally known nowadays as 'West Greek'.

(*c*) The phenomena which occur in a given dialect usually show the influence of dialects which are geographically close but genetically of different origin. Thus Dorian Halikarnassos wrote an Ionic dialect by the fifth century B.C.; the Doric dialects in general use τοί and ταί for the plural of the article, but the Dorian Cretans use οἱ and αἱ, like the Ionic dialects of the Aegean islands; the Ionian Chians wrote λέγοισι, φέροισι, etc., like the Aeolians of Lesbos, not λέγουσι, φέρουσι etc., like the other Ionians.

E5. If we constructed a time-and-place 'map' of the distribution of linguistic phenomena in literature, we should find much of it greatly at variance with the map based on inscriptions, for the language used by a writer was not primarily determined by where and when he lived but by the tradition of the literary genre in which he was writing; nor did a writer (especially a poet) feel compelled to restrict himself to words and forms which were actually used in ordinary speech anywhere in his own time. When we first encounter epic language in Homer it is highly artificial, employing elements from different stages of the development of Ionic, non-Ionic elements, and poetic distortions. Hesiod, a Boeotian, and Tyrtaios, a Spartan, used Homer's language for didactic hexameters and elegiacs respectively. Pindar, like Hesiod, was a Boeotian, but the language which he used for his choral lyric shows no specifically Boeotian characteristics; it draws upon the choral lyric composed by other poets (from the Peloponnese, the Aegean islands and Sicily) during the previous two hundred years. But however true it is that a poet was under no artistic obligation to use, even to the slightest extent, the dialect of his own state, it is equally true that he was under no obligation to refrain from using it to whatever extent he wished. It was open to a poet to create a new genre by a new mixture of ingredients drawn from the literary past and from the regional dialects of his own time.

E6. One does not have to read very far in Theokritos to discover that his language includes a considerable number of alternatives. For example, in I.68 οὐ γὰρ δὴ ποταμοῖο μέγαν ῥόον εἶχετ' Ἀνάπῳ, the endings -οιο and -ω are alternatives for the genitive singular (Attic -ου) of second declension nouns. Again I.5 begins αἴ κα δ' αἶγα λάβῃ and I.10 ends αἰ δέ κ' ἀρέσκῃ: the modal particles κᾱ, which cannot be elided, and κε, which can, are both the equivalent of·

the Attic ἄν, and the different orders αἴ κα δέ and αἰ
δέ κε must also be treated as alternatives, since in
inscriptions the placing of δέ between αἰ or εἰ and
the modal particle is confined to certain regions.
Now, since -οιο and -ω scan differently (and so do κᾱ
and κε), each of them is 'metrically guaranteed' vis-à-
vis the other; if one of them is corrupted to the other
through manuscript error, we can detect the error
because the resulting line does not scan, and so we can
confidently suggest what the poet must have written.
Also, if the inconsistencies in Theokritos's language
were confined to pairs of alternatives which scan
differently, there would be no problems in setting out
the facts of his language, for all Greek poets (not least
Homer) liked to have available to them alternative
forms which scanned differently (e.g. Ἀχιλεύς and
Ἀχιλλεύς, Πατρόκλου and Πατροκλῆος, etc.). The diffi-
culties actually arise from the fact that a very large
number of alternative forms do *not* scan differently;
one could, for example, 'Atticize' the first three lines
of poem I without encountering any metrical obstacle,
thus:

ἡδύ τι τὸ ψιθύρισμα καὶ ἡ πίτυς, αἰπόλ᾽, ἐκείνη
ἡ πρὸς ταῖς πηγαῖσι μελίζεται, ἡδὺ δὲ καὶ σὺ
συρίζεις· μετὰ Πᾶνα τὸ δεύτερον ἆθλον ἀποίσει.

To raise in these circumstances the question 'What did
Theokritos really write?' may seem hypercritical, the
creation of a pseudo-problem, but it is in fact a very
real problem; not only do manuscripts differ from one
another in respect of alternative forms which are
metrically identical, but in the same manuscript the

poems differ from one another, and even within the same poem the degree of inconsistency in the presentation of metrically equivalent forms can be very high.

E7. The main reasons why we find inconsistency in the use of metrically equivalent forms are:

(*a*) Copyists naturally tend, by unconscious error, to substitute familiar for unfamiliar forms. This can be shown clearly in the comparatively small number of passages where the error results in a line that does not scan. E.g. in I.60 τῷ κά τυ μάλα πρόφρων ἀρεσαίμαν and I.62 κοὔτι τυ κερτομέω, in both of which τυ = Attic σε, most manuscripts have substituted the more familiar word τοι; but the error is detectable both grammatically (κερτομεῖν always governs an accusative, and ἀρέσκεσθαι often does) and metrically (τοι is long, τυ short).

(*b*) Scholarly editors in ancient and medieval times, together with copyists who were interested in the linguistic forms of what they were writing, were apt to alter familiar forms to unfamiliar in the belief that they were restoring what the poet wrote. Systematic changes of this kind can be detected:

(i) When the result does not scan. So, for example, in Pindar *Pyth.* 3.46 some manuscripts have the epic form νούσους, but the metrical responsion shows that Pindar must have intended νόσους.

(ii) When the result is nonsense. II.45f. Θησέα φαντὶ / ἐν Δίᾳ λασθῆμεν is a striking case in point. The infinitive ending -μεν here is equivalent to the Attic -ναι. But since the transmitted text of Theokritos presented -μες as equivalent to the Attic -μεν in the first person plural (e.g. I.16 δεδοίκαμες = δεδοίκαμεν = 'we fear'), the infinitive λασθῆμεν appears in some manuscripts as λασθῆμες, which is meaningless and must be the product of a belief that -μες should always be substituted for -μεν in Theokritos.

(iii) When there are several variants for the same word in the same passage, and the poet can hardly have written more than one of them. E.g. in I.36, 'she looks at one man, smiling', the manuscripts present for 'smiling' γελᾶσα, γελεῦσα, γελοῖσα and γελῶσα: only one of these, γελῶσα, is the familiar Attic form; the other three are non-Attic, and at least two of them must originate in different ideas of what the poet 'ought' to have written.

(iv) Rarely, when the form imposes a little too great a strain on our philological credulity, e.g. (some MSS.) IV.28 ἐπάξᾱ < ἐπάξαο (Att. ἐπάξω: cf. V.6 ἐκτάσω); ᾱο > ᾱ in Doric dialects, but ᾰο always > ω. The case is different with (e.g.) VII.51 ἐξεπόνᾱσα (= -νη-, ∼ πονεῖν); cf. E10(e).

(c) Since the regional dialects of Theokritos's time all contained a wide range of metrically equivalent forms (cf. E3), the more he drew on contemporary language the more inconsistency we should expect in his poems. Acknowledgment of this fact, however, is quite unhelpful in respect of any one word (just as, if we knew that a list of statements was 50% true, we should still not know whether any particular statement selected from the list was true or false) — particularly as it would be begging the question to start off with an assumption about the extent to which Theokritos drew on contemporary language.

(*d*) Presumably Theokritos's linguistic preferences were not identical throughout his literary career. We can see, after all, that in poems XI and XV his metrical treatment of the fourth foot of the dactylic hexameter differs from his treatment of it in the other poems (cf. **D2**[*b*]), and it seems only reasonable to suppose that his treatment of alternative linguistic forms varied from time to time. But since we do not know the order in which he wrote the poems, the supposition, however reasonable, does not help with particular cases.

(*e*) We sometimes have reason to believe that a poet's choice between alternative forms was dictated by considerations of euphony. Pindar, for example, normally uses τίν as the dative of the second person singular pronoun, but we find σοί in passages where either or both of the adjacent syllables contains the sound τ. Bacchylides normally uses -ουσι for the third person plural ending of the verb (e.g. λέγουσι), but occasionally -οντι, and it is perhaps no coincidence that when he uses -οντι the preceding syllable contains the sound σ. We must recognise frankly that we know very little about a Greek poet's likes and dislikes in the juxtaposition of sounds; but it should not surprise us that in VII.108 the ancient text (two papyri) has μαστίζοιεν, not μαστίσδοιεν, or that in II.10 it has νῦν δέ μιν for the medieval text's νῦν δέ νιν.

(*f*) Sometimes there is reason to think that the form of a word is determined by its poetical associations. Bacchylides, for example, always uses -αις or -αισι for the dative plural of the first declension, with a solitary exception, 13.135 ἐν κλισίῃσι: not only the word κλισίη, but the actual phrase ἐν κλισίῃσι, is Homeric, and an editor who 'ironed out' the text of Bacchylides by substituting ἐν κλισίαισι could justly be accused of insensitivity to literary associations. Similarly in Theokritos IV.8, where the manuscripts present us with βίην καὶ κάρτος, the chances are that the poet wrote βίην, not βίαν, with the Homeric phrase κάρτος τε βίη τε in mind.

E8. When we possess both medieval manuscripts and fragmentary ancient texts of a poet, we usually find that the corruption of unfamiliar to familiar forms (cf. **E7**[a]) has not gone so far in the ancient texts and that the degree of linguistic consistency is higher in an ancient text than in a medieval text. Certainly in Pindar, whereas the medieval texts vary a great deal between -ᾱς, -ᾱσα and -αις, -αισα for the aorist participle (e.g. λύσαις, λύσαισα), the ancient fragments are solid for -αις, -αισα. We might therefore expect to find that the ancient fragments of Theokritos would present us with a comparatively consistent language which we could take as an editorial canon, rejecting the evidence of the medieval manuscripts when they do not conform to this canon. Unfortunately, the most substantial ancient fragments of Theokritos are very late in date, c. 500 A.D., and although they sometimes present us with unfamiliar forms which have been lost in the medieval tradition they also show a high degree of inconsistency and plenty of signs that the processes of corruption described in **E7** (a) and (b) above had already gone far. For example, the famous Antinoe papyrus at II.143 has ἤλθομες, where the medieval manuscripts (in keeping with what we usually find elsewhere in Theokritos) have ἤνθομες: at XIV.26 the copyist of the papyrus wrote κεῖνον, and a corrector substituted τῆνον (which is what the medieval manuscripts have); and at XIV.45 it has μᾶνες for 'months', like nearly all the medieval manuscripts, but in all known Greek dialects 'month' was μήν, μής or μείς, with a stem μην-, and μᾶνες is the work of someone who thought that the text of Theokritos should always have ᾱ where the Attic Koine had η.

An editor must therefore reconcile himself to a high degree of uncertainty, and hope that one day we shall find a substantial ancient text datable to within a century or less of Theokritos's own lifetime (not an impossibility; good literary papyri written in the third century B.C. exist). For any given passage, the editor's starting-point should be the ancient text, if an ancient fragment is available; having considered it, he may often find good reason to reject it and print a medieval reading or a modern conjecture, but rejection of the oldest known reading always carries the onus of proof. Among 'good reasons' I would include striking linguistic inconsistency in the absence of any apparent considerations of euphony, associations or style which might justify it; and in defining 'consistency' it is rational to take into account not only Theokritos's own work but other poetry which has been transmitted in essentially the same linguistic form; his imitators, whether identifiable (Moschos and Bion) or anonymous, and the fifth and sixth hymns of Kallimachos, together with some of Kallimachos's epigrams.

E9.(*a*) The ingredients of Theokritos's language (excluding poems XXVIII–XXXI, the language of which is explained on pp. 268f.) can be assigned to four sources:

(i) Epic, which itself contains many ingredients besides Ionic (cf. **E5**).

(ii) The work of earlier writers who were, like Theokritos himself, Syracusans: Epicharmos, who wrote comedies in verse in the first quarter of the fifth century B.C.; minor contemporaries and successors of Epicharmos in the same genre; and Sophron, who wrote prose mimes in the fifth century. The work of these writers is known to us only from fragments and citations.

(iii) Choral lyric — particularly Pindar; but we must remember that the works of Stesichoros and Simonides, almost wholly lost to us, were available in their entirety to Theokritos.

(iv) Individual Doric dialects of his own time.

A mixture may occur in the same word; e.g. in IV.57 κομόωντι ('grow vigorously', of plants) has the third person plural ending -ντι, characteristic of (ii), (iv) and sometimes of (iii), combined with the development κομαο->κομοω- which is characteristic of (i), occasional in (iii), and unknown in prose literature or prose inscriptions.

(*b*) The partition of phenomena between the four sources is not quite as neat as it might seem, for many phenomena are common to (ii)–(iv) against (i) — e.g. the retention of original $\bar{a}$, which Ionic and Attic changed to η — and many more are common to all four sources against the Attic Koine, e.g. dative

plurals of the third declension in -εσσι, or the retention
of -ι- in the declension of nouns such as πόλις and
μάντις (e.g. πόλιος = πόλεως, μάντιες = μάντεις). This
means that there is a great deal in Theokritos which
to Athenian ears would have sounded 'poetic', but
to a Koan, Rhodian or Syracusan would have been
everyday language, e.g. I.22 τᾶν = τῶν (fem.), 23 ταὶ
δρύες = αἱ δρύες, 45 ὅσσον = ὅσον, etc. The same con-
sideration applies also to vocabulary; for example,
when in V.28 the South Italian goatherd prays that
the Nymphs may be (τελέθοιεν) gracious to him, he
uses a verb which to an Athenian would have been
associated with elevated poetry, especially epic. But
this verb occurs in a documentary inscription of a
Dorian city in South Italy, Herakleia (ὅτι κα τελέθει
ψαφισθέν, 'whatever has been voted'); Xenophon in
the *Anabasis* twice puts it into the mouth of a Spartan
speaker; and Epicharmos uses it (fr. 170.17) in a pas-
sage of dialogue. We have enough inscriptions to show
us that different localities differed significantly in voca-
bulary even in the third century B.C., and it would
be prudent to assume that perhaps as many as half
the words in Theokritos which seem to us 'poetic'
when we consider them from an Attic standpoint
were not so from a Dorian standpoint. The verb λῆν
(=Attic ἐθέλειν) is of particular interest; Theokritos
uses it constantly, and so did Epicharmos; it appears
in the inscriptions of Doric states, and in Aristo-
phanes' caricatures of Doric-speakers; yet not only
epic poets but also lyric poets avoided it entirely, as if
it carried a stigma of 'colloquial' or 'provincial' status
incompatible with the dignity of their poetry.

(*c*) From what has been said so far it might seem that the language of Theokritos is essentially that of Syracuse or Kos in the early third century B.C., flavoured with epic forms whenever these were metrically useful. But unless his language (and that of the other poets mentioned at the end of **E8** above) has been radically and systematically altered at an early stage of the transmission, so simplified a statement is indefensible. That much is clear from certain relations between sources (ii), (iii) and (iv), namely:

1. The predominant form of the genitive singular of the second declension in Theokritos is -ω (Attic -ου), and that of the accusative plural -ως (Attic -ους) or -ος. But the Dorian communities of Sicily, together with Kos, Rhodes and the neighbouring islands, uniformly show -ου and -ους (or -ος), and so do the fragments of Epicharmos and Sophron. In using -ω and -ως, therefore, Theokritos is adopting a characteristic of Kyrene, South Italy and the Peloponnese.

2. In the active infinitive ending he shows the opposite affinities. In general, dialects which have -ου and -ους (or -ος) in second declension nouns have -ειν (or -εν) in the infinitive, while -ω and -ως (or -ος) go with infinitive -ην (or -εν). The Theokritos text almost always shows -ειν, occasionally -εν, and -ην appears only rarely as a variant.

3. The Theokritos text usually presents us with Μοῖσα (surprisingly, the oldest extant scrap of poem I has Μοῦσα!) and with -οισα in the feminine of participles in -ων (e.g. φέροισα = φέρουσα), but not with -αισα in the feminine of participles in -ας. The distri-

bution of these forms among regional dialects is very restricted: they occur in Lesbos (which was Aeolian) and at Kyrene (which was Dorian), and nowhere else, certainly not among the Dorians of Sicily or the Dodecanese. In poetry, the archaic Spartan poet Alkman used -οισα but not Μοῖσα: Pindar used Μοῖσα, -οισα and -αισα (also masc. -αις); Epicharmos and Sophron used none of these forms.

4. The Theokritos text usually spells medial ζ as σδ. This spelling is found also in the texts of the Lesbian poets, Sappho and Alkaios, in whose dialect the letter ζ was used for a sound like our *j* (e.g. Ζόννυσος = Διόνυσος); possibly the spelling σδ was used in Theokritos's time in current texts of some choral lyric poets (e.g. Alkman), but our evidence for this is inadequate. Inscriptions of the period throw no light on the question.

5. In three passages, I.3, I.19 and IV.3, we find -ες instead of -εις in the second person singular of a present tense (in IV.3 -εις appears as a variant). None of the three is metrically guaranteed, but Σ draws attention to the form in I.3. So far as our evidence goes, this form is confined to Kyrene and Cyprus.

6. For the first and second person plural pronouns we find accus. ἁμέ and ἄμμε, ὑμέ and ὔμμε, dative ἁμίν and ἄμμιν, ὑμίν and ὔμμιν. The first member of each pair is Doric, the second Aeolic and common in epic. Why Theokritos should have used both series (if he really did) is not at all clear; it is not a matter of metrical convenience, for in the accusative the forms are metrically identical and in the dative ἁμιν and

ὗμιν, with short iota, were accepted by ancient grammarians in the text of Sophron.

From these data it appears that Theokritos did not take as the Doric ingredient of his language any one Doric dialect as it was in his own time, nor did he confine himself to the language of Epicharmos and Sophron, but 'shopped around' both in the dialects of his own day and in lyric poetry which had Dorian associations.

E10. The chief respects in which Theokritos's language differs *both* from epic[1] *and* from the Attic Koine are these:

(a) Substantives, first declension. Gen. sing. masc. -ᾱ, e.g. II.70 Θευμαρίδα = Θεομαρίδου; acc. plur. sometimes -ᾰς, e.g. I.134 ὄχνας ἐνείκαι; gen. plur. -ᾶν, e.g. I.12 Νυμφᾶν.

Second declension. Gen. sing. -ω, e.g. I.21 Πριήπω = Πριάπου; acc. plur. either -ως, e.g. I.88 τάκεται ὀφθαλμώς, or -ος, e.g. I.90 τὰς παρθένος.

(b) Personal pronouns. First person sing. nom. sometimes ἐγών, e.g. I.14 ἐγὼν ἐν τῷδε νομευσῶ; dat. ἐμίν, e.g. II.144 ἐμὶν ἀπεμέμψατο (but in IV.30. δῶρον ἐμοί νιν ἔλειπεν for a very obvious euphonic reason).

Second person sing. nom. τύ, e.g. I.2f. ἁδὺ δὲ καὶ τὺ / συρίσδες; acc. emphatic τέ, e.g. I.5 ἐς τὲ καταρρεῖ, enclitic τυ, e.g. I.78 τίς τυ κατατρύχει; gen. emphatic τεῦς, e.g. II.126 τὸ καλὸν στόμα τεῦς ἐφίλησα, or τεοῦς, e.g. XI.25 ἠράσθην μὲν ἔγωγε τεοῦς (but in IV.38 μόνας σέθεν οὐδὲ θανοίσας to avoid $\frac{4}{}$ – |, cf. **D2** [b]), enclitic

---

[1] The definition 'different from epic' disregards phenomena which are exceptional in epic.

τευ, e.g. V.19 οὔ τευ τὰν σύριγγα: dat. emphatic τίν, e.g. II.20 καὶ τὶν ἐπίχαρμα τέτυγμαι, enclitic τοι. In XI.39 and XI.55, however, τίν must be accusative.

First person plur. sometimes nom. ἁμές, acc. ἁμέ, but never metrically guaranteed against ἄμμες and ἄμμε.

Second person plural similarly ὑμές, ὑμέ, never guaranteed.

(c) Verb persons. First person plural active -μες, e.g. II.5 πότερον τεθνάκαμες ἦ ζωοὶ εἰμές = ... τεθνήκαμεν ... ἐσμέν.

Third person singular active in athematic verbs -τι, e.g. I.51 φᾱτί = φησί, III.48 τίθητι = τίθησι.

Third person plural active in primary tenses -ντι, e.g. I.38 μοχθίζοντι = μοχθίζουσι, I.43 ᾠδήκαντι = ᾠδήκᾱσι, II.45 φαντί = φᾱσί.

(d) Infinitives. Thematic active sometimes -εν, e.g. V.7 ποππύσδεν ἔχοντι = ποππύζειν . . .; -ην appears sporadically as a variant on -ειν (cf. E9[b] 2 above).

Athematic active and passive -μεν, e.g. V.21 θέμεν = θεῖναι.

(e) Contracted verbs. Alpha stems: α + ε become η, hence e.g. I.49 φοιτῇ = φοιτᾷ, IV.11 λυσσῆν = λυσσᾶν. ε + ο and ε + ου become ευ. α + an o-vowel sometimes appear to contract to ευ, e.g. I.81 ἀνηρώτευν, VI.31 ἐσορεῦσα, VII.55 ὀπτεύμενον: this phenomenon should perhaps be regarded as part of a tendency for alpha-stems and epsilon-stems to encroach on each other's conjugations, as is well attested in Doric inscriptions from Sicily and the Dodecanese in this period, e.g. τιμεῖν = τιμᾶν (Akragas), τιμεῖ = τιμᾷ (Kalydna), τιμοῦντες and δαπανοῦντας (Kameiros). Conversely,

some epsilon-stems show ᾱ, not η, in the aorist, e.g.
VII.51 ἐξεπόνᾱσα (~ἐκπονεῖν). This may in some cases
be 'hyper-dorism' (cf. E7[b]) on the part of an ancient
editor (or conceivably on the part of Theokritos), but
the relationship -εῖν ~-ᾱσαι is sporadically attested in
inscriptions (and on its occurrence in lyric cf. K.
Strunk, *Glotta* xlii [1964], 165ff.)[1].

Athematic conjugation. Occasionally thematic
verbs of which the stem ends in a vowel are conju-
gated athematically, e.g. VII.40 νίκημι = νικῶ, VI.8
ποθόρησθα = προσορᾷς, I.85 ζάτεισ' (<*ζάτε-νσα) =
ζητοῦσα (most manuscripts have the banal variant
ζατοῖσ'), I.90 γελᾶντι = γελῶσι (banal variants γελεῦντι
and γελῶντι), X.56 μοχθέντας (so the ancient text avail-
able for the last few lines of the poem; the medieval text
has μοχθεῦντας). This phenomenon is normal in Lesbos,
Thessaly, Arkadia and Cyprus (none of which are
Dorian), but at Kyrene also we find τελεσφορέντες,
γυμνασιαρχέντας (= -οῦντες, -οῦντας), and (more im-
portant) ἐλᾶντι and ἐλάντω at Kos.

(*f*) Future stem. The addition of ε to the future
stem, with resulting contraction of vowels (not un-
known in Attic, e.g. φευξεῖσθαι ~φεύγειν) is often metri-
cally attested, e.g., II.8 βᾱσεῦμαι = βήσομαι, XV.133
οἰσεῦμες = οἴσομεν, though sometimes the absence of
ε is equally guaranteed, e.g. II.3 καταδήσομαι ἄνδρα.
(Cf. ἀξιώσοντα, διαλυσοῦντι and διακρινεῦντι all in the
same inscription of Kalydna). In the first and second

---

[1] In Menander, *Aspis* 464, a Doric-speaking doctor says
νόσᾱμα for νόσημα (~νοσεῖν); this may be indiscriminate carica-
ture on the part of an Athenian poet writing for an Athenian
audience.

persons singular, of course, the difference is only one of accent, e.g. I.3 ἀποισῇ, I.14 νομευσῶ.

(g) Aorist stem. Aorist ξ corresponds to imperfective ζ, e.g. I.12 καθίξας (~καθίζειν), XIV.28 ἐξήταξα (~ἐξετάζειν). So (e.g.) ἐξοδιάξαι, κατασκευάξαι in the Dodecanese.

(h) Perfect. In the singular and in the infinitive the perfect is treated like a present, e.g. I.102 δεδύκειν = δεδυκέναι, XV.58 δεδοίκω = δέδοικα, XI.1 πεφύκει = πέφυκε. This was normal in Sicily and the Dodecanese, to judge from γεγόνειν (Akragas) and ἀποδεδώκεν (Knidos; the context proves that it is an infinitive).

(i) The verb 'be'. ἐντί = εἰσί, ἧς = ἦν (third person sing.), ἧμεν (commonly with a variant εἶμεν) = εἶναι.

(j) Original ᾱ is preserved throughout (epic η, Attic usually η). The phenomena -σδ- = -ζ- and -οισα = -ουσα have been discussed above (E9[c] 3 and 4).

(k) A substantial number of individual words (e.g. αἰ, λῆν) which cannot be subsumed under general rules of phonological correspondence come into the category 'different both from epic and from the Attic Koine'; these will be found in the vocabulary at the end of the book.

F. Style

F1. The most prominent single characteristic of Theokritos's style is his repetition or partial repetition of words. This takes the following forms:

(a) Simple repetition, which may be symbolised as AAB = AB, e.g.

I.12 λῆς ποτὶ τᾶν Νυμφᾶν, λῆς, αἰπόλε, κτλ.

Cf. I.15f. (οὐ θέμις), I.64 (ἄρχετε, in the refrain), I.66 (πᾷ ποκα), I.127 al. (λήγετε, refrain), I.144f. (χαίρετε), II.118 (ἦνθον), V.44 (ἕρπε), V.61f. (τίς), VII.118f. (βάλλετε), XI.60 (νῦν), XVIII.50ff. (Λατώ, Κύπρις, Ζεύς), XXIV.40 (ἔστι); with negations, exclamations or vocatives: I.123 (Πάν), IV.54 (ναί), V.14f. (οὐ), 17ff. (οὐ), 86 (φεῦ), VI.8 (τάλαν), 22 (οὐ), VII.38 (οὐ), XI.29 (οὐ), 72 (Κύκλωψ). In XIV.24 ἔστι Λύκος, Λύκος ἐστί a whole clause is excitedly repeated.

(b) Repetition of a word when a clause is added, e.g.

I.29f.   μαρύεται ὑψόθι κισσός,
κισσὸς ἑλιχρύσῳ κεκονιμένος.

Cf. I.95f. (γελάοισα), VII.59 (ἀλκυόνες).

(c) The repetition of a noun where a pronoun would have sufficed, or of a participle where (e.g.) 'then' or 'that' would have sufficed, e.g.

I.5f.   ἐς τὲ καταρρεῖ
ἁ χίμαρος· χιμάρω δὲ καλὸν κρέας κτλ.

II.113 ἕζετ' ἐπὶ κλιντῆρι καὶ ἑζόμενος φάτο μῦθον.

Cf. I.65 (Θύρσιδος), II.23 (Δέλφιδι), II.131 (Κύπριν), XI.63 (ἐξενθοῖσα), XVI.109 (χαρίτεσσιν).
Similar in character, though not so simple, are: I.93 (ἄνυε), VI.5 (πρᾶτος), XI.10 (ἤρατο~8), XXVI.30 (εὐαγέεσσιν).

(d) Anaphora, the repetition of a word in successive clauses, which may be symbolised as AB + AC = A(B + C), e.g.

I.71f. τῆνον μὲν θῶες, τῆνον λύκοι ὠρύσαντο,
τῆνον χὠκ δρυμοῖο λεών ἔκλαυσε θανόντα.

74f. πολλαί οἱ πὰρ ποσσὶ βόες, πολλοὶ δέ τε ταῦροι,
πολλαὶ δὲ δαμάλαι καὶ πόρτιες ὠδύραντο.

Cf. I.1ff., 4f., 67, 78, 100f., 105f., 116f., 132, 146f., II.33, 43, 98, 165, III.24, IV.31, 45f., V.38, 45f., 53f., 58f., 60, 104, VI.36, VII.35, 84, 143, 149ff., XI.45ff., XIII.59, XIV.47, XV.5, 6, 82, 112f., XVI.13, 25, 33ff., 48f., XVIII.10f., 49, XXII.1ff. In certain cases the repeated word is not symmetrically placed, e.g. I.80, III.3f.; there are others in which a cognate word is substituted for a direct repetition, e.g. III.49f. (ζαλωτός~ζαλῶ); there are very many passages in which the effect of anaphora is achieved by the repetition of ὦ (e.g. I.115), of a preposition (e.g. VII.88) or even of the definite article, which accounts for the 'family resemblance' between I.141, XV.43 and XV.86.

(e) In dialogue, the picking up of a word used by the previous speaker, e.g. IV.13f., 44~41, V.35~31, 44f., 118~116, 140f., X.8f., 20f., XIV.2, XXII54f., 56f.

(f) Repetition (usually symmetrical) on a much larger scale is peculiarly characteristic of Theokritos, e.g.

I.87ff.
ὡπόλος, ὄκκ' ἐσορῇ τὰς μηκάδας οἷα βατεῦνται,
τάκεται ὀφθαλμὼς ὅτι οὐ τράγος αὐτὸς ἔγεντο.
ἄρχετε κτλ.
καὶ τὺ δ' ἐπεί κ' ἐσορῇς τὰς παρθένος οἷα γελᾶντι,
τάκεαι ὀφθαλμὼς ὅτι οὐ μετὰ ταῖσι χορεύεις.

Cf. I.97f., 120f., II.38ff., V.68ff., 112ff., XI.22f., XVI.3f., XVIII.43ff., XXII.25f., XXIV.7ff., XXVI.

18ff. The phenomenon appears in a slightly exag-
gerated (and thus cruder) form in the bucolic poetry
written in imitation of Theokritos, e.g. VIII.11f.

VIII.11f.

—χρῇσδεις ὧν ἐσιδεῖν; χρῇσδεις καταθεῖναι ἄεθλον;
—χρῇσδω τοῦτ᾽ ἐσιδεῖν, χρῇσδω καταθεῖναι ἄεθλον.

28f.

χοὶ μὲν παῖδες ἄυσαν, ὁ δ᾽ αἰπόλος ἦνθ᾽ ὑπακούσας·
χοὶ μὲν παῖδες ἀείδεν, ὁ δ᾽ αἰπόλος ἤθελε κρίνειν.

XXVII.37f., Verg. Ecl. 4.58ff., 7.61ff., Calp. Sic.
3.51ff. (cf. R. Gimm, De Vergilii stilo bucolico [Leipzig,
1910])

F2. Of the types of repetition classified in **F1,** (a) and
(e) are familiar to us in comedy, (b) in epic, (c) in
Herodotos (and cf. Ap. Rh. ii. 305, 393f., 422), and
(d) in many Classical and Hellenistic authors (includ-
ing Kallimachos and Aratos and, to a lesser degree,
Apollonios). Theokritos is, however, exceptional in
his predilection for (a) and (d), and his use of (b), (c)
and (e) in addition helps to give much of his poetry a
resemblance to a complicated pattern in which certain
symmetrical motifs constantly recur. Type (f) has a
much more limited distribution in Greek poetry than
the other types. It occurs sporadically in epic, notably
in similes (Il. xviii.219ff., xix.357ff., xxiii.222ff., Od.
iv.339f., x.216ff.); where the words describe an equal
balance of forces and sound is matched to sense (Il.
xii.417ff., xxiii.719f.; cf. Kallim. H.4.84f.); in a
formalised lamentation (Il. xxiv.762f. ∼ 748f.); in
question and answer (Il. vi.379ff.); and in a catalogue

(*Il.* xiv.317ff.). Parallels for this epic usage may be found in a much earlier and less sophisticated work, the Mesopotamian Epic of Gilgamesh; considering the total bulk of the *Iliad* and *Odyssey*, it is remarkable that we cannot glean more examples from them. In literature of the Classical period repetition of type (*f*) appears, naturally enough, in comic scenes (e.g. Ar. *Ach.* 1097ff.) where the poet wishes to emphasise the symmetrical and antithetical nature of what he is portraying. Those scenes apart, its Classical appearances are confined to:

(i) Lamentations, e.g Soph. *Trach.* 947ff.

(ii) Wedding-songs, viz. Sappho fr. 115

τίῳ σ' ὦ φίλε γάμβρε, μάλιστ' ἐϊκάσδω;
ὄρπακι βραδίνῳ σε μάλιστ' ἐϊκάσδω.

and Ar. *Peace* 1338f.

τί δράσομεν αὐτήν; τρυγήσομεν αὐτήν.

(note the question and answer in both cases).

(iii) An anonymous skolion, *PMG* 904

ἁ ὖς τὰν βάλανον τὰν μὲν ἔχει, τὰν δ' ἔραται λαβεῖν·
κἀγὼ παῖδα καλὴν τὴν μὲν ἔχω, τὴν δ' ἔραμαι λαβεῖν.

(iv) A children's game, *PMG* 852

ποῦ μοι τὰ ῥόδα, ποῦ μοι τὰ ἴα, ποῦ μοι τὰ καλὰ σέλινα;
ταδὶ τὰ ῥόδα, ταδὶ τὰ ἴα, ταδὶ τὰ καλὰ σέλινα.

It is not, in my view, a coincidence that of the twelve Theokritean examples cited above I.87ff. is a jocular εἰκών (a popular humorous form, v.n. ad loc.), II.38ff. is a magical spell, XVI.3f. occurs at the outset of a poem which is probably (cf. p. 218) based on a

children's begging-song, XVIII.43ff. is part of a
wedding-song, XXII.25f. is a highly formal ritual
element in a hymn, and XXIV.7ff. is a lullaby. There
is a case for saying that repetition of type (f) is a
primitive form which was eschewed by Classical
literature and by poets such as Apollonios (cf. iii.
648ff., where an opportunity is not taken), just as a
too obvious symmetry was eschewed by Classical
sculptors and painters, but flourished in the sub-
literary compositions produced for social and ritual
occasions and appealed greatly to Theokritos. XXVI.
18ff. is a striking (and not altogether pleasing)
intrusion of this type of repetition into a poem which
is neither bucolic nor, apparently, ritual. The type
does not occur in realistic conversation (note how an
opportunity for it is not taken in XV.89 ~87), and in
II.23ff., 43ff., 48ff., 54f. what could have been a
monotonous recurrence of magical formalism is
replaced by elegant variations.

F3. In I and II Theokritos uses the refrain as a formal
device. This too was taken up by later poets as
eminently bucolic (Moschos 3, Verg. *Ecl.* 8). No
doubt it was a prominent feature of sub-literary
composition among the Greeks, as among many other
peoples, and a short refrain is found in wedding-songs,
but it must not be forgotten that it was also charac-
teristic of paians and of some hymns (e.g. *POxy*
2442 fr. 32 [Pindar] ἰηιὲ βασίλειαν Ὀλυμπίων νύμφαν
ἀριστοπ.[.].ν). In XVIII, where we might expect
repetition of the wedding-song refrain, it appears only
in the last line.

F4. X, XIV and XV, which depict the conversation of ordinary people, are full of colloquial expressions, often elliptic and allusive, of proverbs, and of clichés (cf. pp. 167, 189 and 197). The same characteristics appear in V.21ff., 31, 38f., 78f. and VI.18, but not in I and (surprisingly) very rarely in IV.

F5. Epic morphology ('accidence', 'inflection'), syntax and vocabulary are only to be expected in the heroic poems, but they are also conspicuous on the lips of Theokritean herdsmen; cf. also II.29 and 126. Theokritos adopts epic phraseology in all genres, e.g. VII.137 (κατειβόμενον κελάρυζε), 139 (ἔχον πόνον), XI.27 (ὁδὸν ἁγεμόνευον), XVI.2 (κλέα ἀνδρῶν), though he does not always mean by a phrase what Homer meant by it, e.g. IV.7 (ἐν ὀφθαλμοῖσιν ὀπώπει). Much of his phraseology is not directly or obviously borrowed from Homer but nevertheless modelled on a Homeric original (and, like the directly borrowed phrases, occupying the same place in the verse), e.g. V.44 καὶ ὕστατα βουκολιαξῇ, VI.23f. ὁ μάντις . . . ἐχθρὰ φέροι ποτὶ οἶκον ὅπως τεκέεσσι φυλάσσοι, XIII.44 δειναὶ θεαὶ ἀγροιώταις, XV.50 κακὰ παίχνια, XVI.34 πολλοὶ ἐν Ἀντιόχοιο δόμοις κτλ., XXIV.61 ξηρὸν ὑπαὶ δείους. Sometimes what may look Homeric proves on examination to be a deliberate distortion of a Homeric idea or cliché (cf. **F7**), e.g. XVI.48f. κομόωντας / Πριαμίδας, 56 περίσπλαγχνος Λαέρτης, 74 Ἀχιλεύς . . . μέγας ἢ βαρὺς Αἴας. A Homeric simile sometimes provides the point of departure for a simile which takes a different course, e.g. VI.15ff., XIV.32f.

F6. XI and XIII present mythological material as illustrating a generalisation. This is a traditional technique of Greek poetry from epic onwards, e.g. *Il.* v.382ff. ('for many . . .'), xviii.117ff. ('for not even . . .'), xix.87ff. and xxiv.602ff. ('for even . . .'), *Od.* xxi.293ff. ('for others too . . .'), Aisch. *Cho.* 603ff.; cf. in general R. Oehler, *Mythologische Exempla in der älteren griechischen Dichtung* (Aarau, 1925). Theokritos employs this technique notably in III.40ff., VII.148ff., XV.137ff., XVI. 48ff., 74f., XXII.215ff., more succinctly in II.15ff., 45f.; in XXIV.105ff. the catalogue of the teachers of Herakles is not itself an *exemplum* but has a formal resemblance to passages which are (cf. the list of the loves of Zeus in *Il.* xiv.315ff., or the list of poets in Hermesianax [*Coll. Alex.*] fr. 7). The readiness with which mythological references could be used in ordinary speech is illustrated by XV.61, 92; I.105ff. is a special case in which ridicule and vilification are founded on mythological allusion.

F7. A poet in the time of Theokritos had a very great store of myth available to him in the poetry of the preceding five centuries, and could, if he chose, challenge his readers intellectually by recherché allusions. At the same time it must be remembered that all poets had always assumed the right of creative variation of inherited mythology; we should not imagine, when we encounter in Theokritos something which is unfamiliar to us, that we are witnessing for the first time 'sophisticated' manipulation of 'canonical' stories. We are seldom in a position to know whether Theokritos is offering us his own invention or the product of his reading, e.g. in II.16, XXII.206, XXIV.108, 116, 129. He undoubtedly shows an interest in little-known cults (VII.106f., 115f.) and their aetiology (XVIII.47f.), and occasionally attaches unusual epithets to well-known divinities (XVIII.50, XXII.24, 36; cf. **F5**).

F8. Obscurity of mythological reference need not make much difference to the reader who is content with the vaguely archaic or exotic associations of proper names, or even with their attractive sound; obscurity of thought and imagery is a different matter, and there are passages (predominantly in the heroic poems) of which the interpretation remains controversial: I.136, XV.101., XVI.2ff., 39, 66f., XXII.6ff., 218ff., XXIV.11f., XXVI.4, 29f. In certain other passages it may be that the poet is guilty of carelessness in visualising what he is describing: II.144, XIII.68f., XXII.164, 179, 191, XXIV.31.

F9. Two features of word order should be mentioned here, not because they are un-Greek but because they are both very common in Theokritos and may cause the reader difficulty if he is not prepared for them.

(*a*) The article at the beginning of a clause may be widely separated from its noun, e.g.

I.107   αἱ δὲ καλὸν βομβεῦντι ποτὶ σμάνεσσι μέλισσαι.

Often an adjective or some other qualification may follow the article immediately, e.g.

I.20   καὶ τᾶς βουκολικᾶς ἐπὶ τὸ πλέον ἵκεο μοίσας.

(*b*) The ingredients of a finite clause and a participial or subordinate clause are often interlaced, e.g.

IV.53 εἰς ταύταν ἐτύπην χασμεύμενος (= εἰς ταύταν χασμεύμενος ⋮ ἐτύπην)

XVI.16f. πόθεν οἴσεται ἀθρεῖ ἄργυρον (= ἀθρεῖ ⋮ πόθεν οἴσεται ἄργυρον)

XXIV.82f. δώδεκά οἱ τελέσαντι πεπρωμένον ἐς Διὸς οἰκεῖν μόχθους (= πεπρωμένον οἱ ⋮⋮ δώδεκα μόχθους τελέσαντι ⋮ ἐς Διὸς οἰκεῖν).

G. Bucolic Poetry

G1. Theokritos's claim to recognition as an original genius rests primarily upon the poems in which he portrays herdsmen and other countrymen in a rural setting. Of these poems, IV and XIV are portrayals in verse — like the mimes of Herodas, or Attic drama — of what would in actuality have been ordinary speech; I, III, V, VI, VII, X and XI include within themselves songs ostensibly sung by one or both of the characters (cf. the reference to singing in IV.28–33). A mere rustic mime is not bucolic poetry; the portrayal of musical and poetical rustics is.

G2. The terms 'bucolic song' (βουκολικὰ ἀοιδά) and 'bucolic Muse' (βουκολικὰ Μοῖσα) are applied to the song of Thyrsis in I (20, 70, etc.) and to the pair of songs sung by Simichidas and Lykidas in VII (49). The verb βουκολιάζεσθαι is used of the singers in VII (36) and of the herdsmen who compete in V (44, 60), and the noun βουκολιαστάς has the same reference in V.67. Before Theokritos, βουκόλος normally meant 'cowherd'; it is distinguished from ποιμήν, 'shepherd', and αἰπόλος 'goatherd', in Kratinos (CAF) fr. 281 and in Plato (cf. I.80). The derived verb is βουκολεῖν, which had also a metaphorical sense, 'look after', 'keep under control', in Classical poetry; it acquired a wide concrete sense at an early date, for mares βουκολέοντο in Homer (*Il.* xx.221), and Eupolis (*CAF*) fr. 18 makes 'goats' the object of the middle verb βουκολεῖσθαι. Not knowing the context, we cannot know whether Eupolis intended humorous effect, but clearly Aristotle had no such intention in *Hist. Anim.* 611ª28 'if βουκόλοι fail to find one goat . . .', where βουκόλος is 'herdsman', not 'cowherd'. Theokritos's verb βουκολιάζεσθαι was probably his own invention and modelled on verbs which denote various types of utterance, e.g. φροιμιάζεσθαι, 'speak (or sing) by way of preface', παροιμιάζεσθαι, 'speak in proverbs', and παρρησιάζεσθαι, 'speak frankly' (all these are Classical; later, we find μυθιάζεσθαι, 'tell stories', in Babrios). The nouns βουκολιασμός and βουκολισμός do not appear until very late.

G3. The subject-matter of the songs of herdsmen in Theokritos is sometimes their own love-affairs and their rustic environment, sometimes (as in I, and cf. VII.71ff.) the comparable joys and sorrows of legendary characters, especially Daphnis. Daphnis was himself a cowherd (I.116ff., VII.73) and is himself a singing character in VI. Komatas is referred to in VII.78ff. as a legendary goatherd and a singer of matchless skill; 'Komatas' is also the name of the goatherd who wins the singing-match in V, and although V is located in South Italy its 'dramatic date' is so vague that we cannot be sure whether the victorious goatherd is the legendary character of VII.78ff. or a

contemporary character appropriately named. Of all
the bucolic poems only VII and XIV unmistakably
portray the present. Poem I suggests the present, if
only because the death of Daphnis is treated more as
a legend than as a contemporary event. IV has the
flavour of actuality; VI is located in the mythical
past, and so is the song of Polyphemos in XI, although
the introduction of the poem is addressed to a friend
of Theokritos; III, V and X are timeless. Indeed, the
continuity and community of character between
legendary singing herdsmen and contemporary sing-
ing herdsmen which I and VII put before us may be
felt to condemn the question 'When?' as irrelevant.
The extent to which the same proper names are
mentioned in different poems is another pertinent
consideration (Amaryllis, II.1 and IV.36; Tityros,
III.2 and VII.72; Korydon, IV.1 and V.6; Philondas,
IV.1 and V.114). An artful scattering of these names,
and of the names of people of whom we are told no
more, conveys the impression that we are being
vouchsafed random glimpses of rustic life.

G4. The timelessness of the poems is accentuated by
the highly selective picture of rustic life which they
convey. In Theokritos's own lifetime Sicily and South
Italy were repeatedly devastated and impoverished
by war and pillage; yet his herdsmen never betray any
awareness that their animals are in danger of being
slaughtered by hungry mercenaries (this is particularly
striking in V, which is set in the region of Thourioi,
and it is an important indication that Theokritean
bucolic is not a figurative portrayal of political issues).

They acknowledge the existence of wolves which
threaten their flocks and of animals and insects which
devour the crops, but these dangers to the country-
man's livelihood are never allowed too near the centre
of the stage. We hear much more of the superabundant
fertility of flocks and herds, their prodigious yield of
milk and wool, the delicious colour and scent and
softness of flowers and herbs, the soothing concert of
birds and bees, the cool greenery overshadowing a
spring. It is evident that Theokritos did not set himself
to portray the countryman's environment in all its
aspects, but to treat certain of those aspects as the
material out of which the ideal world of bucolic
poetry could be constructed. Description of idealised
rural scenes, appropriate enough in bucolic, intrudes
also into the heroic poems, e.g. at XIII.39ff., XVI.
90ff., XXII.37ff. — where, however, it is possible also
to discern the influence of much earlier models, e.g.
the description of Kalypso's dwelling in *Od.* v.63ff.
(On the whole question, cf. G. Schönbeck, *Der Locus
Amoenus von Homer bis Horaz* [Heidelberg, 1962]).

G5. Theokritos's countrymen, although (unlike char-
acters in the pastoral poetry of later times) they
do not moralize about the superiority of their life to
that of the city-dweller, are intensely conscious of its
beauties and comforts and extremely fluent in
describing these in terms appropriate to a man who
has come out on a fine day after long confinement in a
city. As poets, they are as skilful and as elegant as
Theokritos can make them; and they know their
Homer — Komatas's words 'may I be Melanthios!'

(V.150) are meaningful only to someone who
remembers the fate of Melanthios in the Odyssey.
But to offset the literary sophistication with which he
endows his characters, Theokritos throws into strong
relief — a little self-consciously, many readers feel —
the hardness and coarseness of countrymen. (So in
Antipatros [GP] 8.3 a 'drunken goatherd' is sexually
the least fastidious of all men). Battos in IV is a
'debunker' more attached to his goats than to people,
an admirer of lecherous old men and malevolent
towards the people of a neighbouring village; Milon
in X jocularly and unfeelingly tries to bully his friend
out of love-sickness; Lakon and Komatas in V accuse,
abuse and ridicule each other with no holds barred;
Aischinas in XIV punches his girl-friend in the face
when he has reason to suspect her of being in love with
another man. Occasional references to the behaviour
of the herds and flocks call our attention (I.151,
III.3f., IV.1f., 15ff., 44ff., V.1ff., 147ff.) to the back-
ground against which the poetry is set. The foci of the
countryman's religion are Pan, Hermes, Priapos, the
Nymphs and (in view of that aspect of the countryman
in which Theokritos is most interested) the Muses;
Zeus (as controller of the weather, and as a god
named in oaths and adjurations), Aphrodite and Eros
(as deities who affect all human life) are acknow-
ledged, but Artemis and Dionysos are conspicuously
absent, despite the long-standing associations of the
former with wild life and of the latter with the culture
of vines and fruit. Hermes was widely associated with
herdsmen (cf. Leonidas [HE] 81.1, where he is
ἐπίσκοπος of goats), as also with travellers in lonely

places. The worship of Pan had spread from its centre in Arkadia throughout the Greek world from the early fifth century onwards, and we often find Hermes and Pan associated in Hellenistic epigrams on rural themes, e.g. Leonidas (*HE*) 3. Priapos (*Πρίηπος*) was originally a local divinity at Lampsakos on the Hellespont; the earliest extant mention of him is in an Athenian comic poet of the late fourth century, Xenarchos (*CAF*) fr. 10. In his original home his cult had something in common with that of Dionysos (Ath. 30B), and at Alexandria he was associated with Dionysos in the time of Ptolemy Philadelphos (Ath. 201B). He took over the functions of many local godlings who protected crops and fruit; cf. *Epigr.* 4 n. and H. Herter, *De Priapo* (Giessen, 1932). The prominence of some gods rather than others in the prayers, sacrifices, dedications and allusions of a given category of people is determined not by a systematic dogma about the relative importance of different gods but by the activities in which that category of people is primarily engaged; if Theokritos had chosen to represent his herdsmen as devoting some of their time to hunting, we should have heard more about Artemis.

G6. The scholia on Theokritos begin with an essay by an ancient scholar (his identity cannot be established) on the 'invention' (*εὕρεσις*) of bucolic poetry. It is noteworthy that this essay looks not to poets earlier than Theokritos but exclusively to cult, and it considers the claims of three festivals: that of Artemis Karyatis in Lakonia, in which 'countrymen' (*ἄγροικοι*) 'sang their own songs'; that of Artemis at Tyndaris in

Sicily, performed by 'the locals' (οἱ ἐπιχώριοι); and
a third festival of Artemis at Syracuse itself, in which
'countrymen' (ἄγροικοι) sang in two or more com-
panies, one of which was eventually declared the
winner. The author of the essay regards the foundation
of this last festival (the aetiological story connects it
with the healing of an episode of civic strife) as the
true origin of bucolic. Modern works of reference
persist in implying, even in stating, that the partici-
pants in the festival were called βουκολιασταί, but
the anonymous author does not say that, and there is
no reason to think that it was so.[1] Since, as we have
seen, Theokritos's herdsmen never mention Artemis,
it is at first sight strange that the ancient scholar
should have considered her festivals. But, of course,
he was quite reasonably looking not for songs *about*
countrymen but for songs *by* countrymen; festivals of
Artemis were the only traditional context in which he
found mention of them; and since Theokritos was a
Syracusan, the scholar naturally decided in favour of
a Syracusan festival at which competitive singing by
countrymen played an important part. He is open to
criticism not for any inadequacy in his research but
for having made an unjustified initial assumption that
the origin of bucolic was to be sought in cult.

G7. This is not to say that there existed a pre-
Theokritean bucolic which measured up to the high

---

[1] The late grammarian Diomedes says that *bucolicon* was the
name given to the singing at the festival of Artemis Karyatis, but
he seems to be grafting on to the theory of origins a quite different
point, the use of the term for 'cowherd' to include all kinds of
herdsmen, *quoniam boues pecora praestarent magnitudine.*

technical standards of literary poetry. The most we can say is that certain poets who *may* have written before Theokritos show an interest in rustic themes:

(*a*) Anyte, an Arkadian woman, composed epigrams on a wide range of subjects which include dedications to Pan and springs in the countryside.[1]

(*b*) Lykophronides, a lyric poet who is probably to be dated before 300 B.C., portrayed in one poem a goatherd in love.

(*c*) The epigrams of Leonidas of Taras include some rustic dedications; one of them, (*HE*) 19, is an epitaph for a certain Kleitagora, who asks herdsmen to pipe and graze their flocks by her grave and offer flowers on it. But although Leonidas may have been older than Theokritos, there are indications that some of his epigrams are to be dated no earlier than *c*. 275–270.

On Hermesianax cf. **G9** below. The fact that no one in antiquity regarded any poet earlier than Theokritos as having written bucolic poetry is a warning to us not to underrate the originality of Theokritos or to overrate the bucolic element in the poets mentioned above.

G8. The hypothesis that Theokritos derived his basic inspiration neither from previous poets nor from ritual, but from the everyday practice of Sicilian herdsmen, and that he elevated a traditional popular art-form to a very high artistic level, receives some support from the following considerations:

---

[1] Reitzenstein's statement (*Real-Enzykl.* i.2655) that Anyte represents a school of Peloponnesian poetry 'which is recognised by Mnasalkas [*Anth.Pal.*] ix.324 as *Hirtenpoesie*' is not justified by the epigram (Mnasalkes [*HE*] 16) to which he refers.

(*a*) Symmetrical repetition, discussed in **F2** above, is proportionately very much rarer in archaic and classical epic, lyric and drama than in Theokritos. Since it is a characteristic of folksongs, games, wedding-songs, lullabies, spells and other subliterate categories of poetry, we can assume with confidence that it was also characteristic of the songs actually composed and sung by herdsmen. In adopting it, Theokritos must have been deliberately drawing (as any reader of his own day would have observed) upon subliterate poetry as a source of new and attractive forms which could be imposed in moderation upon sophisticated matter; this taste was not shared to any significant degree by Kallimachos, Apollonios or Aratos. One might perhaps compare the way in which Albeniz and Granados adopted forms characteristic of Spanish folk-music as a basis for their sophisticated and technically difficult compositions.

(*b*) Herdsmen, who often have time on their hands, do in fact sing and play pipes and it would be surprising if ancient Greek herdsmen were an exception (cf. the shepherd and his Pan-pipes mentioned in Soph. *Phil.* 213f.). The singing-match which is the subject of poem V has a close parallel in the modern Sicilian *botta e risposta*, which is fiercely abusive and obscene, like that of Lakon and Komatas (cf. Gavin Maxwell, *The Ten Pains of Death* [London, 1959], 49f.). The competitive improvization of verses has been observed also in other parts of Italy and in Austria (cf. R. Merkelbach, *Rhein. Mus.* N.F. xcix [1956], 98ff.).

(*c*) However great the artistic gulf between the elegant poetry of Theokritos and the authentic productions of Greek herdsmen, there was much in Greek tradition to support the belief that legendary herdsmen must have been superlative poets, and to justify conventional treatment of contemporary herdsmen as heirs to a great tradition. Hesiod, when the Muses appeared to him and endowed him with the gift of poetry, was 'looking after the lambs beneath Helikon' (Hes. *Theog.* 23). Archilochos's meeting with the Muses, as recounted in the narrative inscription of the third century B.C. discovered on Paros in 1950 (*Suppl. Epigr. Gr.* xv [1958] 517.II.22ff.), took place when he had been sent by his father to drive a cow to market. The herdsman of Theokritos's own time would normally have been a labourer or a slave; but when Simichidas in VII.91f. says of himself, 'Much else the Nymphs taught me when I was tending my herd in the mountains' he is associating himself with Hesiod; he will not have forgotten that Anchises was a herdsman when Aphrodite gave herself to him, that Paris was a herdsman when he was called upon to judge between the three goddesses, and that in *Od.* xiii.221ff. Athena appears to Odysseus 'in the form of a young man, a shepherd of flocks, supple in body, such as are the sons of kings'.

G9. The legendary element in Theokritos's bucolic seems to be derived from his own homeland, Sicily. Daphnis is located in Eastern Sicily in I.66ff., 117f., in northern Sicily in VII.73ff. In VI Daphnis and Damoitas take a Sicilian subject for their songs, Polyphemos and Galateia (cf. XI.7, 47f.). The Sicilian historian Timaios, an older contemporary of

Theokritos, certainly regarded Daphnis as pasturing cattle in the region of Etna (*FGrHist* 566, fr. 83). Admittedly, Kallimachos implies in *Epigr.* 22.3f. that Cretan herdsmen sang of Daphnis; and Hermesianax located his own story of Daphnis and Menalkas ([*Coll. Alex.*] frr. 2f.) in Euboia. Kallimachos, however, may be simply paying a compliment to Theokritos, implying that in consequence of Theokritos's bucolic Daphnis would be a natural subject for the songs of herdsmen anywhere; Theokritos may indeed be paying the same compliment to himself when in VII he represents the 'Kydonian' herdsman Lykidas, encountered on Kos, as devoted to poetry about Daphnis, or when he makes the name of Daphnis familiar to South Italian herdsmen in V.20, 81. We do not know whether Hermesianax inherited or invented the legend which made Daphnis Euboian, but there is no good reason why Daphnis should not be both Euboian and Sicilian, for Chalkis played an important part in the foundation of colonies in the central Mediterranean. One of these colonies was Zankle (Messene), which in turn founded Himera on the river Himeras (Thuc. vi.5.1); and it so happens that the first poet known to have named Daphnis was Stesichoros, who was a native of Himera and died at Katane.[1] The evidence for this is Aelian, *Var.Hist*, x.18, who, having told the legend of the Sicilian cowherd Daphnis, says 'this was the origin of bucolic songs, and their subject (ὑπόθεσις) was the blinding

[1] The name 'Daphnis' was borne by an Athenian named in a magical curse in the fourth century B.C. (W. Peek, *Kerameikos* iii [Berlin, 1941], 97f.).

of Daphnis. And' (*sc.* 'they say that . . .'; the whole passage is introduced by λέγουσι, and reverts at the end to *oratio obliqua*) 'Stesichoros of Himera was the originator of this genre of poetry'. The ancient scholar whose investigation of the origin of bucolic appears as a preface to the scholia on Theokritos says nothing of Stesichoros, and the reason for this may be very simple: Stesichoros can have told the story, or part of the story, of Daphnis in a lyric poem, but need not have represented Daphnis as composing songs, nor need the lyric poem have been presented as the utterance of a herdsman. In Timaios's version of the legend, however, Daphnis was a skilled player on the pan-pipes as well as a cowherd. As such, he was not unique among legendary characters of Sicilian folklore; according to Athenaios 619AB the inventor of a herdsmen's work-song (βουκολιασμός) was a Sicilian cowherd named Diomos, 'of whom Epicharmos speaks in his *Alkyoneus* and in his *Odysseus Shipwrecked*' (frr. 4, 105). We do not know what Epicharmos said about Diomos (a hero whom we encounter also at Delphi and in Attica), but Athenaios's statement suggests that Epicharmos alluded to Diomos as a legendary singing herdsman; and this helps to root the subject-matter of Theokritos's bucolic very deeply in the folklore of the Greeks of Sicily. Kallim. *Epigr.* 22, where is suggested that Cretan herdsmen will in future sing no more of Daphnis, but of Astakides, who has been 'carried off by a Nymph' (cf. p. 84) was no doubt written after the bucolic of Theokritos had become well-known.

H. Some Aspects of Hellenistic Poetry

H1. If a substantial fragment of a hitherto unknown Greek poem were discovered tomorrow, how should we decide whether it belonged to the Classical or to the Hellenistic period? If it contained a number of words and linguistic forms which happen to be first attested in the third century B.C., and if it followed metrical rules first observable at a comparable date, the assignation of it to the Hellenistic period on formal grounds would follow, and in default of any fresh evidence it it unlikely that the question would be reopened. But if it showed no obvious formal affinities of the kind described, we might find that the application of other criteria was indecisive.

(*a*) New words and new senses of words. But the same can be said of almost all the large fragments of archaic lyric and classical tragedy discovered in recent times; the adaptation of obscure words and the invention of new compounds are not specially characteristic of Hellenistic poetry.

(*b*) The incorporation of epic words and phrases. But this is characteristic of archaic elegy.

(*c*) The use of epic material to a different point. But this too is a very old characteristic of Greek poetry; Mimnermos (D³) fr.2.8, adapting *Il.* vii.451 ὅσον τ’ ἐπικίδναται ἠώς, 'for as long as the sun goes on dawning' (i.e. 'for ever'), gives it (as ὅσον τ’ ἐπὶ γῆν κίδναται ἠέλιος) the quite different point 'only for a day'. Theokritos's use of epic passages with alteration of the point (cf. IV.7, VI.23f. nn.) is of the same character.

(*d*) Mythological allusions which presuppose knowledge of the relevant story on the hearer's part. Allusion of this kind is as old as Homer; cf. *Od.* iii. 306f., where we are told that Orestes 'came back from Athens after seven years and killed Aigisthos' (what was he doing at Athens?), or *Od.* xi.291ff., where Melampous is alluded to only as 'the noble seer', and his imprisonment (a complicated story, as we encounter it in later literature) is passed over in two words. Indeed, it can be argued (M. M. Willcock, *CQ* N.S. xiv [1964], 142ff.) that some mythological narratives in Homer include inventive modifications to suit the context.

(*e*) 'Humanization' of the gods and a flippant attitude to mythology. But what of the seduction of Zeus by Hera in *Il.* xiv.277ff., when Zeus desires Hera as much he did when they were both young and went to bed together 'escaping their parents' notice' (295f.)? Or *H. Hom.* 4 in which Apollo passes on to Hermes the methods of divination which, he says (556f.), 'I learned when I was a boy and looking after the cattle, and my father didn't mind'?

H2. The least profitable way of attempting to characterize Hellenistic poetry as a whole is to begin with second-hand generalizations about it (or about Greek morals, politics or intellectual developments), find passages in Hellenistic poetry which bear out these generalizations, and omit to ask to what extent archaic and classical poetry bear out the same generalizations. The nature of the problem can best be illustrated by the following true story. Some years ago in Oxford a number of professional scholars were

discussing the problem posed by the works of the
Boeotian poetess Korinna, and in particular the
problem of her date, for there is evidence that she was
a contemporary of Pindar and there are also some
considerations which suggest that she may, on the
contrary, have lived in Hellenistic times. The company
included two men of exceptional learning and
experience in the study of Greek poetry; I will call
them X and Y. X, speaking of the poem in which
Korinna represents the mountains Helikon and
Kithairon as having engaged in a singing-contest,
said 'I feel that this naivety is not genuine; it is a
Hellenistic pseudo-naivety'. Y, who was hard of
hearing, nodded vigorously: 'I entirely agree. This
naivety cannot be Hellenistic; it must be archaic!'
The point of the story is not simply that two men who
knew far more about Greek poetry than most of us
were able to disagree so radically (and since Y thought
he was agreeing with X, *odium philologicum* is clearly
ruled out); what tells us most about Hellenistic
poetry is the fact that it was possible to raise and dis-
cuss such a question. Theokritos, Kallimachos and
Apollonios Rhodius were separated by more than
four generations from the deaths of Sophokles,
Euripides, Sokrates and Thucydides; by two from the
death of Plato, and by one from the death of Aristotle.
What had happened to make it possible for us to talk
at all about dating a *naive* poet in the third century
B.C.? The great Hellenistic poets, Theokritos and his
contemporaries, were saturated in the poetry of the
preceding centuries; they studied it both intelligently
and lovingly; in choosing material for their own

poems they displayed a deep and wide knowledge of myth and cult; like most Greeks, they had a sharp eye and ear for how human beings feel and talk and act; in writing, they set themselves, and attained, very high technical standards. These are all great virtues, but there are others which they lacked: they did not bring their intelligence to bear upon profound issues which excite the intellect and the emotions simultaneously, and they treated poetry as if its province had been defined at some date in the past and it had been forbidden to advance in certain directions or to penetrate below a certain phenomenological level. If we can put ourselves into the place of educated Athenians at the end of the fifth century B.C., a period in which philosophical, political, religious, scientific and historical thinking were developing at an almost explosive pace, we may, I think, be able to recapture the surprise we should have felt if someone had asserted that a century and a half later one distinguished poet would be writing, 'And if you do this for me, Pan, may the boys of Arkadia not flog your sides and shoulders with squills when meat is short' (Theokr. VII.106ff.), and another describing how Athena with her mighty hands pushed apart the Symplegades to allow the Argo to pass between them (Ap.Rh. ii.598f.) or how Eros flew down to earth like a gadfly (id. iii.275ff.), a passage whose concrete detail may remind us of *Il.* 1.46f.[1]

[1] One can imagine, too, the despair of Thucydides if he had foreseen the drivel which Timaios (*FGrHist* 566) was to write about the mutilation of the herms (fr. 102, criticised by Plu. *Nic.* 1), a good example of the backwash of poetic convention into historiography.

H3. There are good reasons why we should treat the brief career of Alexander the Great as the point of transition from the Classical to the Hellenistic age; it brought about so many lasting changes in the political, social and cultural structure of the Greek world. If, however, we assume that the character of Hellenistic poetry must have resulted from these great changes, we overlook the fact that we can define the character of a literary category only by comparing it with something else, preferably with what immediately preceded it, and most of what is commonly said about Hellenistic poetry arises from comparing it — across a great gap — with the poetry of the *fifth* century B.C. The last two comedies of Aristophanes, *Women in Assembly* (392) and *Wealth* (388), are separated from Menander's *Dyskolos* (316) by two generations. Unless the *Rhesos* is not what it purports to be, an early play of Euripides, but a fourth-century tragedy of unknown authorship (and opinions on this are divided), we possess no tragedy later than *Oedipus at Kolonos*, which was produced (after Sophokles' death) in 401. The *Persians* of Timotheos (*c.* 450–360), much of which is preserved in a good early papyrus, could belong to the fourth century but may well be earlier. We know the names of many fourth-century poets, but we possess a disappointingly small number of citations from genres other than comedy; and in any case, citations really tell us very little about the design and spirit of works as a whole. We are thus virtually deprived of all means of evaluating the development of serious poetry between the end of the fifth century and the early third. What little we know of Anti-

machos of Kolophon (admired by Plato, but not by
everyone) or of tragedians such as Chairemon and
Theodektes rather suggests that if we one day
discovered a great deal more of them and of their
contemporaries we should be able to assert with
confidence (as I am inclined to risk asserting even now)
that Hellenistic poetry began not with the great
Alexandrians but with the deaths of Euripides and
Sophokles.

H4. No two genres of poetry within the same culture
necessarily develop in step. In Attic comedy, for
example, creative innovation was vigorous throughout
the fourth century, whereas in tragedy it seems that
the creative impulse withered early. The revival of
fifth-century tragedies at the dramatic festivals is
known to have begun at least by 386, and about 330,
on the motion of Lykurgos, the Athenian state assumed
responsibility for custody of a canonical text of
Aischylos, Sophokles and Euripides, from which the
actors were forbidden to diverge. The formation of a
classical canon of this kind is of the highest importance
in the history of literature; it marks the transition from
a 'primary' to a 'secondary' stage in the genre con-
cerned. The Hellenistic poet's awareness that he was
living in a secondary stage was predetermined by the
fact that during the fourth century Athens was the
literary centre of the Greek world, and fourth-century
Athenians tended to look back with intense nostalgia
to the wealth and power which their city had enjoyed
in the previous century.

H5. Study of the technical aspects of classical poetry

was the natural accompaniment of the formation of the concept of a classical canon. It appears from references to him in the Homeric scholia that Antimachos of Kolophon did not merely read Homer, but studied him, adopting for his own use unusual words which he found in Homeric epic. Thus the strictly philological study of Homer can be taken well back into the fourth century (exegesis and criticism of the content go much further back). The *Poetics* of Aristotle (who died in 322) was an attempt to apply to poetry the kind of technical analysis and appraisal which had for more than a century been applied to oratory. Philitas of Kos, a contemporary of Alexander the Great and tutor to the young Ptolemy Philadelphos, collected and explained rare epic words; he was at the same time a poet, of whom Theokr. VII.40 speaks admiringly. Thus, although Alexandria in the early third century witnessed a remarkable widening and deepening of the study and exegesis of poetry and the application of the products of this study to the writing of original poetry, it must be remembered that Theokritos grew up in a culture in which a close relationship between poetry and scholarship was already established. (Cf. R. Pfeiffer, *History of Classical Scholarship*, 87ff., and *JHS* lxxv [1955], 69.)

The Poems

NOTES ON THE APPARATUS CRITICUS

THE purpose of the brief and highly selective apparatus is
to indicate the more important passages in which a choice
has been made between transmitted readings, in which all
transmitted readings have been rejected in favour of an
emendation, or in which different choices or emendations
are deserving of consideration. The following symbols are
used:

$\mathbf{a}$ = the only ancient fragment, or all the ancient frag-
ments, available for the passage in question

a = at least one out of two or more ancient fragments
available, or at least one out of two or more readings
offered by the same ancient fragment

$\mathbf{b}$ = apparently the only reading known to the com-
mentators from whose work the scholion on the pas-
sage is derived

b = one out of two or more readings recognised in the
scholion

$\mathbf{c}$ = the only reading found in the citation(s) of the
passage in question by another author or authors

c = the reading found in at least one other author's
citation

$\mathbf{m}$ = all the medieval manuscripts

m = at least one of the medieval manuscripts

m = a reading probably to be attributed to medieval
conjecture

z = modern conjectural emendation

$\mathbf{a}$, a, $\mathbf{b}$, b do not always apply, since there is much of the
text for which we have no ancient evidence, and the scholia
on some poems are very scanty; $\mathbf{c}$, c apply very seldom.

I

ΘΥΡΣΙΣ

ἁδύ τι τὸ ψιθύρισμα καὶ ἁ πίτυς, αἰπόλε, τήνα
ἁ ποτὶ ταῖς παγαῖσι μελίσδεται, ἁδὺ δὲ καὶ τύ
συρίσδες· μετὰ Πᾶνα τὸ δεύτερον ἆθλον ἀποισῇ.
αἴ κα τῆνος ἕλῃ κεραὸν τράγον, αἶγα τὺ λαψῇ·
αἴ κα δ᾽ αἶγα λάβῃ τῆνος γέρας, ἐς τὲ καταρρεῖ   5
ἁ χίμαρος· χιμάρῳ δὲ καλὸν κρέας, ἔστε κ᾽ ἀμέλξῃς.

ΑΙΠΟΛΟΣ

ἅδιον, ὦ ποιμήν, τὸ τεὸν μέλος ἢ τὸ καταχές
τῆν᾽ ἀπὸ τᾶς πέτρας καταλείβεται ὑψόθεν ὕδωρ.
αἴ κα ταὶ Μοῖσαι τὰν οἴιδα δῶρον ἄγωνται,
ἄρνα τὺ σακίταν λαψῇ γέρας· αἰ δέ κ᾽ ἀρέσκῃ   10
τήναις ἄρνα λαβεῖν, τὺ δὲ τὰν ὄιν ὕστερον ἀξῇ.

ΘΥΡΣΙΣ

λῇς ποτὶ τᾶν Νυμφᾶν, λῇς, αἰπόλε, τεῖδε καθίξας,
ὡς τὸ κάταντες τοῦτο γεώλοφον αἴ τε μυρῖκαι,
συρίσδεν; τὰς δ᾽ αἶγας ἐγὼν ἐν τῷδε νομευσῶ.

ΑΙΠΟΛΟΣ

οὐ θέμις, ὦ ποιμήν, τὸ μεσαμβρινὸν οὐ θέμις ἄμμιν 15
συρίσδεν. τὸν Πᾶνα δεδοίκαμες· ἦ γὰρ ἀπ᾽ ἄγρας
τανίκα κεκμακὼς ἀμπαύεται· ἔστι δὲ πικρός,
καί οἱ ἀεὶ δριμεῖα χολὰ ποτὶ ῥινὶ κάθηται.
ἀλλὰ τὺ γὰρ δή, Θύρσι, τὰ Δάφνιδος ἄλγε᾽ ἀείδες
καὶ τᾶς βουκολικᾶς ἐπὶ τὸ πλέον ἵκεο μοίσας,   20
δεῦρ᾽ ὑπὸ τὰν πτελέαν ἐσδώμεθα τῶ τε Πριήπω

3

καὶ τᾶν κρανίδων κατεναντίον, ᾇπερ ὁ θῶκος
τῆνος ὁ ποιμενικὸς καὶ ταὶ δρύες. αἱ δέ κ' ἀείσῃς
ὡς ὅκα τὸν Λιβύαθε ποτὶ Χρόμιν ᾇσας ἐρίσδων,
αἶγά τέ τοι δωσῶ διδυματόκον ἐς τρὶς ἀμέλξαι,   25
ἃ δύ' ἔχοισ' ἐρίφως ποταμέλγεται ἐς δύο πέλλας,
καὶ βαθὺ κισσύβιον κεκλυσμένον ἀδέι κηρῷ,
ἀμφῶες, νεοτευχές, ἔτι γλυφάνοιο ποτόσδον.
τῶ ποτὶ μὲν χείλη μαρύεται ὑψόθι κισσός,
κισσὸς ἑλιχρύσῳ κεκονιμένος· ἁ δὲ κατ' αὐτόν†   30
καρπῷ ἕλιξ εἰλεῖται ἀγαλλομένα κροκόεντι.
ἔντοσθεν δὲ γυνά τι θεῶν δαίδαλμα τέτυκται,
ἀσκητὰ πέπλῳ τε καὶ ἄμπυκι· πὰρ δέ οἱ ἄνδρες
καλὸν ἐθειράζοντες ἀμοιβαδὶς ἄλλοθεν ἄλλος
νεικείουσ' ἐπέεσσι· τὰ δ' οὐ φρενὸς ἅπτεται αὐτᾶς· 35
ἀλλ' ὅκα μὲν τῆνον ποτιδέρκεται ἄνδρα γέλαισα,
ἄλλοκα δ' αὖ ποτὶ τὸν ῥιπτεῖ νόον· οἱ δ' ὑπ' ἔρωτος
δηθὰ κυλοιδιόωντες ἐτώσια μοχθίζοντι.
τοῖς δὲ μέτα γριπεύς τε γέρων πέτρα τε τέτυκται
λεπράς, ἐφ' ᾇ σπεύδων μέγα δίκτυον ἐς βόλον ἕλκει 40
ὁ πρέσβυς, κάμνοντι τὸ καρτερὸν ἀνδρὶ ἐοικώς.
φαίης κεν γυίων νιν ὅσον σθένος ἐλλοπιεύειν,
ὧδέ οἱ ᾠδήκαντι κατ' αὐχένα πάντοθεν ἶνες
καὶ πολιῷ περ ἐόντι· τὸ δὲ σθένος ἄξιον ἅβας.
τυτθὸν δ' ὅσσον ἄπωθεν ἁλιτρύτοιο γέροντος   45
περκναῖσι σταφυλαῖσι καλὸν βέβριθεν ἀλωά,
τὰν ὀλίγος τις κῶρος ἐφ' αἱμασιαῖσι φυλάσσει
ἥμενος· ἀμφὶ δέ νιν δύ' ἀλώπεκες ἁ μὲν ἀν' ὄρχως
φοιτῇ σινομένα τὰν τρώξιμον, ἁ δ' ἐπὶ πήρᾳ
πάντα δόλον τεύχοισα τὸ παιδίον οὐ πρὶν ἀνησεῖν 50
φατὶ πρὶν ἀκράτιστον ἐπὶ ξηροῖσι καθίξῃ.

30 Susp. z   46 περκναῖσι z:]ε[**a**: πυρναίαις **m**   50 κεύθοισα b
51 πρὶν z: πρὶν ἢ **m**

αὐτὰρ ὅγ' ἀνθερίκοισι καλὰν πλέκει ἀκριδοθήκαν
σχοίνῳ ἐφαρμόσδων· μέλεται δέ οἱ οὔτε τι πήρας
οὔτε φυτῶν τοσσῆνον ὅσον περὶ πλέγματι γαθεῖ.
παντᾷ δ' ἀμφὶ δέπας περιπέπταται ὑγρὸς ἄκανθος,   55
αἰπολικὸν θάημα· τέρας κέ τυ θυμὸν ἀτύξαι.
τῶ μὲν ἐγὼ πορθμῆι Καλυδνίῳ αἶγά τ' ἔδωκα
ὦνον καὶ τυρόεντα μέγαν λευκοῖο γάλακτος·
οὐδέ τι πω ποτὶ χεῖλος ἐμὸν θίγεν, ἀλλ' ἔτι κεῖται
ἄχραντον. τῷ κά τυ μάλα πρόφρων ἀρεσαίμαν   60
αἴ κα μοι τύ, φίλος, τὸν ἐφίμερον ὕμνον ἀείσῃς.
κοὔτι τυ κερτομέω. πόταγ', ὠγαθέ· τὰν γὰρ ἀοιδάν
οὔ τι πᾳ εἰς Ἀίδαν γε τὸν ἐκλελάθοντα φυλαξεῖς.

ΘΥΡΣΙΣ

ἄρχετε βουκολικᾶς, Μοῖσαι φίλαι, ἄρχετ' ἀοιδᾶς.

Θύρσις ὅδ' ὡξ Αἴτνας, καὶ Θύρσιδος ἀδέα φωνά.   65
πᾷ ποκ' ἄρ' ἦσθ', ὅκα Δάφνις ἐτάκετο, πᾷ ποκα, Νύμφαι;
ἦ κατὰ Πηνειῶ καλὰ τέμπεα, ἢ κατὰ Πίνδω;
οὐ γὰρ δὴ ποταμοῖο μέγαν ῥόον εἴχετ' Ἀνάπω,
οὐδ' Αἴτνας σκοπιάν, οὐδ' Ἄκιδος ἱερὸν ὕδωρ.

ἄρχετε βουκολικᾶς, Μοῖσαι φίλαι, ἄρχετ' ἀοιδᾶς.   70
τῆνον μὰν θῶες, τῆνον λύκοι ὠρύσαντο,
τῆνον χὠκ δρυμοῖο λέων ἔκλαυσε θανόντα.

ἄρχετε βουκολικᾶς, Μοῖσαι φίλαι, ἄρχετ' ἀοιδᾶς.
πολλαί οἱ πὰρ ποσσὶ βόες, πολλοὶ δέ τε ταῦροι,
πολλαὶ δὲ δαμάλαι καὶ πόρτιες ὠδύραντο.   75

ἄρχετε βουκολικᾶς, Μοῖσαι φίλαι, ἄρχετ' ἀοιδᾶς.
ἦνθ' Ἑρμᾶς πράτιστος ἀπ' ὤρεος, εἶπε δὲ 'Δάφνι,
τίς τυ κατατρύχει; τίνος, ὠγαθέ, τόσσον ἔρασαι;'

52 ἀκριδοθήραν m   56 αἰολικὸν b   57 Καλυδνίῳ b: Καλυδωνίῳ mb

ἄρχετε βουκολικᾶς, Μοῖσαι φίλαι, ἄρχετ' ἀοιδᾶς.

ἦνθον τοὶ βοῦται, τοὶ ποιμένες, ᾠπόλοι ἦνθον·   80
πάντες ἀνηρώτευν τί πάθοι κακόν. ἦνθ' ὁ Πρίηπος
κἤφα 'Δάφνι τάλαν, τί τὺ τάκεαι; ἁ δέ τυ κώρα
πάσας ἀνὰ κράνας, πάντ' ἄλσεα ποσσὶ φορεῖται —

ἄρχετε βουκολικᾶς, Μοῖσαι φίλαι, ἄρχετ' ἀοιδᾶς —

ζάτεισ'· ἁ δύσερώς τις ἄγαν καὶ ἀμήχανος ἐσσί.   85
βούτας μὲν ἐλέγευ, νῦν δ' αἰπόλῳ ἀνδρὶ ἔοικας.
ᾠπόλος, ὅκκ' ἐσορῇ τὰς μηκάδας οἷα βατεῦνται,
τάκεται ὀφθαλμὼς ὅτι οὐ τράγος αὐτὸς ἔγεντο.

ἄρχετε βουκολικᾶς, Μοῖσαι φίλαι, ἄρχετ' ἀοιδᾶς.

καὶ τὺ δ' ἐπεί κ' ἐσορῇς τὰς παρθένος οἷα γελᾶντι, 90
τάκεαι ὀφαλμὼς ὅτι οὐ μετὰ ταῖσι χορεύεις.'
τὼς δ' οὐδὲν ποτελέξαθ' ὁ βουκόλος, ἀλλὰ τὸν αὑτῶ
ἄννε πικρὸν ἔρωτα καὶ ἐς τέλος ἄννε μοίρας.

ἄρχετε βουκολικᾶς, Μοῖσαι, πάλιν ἄρχετ' ἀοιδᾶς.

ἦνθέ γε μὰν ἁδεῖα καὶ ἁ Κύπρις γελάοισα,   95
λάθρη μὲν γελάοισα, βαρὺν δ' ἀνὰ θυμὸν ἔχοισα,
κεῖπε 'τύ θην τὸν Ἔρωτα κατεύχεο, Δάφνι, λυγιξεῖν·
ἦ ῥ' οὐκ αὐτὸς Ἔρωτος ὑπ' ἀργαλέω ἐλυγίχθης;'

ἄρχετε βουκολικᾶς, Μοῖσαι, πάλιν ἄρχετ' ἀοιδᾶς.

τὰν δ' ἄρα χὠ Δάφνις ποταμείβετο· 'Κύπρι βαρεῖα, 100
Κύπρι νεμεσσατά, Κύπρι θνατοῖσιν ἀπεχθής,
ἤδη γὰρ φράσδη πάνθ' ἄλιον ἄμμι δεδύκειν;
Δάφνις κἠν Ἀίδα κακὸν ἔσσεται ἄλγος Ἔρωτι.

ἄρχετε βουκολικᾶς, Μοῖσαι, πάλιν ἄρχετ' ἀοιδᾶς.

οὐ λέγεται τὰν Κύπριν ὁ βουκόλος — ; ἕρπε ποτ' Ἴδαν, 105

95 ἁ δῖα b

ἕρπε ποτ' 'Αγχίσαν· τηνεὶ δρύες ἠδὲ κύπειρος,
αἱ δὲ καλὸν βομβεῦντι ποτὶ σμάνεσσι μέλισσαι.

ἄρχετε βουκολικᾶς, Μοῖσαι, πάλιν ἄρχετ' ἀοιδᾶς.

ὡραῖος χὤδωνις, ἐπεὶ καὶ μῆλα νομεύει
καὶ πτῶκας βάλλει καὶ θηρία πάντα διώκει.   110

ἄρχετε βουκολικᾶς, Μοῖσαι, πάλιν ἄρχετ' ἀοιδᾶς.

αὖτις ὅπως στασῇ Διομήδεος ἆσσον ἰοῖσα,
καὶ λέγε "τὸν βούταν νικῶ Δάφνιν, ἀλλὰ μάχευ μοι".

ἄρχετε βουκολικᾶς, Μοῖσαι, πάλιν ἄρχετ' ἀοιδᾶς.

ὦ λύκοι, ὦ θῶες, ὦ ἀν' ὤρεα φωλάδες ἄρκτοι,   115
χαίρεθ'· ὁ βουκόλος ὔμμιν ἐγὼ Δάφνις οὐκέτ' ἀν' ὕλαν,
οὐκέτ' ἀνὰ δρυμώς, οὐκ ἄλσεα. χαῖρ', 'Αρέθοισα,
καὶ ποταμοὶ τοὶ χεῖτε καλὸν κατὰ Θύβριδος ὕδωρ.

ἄρχετε βουκολικᾶς, Μοῖσαι, πάλιν ἄρχετ' ἀοιδᾶς.

Δάφνις ἐγὼν ὅδε τῆνος ὁ τὰς βόας ὦδε νομεύων,   120
Δάφνις ὁ τὼς ταύρως καὶ πόρτιας ὦδε ποτίσδων.

ἄρχετε βουκολικᾶς, Μοῖσαι, πάλιν ἄρχετ' ἀοιδᾶς.

ὦ Πὰν Πάν, εἴτ' ἐσσὶ κατ' ὤρεα μακρὰ Λυκαίω,
εἴτε τύγ' ἀμφιπολεῖς μέγα Μαίναλον, ἔνθ' ἐπὶ νᾶσον
τὰν Σικελάν, Ἑλίκας δὲ λίπε ῥίον αἰπύ τε σᾶμα   125
τῆνο Λυκαονίδαο, τὸ καὶ μακάρεσσιν ἀγητόν.

λήγετε βουκολικᾶς, Μοῖσαι, ἴτε λήγετ' ἀοιδᾶς.

ἔνθ', ὦναξ, καὶ τάνδε φέρευ πακτοῖο μελίπνουν
ἐκ κηρῶ σύριγγα καλὸν περὶ χεῖλος ἑλικτάν·
ἦ γὰρ ἐγὼν ὑπ' Ἔρωτος ἐς Ἀιδαν ἕλκομαι ἤδη.   130

λήγετε βουκολικᾶς, Μοῖσαι, ἴτε λήγετ' ἀοιδᾶς.

106f. ἠδὲ . . . αἱ δὲ z: ὦδε . . . ὦδε m   130 Ἀιδος m

νῦν ἴα μὲν φορέοιτε βάτοι, φορέοιτε δ' ἄκανθαι,
ἁ δὲ καλὰ νάρκισσος ἐπ' ἀρκεύθοισι κομάσαι,
πάντα δ' ἄναλλα γένοιτο, καὶ ἁ πίτυς ὄχνας ἐνείκαι,
Δάφνις ἐπεὶ θνάσκει, καὶ τὰς κύνας ὥλαφος ἕλκοι, 135
κἠξ ὀρέων τοὶ σκῶπες ἀηδόσι γαρύσαιντο.'

λήγετε βουκολικᾶς, Μοῖσαι, ἴτε λήγετ' ἀοιδᾶς.

χὠ μὲν τόσσ' εἰπὼν ἀπεπαύσατο· τὸν δ' Ἀφροδίτα
ἤθελ' ἀνορθῶσαι· τά γε μὰν λίνα πάντα λελοίπει
ἐκ Μοιρᾶν, χὠ Δάφνις ἔβα ῥόον. ἔκλυσε δίνα   140
τὸν Μοίσαις φίλον ἄνδρα, τὸν οὐ Νύμφαισιν ἀπεχθῆ.

λήγετε βουκολικᾶς, Μοῖσαι, ἴτε λήγετ' ἀοιδᾶς.

καὶ τὺ δίδου τὰν αἶγα τό τε σκύφος, ὥς κεν ἀμέλξας
σπείσω ταῖς Μοίσαις. ὦ χαίρετε πολλάκι, Μοῖσαι,
χαίρετ'· ἐγὼ δ' ὕμμιν καὶ ἐς ὕστερον ἅδιον ᾀσῶ. 145

ΑΙΠΟΛΟΣ

πλῆρές τοι μέλιτος τὸ καλὸν στόμα, Θύρσι, γένοιτο,
πλῆρες δὲ σχαδόνων, καὶ ἀπ' Αἰγίλω ἰσχάδα τρώγοις
ἁδεῖαν, τέττιγος ἐπεὶ τύγα φέρτερον ᾄδεις.
ἠνίδε τοι τὸ δέπας· θᾶσαι, φίλος, ὡς καλὸν ὄσδει·
Ὡρᾶν πεπλύσθαι νιν ἐπὶ κράναισι δοκησεῖς.   150
ὧδ' ἴθι, Κισσαίθα· τὺ δ' ἄμελγέ νιν. αἱ δὲ χίμαιραι,
οὐ μὴ σκιρτασεῖτε, μὴ ὁ τράγος ὕμμιν ἀναστῇ.

II

πᾷ μοι ταὶ δάφναι; φέρε, Θεστυλί. πᾷ δὲ τὰ φίλτρα;
στέψον τὰν κελέβαν φοινικέῳ οἰὸς ἀώτῳ,
ὡς τὸν ἐμὸν βαρὺν εὖντα φίλον καταδήσομαι ἄνδρα,
ὅς μοι δωδεκαταῖος ἀφ' ὧ τάλας οὐδὲ ποθίκει,
οὐδ' ἔγνω πότερον τεθνάκαμες ἢ ζοοὶ εἰμές,   5
οὐδὲ θύρας ἄραξεν ἀνάρσιος. ἦ ῥά οἱ ἀλλᾷ
ᾤχετ' ἔχων ὅ τ' Ἔρως ταχινὰς φρένας ἅ τ' Ἀφροδίτα.
βασεῦμαι ποτὶ τὰν Τιμαγήτοιο παλαίστραν
αὔριον ὥς νιν ἴδω, καὶ μέμψομαι οἷά με ποιεῖ.
νῦν δέ μιν ἐκ θυέων καταδήσομαι. ἀλλά, Σελάνα,   10
φαῖνε καλόν· τὶν γὰρ ποταείσομαι ἄσυχα, δαῖμον,
τᾷ χθινίᾳ θ' Ἑκάτᾳ, τὰν καὶ σκύλακες τρομέοντι
ἐρχομέναν νεκύων ἀνά τ' ἠρία καὶ μέλαν αἷμα.
χαῖρ', Ἑκάτα δασπλῆτι, καὶ ἐς τέλος ἄμμιν ὀπάδει,
φάρμακα ταῦτ' ἔρδοισα χερείονα μήτε τι Κίρκας   15
μήτε τι Μηδείας μήτε ξανθᾶς Περιμήδας.

ἶυγξ, ἕλκε τὺ τῆνον ἐμὸν ποτὶ δῶμα τὸν ἄνδρα.

ἄλφιτά τοι πρᾶτον πυρὶ τάκεται. ἀλλ' ἐπίπασσε,
Θεστυλί. δειλαία, πᾷ τὰς φρένας ἐκπεπότασαι;
ἦ ῥά γε θην, μυσαρά, καὶ τὶν ἐπίχαρμα τέτυγμαι;   20
πάσσ' ἅμα καὶ λέγε ταῦτα· 'τὰ Δέλφιδος ὀστία πάσσω'.

ἶυγξ, ἕλκε τὺ τῆνον ἐμὸν ποτὶ δῶμα τὸν ἄνδρα.

Δέλφις ἔμ' ἀνίασεν· ἐγὼ δ' ἐπὶ Δέλφιδι δάφναν
αἴθω· χὡς αὕτα λακεῖ μέγα καππυρίσασα
κἠξαπίνας ἄφθη κοὐδὲ σποδὸν εἴδομες αὐτᾶς,   25
οὕτω τοι καὶ Δέλφις ἐνὶ φλογὶ σάρκ' ἀμαθύνοι.

10 ἐκ θυμοῦ a   18 κάεται b

ἴυγξ, ἕλκε τὺ τῆνον ἐμὸν ποτὶ δῶμα τὸν ἄνδρα. 27

νῦν θυσῶ τὰ πίτυρα. τὺ δ', "Αρτεμι, καὶ τὸν ἐν
  "Αιδα   28[33]
κινήσαις ἀδάμαντα καὶ εἴ τι περ ἀσφαλὲς ἄλλο — 29[34]
Θεστυλί, ταὶ κύνες ἄμμιν ἀνὰ πτόλιν ὠρύονται· 30[35]
ἁ θεὸς ἐν τριόδοισι· τὸ χαλκέον ὡς τάχος ἄχει. 31[36]

ἴυγξ, ἕλκε τὺ τῆνον ἐμὸν ποτὶ δῶμα τὸν ἄνδρα. 32[37]

ἠνίδε σιγῇ μὲν πόντος, σιγῶντι δ' ἀῆται· 33[38]
ἁ δ' ἐμὰ οὐ σιγῇ στέρνων ἔντοσθεν ἀνία, 34[39]
ἀλλ' ἐπὶ τήνῳ πᾶσα καταίθομαι ὅς με τάλαιναν 35[40]
ἀντὶ γυναικὸς ἔθηκε κακὰν καὶ ἀπάρθενον ἦμεν. 36[41]

ἴυγξ, ἕλκε τὺ τῆνον ἐμὸν ποτὶ δῶμα τὸν ἄνδρα. 37[42]

ὡς τοῦτον τὸν κηρὸν ἐγὼ σὺν δαίμονι τάκω, 38[28]
ὣς τάκοιθ' ὑπ' ἔρωτος ὁ Μύνδιος αὐτίκα Δέλφις. 39[29]
χὣς δινεῖθ' ὅδε ῥόμβος ὁ χάλκεος ἐξ Ἀφροδίτας, 40[30]
ὣς τῆνος δινοῖτο ποθ' ἁμετέραισι θύραισιν. 41[31]

ἴυγξ, ἕλκε τὺ τῆνον ἐμὸν ποτὶ δῶμα τὸν ἄνδρα. 42[32]

ἐς τρὶς ἀποσπένδω καὶ τρὶς τάδε, πότνια, φωνῶ· 43
εἴτε γυνὰ τήνῳ παρακέκλιται εἴτε καὶ ἀνήρ,
τόσσον ἔχοι λάθας ὅσσον ποκὰ Θησέα φαντί 45
ἐν Δίᾳ λασθῆμεν εὐπλοκάμῳ Ἀριάδνας.

ἴυγξ, ἕλκε τὺ τῆνον ἐμὸν ποτὶ δῶμα τὸν ἄνδρα.

ἱππομανὲς φυτόν ἐστι παρ' Ἀρκάσι, τῷ δ' ἔπι πᾶσαι
καὶ πῶλοι μαίνονται ἀν' ὤρεα καὶ θοαὶ ἵπποι·
ὡς καὶ Δέλφιν ἴδοιμι, καὶ ἐς τόδε δῶμα περάσαι 50
μαινομένῳ ἴκελος λιπαρᾶς ἔκτοσθε παλαίστρας.

38-42 hic am : post 27 m

ἴυγξ, ἕλκε τὺ τῆνον ἐμὸν ποτὶ δῶμα τὸν ἄνδρα.

τοῦτ' ἀπὸ τᾶς χλαίνας τὸ κράσπεδον ὤλεσε Δέλφις,
ὡγὼ νῦν τίλλοισα κατ' ἀγρίῳ ἐν πυρὶ βάλλω.
αἰαῖ Ἔρως ἀνιαρέ, τί μευ μέλαν ἐκ χροὸς αἷμα   55
ἐμφὺς ὡς λιμνᾶτις ἅπαν ἐκ βδέλλα πέπωκας;

  ἴυγξ, ἕλκε τὺ τῆνον ἐμὸν ποτὶ δῶμα τὸν ἄνδρα.

σαύραν τοι τρίψαισα κακὸν ποτὸν αὔριον οἰσῶ.
Θεστυλί, νῦν δὲ λαβοῖσα τὺ τὰ θρόνα ταῦθ' ὑπόμαξον
τᾶς τήνω φλιᾶς καθ' ὑπέρτερον ἇς ἔτι καὶ νύξ,   60
  .   .   .   .
καὶ λέγ' ἐπιτρύζοισα 'τὰ Δέλφιδος ὀστία μάσσω'.   62

  ἴυγξ, ἕλκε τὺ τῆνον ἐμὸν ποτὶ δῶμα τὸν ἄνδρα.

νῦν δὴ μώνα ἐοῖσα πόθεν τὸν ἔρωτα δακρύσω;
ἐκ τίνος ἄρξωμαι; τίς μοι κακὸν ἄγαγε τοῦτο;   65
ἦνθ' ἁ τωὐβούλοιο καναφόρος ἄμμιν Ἀναξώ
ἄλσος ἐς Ἀρτέμιδος, τᾷ δή ποκα πολλὰ μὲν ἄλλα
θηρία πομπεύεσκε περισταδόν, ἐν δὲ λέαινα.

  φράζεό μευ τὸν ἔρωθ' ὅθεν ἵκετο, πότνα Σελάνα.

καί μ' ἁ Θευμαρίδα Θρᾷσσα τροφός, ἁ μακαρῖτις,   70
ἀγχίθυρος ναίοισα κατεύξατο καὶ λιτάνευσε
τὰν πομπὰν θάσασθαι· ἐγὼ δέ οἱ ἁ μεγάλοιτος
ὡμάρτευν βύσσοιο καλὸν σύροισ'· χιτῶνα
κἀμφιστειλαμένα τὰν ξυστίδα τὰν Κλεαρίστας.

  φράζεό μευ τὸν ἔρωθ' ὅθεν ἵκετο, πότνα Σελάνα.   75

ἤδη δ' εὖσα μέσαν κατ' ἀμαξιτόν, ᾇ τὰ Λύκωνος,
εἶδον Δέλφιν ὁμοῦ τε καὶ Εὐδάμιππον ἰόντας·

59 ἀπόμορξον b   60 νύξ z: νῦν am   '61' ἐκ θυμῷ δέδεμαι·
ὁ δέ μευ λόγον οὐδένα ποιεῖ m   62 ἐπιφθύζοισα a(b)   μάσσω z:
καίω a: πάσσω m   67 δὴ τόκα z   72 μεγάλατος z

τοῖς δ' ἦς ξανθοτέρα μὲν ἑλιχρύσοιο γενειάς
στήθεα δὲ στίλβοντα πολὺ πλέον ἢ τύ, Σελάνα,
ὡς ἀπὸ γυμνασίοιο καλὸν πόνον ἄρτι λιπόντων.   80

  φράζεό μευ τὸν ἔρωθ' ὅθεν ἵκετο, πότνα Σελάνα.

χὠς ἴδον ὡς ἐμάνην, ὥς μοι πυρὶ θυμὸς ἰάφθη
δειλαίας, τὸ δὲ κάλλος ἐτάκετο. οὐκέτι πομπᾶς
τήνας ἐφρασάμαν, οὐδ' ὡς πάλιν οἴκαδ' ἀπῆνθον
ἔγνων, ἀλλά με τις καπυρὰ νόσος ἐξεσάλαξεν   85
κείμαν δ' ἐν κλιντῆρι δέκ' ἄματα καὶ δέκα νύκτας.

  φράζεό μευ τὸν ἔρωθ' ὅθεν ἵκετο, πότνα Σελάνα.

καί μευ χρὼς μὲν ὁμοῖος ἐγίνετο πολλάκι θάψῳ,
ἔρρευν δ' ἐκ κεφαλᾶς πᾶσαι τρίχες, αὐτὰ δὲ λοιπά
ὀστί' ἔτ' ἦς καὶ δέρμα. καὶ ἐς τίνος οὐκ ἐπέρασα,   90
ἢ ποίας ἔλιπον γραίας δόμον ἄτις ἐπᾷδεν;
ἀλλ' ἦς οὐδὲν ἐλαφρόν, ὁ δὲ χρόνος ἄνυτο φεύγων.

  φράζεό μευ τὸν ἔρωθ' ὅθεν ἵκετο, πότνα Σελάνα.

χοὔτω τᾷ δώλᾳ τὸν ἀλαθέα μῦθον ἔλεξα·
'εἰ δ' ἄγε, Θεστυλί, μοι χαλεπᾶς νόσω εὑρέ τι μᾶχος.   95
πᾶσαν ἔχει με τάλαιναν ὁ Μύνδιος· ἀλλὰ μολοῖσα
τήρησον ποτὶ τὰν Τιμαγήτοιο παλαίστραν·
τηνεὶ γὰρ φοιτῇ, τηνεὶ δέ οἱ ἁδὺ καθῆσθαι.

  φράζεό μευ τὸν ἔρωθ' ὅθεν ἵκετο, πότνα Σελάνα.

κἠπεί κα νιν ἐόντα μάθῃς μόνον, ἄσυχα νεῦσον,   100
κεἴφ' ὅτι "Σιμαίθα τυ καλεῖ", καὶ ὑφαγέο τεῖδε'.
ὣς ἐφάμαν· ἁ δ' ἦνθε καὶ ἄγαγε τὸν λιπαρόχρων
εἰς ἐμὰ δώματα Δέλφιν· ἐγὼ δέ νιν ὡς ἐνόησα
ἄρτι θύρας ὑπὲρ οὐδὸν ἀμειβόμενον ποδὶ κούφῳ —

82 μευ am   85 ἐξεσάλαξεν ab: ἐξαλάπαξεν m   101 ὑφαγέο
m: ἀφαγέο am

φράζεό μευ τὸν ἔρωθ' ὅθεν ἵκετο, πότνα Σελάνα — 105

πᾶσα μὲν ἐψύχθην χιόνος πλέον, ἐκ δὲ μετώπω
ἱδρώς μευ κοχύδεσκεν ἶσον νοτίαισιν ἐέρσαις,
οὐδέ τι φωνᾶσαι δυνάμαν, οὐδ' ὅσσον ἐν ὕπνῳ
κνυζεῦνται φωνεῦντα φίλαν ποτὶ ματέρα τέκνα·
ἀλλ' ἐπάγην δαγῦδι καλὸν χρόα πάντοθεν ἶσα.   110

    φράζεό μευ τὸν ἔρωθ' ὅθεν ἵκετο, πότνα Σελάνα.

καί μ' ἐσιδὼν ὥστοργος ἐπὶ χθονὸς ὄμματα πάξας
ἕζετ' ἐπὶ κλιντῆρι καὶ ἑζόμενος φάτο μῦθον·
'ἦ ῥά με, Σιμαίθα, τόσον ἔφθασας, ὅσσον ἐγώ θην
πρᾶν ποκα τὸν χαρίεντα τράχων ἔφθασσα Φιλῖνον,   115
ἐς τὸ τεὸν καλέσασα τόδε στέγος ἢ 'μὲ παρῆμεν.

    φράζεό μευ τὸν ἔρωθ' ὅθεν ἵκετο, πότνα Σελάνα.

ἦνθον γάρ κεν ἐγώ, ναὶ τὸν γλυκὺν ἦνθον Ἔρωτα,
ἢ τρίτος ἠὲ τέταρτος ἐὼν φίλος αὐτίκα νυκτός,
μᾶλα μὲν ἐν κόλποισι Διωνύσοιο φυλάσσων,   120
κρατὶ δ' ἔχων λεύκαν, Ἡρακλέος ἱερὸν ἔρνος,
πάντοθι πορφυρέαισι περὶ ζώστραισιν ἑλικτάν.

    φράζεό μευ τὸν ἔρωθ' ὅθεν ἵκετο, πότνα Σελάνα.

καί κ', εἰ μέν μ' ἐδέχεσθε, τάδ' ἦς φίλα (καὶ γὰρ ἐλαφρός
καὶ καλὸς πάντεσσι μετ' ἀιθέοισι καλεῦμαι),   125
εὗδόν τ' εἴ κε μόνον τὸ καλὸν στόμα τεῦς ἐφίλησα·
εἰ δ' ἄλλα μ' ὠθεῖτε καὶ ἁ θύρα εἴχετο μοχλῷ,
πάντως κα πελέκεις καὶ λαμπάδες ἦνθον ἐφ' ὑμέας.

    φράζεό μευ τὸν ἔρωθ' ὅθεν ἵκετο, πότνα Σελάνα.

νῦν δὲ χάριν μὲν ἔφαν τᾷ Κύπριδι πρᾶτον ὀφείλειν, 130
καὶ μετὰ τὰν Κύπριν τύ με δευτέρα ἐκ πυρὸς εἵλευ,
ὦ γύναι, ἐσκαλέσαισα τεὸν ποτὶ τοῦτο μέλαθρον

118 καὶ ἐγώ a: κἠγώ m   128 κα z: καὶ am

αὔτως ἡμίφλεκτον· Ἔρως δ' ἄρα καὶ Λιπαραίω
πολλάκις Ἀφαίστοιο σέλας φλογερώτερον αἴθει.

φράζεό μευ τόν ἔρωθ' ὅθεν ἵκετο, πότνα Σελάνα. 135

σὺν δὲ κακαῖς μανίαις καὶ παρθένον ἐκ θαλάμοιο
καὶ νύμφαν ἐφόβησ' ἔτι δέμνια θερμὰ λιποῖσαν
ἀνέρος'. ὡς ὁ μὲν εἶπεν· ἐγὼ δέ μιν ἁ ταχυπειθής
χειρὸς ἐφαψαμένα μαλακῶν ἔκλιν' ἐπὶ λέκτρων.
καὶ ταχὺ χρὼς ἐπὶ χρωτὶ πεπαίνετο, καὶ τὰ πρόσωπα 140
θερμότερ' ἦς ἢ πρόσθε, καὶ ἐψιθυρίσδομες ἁδύ.
ὡς καί τοι μὴ μακρὰ φίλα θρυλέοιμι Σελάνα,
ἐπράχθη τὰ μέγιστα καὶ ἐς πόθον ἤνθομες ἄμφω.
κοὔτε τι τῆνος ἐμὶν ἀπεμέμψατο μέσφα τό γ' ἐχθές,
οὔτ' ἐγὼ αὖ τήνῳ. ἀλλ' ἦνθέ μοι ἅ τε Φιλίστας 145
μάτηρ τᾶς ἀμᾶς αὐλητρίδος ἅ τε Μελιξοῦς
σάμερον, ἀνίκα πέρ τε ποτ' ὠρανὸν ἔτραχεν ἵπποι
Ἀῶ τὰν ῥοδόεσσαν ἀπ' ὠκεανοῖο φέροισαι,
κεἶπέ μοι ἄλλα τε πολλὰ καὶ ὡς ἄρα_ Δέλφις ἔραται.
κεἶτε νιν αὖτε γυναικὸς ἔχει πόθος εἴτε καὶ ἀνδρός, 150
οὐκ ἔφατ' ἀτρεκὲς ἴδμεν, ἀτὰρ τόσον· αἰὲν Ἔρωτος
ἀκράτω ἐπεχεῖτο καὶ ἐς τέλος ᾤχετο φεύγων,
καὶ φάτο οἱ στεφάνοισι τὰ δώματα τῆνα πυκαξεῖν.
ταῦτά μοι ἁ ξείνα μυθήσατο, ἔστι δ' ἀλαθής.
ἦ γάρ μοι καὶ τρὶς καὶ τετράκις ἄλλοκ' ἐφοίτη, 155
καὶ παρ' ἐμὶν ἐτίθει τὰν Δωρίδα πολλάκις ὄλπαν·
νῦν δέ τε δωδεκαταῖος ἀφ' ὧτέ νιν οὐδὲ ποτεῖδον.
ἦ ῥ' οὐκ ἄλλο τι τερπνὸν ἔχει, ἀμῶν δὲ λέλασται;
νῦν μὲν τοῖς φίλτροις καταδήσομαι· αἰ δ' ἔτι κά με
λυπῇ, τὰν Ἀίδαο πύλαν, ναὶ Μοίρας, ἀραξεῖ· 160

---

134 φοβερώτερον a   141 ἁδύ m: ἤδη a   ὡς κεν a: χῶς κα m
144 κοὔτε τι am: κούκέτι m   148 ῥοδόπαχυν m   157 δέ τε
m: μὰν a

τοῖά οἱ ἐν κίστᾳ κακὰ φάρμακα φαμὶ φυλάσσειν,
'Ασσυρίω, δέσποινα, παρὰ ξείνοιο μαθοῖσα.
ἀλλὰ τὺ μὲν χαίροισα ποτ' ὠκεανὸν τρέπε πώλως,
πότνι'· ἐγὼ δ' οἰσῶ τὸν ἐμὸν πόθον ὥσπερ ὑπέσταν.
χαῖρε, Σελαναία λιπαρόθρονε, χαίρετε δ' ἄλλοι   165
ἀστέρες, εὐκάλοιο κατ' ἄντυγα Νυκτὸς ὀπαδοί.

164 πόνον m

III

κωμάσδω ποτὶ τὰν 'Αμαρυλλίδα, ταὶ δέ μοι αἶγες
βόσκονται κατ' ὄρος, καὶ ὁ Τίτυρος αὐτὰς ἐλαύνει.
Τίτυρ', ἐμὶν τὸ καλὸν πεφιλημένε, βόσκε τὰς αἶγας,
καὶ ποτὶ τὰν κράναν ἄγε, Τίτυρε· καὶ τὸν ἐνόρχαν,
τὸν Λιβυκὸν κνάκωνα, φυλάσσεο μή τυ κορύψῃ.   5

ὦ χαρίεσσ' 'Αμαρυλλί, τί μ' οὐκέτι τοῦτο κατ' ἄντρον
παρκύπτοισα καλεῖς, τὸν ἐρωτύλον; ἦ ῥά με μισεῖς;
ἦ ῥά γε τοι σιμὸς καταφαίνομαι ἐγγύθεν ἦμεν,
νύμφα, καὶ προγένειος; ἀπάγξασθαί με ποησεῖς.
ἠνίδε τοι δέκα μᾶλα φέρω· τηνῶθε καθεῖλον   10
ὦ μ' ἐκέλευ καθελεῖν τύ, καὶ αὔριον ἄλλα τοι οἰσῶ.
θᾶσαι μάν. θυμαλγὲς ἐμὶν ἄχος. αἴθε γενοίμαν
ἁ βομβεῦσα μέλισσα καὶ ἐς τεὸν ἄντρον ἱκοίμαν,
τὸν κισσὸν διαδὺς καὶ τὰν πτέριν ἅ τυ πυκάσδει.
νῦν ἔγνων τὸν Ἔρωτα· βαρὺς θεός· ἦ ῥα λεαίνας   15
μαζὸν ἐθήλαζεν, δρυμῷ τέ νιν ἔτραφε μάτηρ,
ὅς με κατασμύχων καὶ ἐς ὀστίον ἄχρις ἰάπτει.
ὦ τὸ καλὸν ποθορεῦσα, τὸ πᾶν λίθος, ὦ κυάνοφρυ
νύμφα, πρόσπτυξαί με τὸν αἰπόλον ὥς τυ φιλήσω.

12 ἐμὶν a: ἐμὸν m   18 λίπος b

ἔστι καὶ ἐν κενεοῖσι φιλήμασιν ἀδέα τέρψις.   20
τὸν στέφανον τῖλαί με κατ' αὐτίκα λεπτὰ ποησεῖς,
τόν τοι ἐγών, Ἀμαρυλλὶ φίλα, κισσοῖο φυλάσσω,
ἀμπλέξας καλύκεσσι καὶ εὐόδμοισι σελίνοις.

ὤμοι ἐγών, τί πάθω, τί ὁ δύσσοος; οὐχ ὑπακούεις.
τὰν βαίταν ἀποδὺς ἐς κύματα τηνῶ ἁλεῦμαι,   25
ὧπερ τὼς θύννως σκοπιάζεται Ὄλπις ὁ γριπεύς·
καὶ κα δὴ 'ποθάνω, τό γε μὲν τεὸν ἁδὺ τέτυκται.
ἔγνων πρᾶν ὅκα μοι μεμναμένῳ εἰ φιλέεις με
οὐδὲ τὸ τηλέφιλον ποτεμάξατο τὸ πλατάγημα,
ἀλλ' αὕτως ἁπαλῷ ποτὶ πάχεϊ ἐξεμαράνθη.   30
εἶπε καὶ Ἀγροιὼ τἀλαθέα κοσκινόμαντις,
ἁ πρᾶν ποιολογεῦσα παραιβάτις, οὕνεκ' ἐγὼ μέν
τὶν ὅλος ἔγκειμαι, τὺ δέ μευ λόγον οὐδένα ποιῇ.
ἦ μάν τοι λευκὰν διδυματόκον αἶγα φυλάσσω,
τάν με καὶ ἁ Μέρμνωνος ἐριθακὶς ἁ μελανόχρως   35
αἰτεῖ· καὶ δωσῶ οἱ, ἐπεὶ τύ μοι ἐνδιαθρύπτῃ.
ἅλλεται ὀφθαλμός μευ ὁ δεξιός· ἆρά γ' ἰδησῶ
αὐτάν; ἀσεῦμαι ποτὶ τὰν πίτυν ὧδ' ἀποκλινθείς,
καί κε μ' ἴσως ποτίδοι, ἐπεὶ οὐκ ἀδαμαντίνα ἐστίν.

Ἱππομένης, ὅκα δὴ τὰν παρθένον ἤθελε γᾶμαι,   40
μᾶλ' ἐν χερσὶν ἑλὼν δρόμον ἄνυεν· ἁ δ' Ἀταλάντα
ὡς ἴδεν, ὡς ἐμάνη, ὡς ἐς βαθὺν ἅλατ' ἔρωτα.
τὰν ἀγέλαν χὠ μάντις ἀπ' Ὄθρυος ἆγε Μελάμπους
ἐς Πύλον· ἁ δὲ Βίαντος ἐν ἀγκοίναισιν ἐκλίνθη
μάτηρ ἁ χαρίεσσα περίφρονος Ἀλφεσιβοίας.   45
τὰν δὲ καλὰν Κυθέρειαν ἐν ὤρεσι μῆλα νομεύων
οὐχ οὕτως Ὤδωνις ἐπὶ πλέον ἄγαγε λύσσας
ὥστ' οὐδὲ φθίμενόν νιν ἄτερ μαζοῖο τίθητι;
ζαλωτὸς μὲν ἐμὶν ὁ τὸν ἄτροπον ὕπνον ἰαύων

27 δὴ z: μὴ m   μὲν z: μὰν m

Ἐνδυμίων· ζαλῶ δέ, φίλα γύναι, Ἰασίωνα, 50
ὃς τόσσων ἐκύρησεν ὅσ᾽ οὐ πευσεῖσθε βέβαλοι.

ἀλγέω τὰν κεφαλάν, τὶν δ᾽ οὐ μέλει. οὐκέτ᾽ ἀείδω,
κεισεῦμαι δὲ πεσών, καὶ τοὶ λύκοι ὧδέ μ᾽ ἔδονται.
ὡς μέλι τοι γλυκὺ τοῦτο κατὰ βρόχθοιο γένοιτο.

IV

ΒΑΤΤΟΣ

εἰπέ μοι, ὦ Κορύδων, τίνος αἱ βόες; ἦ ῥα Φιλώνδα;

ΚΟΡΥΔΩΝ

οὔκ, ἀλλ᾽ Αἴγωνος· βόσκειν δέ μοι αὐτὰς ἔδωκεν.
ΒΑ. ἦ πᾷ ψε κρύβδαν τὰ ποθέσπερα πάσας ἀμέλγες;
ΚΟ. ἀλλ᾽ ὁ γέρων ὑφίητι τὰ μοσχία κἠμὲ φυλάσσει.
ΒΑ. αὐτὸς δ᾽ ἐς τίν᾽ ἄφαντος ὁ βουκόλος ᾤχετο χώραν; 5
ΚΟ. οὐκ ἄκουσας; ἄγων νιν ἐπ᾽ Ἀλφεὸν ᾤχετο Μίλων.
ΒΑ. καὶ πόκα τῆνος ἔλαιον ἐν ὀφθαλμοῖσιν ὀπώπει;
ΚΟ. φαντί νιν Ἡρακλῆι βίην καὶ κάρτος ἐρίσδειν.
ΒΑ. κἤμ᾽ ἔφαθ᾽ ἁ μάτηρ Πολυδεύκεος ἦμεν ἀμείνω.
ΚΟ. κᾤχετ᾽ ἔχων σκαπάναν τε καὶ εἴκατι τουτόθε μῆλα 10
ΒΑ. πείσαι κα Μίλων καὶ τὼς λύκος αὐτίκα λυσσῆν.
ΚΟ. ταὶ δαμάλαι δ᾽ αὐτὸν μυκώμεναι αἵδε ποθεῦντι.
ΒΑ. δείλαιαί γ᾽ αὗται, τὸν βουκόλον ὡς κακὸν εὗρον.
ΚΟ. ἦ μὰν δείλαιαί γε, καὶ οὐκέτι λῶντι νέμεσθαι.
ΒΑ. τήνας μὲν δή τοι τᾶς πόρτιος αὐτὰ λέλειπται 15
  τὠστία. μὴ πρώκας σιτίζεται ὥσπερ ὁ τέττιξ;
ΚΟ. οὐ Δᾶν, ἀλλ᾽ ὅκα μέν νιν ἐπ᾽ Αἰσάροιο νομεύω
  καὶ μαλακῶ χόρτοιο καλὰν κώμυθα δίδωμι,
  ἄλλοκα δὲ σκαίρει τὸ βαθύσκιον ἀμφὶ Λάτυμνον.

ΒΑ. λεπτὸς μὰν χὠ ταῦρος ὁ πυρρίχος. αἴθε λάχοιεν   20
   τοὶ τῶ Λαμπριάδα, τοὶ δαμόται ὄκκα θύωντι
   τᾷ ῞Ηρᾳ, τοιόνδε· κακοχράσμων γὰρ ὁ δᾶμος.

ΚΟ. καὶ μὰν ἐς στομάλιμνον ἐλαύνεται ἔς τε τὰ Φύσκω,
   καὶ ποτὶ τὸν Νήαιθον, ὅπᾳ καλὰ πάντα φύοντι,
   αἰγίπυρος καὶ κνύζα καὶ εὐώδης μελίτεια.   25

ΒΑ. φεῦ φεῦ βασεῦνται καὶ ταὶ βόες, ὦ τάλαν Αἴγων,
   εἰς ᾽Αίδαν ὄκα καὶ τὺ κακᾶς ἠράσσαο νίκας,
   χὰ σῦριγξ εὐρῶτι παλύνεται, ἄν ποκ᾽ ἐπάξω.

ΚΟ. οὐ τήνα γ᾽, οὐ Νύμφας, ἐπεὶ ποτὶ Πῖσαν ἀφέρπων
   δῶρον ἐμοί νιν ἔλειπεν· ἐγὼ δέ τις εἰμὶ μελικτάς,   30
   κεῦ μὲν τὰ Γλαύκας ἀγκρούομαι, εὖ δὲ τὰ Πύρρω.
   αἰνέω τάν τε Κρότωνα — ᾽καλὰ πόλις ἅ τε
      Ζάκυνθος . . .᾽ —
   καὶ τὸ ποταῷον τὸ Λακίνιον, ἆπερ ὁ πύκτας
   Αἴγων ὀγδώκοντα μόνος κατεδαίσατο μάζας.
   τηνεὶ καὶ τὸν ταῦρον ἀπ᾽ ὤρεος ἆγε πιάξας   35
   τᾶς ὁπλᾶς κῆδωκ᾽ ᾽Αμαρυλλίδι, ταὶ δὲ γυναῖκες
   μακρὸν ἀνάυσαν, χὠ βουκόλος ἐξεγέλασσεν.

ΒΑ. ὦ χαρίεσσ᾽ ᾽Αμαρυλλί, μόνας σέθεν οὐδὲ θανοίσας
   λασεύμεσθ᾽· ὅσον αἶγες ἐμὶν φίλαι, ὅσσον ἀπέσβης.
   αἰαῖ τῶ σκληρῶ μάλα δαίμονος ὅς με λελόγχει.   40

ΚΟ. θαρσεῖν χρή, φίλε Βάττε· τάχ᾽ αὔριον ἔσσετ᾽ ἄμεινον.
   ἐλπίδες ἐν ζωοῖσιν, ἀνέλπιστοι δὲ θανόντες,
   χὠ Ζεὺς ἄλλοκα μὲν πέλει αἴθριος, ἄλλοκα δ᾽ ὕει.

ΒΑ. θαρσέω. βάλλε κάτωθε τὰ μοσχία· τᾶς γὰρ ἐλαίας
   τὸν θαλλὸν τρώγοντι τὰ δύσσοα.   *ΚΟ.* σίτθ᾽, ὁ
      Λέπαργος,   45
   σίτθ᾽, ἁ Κυμαίθα, ποτὶ τὸν λόφον. οὐκ ἐσακούεις;
   ἡξῶ, ναὶ τὸν Πᾶνα, κακὸν τέλος αὐτίκα δωσῶν,
   εἰ μὴ ἄπει τουτῶθεν. ἴδ᾽ αὖ πάλιν ἅδε ποθέρπει.

28 ἐπάξα m

αἴθ᾽ ἦς μοι ῥοικόν τι λαγωβόλον ὥς τυ πάταξα.

ΒΑ. θᾶσαί μ᾽, ὦ Κορύδων, ποττῶ Διός· ἀ γὰρ ἄκανθα 50
    ᾽ρμοῖ μ᾽ ὧδ᾽ ἐπάταξ᾽ ὑπὸ τὸ σφυρόν. ὡς δὲ βαθεῖαι
    τἀτρακτυλλίδες ἐντί. κακῶς ἀ πόρτις ὄλοιτο·
    εἰς ταύταν ἐτύπην χασμεύμενος. ἦ ῥά γε λεύσσεις;

ΚΟ. ναὶ ναί, τοῖς ὀνύχεσσιν ἔχω τέ νιν· ἄδε καὶ αὐτά.

ΒΑ. ὁσσίχον ἐστὶ τὸ τύμμα, καὶ ἁλίκον ἄνδρα δαμάσδει. 55

ΚΟ. εἰς ὄρος ὄκχ᾽ ἕρπῃς, μὴ νήλιπος ἔρχεο, Βάττε·
    ἐν γὰρ ὄρει ῥάμνοι τε καὶ ἀσπάλαθοι κομόωντι.

ΒΑ. εἶπ᾽ ἄγε μ᾽, ὦ Κορύδων, τὸ γερόντιον ἦ ῥ᾽ ἔτι μύλλει
    τήναν τὰν κυάνοφρυν ἐρωτίδα τᾶς ποκ᾽ ἐκνίσθη;

ΚΟ. ἀκμάν γ᾽, ὦ δείλαιε· πρόαν γε μὲν αὐτὸς ἐπενθὼν 60
    καὶ ποτὶ τᾷ μάνδρᾳ κατελάμβανον ἇμος ἐνήργει.

ΒΑ. εὖ γ᾽, ὤνθρωπε φιλοῖφα. τό τοι γένος ἢ Σατυρίσκοις
    ἐγγύθεν ἢ Πάνεσσι κακοκνάμοισιν ἐρίσδει.

57 κάκτοι b   61 τὰν μάκτραν (sic) b

V

ΚΟΜΑΤΑΣ

αἶγες ἐμαί, τῆνον τὸν ποιμένα, τὸν Συβαρίταν,
φεύγετε, τὸν Λάκωνα· τό μευ νάκος ἐχθὲς ἔκλεψεν.

ΛΑΚΩΝ

οὐκ ἀπὸ τᾶς κράνας; σίττ᾽, ἀμνίδες· οὐκ ἐσορῆτε
τόν μευ τὰν σύριγγα πρόαν κλέψαντα Κομάταν;

ΚΟ. τὰν ποίαν σύριγγα; τὺ γάρ ποκα, δῶλε Σιβύρτα, 5
    ἐκτάσω σύριγγα; τί δ᾽ οὐκέτι σὺν Κορύδωνι
    ἀρκεῖ τοι καλάμας αὐλὸν ποππύσδεν ἔχοντι;

ΛΑ. τάν μοι ἔδωκε Λύκων, ὠλεύθερε. τὶν δὲ τὸ ποῖον
Λάκων ἀγκλέψας ποκ' ἔβα νάκος; εἰπέ, Κομάτα·
οὐδὲ γὰρ Εὐμάρᾳ τῷ δεσπότᾳ ἦς τοι ἐνεύδειν. 10
ΚΟ. τὸ Κροκύλος μοι ἔδωκε, τὸ ποικίλον, ἁνίκ' ἔθυσε
ταῖς Νύμφαις τὰν αἶγα· τὺ δ', ὦ κακέ, καὶ τόκ'
ἐτάκευ
βασκαίνων, καὶ νῦν με τὰ λοίσθια γυμνὸν ἔθηκας.
ΛΑ. οὐ μαὐτὸν τὸν Πᾶνα τὸν ἄκτιον, οὐ τέ γε Λάκων
τὰν βαίταν ἀπέδυσ' ὁ Καλαιθίδος· ἦ κατὰ τήνας 15
τᾶς πέτρας, ὤνθρωπε, μανεὶς εἰς Κρᾶθιν ἁλοίμαν.
ΚΟ. οὐ μάν, οὐ ταύτας τὰς λιμνάδας, ὠγαθέ, Νύμφας,
αἴτε μοι ἵλαοί τε καὶ εὐμενέες τελέθοιεν,
οὔ τευ τὰν σύριγγα λαθὼν ἔκλεψε Κομάτας.
ΛΑ. αἴ τοι πιστεύσαιμι, τὰ Δάφνιδος ἄλγε' ἀροίμαν. 20
ἀλλ' ὦν αἴ κα λῇς ἔριφον θέμεν, ἔστι μὲν οὐδέν
ἱερόν, ἀλλά γε τοι διαείσομαι ἔστε κ' ἀπείπῃς.
ΚΟ. ὗς ποτ' Ἀθαναίαν ἔριν ἤρισεν. ἠνίδε κεῖται
ὦριφος· ἀλλ' ἄγε καὶ τύ τιν' εὔβοτον ἀμνὸν ἔρειδε.
ΛΑ. καὶ πῶς, ὦ κίναδος τύ, τάδ' ἔσσεται ἐξ ἴσω ἄμμιν; 25
τίς τρίχας ἀντ' ἐρίων ἐποκίξατο; τίς δὲ παρεύσας
αἰγὸς πρατοτόκοιο κακὰν κύνα δήλετ' ἀμέλγειν;
ΚΟ. ὅστις νικασεῖν τὸν πλατίον ὡς τὺ πεποίθεις,
σφὰξ βομβέων τέττιγος ἐναντίον. ἀλλὰ γὰρ οὔτι
ὦριφος ἰσοπαλής τοι, ἴδ' ὁ τράγος οὗτος· ἔρισδε. 30
ΛΑ. μὴ σπεῦδ'· οὐ γάρ τοι πυρὶ θάλπεαι. ἄδιον ᾀσῇ
τεῖδ' ὑπὸ τὰν κότινον καὶ τἄλσεα ταῦτα καθίξας.
ψυχρὸν ὕδωρ τουτεὶ καταλείβεται· ὧδε πεφύκει
ποία, χἀ στιβὰς ἅδε, καὶ ἀκρίδες ὧδε λαλεῦντι.
ΚΟ. ἀλλ' οὔτι σπεύδω· μέγα δ' ἄχθομαι εἰ τύ με
τολμῇς 35
ὄμμασι τοῖς ὀρθοῖσι ποτιβλέπεν, ὅν ποκ' ἐόντα

22 ἀλλ' ἄγε τοι m   25 κίναδος τύ z: κίναδ' εὖ vel sim. m

παῖδ' ἔτ' ἐγὼν ἐδίδασκον. ἴδ' ἁ χάρις ἐς τί ποχ' ἔρπει·
θρέψαι καὶ λυκιδεῖς, θρέψαι κύνας, ὥς τυ φάγωντι.

ΛΑ. καὶ πόκ' ἐγὼν παρὰ τεῦς τι μαθὼν καλὸν ἢ καὶ
    ἀκούσας
    μέμναμ', ὦ φθονερὸν τὺ καὶ ἀπρεπὲς ἀνδρίον
    αὔτως;   40

ΚΟ. ἁνίκ' ἐπύγιζόν τυ, τὺ δ' ἄλγεες· αἱ δὲ χίμαιραι
    αἵδε κατεβληχῶντο, καὶ ὁ τράγος αὐτὰς ἐτρύπη.

ΛΑ. μὴ βάθιον τήνω πυγίσματος, ὑβέ, ταφείης.
    ἀλλὰ γὰρ ἔρφ', ὧδ' ἔρπε, καὶ ὕστατα βουκολιαξῇ.

ΚΟ. οὐχ ἐρψῶ τηνεί. τουτεὶ δρύες, ὧδε κύπειρος,   45
    ὧδε καλὸν βομβεῦντι ποτὶ σμάνεσσι μέλισσαι,
    ἔνθ' ὕδατος ψυχρῶ κρᾶναι δύο, ταὶ δ' ἐπὶ δένδρει
    ὄρνιχες λαλαγεῦντι, καὶ ἁ σκιὰ οὐδὲν ὁμοία
    τᾷ παρὰ τίν· βάλλει δὲ καὶ ἁ πίτυς ὑψόθε
    κώνοις.

ΛΑ. ἦ μὰν ἀρνακίδας τε καὶ εἴρια τεῖδε πατησεῖς,   50
    αἴ κ' ἔνθῃς, ὕπνω μαλακώτερα· ταὶ δὲ τραγεῖαι
    ταὶ παρὰ τὶν ὄσδοντι κακώτερον ἢ τύ περ
    ὄσδεις.
    στασῶ δὲ κρατῆρα μέγαν λευκοῖο γάλακτος
    ταῖς Νύμφαις, στασῶ δὲ καὶ ἁδέος ἄλλον ἐλαίω.

ΚΟ. αἰ δέ κε καὶ τὺ μόλῃς, ἁπαλὰν πτέριν ὧδε
    πατησεῖς   55
    καὶ γλάχων' ἀνθεῦσαν· ὑπεσσεῖται δὲ χιμαιρᾶν
    δέρματα τᾶν παρὰ τὶν μαλακώτερα τετράκις
    ἀρνᾶν.
    στασῶ δ' ὀκτὼ μὲν γαυλὼς τῷ Πανὶ γάλακτος,
    ὀκτὼ δὲ σκαφίδας μέλιτος πλέα κηρί' ἐχοίσας.

ΛΑ. αὐτόθε μοι ποτέρισδε καὶ αὐτόθε βουκολιάσδευ· 60
    τὰν σαυτῶ πατέων ἔχε τὰς δρύας. ἀλλὰ τίς ἄμμε,

57 πολλάκις am   ἀρνᾶν z: ἀρνῶν am

τίς κρινεῖ; αἴθ' ἔνθοι ποχ' ὁ βουκόλος ὧδε
      Λυκώπας.
ΚΟ. οὐδὲν ἐγὼ τήνω ποτιδεύομαι· ἀλλὰ τὸν ἄνδρα,
      αἰ λῇς, τὸν δρυτόμον βωστρήσομες, ὃς τὰς
        ἐρείκας
      τήνας τὰς παρὰ τὶν ξυλοχίζεται· ἔστι δὲ
        Μόρσων.   65
ΛΑ. βωστρέωμες.
ΚΟ.   τὺ κάλει νιν.
ΛΑ.   ἴθ' ὦ ξένε, μικκὸν ἄκουσον
      τεῖδ' ἐνθών· ἄμμες γὰρ ἐρίδομες ὅστις ἀρείων
      βουκολιαστάς ἐστι. τὺ δ', ὠγαθέ, μήτ' ἐμέ,
        Μόρσων,
      ἐν χάριτι κρίνῃς, μήτ' ὢν τύγα τοῦτον ὀνάσῃς.
ΚΟ. ναί, ποτὶ τᾶν Νυμφᾶν, Μόρσων φίλε, μήτε
        Κομάτᾳ   70
      τὸ πλέον ἰθύνῃς, μήτ' ὢν τύγα τῷδε χαρίξῃ.
      ἅδε τοι ἁ ποίμνα τῶ Θουρίω ἐστὶ Σιβύρτα,
      Εὐμάρα δὲ τὰς αἶγας ὁρῇς, φίλε, τῶ Συβαρίτα.
ΛΑ. μὴ τύ τις ἠρώτη, ποττῶ Διός, αἴτε Σιβύρτα
      αἴτ' ἐμόν ἐστι, κάκιστε, τὸ ποίμνιον; ὡς λάλος
        ἐσσί.   75
ΚΟ. βέντισθ' οὗτος, ἐγὼ μὲν ἀλαθέα πάντ' ἀγορεύω
      κοὐδὲν καυχέομαι· τύγα μὰν φιλοκέρτομος ἐσσί.
ΛΑ. εἶα λέγ', εἴ τι λέγεις, καὶ τὸν ξένον ἐς πόλιν αὖθις
      ζῶντ' ἄφες· ὦ Παιάν, ἦ στωμύλος ἦσθα,
        Κομᾶτα.

ΚΟ. ταὶ Μοῖσαί με φιλεῦντι πολὺ πλέον ἢ τὸν
        ἀοιδόν   80
      Δάφνιν· ἐγὼ δ' αὐταῖς χιμάρως δύο πρᾶν ποκ'
        ἔθυσα.

ΛΑ. καὶ γὰρ ἔμ' Ὠπόλλων φιλέει μέγα, καὶ καλὸν
αὐτῷ
κριὸν ἐγὼ βόσκω· τὰ δὲ Κάρνεα καὶ δὴ
ἐφέρπει.

ΚΟ. πλὰν δύο τὰς λοιπὰς διδυματόκος αἶγας ἀμέλγω,
καί μ' ἁ παῖς ποθορεῦσα, 'τάλαν,' λέγει, 'αὐτὸς
ἀμέλγεις;' 85

ΛΑ. φεῦ φεῦ, Λάκων τοι ταλάρως σχεδὸν εἴκατι
πληροῖ
τυρῶ, καὶ τὸν ἄναβον ἐν ἄνθεσι παῖδα μολύνει.

ΚΟ. βάλλει καὶ μάλοισι τὸν αἰπόλον ἁ Κλεαρίστα
τὰς αἶγας παρελᾶντα καὶ ἁδύ τι ποππυλιάσδει.

ΛΑ. κἠμὲ γὰρ ὁ Κρατίδας τὸν ποιμένα λεῖος
ὑπαντῶν 90
ἐκμαίνει· λιπαρὰ δὲ παρ' αὐχένα σείετ' ἔθειρα.

ΚΟ. ἀλλ' οὐ συμβλήτ' ἐστὶ κυνόσβατος οὐδ' ἀνεμώνα
πρὸς ῥόδα, τῶν ἄνδηρα παρ' αἱμασιαῖσι πεφύκει.

ΛΑ. οὐδὲ γὰρ οὐδ' ἀκύλοις ὀρομαλίδες· αἱ μὲν
ἔχοντι
λεπτὸν ἀπὸ πρίνοιο λεπύριον, αἱ δὲ μελιχραί. 95

ΚΟ. κἠγὼ μὲν δωσῶ τᾷ παρθένῳ αὐτίκα φάσσαν,
ἐκ τᾶς ἀρκεύθω καθελών· τηνεὶ.γὰρ ἐφίσδει.

ΛΑ. ἀλλ' ἐγὼ ἐς χλαῖναν μαλακὸν πόκον, ὁππόκα πέξω
τὰν οἶν τὰν πέλλαν, Κρατίδᾳ δωρήσομαι αὐτός.

ΚΟ. σίττ' ἀπὸ τᾶς κοτίνω, ταὶ μηκάδες· ὧδε
νέμεσθε 100
ὡς τὸ κάταντες τοῦτο γεώλοφον αἵ τε μυρῖκαι.

ΛΑ. οὐκ ἀπὸ τᾶς δρυός, οὗτος ὁ Κώναρος ἅ τε
Κιναίθα;
τουτεὶ βοσκησεῖσθε ποτ' ἀντολὰς ὡς ὁ Φάλαρος.

ΚΟ. ἔστι δέ μοι γαυλὸς κυπαρίσσινος, ἔστι δὲ κρατήρ,

101 αἵ τε z: ᾷτε m

ἔργον Πραξιτέλευς· τᾷ παιδὶ δὲ ταῦτα
φυλάσσω. 105

ΛΑ. χἀμὶν ἐστι κύων φιλοποίμνιος ὃς λύκος ἄγχει,
ὃν τῷ παιδὶ δίδωμι τὰ θηρία πάντα διώκειν.

ΚΟ. ἀκρίδες, αἳ τὸν φραγμὸν ὑπερπαδῆτε τὸν ἁμόν,
μή μευ λωβάσησθε τὰς ἀμπέλος· ἐντὶ γὰρ αὖαι.

ΛΑ. τοὶ τέττιγες, ὁρῆτε τὸν αἰπόλον ὡς ἐρεθίζω· 110
οὕτω κὔμμες θην ἐρεθίζετε τὼς καλαμευτάς.

ΚΟ. μισέω τὰς δασυκέρκος ἀλώπεκας, αἳ τὰ Μίκωνος
αἰεὶ φοιτῶσαι τὰ ποθέσπερα ῥαγίζοντι.

ΛΑ. καὶ γὰρ ἐγὼ μισέω τὼς κανθάρος, οἳ τὰ
Φιλώνδα
σῦκα κατατρώγοντες ὑπανέμιοι φορέονται. 115

ΚΟ. ἦ οὐ μέμνασ’ ὅκ’ ἐγών τυ κατήλασα, καὶ τὺ
σεσαρὼς
εὖ ποτεκιγκλίζευ καὶ τᾶς δρυὸς εἴχεο τήνας;

ΛΑ. τοῦτο μὲν οὐ μέμναμ’· ὅκα μάν ποκα τεῖδέ τυ
δήσας
Εὐμάρας ἐκάθηρε, καλῶς μάλα τοῦτό γ’ ἴσαμι.

ΚΟ. ἤδη τις, Μόρσων, πικραίνεται· ἢ οὐχὶ
παρῄσθεν; 120
σκίλλας ἰὼν γραίας ἀπὸ σάματος αὐτίκα τίλλοις.

ΛΑ. κἠγὼ μὰν κνίζω, Μόρσων, τινά· καὶ τὺ δὲ
λεύσσεις.
ἐνθὼν τὰν κυκλάμινον ὄρυσσέ νυν ἐς τὸν
Ἄλεντα.

ΚΟ. Ἱμέρα ἀνθ’ ὕδατος ῥείτω γάλα, καὶ τὺ δέ,
Κρᾶθι,
οἴνῳ πορφύροις, τὰ δέ τοι σία καρπὸν ἐνείκαι. 125

ΛΑ. ῥείτω χἀ Συβαρῖτις ἐμὶν μέλι, καὶ τὸ πότορθρον
ἁ παῖς ἀνθ’ ὕδατος τᾷ κάλπιδι κηρία βάψαι.

109 ἄζαι b   116 ἦ om. m   120 ἦ om. m

KO. ταὶ μὲν ἐμαὶ κύτισόν τε καὶ αἴγιλον αἶγες
    ἔδοντι,
  καὶ σχῖνον πατέοντι καὶ ἐν κομάροισι κέονται.

ΛΑ. ταῖσι δ' ἐμαῖς οἴεσσι πάρεστι μὲν ἁ
    μελίτεια   130
  φέρβεσθαι, πολλὸς δὲ καὶ ὡς ῥόδα κισθὸς
  ἐπανθεῖ.

KO. οὐκ ἔραμ' Ἀλκίππας, ὅτι με πρᾶν οὐκ
    ἐφίλησε
  τῶν ὤτων καθελοῖσ' ὅκα οἱ τὰν φάσσαν ἔδωκα.

ΛΑ. ἀλλ' ἐγὼ Εὐμήδευς ἔραμαι μέγα· καὶ γὰρ ὅκ'
    αὐτῷ
  τὰν σύριγγ' ὤρεξα, καλόν τί με κάρτ'
  ἐφίλησεν.   135

KO. οὐ θεμιτόν, Λάκων, ποτ' ἀηδόνα κίσσας
    ἐρίσδειν,
  οὐδ' ἔποπας κύκνοισι· τὺ δ', ὦ τάλαν, ἐσσὶ
  φιλεχθής.

ΜΟΡΣΩΝ

παύσασθαι κέλομαι τὸν ποιμένα. τὶν δέ, Κομᾶτα,
δωρεῖται Μόρσων τὰν ἀμνίδα· καὶ τὺ δὲ θύσας
ταῖς Νύμφαις Μόρσωνι καλὸν κρέας αὐτίκα
  πέμψον.   140

KO. πεμψῶ, ναὶ τὸν Πᾶνα. φριμάσσεο, πᾶσα
    τραγίσκων
  νῦν ἀγέλα· κἠγὼν γὰρ ἴδ' ὡς μέγα τοῦτο
  καχαξῶ
  καττῶ Λάκωνος τῶ ποιμένος, ὅττι ποκ' ἤδη
  ἀννυσάμαν τὰν ἀμνόν· ἐς ὠρανὸν ὔμμιν ἀλεῦμαι.
  αἶγες ἐμαί, θαρσεῖτε, κερουχίδες· αὔριον ὔμμε   145

131 ῥοδάκισσος b

πάσας ἐγὼ λουσῶ Συβαρίτιδος ἔνδοθι λίμνας.
οὗτος ὁ λευκίτας ὁ κορυπτίλος, εἴ τιν' ὀχευσεῖς
τᾶν αἰγῶν, φλασσῶ τυ, πρὶν ἢ ἐμὲ καλλιερῆσαι
ταῖς Νύμφαις τὰν ἀμνόν. ὁ δ' αὖ πάλιν. ἀλλὰ
   γενοίμαν,
αἰ μή τυ φλάσσαιμι, Μελάνθιος ἀντὶ Κομάτα. 150

146 κράνας am

VI

Δαμοίτας καὶ Δάφνις ὁ βουκόλος εἰς ἕνα χῶρον
τὰν ἀγέλαν ποκ', "Αρατε, συνάγαγον· ἧς δ' ὁ μὲν αὐτῶν
πυρρός, ὁ δ' ἡμιγένειος· ἐπὶ κράναν δέ τιν' ἄμφω
ἑσδόμενοι θέρεος μέσῳ ἄματι τοιάδ' ἄειδον.
πρᾶτος δ' ἄρξατο Δάφνις, ἐπεὶ καὶ πρᾶτος ἔρισδεν. 5

βάλλει τοι, Πολύφαμε, τὸ ποίμνιον ἁ Γαλάτεια
μάλοισιν, δυσέρωτα καὶ αἰπόλον ἄνδρα καλεῦσα·
καὶ τύ νιν οὐ ποθόρησθα, τάλαν τάλαν, ἀλλὰ κάθησαι
ἀδέα συρίσδων. πάλιν ἄδ', ἴδε, τὰν κύνα βάλλει,
ἅ τοι τᾶν ὀίων ἕπεται σκοπός· ἁ δὲ βαύσδει   10
εἰς ἅλα δερκομένα, τὰ δέ νιν καλὰ κύματα φαίνει
ἅσυχα καχλάζοντος ἐπ' αἰγιαλοῖο θέοισαν.
φράζεο μὴ τᾶς παιδὸς ἐπὶ κνάμαισιν ὀρούσῃ
ἐξ ἁλὸς ἐρχομένας, κατὰ δὲ χρόα καλὸν ἀμύξῃ.
ἁ δὲ καὶ αὐτόθε τοι διαθρύπτεται· ὡς ἀπ' ἀκάνθας 15
ταὶ καπυραὶ χαῖται, τὸ καλὸν θέρος ἀνίκα φρύγει,
καὶ φεύγει φιλέοντα καὶ οὐ φιλέοντα διώκει,
καὶ τὸν ἀπὸ γραμμᾶς κινεῖ λίθον· ἦ γὰρ ἔρωτι
πολλάκις, ὦ Πολύφαμε, τὰ μὴ καλὰ καλὰ πέφανται.

11 ῥαίνει b

τῷ δ' ἐπὶ Δαμοίτας ἀνεβάλλετο καὶ τάδ' ἄειδεν.   20

εἶδον, ναὶ τὸν Πᾶνα, τὸ ποίμνιον ἀνίκ' ἔβαλλε,
κοὔ μ' ἔλαθ', οὐ τὸν ἐμὸν τὸν ἕνα γλυκύν, ᾧ
    ποθορῷμι
ἐς τέλος· αὐτὰρ ὁ μάντις ὁ Τήλεμος ἔχθρ' ἀγορεύων
ἐχθρὰ φέροι ποτὶ οἶκον ὅπως τεκέεσσι φυλάσσοι.
ἀλλὰ καὶ αὐτὸς ἐγὼ κνίζων πάλιν οὐ ποθόρημι,   25
ἀλλ' ἄλλαν τινὰ φαμὶ γυναῖκ' ἔχεν· ἁ δ' ἀΐοισα
ζαλοῖ μ', ὦ Παιάν, καὶ τάκεται, ἐκ δὲ θαλάσσας
οἰστρεῖ παπταίνοισα ποτ' ἄντρα τε καὶ ποτὶ ποίμνας.
σίξα δ' ὑλακτεῖν νιν καὶ τᾷ κυνί· καὶ γὰρ ὅκ' ἤρων,
αὐτᾶς ἐκνυζεῖτο ποτ' ἰσχία ῥύγχος ἔχοισα.   30
ταῦτα δ' ἴσως ἐσορεῦσα ποεῦντά με πολλάκι πεμψεῖ
ἄγγελον. αὐτὰρ ἐγὼ κλαξῶ θύρας ἔστε κ' ὀμόσσῃ
αὐτά μοι στορεσεῖν καλὰ δέμνια τᾶσδ' ἐπὶ νάσω·
καὶ γάρ θην οὐδ' εἶδος ἔχω κακὸν ὥς με λέγοντι.
ἦ γὰρ πρᾶν ἐς πόντον ἐσέβλεπον, ἦς δὲ γαλάνα,   35
καὶ καλὰ μὲν τὰ γένεια, καλὰ δέ μευ ἁ μία κώρα,
ὡς παρ' ἐμὶν κέκριται, κατεφαίνετο, τῶν δέ τ' ὀδόντων
λευκοτέραν αὐγὰν Παρίας ὑπέφαινε λίθοιο.
ὡς μὴ βασκανθῶ δὲ τρὶς εἰς ἐμὸν ἔπτυσα κόλπον·
ταῦτα γὰρ ἁ γραία με Κοτυτταρὶς ἐξεδίδαξε.   40

τόσσ' εἰπὼν τὸν Δάφνιν ὁ Δαμοίτας ἐφίλησε·   42
χὠ μὲν τῷ σύριγγ', ὁ δὲ τῷ καλὸν αὐλὸν ἔδωκεν.
αὔλει Δαμοίτας, σύρισδε δὲ Δάφνις ὁ βούτας·
ὠρχεῦντ' ἐν μαλακᾷ ταὶ πόρτιες αὐτίκα ποίᾳ.   45
νίκη μὲν οὐδάλλος, ἀνήσσατοι δ' ἐγένοντο.

20 καλὸν ἀείδειν bm   22 ποθορῷμι ʒ: ποθορῶμαι m: ποθόρημαι m
29 σίξα ʒ: σῖγα vel sim. m   '41' ἁ πρᾶν ἀμάντεσσι παρ'
Ἱπποκίωνι ποταύλει (=x.16) m

VII

ἦς χρόνος ἁνίκ' ἐγών τε καὶ Εὔκριτος εἰς τὸν Ἅλεντα
εἵρπομες ἐκ πόλιος, σὺν καὶ τρίτος ἄμμιν Ἀμύντας.
τᾷ Δηοῖ γὰρ ἔτευχε θαλύσια καὶ Φρασίδαμος
κἈντιγένης, δύο τέκνα Λυκωπέος, εἴ τι περ ἐσθλόν
χαῶν τῶν ἐπάνωθεν ἀπὸ Κλυτίας τε καὶ αὐτῶ   5
Χάλκωνος, Βούριναν ὃς ἐκ ποδὸς ἆννε κράναν
εὖ ἐνερεισάμενος πέτρᾳ γόνυ· ταὶ δὲ παρ' αὐτάν
αἴγειροι πτελέαι τε ἐΰσκιον ἄλσος ὕφαινον
χλωροῖσιν πετάλοισι κατηρεφέες κομόωσαι.
κοὔπω τὰν μεσάταν ὁδὸν ἄνυμες, οὐδὲ τὸ σᾶμα   10
ἁμῖν τὸ Βρασίλα κατεφαίνετο, καί τιν' ὁδίταν
ἐσθλὸν σὺν Μοίσαισι Κυδωνικὸν εὕρομες ἄνδρα,
οὔνομα μὲν Λυκίδαν, ἦς δ' αἰπόλος, οὐδέ κε τίς νιν
ἠγνοίησεν ἰδών, ἐπεὶ αἰπόλῳ ἔξοχ' ἐῴκει.
ἐκ μὲν γὰρ λασίοιο δασύτριχος εἶχε τράγοιο   15
κνακὸν δέρμ' ὤμοισι νέας ταμίσοιο ποτόσδον,
ἀμφὶ δέ οἱ στήθεσσι γέρων ἐσφίγγετο πέπλος
ζωστῆρι πλακερῷ, ῥοικὰν δ' ἔχεν ἀγριελαίω
δεξιτερᾷ κορύναν. καί μ' ἀτρέμας εἶπε σεσαρώς
ὄμματι μειδιόωντι, γέλως δέ οἱ εἴχετο χείλευς·   20
'Σιμιχίδα, πᾷ δὴ τὺ μεσαμέριον πόδας ἕλκεις,
ἁνίκα δὴ καὶ σαῦρος ἐν αἱμασιαῖσι καθεύδει,
οὐδ' ἐπιτυμβίδιοι κορυδαλλίδες ἠλαίνοντι;
ἦ μετὰ δαῖτ' ἄκλητος ἐπείγεαι, ἤ τινος ἀστῶν
λανὸν ἔπι θρώσκεις; ὥς τοι ποσὶ νισσομένοιο   25
πᾶσα λίθος πταίοισα ποτ' ἀρβυλίδεσσιν ἀείδει.'
τὸν δ' ἐγὼ ἀμείφθην· 'Λυκίδα φίλε, φαντί τυ πάντες
ἦμεν συρικτὰν μέγ' ὑπείροχον ἔν τε νομεῦσιν

5 ἐπάνωθεν z: ἔτ' ἄνωθεν **m**   8 ὕφαινον z: ἔφαινον **m**   24 δαῖτα
κλητός **bm**

ἔν τ' ἀματήρεσσι. τὸ δὴ μάλα θυμὸν ἰαίνει
ἀμέτερον· καίτοι κατ' ἐμὸν νόον ἰσοφαρίζειν   30
ἔλπομαι. ἁ δ' ὁδὸς ἅδε θαλυσιάς· ἦ γὰρ ἑταῖροι
ἀνέρες εὐπέπλῳ Δαμάτερι δαῖτα τελεῦντι
ὄλβω ἀπαρχόμενοι· μάλα γάρ σφισι πίονι μέτρῳ
ἁ δαίμων εὔκριθον ἀνεπλήρωσεν ἀλωάν.
ἀλλ' ἄγε δή, ξυνὰ γὰρ ὁδὸς ξυνὰ δὲ καὶ ἀώς,   35
βουκολιασδώμεσθα· τάχ' ὥτερος ἄλλον ὀνασεῖ.
καὶ γὰρ ἐγὼ Μοισᾶν καπυρὸν στόμα, κἠμὲ λέγοντι
πάντες ἀοιδὸν ἄριστον· ἐγὼ δέ τις οὐ ταχυπειθής,
οὐ Δᾶν· οὐ γάρ πω κατ' ἐμὸν νόον οὔτε τὸν ἐσθλόν
Σικελίδαν νίκημι τὸν ἐκ Σάμω οὔτε Φιλίταν   40
ἀείδων, βάτραχος δὲ ποτ' ἀκρίδας ὥς τις ἐρίσδω.'
ὣς ἐφάμαν ἐπίταδες· ὁ δ' αἰπόλος ἀδὺ γελάσσας,
'τάν τοι', ἔφα, 'κορύναν δωρύττομαι, οὕνεκεν ἐσσί
πᾶν ἐπ' ἀλαθείᾳ πεπλασμένον ἐκ Διὸς ἔρνος.
ὥς μοι καὶ τέκτων μέγ' ἀπέχθεται ὅστις ἐρευνῇ   45
ἶσον ὄρευς κορυφᾷ τελέσαι δόμον Ὠρομέδοντος,
καὶ Μοισᾶν ὄρνιχες ὅσοι ποτὶ Χῖον ἀοιδόν
ἀντία κοκκύζοντες ἐτώσια μοχθίζοντι.
ἀλλ' ἄγε βουκολικᾶς ταχέως ἀρξώμεθ' ἀοιδᾶς,
Σιμιχίδα· κἠγὼ μέν — ὅρη, φίλος, εἴ τοι ἀρέσκει   50
τοῦθ' ὅτι πρᾶν ἐν ὄρει τὸ μελύδριον ἐξεπόνασα.

ἔσσεται Ἀγεάνακτι καλὸς πλόος ἐς Μιτυλήναν,
χὤταν ἐφ' ἑσπερίοις Ἐρίφοις νότος ὑγρὰ διώκῃ
κύματα, χὨρίων ὅτ' ἐπ' ὠκεανῷ πόδας ἴσχει,
αἴ κα τὸν Λυκίδαν ὀπτεύμενον ἐξ Ἀφροδίτας   55
ῥύσηται· θερμὸς γὰρ ἔρως αὐτῶ με καταίθει.
χἀλκυόνες στορεσεῦντι τὰ κύματα τάν τε θάλασσαν
τόν τε νότον τόν τ' εὖρον, ὃς ἔσχατα φυκία κινεῖ,

46 Ὠρομέδοντος **ab**m: Εὐρυμέδοντος m

ἀλκυόνες, γλαυκαῖς Νηρηΐσι ταί τε μάλιστα
ὀρνίχων ἐφίληθεν, ὅσοις τέ περ ἐξ ἁλὸς ἄγρα.   60
'Αγεάνακτι πλόον διζημένῳ ἐς Μιτυλήναν
ὥρια πάντα γένοιτο, καὶ εὔπλοος ὅρμον ἵκοιτο.
κἠγὼ τῆνο κατ' ἆμαρ ἀνήτινον ἢ ῥοδόεντα
ἢ καὶ λευκοΐων στέφανον περὶ κρατὶ φυλάσσων
τὸν Πτελεατικὸν οἶνον ἀπὸ κρατῆρος ἀφυξῶ   65
πὰρ πυρὶ κεκλιμένος, κύαμον δέ τις ἐν πυρὶ φρυξεῖ.
χἀ στιβὰς ἐσσεῖται πεπυκασμένα ἔστ' ἐπὶ πᾶχυν
κνύζᾳ τ' ἀσφοδέλῳ τε πολυγνάμπτῳ τε σελίνῳ.
καὶ πίομαι μαλακῶς μεμναμένος 'Αγεάνακτος
† αὐταῖσιν κυλίκεσσι καὶ ἐς τρύγα χεῖλος ἐρείδων.   70
αὐλησεῦντι δέ μοι δύο ποιμένες, εἷς μὲν 'Αχαρνεύς,
εἷς δὲ Λυκωπίτας· ὁ δὲ Τίτυρος ἐγγύθεν ᾀσεῖ
ὥς ποκα τᾶς Ξενέας ἠράσσατο Δάφνις ὁ βούτας,
χὠς ὄρος ἀμφεπονεῖτο καὶ ὡς δρύες αὐτὸν ἐθρήνευν
'Ιμέρα αἴτε φύοντι παρ' ὄχθαισιν ποταμοῖο,   75
εὖτε χιὼν ὥς τις κατετάκετο μακρὸν ὑφ' Αἷμον
ἢ "Αθω ἢ 'Ροδόπαν ἢ Καύκασον ἐσχατόωντα.
ᾀσεῖ δ' ὥς ποκ' ἔδεκτο τὸν αἰπόλον εὐρέα λάρναξ
ζωὸν ἐόντα κακαῖσιν ἀτασθαλίαισιν ἄνακτος,
ὥς τέ νιν αἱ σιμαὶ λειμωνόθε φέρβον ἰοῖσαι   80
κέδρον ἐς ἀδεῖαν μαλακοῖς ἄνθεσσι μέλισσαι
οὕνεκά οἱ γλυκὺ Μοῖσα κατὰ στόματος χέε νέκταρ.
ὦ μακαριστὲ Κομᾶτα, τύ θην τάδε τερπνὰ πεπόνθεις·
καὶ τὺ κατεκλάσθης ἐς λάρνακα, καὶ τὺ μελισσᾶν
κηρία φερβόμενος ἔτος ὥριον ἐξεπόνασας.   85
αἴθ' ἐπ' ἐμεῦ ζωοῖς ἐναρίθμιος ὤφελες ἦμεν
ὥς τοι ἐγὼν ἐνόμευον ἀν' ὥρεα τὰς καλὰς αἶγας
φωνᾶς εἰσαΐων, τὺ δ' ὑπὸ δρυσὶν ἢ ὑπὸ πεύκαις
ἁδὺ μελισδόμενος κατεκέκλισο, θεῖε Κομᾶτα.'

70 αὐταῖς ἐν z   73 ξανθᾶς b

χὠ μὲν τόσσ' εἰπὼν ἀπεπαύσατο· τὸν δὲ μέτ' αὖθις   90
κἠγὼν τοῖ' ἐφάμαν· 'Λυκίδα φίλε, πολλὰ μὲν ἄλλα
Νύμφαι κἠμὲ δίδαξαν ἀν' ὤρεα βουκολέοντα
ἐσθλά, τά που καὶ Ζηνὸς ἐπὶ θρόνον ἄγαγε φάμα·
ἀλλὰ τόγ' ἐκ πάντων μέγ' ὑπείροχον, ᾧ τυ γεραίρειν
ἀρξεῦμ'· ἀλλ' ὑπάκουσον, ἐπεὶ φίλος ἔπλεο Μοίσαις.   95

Σιμιχίδᾳ μὲν Ἔρωτες ἐπέπταρον· ἦ γὰρ ὁ δειλός
τόσσον ἐρᾷ Μυρτοῦς ὅσον εἴαρος αἶγες ἔρανται.
Ὤρατος δ' ὁ τὰ πάντα φιλαίτατος ἀνέρι τήνῳ
παιδὸς ὑπὸ σπλάγχνοισιν ἔχει πόθον. οἶδεν Ἄριστις,
ἐσθλὸς ἀνήρ, μέγ' ἄριστος, ὃν οὐδέ κεν αὐτὸς ἀείδειν   100
Φοῖβος σὺν φόρμιγγι παρὰ τριπόδεσσι μεγαίροι,
ὡς ἐκ παιδὸς Ἄρατος ὑπ' ὀστίον αἴθετ' ἔρωτι.
τόν μοι, Πάν, Ὁμόλας ἐρατὸν πέδον ὅστε λέλογχας,
ἄκλητον τήνοιο φίλας ἐς χεῖρας ἐρείσαις,
εἴτ' ἔστ' ἄρα Φιλῖνος ὁ μαλθακὸς εἴτε τις ἄλλος.   105
κεἰ μὲν ταῦτ' ἔρδοις, ὦ Πὰν φίλε, μήτι τυ παῖδες
Ἀρκαδικοὶ σκίλλαισιν ὑπὸ πλευράς τε καὶ ὤμως
τανίκα μαστίζοιεν ὅτε κρέα τυτθὰ παρείη·
εἰ δ' ἄλλως νεύσαις, κατὰ μὲν χρόα πάντ' ὀνύχεσσι
δακνόμενος κνάσαιο καὶ ἐν κνίδαισι καθεύδοις·   110
εἴης δ' Ἠδωνῶν μὲν ἐν ὤρεσι χείματι μέσσῳ
Ἕβρον πὰρ ποταμὸν τετραμμένος ἐγγύθεν Ἄρκτω,
ἐν δὲ θέρει πυμάτοισι παρ' Αἰθιόπεσσι νομεύοις
πέτρᾳ ὕπο Βλεμύων, ὅθεν οὐκέτι Νεῖλος ὁρατός.
ὔμμες δ' Ὑετίδος καὶ Βυβλίδος ἁδὺ λιπόντες   115
νᾶμα καὶ Οἰκοῦντα, ξανθᾶς ἕδος αἰπὺ Διώνας,
ὦ μάλοισιν Ἔρωτες ἐρευθομένοισιν ὁμοῖοι,
βάλλετέ μοι τόξοισι τὸν ἱμερόεντα Φιλῖνον,
βάλλετ', ἐπεὶ τὸν ξεῖνον ὁ δύσμορος οὐκ ἐλεεῖ μευ.
καὶ δὴ μὰν ἀπίοιο πεπαίτερος, αἱ δὲ γυναῖκες,   120

"αἰαῖ", φαντί, "Φιλῖνε, τό τοι καλὸν ἄνθος ἀπορρεῖ"
μηκέτι τοι φρουρέωμες ἐπὶ προθύροισιν, Ἄρατε,
μηδὲ πόδας τρίβωμες· ὁ δ' ὄρθριος ἄλλον ἀλέκτωρ
κοκκύσδων νάρκαισιν ἀνιαραῖσι διδοίη·
εἷς δ' ἀπὸ τᾶσδε, φέριστε, Μόλων ἄγχοιτο παλαίστρας.   125
ἄμμιν δ' ἀσυχία τε μέλοι, γραῖα τε παρείη
ἅτις ἐπιφθύζοισα τὰ μὴ καλὰ νόσφιν ἐρύκοι.'

τόσσ' ἐφάμαν· ὁ δέ μοι τὸ λαγωβόλον, ἁδὺ γελάσσας,
ὡς πάρος, ἐκ Μοισᾶν ξεινήϊον ὤπασεν ἦμεν.
χὠ μὲν ἀποκλίνας ἐπ' ἀριστερὰ τὰν ἐπὶ Πύξας   130
εἷρφ' ὁδόν· αὐτὰρ ἐγών τε καὶ Εὔκριτος ἐς Φρασιδάμω
στραφθέντες χὠ καλὸς Ἀμύντιχος ἔν τε βαθείαις
ἁδείας σχοίνοιο χαμευνίσιν ἐκλίνθημες
ἔν τε νεοτμάτοισι γεγαθότες οἰναρέοισι.
πολλαὶ δ' ἄμμιν ὕπερθε κατὰ κρατὸς δονέοντο   135
αἴγειροι πτελέαι τε· τὸ δ' ἐγγύθεν ἱερὸν ὕδωρ
Νυμφᾶν ἐξ ἄντροιο κατειβόμενον κελάρυζε.
τοὶ δὲ ποτὶ σκιαραῖς ὀροδαμνίσιν αἰθαλίωνες
τέττιγες λαλαγεῦντες ἔχον πόνον· ἁ δ' ὀλολυγών
τηλόθεν ἐν πυκιναῖσι βάτων τρύζεσκεν ἀκάνθαις·   140
ἄειδον κόρυδοι καὶ ἀκανθίδες, ἔστενε τρυγών,
πωτῶντο ξουθαὶ περὶ πίδακας ἀμφὶ μέλισσαι.
πάντ' ὦσδεν θέρεος μάλα πίονος, ὦσδε δ' ὀπώρας.
ὄχναι μὲν πὰρ ποσσί, παρὰ πλευραῖσι δὲ μᾶλα
δαψιλέως ἁμῖν ἐκυλίνδετο, τοὶ δ' ἐκέχυντο   145
ὄρπακες βραβίλοισι καταβρίθοντες ἔραζε·
τετράενες δὲ πίθων ἀπελύετο κρατὸς ἄλειφαρ.
Νύμφαι Κασταλίδες Παρνάσιον αἶπος ἔχοισαι,
ἆρά γε πᾳ τοιόνδε Φόλω κατὰ λάϊνον ἄντρον
κρατῆρ' Ἡρακλῆϊ γέρων ἐστάσατο Χίρων;   150

125 ἐπὶ bm   147 ἑπτάενες b

ἀρά γε πα τῆνον τὸν ποιμένα τὸν ποτ' Ἀνάπῳ,
τὸν κρατερὸν Πολύφαμον, ὃς ὤρεσι νᾶας ἔβαλλε,
τοῖον νέκταρ ἔπεισε κατ' αὔλια ποσσὶ χορεῦσαι,
οἷον δὴ τόκα πῶμα διεκρανάσατε, Νύμφαι,
βωμῷ πὰρ Δάματρος ἁλωΐδος; ἇς ἐπὶ σωρῷ   155
αὖτις ἐγὼ πάξαιμι μέγα πτύον, ἁ δὲ γελάσσαι
δράγματα καὶ μάκωνας ἐν ἀμφοτέραισιν ἔχοισα.

152 νᾶας z: λᾶας m

X

ΜΙΛΩΝ

ἐργατίνα Βουκαῖε, τί νῦν, ὦζυρέ, πεπόνθεις;
οὔτε τὸν ὄγμον ἄγειν ὀρθὸν δύνᾳ, ὡς τὸ πρὶν
    ἆγες,
οὔθ' ἅμα λᾳοτομεῖς τῷ πλατίον, ἀλλ' ἀπολείπῃ,
ὥσπερ ὄϊς ποίμνας ἃς τὸν πόδα κάκτος ἔτυψε.
ποῖός τις δείλαν τὺ καὶ ἐκ μέσω ἄματος ἐσσῇ,   5
ὃς νῦν ἀρχόμενος τᾶς αὔλακος οὐκ ἀποτρώγεις;

ΒΟΥΚΑΙΟΣ

Μίλων ὀψαμᾶτα, πέτρας ἀπόκομμ' ἀτεράμνω,
οὐδαμά τοι συνέβα ποθέσαι τινὰ τῶν ἀπεόντων;
MI. οὐδαμά. τίς δὲ πόθος τῶν ἔκτοθεν ἐργάτᾳ ἀνδρί;
BO. οὐδαμά νυν συνέβα τοι ἀγρυπνῆσαι δι' ἔρωτα;   10
MI. μηδέ γε συμβαίη· χαλεπὸν χορίω κύνα γεῦσαι.
BO. ἀλλ' ἐγώ, ὦ Μίλων, ἔραμαι σχεδὸν ἑνδεκαταῖος.
MI. ἐκ πίθω ἀντλεῖς δῆλον· ἐγὼ δ' ἔχω οὐδ' ἅλις ὄξος.
BO. τοιγὰρ τὰ πρὸ θυρᾶν μοι ἀπὸ σπόρω ἄσκαλα πάντα.

2 οὐ τεὸν m

MI. τίς δέ τυ τᾶν παίδων λυμαίνεται;

BO.   ἁ Πολυβώτα,   15
ἃ πρᾶν ἁμάντεσσι παρ' Ἱπποκίωνι ποταύλει.

MI. εὗρε θεὸς τὸν ἀλιτρόν· ἔχεις πάλαι ὧν ἐπεθύμεις·
μάντις τοι τὰν νύκτα χροϊξεῖται καλαμαία.

BO. μωμᾶσθαί μ' ἄρχῃ τύ· τυφλὸς δ' οὐκ αὐτὸς ὁ Πλοῦτος,
ἀλλὰ καὶ ὠφρόντιστος Ἔρως. μὴ δὴ μέγα μυθεῦ. 20

MI. οὐ μέγα μυθεῦμαι· τὺ μόνον κατάβαλλε τὸ λᾷον,
καί τι κόρας φιλικὸν μέλος ἀμβάλευ. ἅδιον οὕτως
ἐργαξῇ. καὶ μὰν πρότερόν ποκα μουσικὸς ἦσθα.

BO. Μοῖσαι Πιερίδες, συναείσατε τὰν ῥαδινάν μοι
παῖδ'· ὧν γάρ χ' ἅψησθε, θεαί, καλὰ πάντα ποεῖτε. 25
Βομβύκα χαρίεσσα, Σύραν καλέοντί τυ πάντες,
ἰσχνάν, ἁλιόκαυστον, ἐγὼ δὲ μόνος μελίχλωρον.
καὶ τὸ ἴον μέλαν ἐστί, καὶ ἁ γραπτὰ ὑάκινθος·
ἀλλ' ἔμπας ἐν τοῖς στεφάνοις τὰ πρᾶτα λέγονται.
ἁ αἶξ τὰν κύτισον, ὁ λύκος τὰν αἶγα διώκει,   30
ἁ γέρανος τὤροτρον· ἐγὼ δ' ἐπὶ τὶν μεμάνημαι.
αἴθε μοι ἦς ὅσσα Κροῖσόν ποκα φαντὶ πεπᾶσθαι·
χρύσεοι ἀμφότεροί κ' ἀνεκείμεθα τᾷ Ἀφροδίτᾳ,
τὼς αὐλὼς μὲν ἔχοισα καὶ ἢ ῥόδον ἢ τύγε μᾶλον,
σχῆμα δ' ἐγὼ καὶ καινὰς ἐπ' ἀμφοτέροισιν ἀμύκλας.   35
Βομβύκα χαρίεσσ', οἱ μὲν πόδες ἀστράγαλοί τευς,
ἁ φωνὰ δὲ τρύχνος· τὸν μὰν τρόπον οὐκ ἔχω εἰπεῖν.

MI. ἦ καλὰς ἄμμε ποῶν ἐλελάθει Βοῦκος ἀοιδάς·
ὡς εὖ τὰν ἰδέαν τᾶς ἁρμονίας ἐμέτρησεν.

ὤμοι τῶ πώγωνος, ὃν ἀλιθίως ἀνέφυσα.　　40
θᾶσαι δὴ καὶ ταῦτα τὰ τῶ θείω Λιτυέρσα.

Δάματερ πολύκαρπε, πολύσταχυ, τοῦτο τὸ
　　λᾶον
εὔεργόν τ' εἴη καὶ κάρπιμον ὅττι μάλιστα.
σφίγγετ', ἀμαλλοδέται, τὰ δράγματα, μὴ παριών
　　τις
εἴπῃ, 'σύκινοι ἄνδρες· ἀπώλετο χοὗτος ὁ
　　μισθός'.　　　　　　　　　　　　　　　　45
ἐς βορέαν ἄνεμον τᾶς κόρθυος ἁ τομὰ ὕμμιν
ἢ ζέφυρον βλεπέτω· πιαίνεται ὁ στάχυς οὕτως.
σῖτον ἀλοιῶντας φεύγειν τὸ μεσαμβρινὸν ὕπνον·
ἐκ καλάμας ἄχυρον τελέθει τημόσδε μάλιστα.
ἄρχεσθαι δ' ἀμῶντας ἐγειρομένω κορυδαλλῶ　　50
καὶ λήγειν εὔδοντος, ἐλινῦσαι δὲ τὸ καῦμα.
εὐκτὸς ὁ τῶ βατράχω, παῖδες, βίος· οὐ
　　μελεδαίνει
τὸν τὸ πιεῖν ἐγχεῦντα, πάρεστι γὰρ ἄφθονον
　　αὐτῷ.
κάλλιον, ὦ 'πιμελητὰ φιλάργυρε, τὸν φακὸν ἕψειν,
μὴ 'πιτάμῃς τὰν χεῖρα καταπρίων τὸ κύμινον.　55

ταῦτα χρὴ μόχθεντας ἐν ἁλίω ἄνδρας ἀείδειν,
τὸν δὲ τεόν, Βουκαῖε, πρέπει λιμηρὸν ἔρωτα
μυθίσδεν τᾷ ματρὶ κατ' εὐνὰν ὀρθρευοίσᾳ.

55 μὴ 'πιτάμῃς **acm**: μή τι τάμῃς m

XI

οὐδὲν ποττὸν ἔρωτα πεφύκει φάρμακον ἄλλο,
Νικία, οὔτ' ἔγχριστον, ἐμὶν δοκεῖ, οὔτ' ἐπίπαστον,
ἢ ταὶ Πιερίδες· κοῦφον δέ τι τοῦτο καὶ ἁδύ
γίνετ' ἐπ' ἀνθρώποις, εὑρεῖν δ' οὐ ῥᾴδιόν ἐστι.
γινώσκειν δ' οἶμαί τυ καλῶς ἰατρὸν ἐόντα　　　　　5
καὶ ταῖς ἐννέα δὴ πεφιλημένον ἔξοχα Μοίσαις.
οὕτω γοῦν ῥάιστα διᾶγ' ὁ Κύκλωψ ὁ παρ' ἁμῖν,
ὡρχαῖος Πολύφαμος, ὅκ' ἤρατο τᾶς Γαλατείας,
ἄρτι γενειάσδων περὶ τὸ στόμα τὼς κροτάφως τε.
ἤρατο δ' οὐ μάλοις οὐδὲ ῥόδῳ οὐδὲ κικίννοις,　　　　　10
ἀλλ' ὀρθαῖς μανίαις, ἁγεῖτο δὲ πάντα πάρεργα.
πολλάκι ταὶ ὄιες ποτὶ τωὔλιον αὐταὶ ἀπῆνθον
χλωρᾶς ἐκ βοτάνας· ὁ δὲ τὰν Γαλάτειαν ἀείδων
αὐτὸς ἐπ' ἀϊόνος κατετάκετο φυκιοέσσας
ἐξ ἀοῦς, ἔχθιστον ἔχων ὑποκάρδιον ἕλκος,　　　　　15
Κύπριδος ἐκ μεγάλας τό οἱ ἥπατι πᾶξε βέλεμνον.
ἀλλὰ τὸ φάρμακον εὗρε, καθεζόμενος δ' ἐπὶ πέτρας
ὑψηλᾶς ἐς πόντον ὁρῶν ἄειδε τοιαῦτα·

ὦ λευκὰ Γαλάτεια, τί τὸν φιλέοντ' ἀποβάλλῃ,
λευκοτέρα πακτᾶς προτιδεῖν, ἁπαλωτέρα ἀρνός,　　　　　20
μόσχω γαυροτέρα, φιαρωτέρα ὄμφακος ὠμᾶς;
φοιτῇς δ' αὖθ' οὕτως ὅκκα γλυκὺς ὕπνος ἔχῃ με,
οἴχῃ δ' εὐθὺς ἰοῖσ' ὅκκα γλυκὺς ὕπνος ἀνῇ με,
φεύγεις δ' ὥσπερ ὄις πολιὸν λύκον ἀθρήσασα;
ἠράσθην μὲν ἔγωγε τεοῦς, κόρα, ἁνίκα πρᾶτον　　　　　25
ἦνθες ἐμᾷ σὺν ματρὶ θέλοισ' ὑακίνθινα φύλλα
ἐξ ὄρεος δρέψασθαι, ἐγὼ δ' ὁδὸν ἁγεμόνευον.
παύσασθαι δ' ἐσιδών τυ καὶ ὕστερον οὐδ' ἔτι πᾳ νῦν

11 ὀλοαῖς bm

ἐκ τήνω δύναμαι· τὶν δ' οὐ μέλει, οὐ μὰ Δί' οὐδέν.
γινώσκω, χαρίεσσα κόρα, τίνος οὕνεκα φεύγεις·   30
οὕνεκά μοι λασία μὲν ὀφρὺς ἐπὶ παντὶ μετώπῳ
ἐξ ὠτὸς τέταται ποτὶ θώτερον ὣς μία μακρά,
εἷς δ' ὀφθαλμὸς ὕπεστι, πλατεῖα δὲ ῥὶς ἐπὶ χείλει.
ἀλλ' οὗτος τοιοῦτος ἐὼν βοτὰ χίλια βόσκω,
κἠκ τούτων τὸ κράτιστον ἀμελγόμενος γάλα πίνω·   35
τυρὸς δ' οὐ λείπει μ' οὔτ' ἐν θέρει οὔτ' ἐν ὀπώρᾳ,
οὐ χειμῶνος ἄκρω· ταρσοὶ δ' ὑπεραχθέες αἰεί.
συρίσδεν δ' ὡς οὔτις ἐπίσταμαι ὧδε Κυκλώπων,
τίν, τὸ φίλον γλυκύμαλον, ἁμᾷ κἠμαυτὸν ἀείδων
πολλάκι νυκτὸς ἀωρί. τράφω δέ τοι ἕνδεκα νεβρώς,   40
πάσας μαννοφόρως, καὶ σκύμνως τέσσαρας ἄρκτων.
ἀλλ' ἀφίκευσο ποθ' ἁμέ, καὶ ἑξεῖς οὐδὲν ἔλασσον,
τὰν γλαυκὰν δὲ θάλασσαν ἔα ποτὶ χέρσον ὀρεχθεῖν·
ἅδιον ἐν τὤντρῳ παρ' ἐμὶν τὰν νύκτα διαξεῖς.
ἐντὶ δάφναι τηνεί, ἐντὶ ῥαδιναὶ κυπάρισσοι,   45
ἔστι μέλας κισσός, ἔστ' ἄμπελος ἁ γλυκύκαρπος,
ἔστι ψυχρὸν ὕδωρ, τό μοι ἁ πολυδένδρεος Αἴτνα
λευκᾶς ἐκ χιόνος ποτὸν ἀμβρόσιον προΐητι.
τίς κα τῶνδε θάλασσαν ἔχειν καὶ κύμαθ' ἕλοιτο;
αἰ δέ τοι αὐτὸς ἐγὼν δοκέω λασιώτερος ἦμεν,   50
ἐντὶ δρυὸς ξύλα μοι καὶ ὑπὸ σποδῷ ἀκάματον πῦρ·
καιόμενος δ' ὑπὸ τεῦς καὶ τὰν ψυχὰν ἀνεχοίμαν
καὶ τὸν ἔν' ὀφθαλμόν, τῶ μοι γλυκερώτερον οὐδέν.
ὤμοι ὅτ' οὐκ ἔτεκέν μ' ἁ μάτηρ βράγχι' ἔχοντα,
ὡς κατέδυν ποτὶ τὶν καὶ τὰν χέρα τεῦς ἐφίλησα,   55
αἰ μὴ τὸ στόμα λῇς, ἔφερον δέ τοι ἢ κρίνα λευκά
ἢ μάκων' ἁπαλὰν ἐρυθρὰ πλαταγώνι' ἔχοισαν·
ἀλλὰ τὰ μὲν θέρεος, τὰ δὲ γίνεται ἐν χειμῶνι,

33 ὕπεστι z: ἔπεστι m   41 μαννοφόρως b: ἀμνοφόρως m
42 ἀφίκευσο bm: ἀφίκευ τὺ m

ὥστ' οὔ κά τοι ταῦτα φέρειν ἅμα πάντ' ἐδυνάθην.
νῦν μάν, ὦ κόριον, νῦν αὐτίκα νεῖν γε μαθεῦμαι,   60
αἴ κα τις σὺν ναΐ πλέων ξένος ὧδ' ἀφίκηται,
ὡς εἰδῶ τί ποχ' ἁδὺ κατοικεῖν τὸν βυθὸν ὕμμιν.
ἐξένθοις, Γαλάτεια, καὶ ἐξενθοῖσα λάθοιο,
ὥσπερ ἐγὼ νῦν ὧδε καθήμενος, οἴκαδ' ἀπενθεῖν·
ποιμαίνειν δ' ἐθέλοις σὺν ἐμὶν ἅμα καὶ γάλ'
          ἀμέλγειν   65
καὶ τυρὸν πᾶξαι τάμισον δριμεῖαν ἐνεῖσα.
ἁ μάτηρ ἀδικεῖ με μόνα, καὶ μέμφομαι αὐτᾷ·
οὐδὲν πήποχ' ὅλως ποτὶ τὶν φίλον εἶπεν ὑπέρ μευ,
καὶ ταῦτ' ἆμαρ ἐπ' ἆμαρ ὁρεῦσά με λεπτύνοντα.
φασῶ τὰν κεφαλὰν καὶ τὼς πόδας ἀμφοτέρως μευ   70
σφύσδειν, ὡς ἀνιαθῇ ἐπεὶ κἠγὼν ἀνιῶμαι.
ὦ Κύκλωψ Κύκλωψ, πᾷ τὰς φρένας ἐκπεπότασαι;
αἴ κ' ἐνθὼν ταλάρως τε πλέκοις καὶ θαλλὸν ἀμάσας
ταῖς ἄρνεσσι φέροις, τάχα κα πολὺ μᾶλλον ἔχοις νῶν.
τὰν παρεοῖσαν ἄμελγε· τί τὸν φεύγοντα διώκεις;   75
εὑρησεῖς Γαλάτειαν ἴσως καὶ καλλίον' ἄλλαν.
πολλαὶ συμπαίσδεν με κόραι τὰν νύκτα κέλονται,
κιχλίζοντι δὲ πᾶσαι, ἐπεί κ' αὐταῖς ὑπακούσω.
δῆλον ὅτ' ἐν τᾷ γᾷ κἠγών τις φαίνομαι ἦμεν.

     οὕτω τοι Πολύφαμος ἐποίμαινεν τὸν ἔρωτα   80
μουσίσδων, ῥᾷον δὲ διᾶγ' ἢ εἰ χρυσὸν ἔδωκεν.

60 αὐτίκα z: αὐτό γα m: τό γε m   69 λεπτύνοντα z: λεπτὸν
ἐόντα m

XIII

οὐχ ἁμῖν τὸν Ἔρωτα μόνοις ἔτεχ', ὡς ἐδοκεῦμες,
Νικία, ᾧτινι τοῦτο θεῶν ποκα τέκνον ἔγεντο·
οὐχ ἁμῖν τὰ καλὰ πράτοις καλὰ φαίνεται ἦμεν,
οἳ θνατοὶ πελόμεσθα, τὸ δ' αὔριον οὐκ ἐσορῶμες·
ἀλλὰ καὶ Ἀμφιτρύωνος ὁ χαλκεοκάρδιος υἱός,   5
ὃς τὸν λῖν ὑπέμεινε τὸν ἄγριον, ἤρατο παιδός,
τοῦ χαρίεντος Ὕλα, τοῦ τὰν πλοκαμίδα φορεῦντος,
καί νιν πάντ' ἐδίδασκε, πατὴρ ὡσεὶ φίλον υἱόν,
ὅσσα μαθὼν ἀγαθὸς καὶ ἀοίδιμος αὐτὸς ἔγεντο·
χωρὶς δ' οὐδέποκ' ἦς, οὔτ' εἰ μέσον ἆμαρ ὄροιτο,   10
οὔθ' ὁπόχ' ἁ λεύκιππος ἀνατρέχοι ἐς Διὸς Ἀώς,
οὔθ' ὁπόκ' ὀρτάλιχοι μινυροὶ ποτὶ κοῖτον ὁρῷεν,
σεισαμένας πτερὰ ματρὸς ἐπ' αἰθαλόεντι πετεύρῳ,
ὡς αὐτῷ κατὰ θυμὸν ὁ παῖς πεπομαμένος εἴη,
†αὐτῷ δ' εὖ ἕλκων† ἐς ἀλαθινὸν ἄνδρ' ἀποβαίη.   15
ἀλλ' ὅτε τὸ χρύσειον ἔπλει μετὰ κῶας Ἰάσων
Αἰσονίδας, οἱ δ' αὐτῷ ἀριστῆες συνέποντο
πασᾶν ἐκ πολίων προλελεγμένοι ὧν ὄφελός τι,
ἵκετο χὠ ταλαεργὸς ἀνὴρ ἐς ἀφνειὸν Ἰωλκόν,
Ἀλκμήνας υἱὸς Μιδεάτιδος ἡρωίνας,   20
σὺν δ' αὐτῷ κατέβαινεν Ὕλας εὔεδρον ἐς Ἀργώ,
ἅτις κυανεᾶν οὐχ ἅψατο συνδρομάδων ναῦς
ἀλλὰ διεξάιξε — βαθὺν δ' εἰσέδραμε Φᾶσιν —
αἰετὸς ὡς μέγα λαῖτμα· ἀφ' οὖ τότε χοιράδες ἔσταν.
ἆμος δ' ἀντέλλοντι Πελειάδες, ἐσχατιαὶ δέ   25
ἄρνα νέον βόσκοντι, τετραμμένου εἴαρος ἤδη,
τᾶμος ναυτιλίας μιμνάσκετο θεῖος ἄωτος
ἡρώων, κοίλαν δὲ καθιδρυθέντες ἐς Ἀργώ

15 αὐτῷ δ' εὖ εἰκώς z: οὕτω δ' εὐκλεῶς z   23 f. βαθὺν ...
Φᾶσιν et ἀφ' οὖ ... ἔσταν transp. z

Ἑλλάσποντον ἵκοντο νότῳ τρίτον ἆμαρ ἀέντι,
εἴσω δ' ὅρμον ἔθεντο Προποντίδος, ἔνθα Κιανῶν   30
αὔλακας εὐρύνοντι βόες τρίβοντες ἄροτρα.
ἐκβάντες δ' ἐπὶ θῖνα κατὰ ζυγὰ δαῖτα πένοντο
δειελινοί, πολλοὶ δὲ μίαν στορέσαντο χαμεύναν.
λειμὼν γάρ σφιν ἔκειτο μέγα στιβάδεσσιν ὄνειαρ,
ἔνθεν βούτομον ὀξὺ βαθύν τ' ἐτάμοντο κύπειρον.   35
κὦχεθ' Ὕλας ὁ ξανθὸς ὕδωρ ἐπιδόρπιον οἴσων
αὐτῷ θ' Ἡρακλῆϊ καὶ ἀστεμφεῖ Τελαμῶνι,
οἳ μίαν ἄμφω ἑταῖροι ἀεὶ δαίνυντο τράπεζαν,
χάλκεον ἄγγος ἔχων. τάχα δὲ κράναν ἐνόησεν
ἡμένῳ ἐν χώρῳ· περὶ δὲ θρύα πολλὰ πεφύκει,   40
κυάνεόν τε χελιδόνιον χλωρόν τ' ἀδίαντον
καὶ θάλλοντα σέλινα καὶ εἰλιτενὴς ἄγρωστις.
ὕδατι δ' ἐν μέσσῳ Νύμφαι χορὸν ἀρτίζοντο,
Νύμφαι ἀκοίμητοι, δειναὶ θεαὶ ἀγροιώταις,
Εὐνίκα καὶ Μαλὶς ἔαρ θ' ὁρόωσα Νύχεια.   45
ἤτοι ὁ κοῦρος ἐπεῖχε ποτῷ πολυχανδέα κρωσσόν
βάψαι ἐπειγόμενος· ταὶ δ' ἐν χερὶ πᾶσαι ἔφυσαν·
πασάων γὰρ ἔρως ἀπαλὰς φρένας ἐξεφόβησεν
Ἀργείῳ ἐπὶ παιδί. κατήριπε δ' ἐς μέλαν ὕδωρ
ἀθρόος, ὡς ὅτε πυρσὸς ἀπ' οὐρανοῦ ἤριπεν ἀστήρ   50
ἀθρόος ἐν πόντῳ, ναύτας δέ τις εἶπεν ἑταίροις
'κουφότερ', ὦ παῖδες, ποιεῖσθ' ὅπλα· πλευστικὸς οὖρος'.
Νύμφαι μὲν σφετέροις ἐπὶ γούνασι κοῦρον ἔχοισαι
δακρυόεντ' ἀγανοῖσι παρεψύχοντ' ἐπέεσσιν·
Ἀμφιτρυωνιάδας δὲ ταρασσόμενος περὶ παιδί   55
ᾤχετο, Μαιωτιστὶ λαβὼν εὐκαμπέα τόξα
καὶ ῥόπαλον, τό οἱ αἰὲν ἐχάνδανε δεξιτερὰ χείρ.
τρὶς μὲν Ὕλαν ἄϋσεν ὅσον βαθὺς ἤρυγε λαιμός,

34 λειμ]ων [σ]φ[ι]ν πα[ρεκειτο a   48 ἀμφεκάλυψεν m   51 ναύτας
z: ναύταις m   ἑταῖρος m   58 βαρὺς m

τρὶς δ' ἄρ' ὁ παῖς ὑπάκουσεν, ἀραιὰ δ' ἵκετο φωνά
ἐξ ὕδατος, παρεὼν δὲ μάλα σχεδὸν εἴδετο πόρρω.   60
νεβροῦ φθεγξαμένας τις ἐν οὔρεσιν ὠμοφάγος λίς   62
ἐξ εὐνᾶς ἔσπευσεν ἑτοιμοτάταν ἐπὶ δαῖτα·
Ἡρακλέης τοιοῦτος ἐν ἀτρίπτοισιν ἀκάνθαις
παῖδα ποθῶν δεδόνητο, πολὺν δ' ἐπελάμβανε χῶρον.   65
σχέτλιοι οἱ φιλέοντες, ἀλώμενος ὅσσ' ἐμόγησεν
οὔρεα καὶ δρυμούς, τὰ δ' Ἰάσονος ὕστερα πάντ' ἦς.
ναῦς γέμεν ἄρμεν' ἔχοισα μετάρσια τῶν παρεόντων,
ἱστία δ' ἡμίθεοι μεσονύκτιον ἐξεκάθαιρον
Ἡρακλῆα μένοντες. ὁ δ' ᾇ πόδες ἆγον εχωρει   70
μαινόμενος· χαλεπὸς γὰρ ἔσω θεὸς ἧπαρ ἄμυσσεν.
οὕτω μὲν κάλλιστος Ὕλας μακάρων ἀριθμεῖται·
Ἡρακλέην δ' ἥρωες ἐκερτόμεον λιποναύταν,
οὕνεκεν ἠρώησε τριακοντάζυγον Ἀργώ,
πεζᾷ δ' ἐς Κόλχους τε καὶ ἄξενον ἵκετο Φᾶσιν.   75

'61' ὡς δ' ὁπότ' ἠϊγένειος ἀπόπροθι λὶς ἐσακούσας m (om. abm)
68 γέμεν z: μὲν **m**   69 αὖτε καθαίρουν z

XIV

ΑΙΣΧΙΝΑΣ

Χαίρειν πολλὰ τὸν ἄνδρα Θυώνιχον.

ΘΥΩΝΙΧΟΣ

ἄλλα τοιαῦτα

Αἰσχίνᾳ. ὡς χρόνιος.

ΑΙ.　　　　　χρόνιος.

ΘΥ.　　　　　　　　τί δέ τοι τὸ μέλημα;

ΑΙ. πράσσομες οὐχ ὡς λῷστα, Θυώνιχε.

ΘΥ.　　　　　　　ταῦτ' ἄρα λεπτός,
χὠ μύσταξ πολὺς οὗτος, αὐσταλέοι δὲ κίκιννοι.
τοιοῦτος πρώαν τις ἀφίκετο Πυθαγορικτάς,　　5
ὠχρὸς κἀνυπόδητος· 'Αθαναῖος δ' ἔφατ' ἦμεν.

ΑΙ. ἤρατο μὰν καὶ τῆνος;

ΘΥ.　　　　　　ἐμὶν δοκεῖ, ὀπτῶ ἀλεύρῳ.

ΑΙ. παίσδεις, ὠγάθ', ἔχων· ἐμὲ δ' ἁ χαρίεσσα
　　　Κυνίσκα
ὑβρίσδει· λασῶ δὲ μανείς ποκα, θρὶξ ἀνὰ
　　　μέσσον.

ΘΥ. τοιοῦτος μὲν ἀεὶ τύ, φίλ' Αἰσχίνα, ἀσυχᾷ ὀξύς,　10
πάντ' ἐθέλων κατὰ καιρόν· ὅμως δ' εἶπον τί τὸ
　　　καινόν.

ΑΙ. 'Ωργεῖος κἠγὼν καὶ ὁ Θεσσαλὸς ἱπποδιώκτας
Ἆγις καὶ Κλεύνικος ἐπίνομες ὁ στρατιώτας
ἐν χώρῳ παρ' ἐμίν. δύο μὲν κατέκοψα νεοσσώς
θηλάζοντά τε χοῖρον, ἀνῷξα δὲ Βίβλινον
　　　αὐτοῖς　　　　　　　　　　　　　　15
εὐώδη τετόρων ἐτέων, σχεδὸν ὡς ἀπὸ λανῶ·
βολβός τις, κοχλίας, ἐξαιρέθη· ἦς πότος ἀδύς.

10 ἄσυχος m　　15 Βίβλινον am: Βύβλινον m

ἤδη δὲ προϊόντος ἔδοξ' ἐπιχεῖσθαι ἄκρατον
ὧτινος ἤθελ' ἕκαστος· ἔδει μόνον ὧτινος εἰπεῖν.
ἀμὲς μὲν φωνεῦντες ἐπίνομες, ὡς ἐδέδοκτο·   20
ἁ δ' οὐδὲν παρεόντος ἐμεῦ. τίν' ἔχειν με δοκεῖς
     νῶν;
'οὐ φθεγξῇ; λύκον εἶδες;' ἔπαιξέ τις. 'ὡς
     σοφός' εἶπεν,
κἠφλέγετ'· εὐμαρέως κεν ἀπ' αὐτᾶς καὶ λύχνον
     ἇψας.

ἔστι Λύκος, Λύκος ἐστί, Λάβα τῶ γείτονος υἱός,
εὐμάκης, ἁπαλός, πολλοῖς δοκέων καλὸς ἦμεν·   25
τούτω τὸν κλύμενον κατεφρύγετο τῆνον ἔρωτα.
χἀμῖν τοῦτο δι' ὠτὸς ἔγεντό ποχ' ἁσυχᾷ οὕτως·
οὐ μὰν ἐξήταξα, μάταν εἰς ἄνδρα γενειῶν.
ἤδη δ' ὦν πόσιος τοὶ τέσσαρες ἐν βάθει ἦμες,
χὠ Λαρισαῖος 'τὸν ἐμὸν Λύκον' ᾆδεν ἀπ'
     ἀρχᾶς,   30
Θεσσαλικόν τι μέλισμα, κακαὶ φρένες· ἁ δὲ
     Κυνίσκα
ἔκλαεν ἐξαπίνας θαλερώτερον ἢ παρὰ ματρί
παρθένος ἑξαετὴς κόλπω ἐπιθυμήσασα.
τᾶμος ἐγώ, τὸν ἴσαις τύ, Θυώνιχε, πὺξ ἐπὶ
     κόρρας
ἤλασα, κἄλλαν αὖθις. ἀνειρύσασα δὲ πέπλως   35
ἔξω ἀποίχετο θᾶσσον. 'ἐμὸν κακόν, οὔ τοι
     ἀρέσκω;
ἄλλος τοι γλυκίων ὑποκόλπιος; ἄλλον ἰοῖσα
θάλπε φίλον. τήνῳ τεὰ δάκρυα μᾶλα ῥέοντι.'
μάστακα δοῖσα τέκνοισιν ὑπωροφίοισι χελιδών
ἄψορρον ταχινὰ πέτεται βίον ἄλλον ἀγείρειν·   40

26 κατεφρύγετο z: καταφ[a: κατετάκετο m   38 τήνω τεὰ
δάκρυα; μᾶλα ῥεόντω z   39 δοῖσα z (b?): δ' οἶα m

ὠκυτέρα μαλακᾶς ἀπὸ δίφρακος ἔπτετο τήνα
ἰθὺ δι' ἀμφιθύρω καὶ δικλίδος, ᾇ πόδες ἆγον.
αἰνός θην λέγεταί τις 'ἔβα ποκὰ ταῦρος ἀν' ὕλαν'.
εἴκατι· ταὶ δ' ὀκτώ, ταὶ δ' ἐννέα, ταὶ δὲ δέκ'
    ἄλλαι·
σάμερον ἑνδεκάτα· ποτίθες δύο, καὶ δύο
    μῆνες   45
ἐξ ὧ ἀπ' ἀλλάλων· οὐδ' εἰ Θρᾳκιστὶ κέκαρμαι
οἶδε. Λύκος νῦν πάντα, Λύκῳ καὶ νυκτὸς
    ἀνῷκται·
ἄμμες δ' οὔτε λόγω τινὸς ἄξιοι οὔτ' ἀριθμητοί,
δύστανοι Μεγαρῆες ἀτιμοτάτᾳ ἐνὶ μοίρᾳ.
κεἰ μὲν ἀποστέρξαιμι, τὰ πάντα κεν ἐς δέον
    ἕρποι.   50
νῦν δὲ πόθεν; μῦς, φαντί, Θυώνιχε, γεύμεθα
    πίσσας,
χὤτι τὸ φάρμακόν ἐστιν ἀμηχανέοντος ἔρωτος
οὐκ οἶδα· πλὰν Σῖμος, ὁ τᾶς ἐπιχάλκω
    ἐρασθείς,
ἐκπλεύσας ὑγιὴς ἐπανῆνθ', ἐμὸς ἁλικιώτας.
πλευσεῦμαι κἠγὼν διαπόντιος· οὔτε κάκιστος 55
οὔτε πρᾶτος ἴσως, ὁμαλὸς δέ τις ὁ στρατιώτας.
ΘΥ. ὤφελε μὲν χωρεῖν κατὰ νῶν τεὸν ὧν ἐπεθύμεις,
    Αἰσχίνα. εἰ δ' οὕτως ἄρα τοι δοκεῖ ὥστ'
    ἀποδαμεῖν,
    μισθοδότας Πτολεμαῖος ἐλευθέρῳ οἷος ἄριστος.
ΑΙ. τἆλλα δ' ἀνὴρ ποῖός τις;
ΘΥ.   <. . .> τοισιν ἄριστος·   60
    εὐγνώμων, φιλόμουσος, ἐρωτικός, εἰς ἄκρον ἁδύς,

41 ἔπτετο z:]το a: ἔδραμε m   43 ποκὰ ταῦρος z: κένταυρος
a: κε(ν) ταῦρος m: καὶ ταῦρος m   45 καὶ δέκα am
53 ὑποχάλκω abm   60].[.]. τοισιναρ a: ἐλευθέρῳ οἷος ἄριστος m

εἰδὼς τὸν φιλέοντα, τὸν οὐ φιλέοντ᾽ ἔτι μᾶλλον,
πολλοῖς πολλὰ διδούς, αἰτεύμενος οὐκ ἀνανεύων,
οἷα χρὴ βασιλῆ· αἰτεῖν δὲ δεῖ οὐκ ἐπὶ παντί,
Αἰσχίνα. ὥστ᾽ εἴ τοι κατὰ δεξιὸν ὦμον
    ἀρέσκει   65
λῶπος ἄκρον περονᾶσθαι, ἐπ᾽ ἀμφοτέροις δὲ
    βεβακώς
τολμασεῖς ἐπιόντα μένειν θρασὺν ἀσπιδιώταν,
ᾇ τάχος εἰς Αἴγυπτον. ἀπὸ κροτάφων
    πελόμεσθα
πάντες γηραλέοι, καὶ ἐπισχερὼ ἐς γένυν ἕρπει
λευκαίνων ὁ χρόνος· ποιεῖν τι δεῖ ᾇς γόνυ
    χλωρόν.   70

XV

ΓΟΡΓΩ

ἔνδοι Πραξινόα;

ΠΡΑΞΙΝΟΑ

        Γοργὼ φίλα, ὡς χρόνῳ. ἔνδοι.
θαῦμ᾽ ὅτι καὶ νῦν ἦνθες. ὅρη δρίφον, Εὐνόα, αὐτᾷ·
ἔμβαλε καὶ ποτίκρανον.
ΓΟ.   ἔχει κάλλιστα.
ΠΡ.   καθίζευ.
ΓΟ. ὦ τᾶς ἀλεμάτω ψυχᾶς· μόλις ὕμμιν ἐσώθην,
Πραξινόα, πολλῷ μὲν ὄχλῳ, πολλῶν δὲ τεθρίππων· 5
παντᾷ κρηπῖδες, παντᾷ χλαμυδηφόροι ἄνδρες·

ἁ δ' ὁδὸς ἄτρυτος· τὺ δ' ἑκαστέρω αἰὲν ἀποικεῖς

ΠΡ. ταῦθ' ὁ πάραρος τῆνος· ἐπ' ἔσχατα γᾶς ἔλαβ' ἐνθών
ἰλεόν, οὐκ οἴκησιν, ὅπως μὴ γείτονες ὦμες
ἀλλάλαις, ποτ' ἔριν, φθονερὸν κακόν, αἰὲν ὁμοῖος. 10

ΓΟ. μὴ λέγε τὸν τεὸν ἄνδρα, φίλα, Δίνωνα τοιαῦτα
τῶ μικκῶ παρεόντος· ὅρη, γύναι, ὡς ποθορῇ τυ.
θάρσει, Ζωπυρίων, γλυκερὸν τέκος· οὐ λέγει ἀπφῦν.

ΠΡ. αἰσθάνεται τὸ βρέφος, ναὶ τὰν πότνιαν.

ΓΟ.   καλὸς ἀπφῦς.

ΠΡ. ἀπφῦς μὰν τῆνός γα πρόαν — λέγομες δὲ πρόαν θην 15
'πάππα, νίτρον καὶ φῦκος ἀπὸ σκανᾶς ἀγοράσδειν' —
ἵκτο φέρων ἅλας ἄμμιν, ἀνὴρ τρισκαιδεκάπαχυς.

ΓΟ. χὠμὸς ταυτᾷ ἔχει· φθόρος ἀργυρίω Διοκλείδας·
ἑπταδράχμως κυνάδας, γραιᾶν ἀποτίλματα πηρᾶν,
πέντε πόκως ἔλαβ' ἐχθές, ἅπαν ῥύπον, ἔργον ἐπ'
    ἔργῳ.   20
ἀλλ' ἴθι, τὠμπέχονον καὶ τὰν περονατρίδα λάζευ.
βᾶμες τῶ βασιλῆος ἐς ἀφνειῶ Πτολεμαίω
θασόμεναι τὸν Ἄδωνιν· ἀκούω χρῆμα καλόν τι
κοσμεῖν τὰν βασίλισσαν.

ΠΡ.   ἐν ὀλβίω ὄλβια πάντα.

ΓΟ. ὧν ἴδες, ὧν εἴπαις κεν ἰδοῖσα τὺ τῶ μὴ ἰδόντι. 25
ἕρπειν ὥρα κ' εἴη.

ΠΡ.   ἀεργοῖς αἰὲν ἑορτά.
Εὐνόα, αἶρε τὸ νῆμα καὶ ἐς μέσον, αἰνόδρυπτε,
θὲς πάλιν· αἱ γαλέαι μαλακῶς χρῄζοντι καθεύδειν.
κινεῦ δή· φέρε θᾶσσον ὕδωρ. ὕδατος πρότερον δεῖ,
ἁ δὲ σμᾶμα φέρει. δὸς ὅμως. μὴ δὴ πολύ, λᾳστρί. 30
ἔγχει ὕδωρ. δύστανε, τί μευ τὸ χιτώνιον ἄρδεις;

7 ἀτρύγετος a   16 πάππα, νίτρον z: πάντα νίτρον am: ἀφρόνιτρον z
ἀγοράσδειν z: ἀγοράσδων am   27 αἰνόδρυπτε am: αἰνόθρυπτε m
30 λᾳστρί z: ἄπληστε am

παῦέ ποχ'· οἷα θεοῖς ἐδόκει, τοιαῦτα νένιμμαι.
ἁ κλᾷξ τᾶς μεγάλας πεῖ λάρνακος; ὧδε φέρ' αὐτάν.
ΓΟ. Πραξινόα, μάλα τοι τὸ καταπτυχὲς ἐμπερόναμα
τοῦτο πρέπει· λέγε μοι, πόσσω κατέβα τοι ἀφ'
ἱστῶ;   35
ΠΡ. μὴ μνάσῃς, Γοργοῖ· πλέον ἀργυρίω καθαρῶ μνᾶν
ἢ δύο· τοῖς δ' ἔργοις καὶ τὰν ψυχὰν ποτέθηκα.
ΓΟ. ἀλλὰ κατὰ γνώμαν ἀπέβα τοι·   τοῦτό κεν εἴπαις.
ΠΡ. τὤμπέχονον φέρε μοι καὶ τὰν θολίαν· κατὰ κόσμον
ἀμφίθες. οὐκ ἀξῶ τυ, τέκνον. Μορμώ, δάκνει
ἵππος.   40
δάκρυ' ὅσσα θέλεις, χωλὸν δ' οὐ δεῖ τυ γενέσθαι.
ἕρπωμες. Φρυγία, τὸν μικκὸν παῖσδε λαβοῖσα,
τὰν κύν' ἔσω κάλεσον, τὰν αὐλείαν ἀπόκλαξον.

ὦ θεοί, ὅσσος ὄχλος. πῶς καὶ πόκα τοῦτο περᾶσαι
χρὴ τὸ κακόν; μύρμακες ἀνάριθμοι καὶ ἄμετροι. 45
πολλά τοι, ὦ Πτολεμαῖε, πεποίηται καλὰ ἔργα
ἐξ ὦ ἐν ἀθανάτοις ὁ τεκών· οὐδεὶς κακοεργός
δαλεῖται τὸν ἰόντα παρέρπων Αἰγυπτιστί,
οἷα πρὶν ἐξ ἀπάτας κεκροτημένοι ἄνδρες ἔπαισδον,
ἀλλάλοις ὁμαλοί, κακὰ παίχνια, πάντες ἀραῖοι. 50
ἀδίστα Γοργώ, τί γενώμεθα; τοὶ πολεμισταί
ἵπποι τῶ βασιλῆος. ἄνερ φίλε, μή με πατήσῃς.
ὀρθὸς ἀνέστα ὁ πυρρός· ἴδ' ὡς ἄγριος. κυνοθαρσής
Εὐνόα, οὐ φευξῇ; διαχρησεῖται τὸν ἄγοντα.
ὠνάθην μεγάλως ὅτι μοι τὸ βρέφος μένει ἔνδον. 55
ΓΟ. θάρσει, Πραξινόα· καὶ δὴ γεγενήμεθ' ὄπισθεν,
τοὶ δ' ἔβαν ἐς χώραν.
ΠΡ.
                              καὐτὰ συναγείρομαι ἤδη.
ἵππον καὶ τὸν ψυχρὸν ὄφιν τὰ μάλιστα δεδοίκω

50 ἀραῖοι z: αεργοι a: αροιοι a: ἐριοί m

ἐκ παιδός. σπεύδωμες· ὄχλος πολὺς ἄμμιν ἐπιρρεῖ.
ΓΟ. ἐξ αὐλᾶς, ὦ μᾶτερ;

ΓΡΑΥΣ

ἐγών, τέκνα.

ΓΟ.   εἶτα παρενθεῖν   60
εὐμαρές;
ΓΡ.   ἐς Τροίαν πειρώμενοι ἦνθον Ἀχαιοί,
κάλλισται παίδων· πείρᾳ θην πάντα τελεῖται.
ΓΟ. χρησμὼς ἁ πρεσβῦτις ἀπῴχετο θεσπιξασα.
ΠΡ. πάντα γυναῖκες ἴσαντι, καὶ ὡς Ζεὺς ἀγάγεθ' Ἥραν.
ΓΟ. θᾶσαι, Πραξινόα, περὶ τὰς θύρας ὅσσος ὅμιλος.   65
ΠΡ. θεσπέσιος. Γοργοῖ, δὸς τὰν χέρα μοι· λάβε καὶ τύ,
Εὐνόα, Εὐτυχίδος· πότεχ' αὐτᾶς μὴ ἀποπλαγχθῇς.
πᾶσαι ἅμ' εἰσένθωμες· ἁπρὶξ ἔχευ, Εὐνόα, ἁμῶν.
οἴμοι δειλαία, δίχα μοι τὸ θερίστριον ἤδη
ἔσχισται, Γοργοῖ. ποττῶ Διός, εἴ τι γένοιο   70
εὐδαίμων, ἄνθρωπε, φυλάσσεο τὠμπέχονόν μευ.

ΞΕΝΟΣ

οὐκ ἐπ' ἐμὶν μέν, ὅμως δὲ φυλάξομαι.
ΠΡ.   ὄχλος ἀλαθέως·
ὠθεῦνθ' ὥσπερ ὕες.
ΞΕ.   θάρσει, γύναι· ἐν καλῷ εἰμές.
ΠΡ. κῆς ὥρας κἤπειτα, φίλ' ἀνδρῶν, ἐν καλῷ εἴης,
ἄμμε περιστέλλων. χρηστῶ κοἰκτίρμονος ἀνδρός.   75
φλίβεται Εὐνόα ἄμμιν· ἄγ', ὦ δειλὰ τύ, βιάζευ.
κάλλιστ'· 'ἔνδοι πᾶσαι', ὁ τὰν νυὸν εἶπ' ἀποκλᾷξας.

ΓΟ. Πραξινόα, πόταγ' ὧδε. τὰ ποικίλα πρᾶτον ἄθρησυν
λεπτὰ καὶ ὡς χαρίεντα· θεῶν περονάματα φασεῖς
ΠΡ. πότνι' Ἀθαναία, ποῖαί σφ' ἐπόνασαν ἔριθοι,   8

ποῖοι ζωογράφοι τἀκριβέα γράμματ' ἔγραψαν.
ὡς ἔτυμ' ἑστάκαντι καὶ ὡς ἔτυμ' ἐνδινεῦντι,
ἔμψυχ', οὐκ ἐνυφαντά. σοφόν τι χρῆμ' ἄνθρωπος.
αὐτὸς δ' ὡς θαητὸς ἐπ' ἀργυρέας κατάκειται
κλισμῷ, πρᾶτον ἴουλον ἀπὸ κροτάφων
    καταβάλλων,   85
ὁ τριφίλητος Ἄδωνις, ὁ κὴν Ἀχέροντι φιληθείς.

ΕΤΕΡΟΣ ΞΕΝΟΣ

παύσασθ', ὦ δύστανοι, ἀνάνυτα κωτίλλοισαι,
τρυγόνες· ἐκκναισεῦντι πλατειάσδοισαι ἄπαντα.
ΠΡ. μᾶ, πόθεν ὤνθρωπος; τί δὲ τὶν εἰ κωτίλαι εἰμές;
πασάμενος ἐπίτασσε· Συρακοσίαις ἐπιτάσσεις.   90
ὡς εἰδῇς καὶ τοῦτο, Κορίνθιαι εἰμὲς ἄνωθεν,
ὡς καὶ ὁ Βελλεροφῶν. Πελοποννασιστὶ λαλεῦμες,
Δωρίσδειν δ' ἔξεστι, δοκῶ, τοῖς Δωριέεσσι.
μὴ φύη, Μελιτῶδες, ὃς ἀμῶν καρτερὸς εἴη,
πλὰν ἑνός. οὐκ ἀλέγω. μή μοι κενεὰν ἀπομάξῃς.   95
ΓΟ. σίγη, Πραξινόα· μέλλει τὸν Ἄδωνιν ἀείδειν
ἁ τᾶς Ἀργείας θυγάτηρ, πολύϊδρις ἀοιδός,
ἅτις καὶ πέρυσιν τὸν ἰάλεμον ἀρίστευσε.
φθεγξεῖταί τι, σάφ' οἶδα, καλόν· διαχρέμπτεται ἤδη.

ΓΥΝΗ ΑΟΙΔΟΣ

δέποιν', ἃ Γολγώς τε καὶ Ἰδάλιον ἐφίλησας   100
αἰπεινάν τ' Ἔρυκα, χρυσῷ παίζοισ' Ἀφροδίτα,
οἷόν τοι τὸν Ἄδωνιν ἀπ' ἀενάω Ἀχέροντος
μηνὶ δυωδεκάτῳ μαλακαὶ πόδας ἄγαγον Ὧραι,
βάρδισται μακάρων Ὧραι φίλαι· ἀλλὰ ποθειναί
ἔρχονται πάντεσσι βροτοῖς αἰεί τι φέροισαι.   105
Κύπρι Διωναία, τὺ μὲν ἀθανάταν ἀπὸ θνατᾶς,

81 ταλαθέα a   99 διαχρέμπτεται a: διαθρύπτεται m

ἀνθρώπων ὡς μῦθος, ἐποίησας Βερενίκαν,
ἀμβροσίαν ἐς στῆθος ἀποστάξασα γυναικός·
τὶν δὲ χαριζομένα, πολυώνυμε καὶ πολύναε,
ἁ Βερενικεία θυγάτηρ Ἑλένᾳ εἰκυῖα   110
Ἀρσινόα πάντεσσι καλοῖς ἀτιτάλλει Ἄδωνιν.
πὰρ μέν οἱ ὥρια κεῖται ὅσα δρυὸς ἄκρα καλεῖται,
πὰρ δ᾽ ἁπαλοὶ κᾶποι πεφυλαγμένοι ἐν ταλαρίσκοις
ἀργυρέοις, Συρίω δὲ μύρω χρύσει᾽ ἀλάβαστρα,
εἴδατά θ᾽ ὅσσα γυναῖκες ἐπὶ πλαθάνω πονέονται   115
ἄνθεα μίσγοισαι λευκῷ παντοῖα μαλεύρω,
ὅσσα τ᾽ ἀπὸ γλυκερῶ μέλιτος τά τ᾽ ἐν ὑγρῷ ἐλαίῳ.
πάντ᾽ αὐτῷ πετεηνὰ καὶ ἑρπετὰ τεῖδε πάρεστι·
χλωραὶ δὲ σκιάδες μαλακῷ βρίθοισαι ἀνήθῳ
δέδμανθ᾽· οἱ δέ τε κῶροι ὑπερπωτῶνται
   Ἔρωτες,   120
οἷοι ἀηδονιδῆες ἀεξομενᾶν ἐπὶ δένδρῳ
πωτῶνται πτερύγων πειρώμενοι ὄζον ἀπ᾽ ὄζω.
ὦ ἔβενος, ὦ χρυσός, ὦ ἐκ λευκῶ ἐλέφαντος
αἰετοὶ οἰνοχόον Κρονίδα Διὶ παῖδα φέροντες,
πορφύρεοι δὲ τάπητες ἄνω᾽ μαλακώτεροι ὕπνω·   125
ἁ Μίλατος ἐρεῖ χὠ τὰν Σαμίαν καταβόσκων,
᾽ἔστρωται κλίνα τὠδώνιδι τῷ καλῷ ἄλλα.
τὸν μὲν Κύπρις ἔχει, τὰν δ᾽ ὁ ῥοδόπαχυς Ἄδωνις.
ὀκτωκαιδεκετὴς ἢ ἐννεακαίδεχ᾽ ὁ γαμβρός·
οὐ κεντεῖ τὸ φίλημ᾽· ἔτι οἱ περὶ χείλεα πυρρά. 130
νῦν μὲν Κύπρις ἔχοισα τὸν αὐτᾶς χαιρέτω ἄνδρα·
ἀῶθεν δ᾽ ἄμμες νιν ἅμα δρόσῳ ἀθρόαι ἔξω
οἰσεῦμες ποτὶ κύματ᾽ ἐπ᾽ ἀϊόνι πτύοντα,
λύσασαι δὲ κόμαν καὶ ἐπὶ σφυρὰ κόλπον ἀνεῖσαι

112 καλεῖται a: φέρονται (vel -τι) m   116 παντοῖ᾽ ἄμ᾽
ἀλεύρῳ am   127 ἀμά z: ἄμμιν z   128 τὸν μὲν z: τὰν μὲν am
133 κλυ[ζοντα a

στήθεσι φαινομένοις λιγυρᾶς ἀρξεύμεθ' ἀοιδᾶς. 135
ἕρπεις, ὦ φίλ' Ἄδωνι, καὶ ἐνθάδε κῆς Ἀχέροντα
ἡμιθέων, ὡς φαντί, μονώτατος. οὔτ' Ἀγαμέμνων
τοῦτ' ἔπαθ' οὔτ' Αἴας ὁ μέγας, βαρυμάνιος ἥρως,
οὔθ' Ἕκτωρ, Ἑκάβας ὁ γεραίτατος εἴκατι παίδων,
οὐ Πατροκλῆς, οὐ Πύρρος ἀπὸ Τροίας
  ἐπανενθών, 140
οὔθ' οἱ ἔτι πρότεροι Λαπίθαι καὶ Δευκαλίωνες,
οὐ Πελοπηϊάδαι τε καὶ Ἄργεος ἄκρα Πελασγοί.
ἴλαος, ὦ φίλ' Ἄδωνι, καὶ ἐς νέωτ'· εὐθυμεύσαις
καὶ νῦν ἦνθες, Ἄδωνι, καὶ ὄκκ' ἀφίκῃ, φίλος ἡξεῖς.

ΓΟ. Πραξινόα, τὸ χρῆμα σοφώτατον ἁ θήλεια· 145
ὀλβία ὄσσα ἴσατι, πανολβία ὡς γλυκὺ φωνεῖ.
ὥρα ὅμως κῆς οἶκον. ἀνάριστος Διοκλείδας·
χὠνὴρ ὄξος ἄπαν, πεινᾶντι δὲ μηδὲ ποτένθῃς.
χαῖρε, Ἄδων ἀγαπατέ, καὶ ἐς χαίροντας ἀφικνεῦ.

XVI

αἰεὶ τοῦτο Διὸς κούραις μέλει, αἰὲν ἀοιδοῖς,
ὑμνεῖν ἀθανάτους, ὑμνεῖν ἀγαθῶν κλέα ἀνδρῶν.
Μοῖσαι μὲν θεαὶ ἐντί, θεοὺς θεαὶ ἀείδοντι·
ἄμμες δὲ βροτοὶ οἴδε, βροτοὺς βροτοὶ ἀείδωμεν.
τίς γὰρ τῶν ὁπόσοι γλαυκὰν ναίουσιν ὑπ' ἀῶ 5
ἡμετέρας Χάριτας πετάσας ὑποδέξεται οἴκῳ
ἀσπασίως, οὐδ' αὖθις ἀδωρήτους ἀποπέμψει;
αἱ δὲ σκυζόμεναι γυμνοῖς ποσὶν οἴκαδ' ἴασι,
πολλά με τωθάζοισαι ὅτ' ἀλιθίην ὁδὸν ἦλθον,

9 ἀλλοτρίην m

ὀκνηραὶ δὲ πάλιν κενεᾶς ἐν πυθμένι χηλοῦ　　　　10
ψυχροῖς ἐν γονάτεσσι κάρη μίμνοντι βαλοῖσαι,
ἔνθ' αἰεί σφισιν ἕδρη ἐπὴν ἄπρακτοι ἵκωνται.
τίς τῶν νῦν τοιόσδε; τίς εὖ εἰπόντα φιλήσει;
οὐκ οἶδ'· οὐ γὰρ ἔτ' ἄνδρες ἐπ' ἔργμασιν ὡς πάρος ἐσθλοῖς
αἰνεῖσθαι σπεύδοντι, νενίκηνται δ' ὑπὸ κερδέων.　　15
πᾶς δ' ὑπὸ κόλπου χεῖρας ἔχων πόθεν οἴσεταί ἀθρεῖ
ἄργυρον, οὐδέ κεν ἰὸν ἀποτρίψας τινὶ δοίη,
ἀλλ' εὐθὺς μυθεῖται· 'ἀπωτέρω ἢ γόνυ κνάμα.'
'αὐτῷ μοί τι γένοιτο.' 'θεοὶ τιμῶσιν ἀοιδούς.'
'τίς δέ κεν ἄλλου ἀκούσαι; ἅλις πάντεσσιν
　　　Ὅμηρος.'　　　　　　　　　　　　　20
'οὗτος ἀοιδῶν λῷστος ὃς ἐξ ἐμεῦ οἴσεται οὐδέν.'
　　δαιμόνιοι, τί δὲ κέρδος ὁ μυρίος ἔνδοθι χρυσός
κείμενος; οὐχ ἅδε πλούτου φρονέουσιν ὄνασις,
ἀλλὰ τὸ μὲν ψυχᾷ, τὸ δέ που τινὶ δοῦναι ἀοιδῶν·
πολλοὺς εὖ ἔρξαι παῶν, πολλοὺς δὲ καὶ ἄλλων　　25
ἀνθρώπων, αἰεὶ δὲ θεοῖς ἐπιβώμια ῥέζειν,
μηδὲ ξεινοδόκον κακὸν ἔμμεναι ἀλλὰ τραπέζῃ
μειλίξαντ' ἀποπέμψαι ἐπὴν ἐθέλωντι νέεσθαι,
Μοισάων δὲ μάλιστα τίειν ἱεροὺς ὑποφήτας,
ὄφρα καὶ εἰν Ἀίδαο κεκρυμμένος ἐσθλὸς ἀκούσῃς,　30
μηδ' ἀκλεὴς μύρηαι ἐπὶ ψυχροῦ Ἀχέροντος
ὡσεί τις μακέλᾳ τετυλωμένος ἔνδοθι χεῖρας
ἀχὴν ἐκ πατέρων πενίην ἀκτήμονα κλαίων.
πολλοὶ ἐν Ἀντιόχοιο δόμοις καὶ ἄνακτος Ἀλεύα
ἁρμαλιὴν ἔμμηνον ἐμετρήσαντο πενέσται.　　　35
πολλοὶ δὲ Σκοπάδαισιν ἐλαυνόμενοι ποτὶ σακούς
μόσχοι σὺν κεραῇσιν ἐμυκήσαντο βόεσσι.
μυρία δ' ἂμ πεδίον Κραννώνιον ἐνδιάασκον
ποιμένες ἔκκριτα μῆλα φιλοξείνοισι Κρεώνδαις.
ἀλλ' οὔ σφιν τῶν ἧδος, ἐπεὶ γλυκὺν ἐξεκένωσαν　40

θυμὸν ἐς εὐρεῖαν σχεδίαν στυγνοῦ Ἀχέροντος,
ἄμναστοι δὲ τὰ πολλὰ καὶ ὄλβια τῆνα λιπόντες
δειλοῖς ἐν νεκύεσσι μακροὺς αἰῶνας ἔκειντο,
εἰ μὴ θεῖος ἀοιδὸς ὁ Κήϊος αἰόλα φωνέων
βάρβιτον ἐς πολύχορδον ἐν ἀνδράσι θῆκ' ὀνομαστούς 45
ὁπλοτέροις· τιμᾶς δὲ καὶ ὠκέες ἔλλαχον ἵπποι
οἵ σφισιν ἐξ ἱερῶν στεφανηφόροι ἦλθον ἀγώνων.
τίς δ' ἂν ἀριστῆας Λυκίων ποτέ, τίς κομόωντας
Πριαμίδας ἢ θῆλυν ἀπὸ χροιᾶς Κύκνον ἔγνω,
εἰ μὴ φυλόπιδας προτέρων ὕμνησαν ἀοιδοί;   50
οὐδ' Ὀδυσεὺς ἑκατόν τε καὶ εἴκατι μῆνας ἀλαθεὶς
πάντας ἐπ' ἀνθρώπους, Ἀΐδαν τ' εἰς ἔσχατον ἐλθὼν
ζωός, καὶ σπήλυγγα φυγὼν ὀλοοῖο Κύκλωπος,
δηναιὸν κλέος ἔσχεν, ἐσιγάθη δ' ἂν ὑφορβὸς
Εὔμαιος καὶ βουσὶ Φιλοίτιος ἀμφ' ἀγελαίαις   55
ἔργον ἔχων αὐτός τε περίσπλαγχνος Λαέρτης,
εἰ μή σφεας ὤνασαν Ἰάονος ἀνδρὸς ἀοιδαί.
    ἐκ Μοισᾶν ἀγαθὸν κλέος ἔρχεται ἀνθρώποισι,
χρήματα δὲ ζώοντες ἀμαλδύνουσι θανόντων.
ἀλλ' ἴσος γὰρ ὁ μόχθος ἐπ' ᾀόνι κύματα μετρεῖν   60
ὅσσ' ἄνεμος χέρσονδε μετὰ γλαυκᾶς ἁλὸς ὠθεῖ,
ἢ ὕδατι νίζειν θολερὰν διαειδέϊ πλίνθον,
καὶ φιλοκερδείᾳ βεβλαμμένον ἄνδρα παρελθεῖν.
χαιρέτω ὅστις τοῖος, ἀνήριθμος δέ οἱ εἴη
ἄργυρος, αἰεὶ δὲ πλεόνων ἔχοι ἵμερος αὐτόν·   65
αὐτὰρ ἐγὼ τιμήν τε καὶ ἀνθρώπων φιλότητα
πολλῶν ἡμιόνων τε καὶ ἵππων πρόσθεν ἑλοίμαν.
δίζημαι δ' ὅτινι θνατῶν κεχαρισμένος ἔλθω
σὺν Μοίσαις· χαλεπαὶ γὰρ ὁδοὶ τελέθουσιν ἀοιδοῖς
κουράων ἀπάνευθε Διὸς μέγα βουλεύοντος.   70
οὔπω μῆνας ἄγων ἔκαμ' οὐρανὸς οὐδ' ἐνιαυτούς·

41 στυγνοῖο γέροντος z

πολλοὶ κινήσουσιν ἔτι τροχὸν ἅματος ἵπποι·
ἔσσεται οὗτος ἀνὴρ ὃς ἐμοῦ κεχρήσετ' ἀοιδοῦ,
ῥέξας ἢ 'Αχιλεὺς ὅσσον μέγας ἢ βαρὺς Αἴας
ἐν πεδίῳ Σιμόεντος ὅθι Φρυγὸς ἠρίον Ἴλου.   75
ἤδη νῦν Φοίνικες ὑπ' ἠελίῳ δύνοντι
οἰκεῦντες Λιβύας ἄκρον σφυρὸν ἐρρίγασιν·
ἤδη βαστάζουσι Συρακόσιοι μέσα δοῦρα,
ἀχθόμενοι σακέεσσι βραχίονας ἰτεῖνοισιν·
ἐν δ' αὐτοῖς Ἱέρων προτέροις ἶσος ἡρώεσσι   80
ζώννυται, ἵππειαι δὲ κόρυν σκιάουσιν ἔθειραι.
αἲ γάρ, Ζεῦ κύδιστε πάτερ καὶ πότνι' 'Αθάνα
κούρη θ' ἣ σὺν ματρὶ πολυκλήρων 'Εφυραίων
εἴληχας μέγα ἄστυ παρ' ὕδασι Λυσιμελείας,
ἐχθροὺς ἐκ νάσοιο κακαὶ πέμψειαν ἀνάγκαι   85
Σαρδόνιον κατὰ κῦμα φίλων μόρον ἀγγέλλοντας
τέκνοις ἠδ' ἀλόχοισιν, ἀριθμητοὺς ἀπὸ πολλῶν.
ἄστεα δὲ προτέροισι πάλιν ναίοιτο πολίταις,
δυσμενέων ὅσα χεῖρες ἐλωβήσαντο κατ' ἄκρας·
ἀγροὺς δ' ἐργάζοιντο τεθαλότας· αἱ δ' ἀνάριθμοι   90
μήλων χιλιάδες βοτάνᾳ διαπιανθεῖσαι
ἂμ πεδίον βληχῶντο, βόες δ' ἀγεληδὸν ἐς αὖλιν
ἐρχόμεναι σκνιφαῖον ἐπισπεύδοιεν ὁδίταν·
νειοὶ δ' ἐκπονέοιντο ποτὶ σπόρον, ἁνίκα τέττιξ
ποιμένας ἐνδίους πεφυλαγμένος ὑψόθι δένδρων   95
ἀχεῖ ἐν ἀκρεμόνεσσιν· ἀράχνια δ' εἰς ὅπλ' ἀράχναι
λεπτὰ διαστήσαιντο, βοᾶς δ' ἔτι μηδ' ὄνομ' εἴη.
ὑψηλὸν δ' Ἱέρωνι κλέος φορέοιεν ἀοιδοί
καὶ πόντου Σκυθικοῖο πέραν καὶ ὅθι πλατὺ τεῖχος
ἀσφάλτῳ δήσασα Σεμίραμις ἐμβασίλευεν.   100
εἷς μὲν ἐγώ, πολλοὺς δὲ Διὸς φιλέοντι καὶ ἄλλους
θυγατέρες, τοῖς πᾶσι μέλοι Σικελὴν 'Αρέθοισαν

72 ἅματος z: ἅρματος m

ὑμνεῖν σὺν λαοῖσι καὶ αἰχμητὴν Ἱέρωνα.
ὦ Ἐτεόκλειοι Χάριτες θεαί, ὦ Μινύειον
Ὀρχομενὸν φιλέοισαι ἀπεχθόμενόν ποτε Θήβαις,   105
ἄκλητος μὲν ἔγωγε μένοιμί κεν, ἐς δὲ καλεύντων
θαρσήσας Μοίσαισι σὺν ἀμετέραισιν ἴοιμ' ἄν·
καλλείψω δ' οὐδ' ὔμμε· τί γὰρ Χαρίτων ἀγαπατὸν
ἀνθρώποις ἀπάνευθεν; ἀεὶ Χαρίτεσσιν ἅμ' εἴην.

XVIII

ἔν ποκ' ἄρα Σπάρτᾳ ξανθότριχι πὰρ Μενελάῳ
παρθενικαὶ θάλλοντα κόμαις ὑάκινθον ἔχοισαι
πρόσθε νεογράπτω θαλάμω χορὸν ἐστάσαντο,
δώδεκα ταὶ πρᾶται πόλιος, μέγα χρῆμα Λακαινᾶν,
ἁνίκα Τυνδαρίδα κατεκλάξατο τὰν ἀγαπατάν   5
μναστεύσας Ἑλέναν ὁ νεώτερος Ἀτρέος υἱῶν.
ἄειδον δ' ἅμα πᾶσαι ἐς ἓν μέλος ἐγκροτέοισαι
ποσσὶ περιπλέκτοις, ὑπὸ δ' ἴαχε δῶμ' ὑμεναίῳ.

οὕτω δή πρωίζὰ κατέδραθες, ὦ φίλε γαμβρέ;
ἦ ῥά τις ἐσσὶ λίαν βαρυγούνατος; ἦ ῥα φίλυπνος;   10
ἦ ῥα πολύν τιν' ἔπινες, ὅκ' εἰς εὐνὰν κατεβάλλευ;
εὕδειν μὰν σπεύδοντα καθ' ὥραν αὐτὸν ἐχρῆν τυ,
παῖδα δ' ἐᾶν σὺν παισὶ φιλοστόργῳ παρὰ ματρί
παίσδειν ἐς βαθὺν ὄρθρον, ἐπεὶ καὶ ἔνας καὶ ἐς ἀῶ
κῆς ἔτος ἐξ ἔτεος, Μενέλαε, τεὰ νυὸς ἅδε.   15
ὄλβιε γάμβρ', ἀγαθός τις ἐπέπταρεν ἐρχομένῳ τοι
ἐς Σπάρταν ἅπερ ὦλλοι ἀριστέες ὡς ἀνύσαιο·
μῶνος ἐν ἡμιθέοις Κρονίδαν Δία πενθερὸν ἑξεῖς.
Ζανός τοι θυγάτηρ ὑπὸ τὰν μίαν ἵκετο χλαῖναν,

8 περιβλέπτοις a   11 κατέβαινες a   16 ἀγαθόν tent. z

οἷα Ἀχαιιάδων γαῖαν πατεῖ οὐδεμί' ἄλλα.　　　20
ἦ μέγα κά τι τέκοιτ' εἰ ματέρι τίκτοι ὁμοῖον.
ἀμὲς δ' αἱ πᾶσαι συνομάλικες, αἷς δρόμος ωὑτός
χρισαμέναις ἀνδριστὶ παρ' Εὐρώταο λοετροῖς,
τετράκις ἑξήκοντα κόραι, θῆλυς νεολαία·
τᾶν οὐδ' ἅτις ἄμωμος ἐπεί χ' Ἑλένᾳ παρισωθῇ.　　25
Ἀὼς ἀντέλλοισα καλὸν διέφανε πρόσωπον,
πότνια Νύξ, τό τε λευκὸν ἔαρ χειμῶνος ἀνέντος·
ὧδε καὶ ἀ χρυσέα Ἑλένα διεφαίνετ' ἐν ἀμῖν.
πιείρᾳ μεγάλα ἅτ' ἀνέδραμε κόσμος ἀρούρᾳ
ἢ κάπῳ κυπάρισσος, ἢ ἅρματι Θεσσαλὸς ἵππος,　　30
ὧδε καὶ ἀ ῥοδόχρως Ἑλένα Λακεδαίμονι κόσμος·
οὐδέ τις ἐκ ταλάρω πανίσδεται ἔργα τοιαῦτα,
οὐδ' ἐπὶ δαιδαλέῳ πυκινώτερον ἄτριον ἱστῷ
κερκίδι συμπλέξαισα μακρῶν ἔταμ' ἐκ κελεόντων.
οὐ μὰν οὐδὲ λύραν τις ἐπίσταται ὧδε κροτῆσαι　　35
Ἄρτεμιν ἀείδοισα καὶ εὐρύστερνον Ἀθάναν
ὡς Ἑλένα, τᾶς πάντες ἐπ' ὄμμασιν ἵμεροι ἐντί.
ὦ καλά, ὦ χαρίεσσα κόρα, τὺ μὲν οἰκέτις ἤδη.
ἀμὲς δ' ἐς δρόμον ἦρι καὶ ἐς λειμώνια φύλλα
ἐρψεῦμες στεφάνως δρεψεύμεναι ἀδὺ πνέοντας,　　40
πολλὰ τεοῦς, Ἑλένα, μεμναμέναι ὡς γαλαθηναί
ἄρνες γειναμένας ὄιος μαστὸν ποθέοισαι.
πρᾶταί τοι στέφανον λωτῶ χαμαὶ αὐξομένοιο
πλέξαισαι σκιαρὰν καταθήσομεν ἐς πλατάνιστον·
πρᾶται δ' ἀργυρέας ἐξ ὄλπιδος ὑγρὸν ἄλειφαρ　　45
λαζύμεναι σταξεῦμες ὑπὸ σκιαρὰν πλατάνιστον·
γράμματα δ' ἐν φλοιῷ γεγράψεται, ὡς παριών τις
ἀννείμῃ Δωριστί· 'σέβευ μ'· Ἑλένας φυτόν εἰμι.'
　χαίροις, ὦ νύμφα· χαίροις, εὐπένθερε γαμβρέ.

22 δ' αἱ m: δὲ a: γὰρ am　　25 τᾶν δ' a　　26 διέφανε z:
διέφαινε am　　27 τό τε z: ἅτε am

Λατὼ μὲν δοίη, Λατὼ κουροτρόφος, ὕμμιν   50
εὐτεκνίαν, Κύπρις δέ, θεὰ Κύπρις, ἶσον ἔρασθαι
ἀλλάλων, Ζεὺς δέ, Κρονίδας Ζεύς, ἄφθιτον ὄλβον,
ὡς ἐξ εὐπατριδᾶν εἰς εὐπατρίδας πάλιν ἔνθῃ.
εὕδετ' ἐς ἀλλάλων στέρνον φιλότητα πνέοντες
καὶ πόθον· ἐγρέσθαι δὲ πρὸς ἀῶ μή 'πιλάθησθε.   55
νεύμεθα κάμμες ἐς ὄρθρον, ἐπεί κα πρᾶτος ἀοιδός
ἐξ εὐνᾶς κελαδήσῃ ἀνασχὼν εὔτριχα δειράν.
'Υμὴν ὦ 'Υμέναιε, γάμῳ ἐπὶ τῷδε χαρείης.

XXII

ὑμνέομεν Λήδας τε καὶ αἰγιόχου Διὸς υἱώ,
Κάστορα καὶ φοβερὸν Πολυδεύκεα πὺξ ἐρεθίζειν
χεῖρας ἐπιζεύξαντα μέσας βοέοισιν ἱμᾶσιν.
ὑμνέομεν καὶ δὶς καὶ τὸ τρίτον ἄρσενα τέκνα
κούρης Θεστιάδος, Λακεδαιμονίους δύ' ἀδελφούς,   5
ἀνθρώπων σωτῆρας ἐπὶ ξυροῦ ἤδη ἐόντων,
ἵππων θ' αἱματόεντα ταρασσομένων καθ' ὅμιλον,
νηῶν θ' αἳ δύνοντα καὶ οὐρανὸν εἰσανιόντα
ἄστρα βιαζόμεναι χαλεποῖς ἐνέκυρσαν ἀήταις.
οἱ δέ σφεων κατὰ πρύμναν ἀείραντες μέγα κῦμα   10
ἠὲ καὶ ἐκ πρώρηθεν ἢ ὅππῃ θυμὸς ἑκάστου
εἰς κοίλην ἔρριψαν, ἀνέρρηξαν δ' ἄρα τοίχους
ἀμφοτέρους· κρέμαται δὲ σὺν ἱστίῳ ἄρμενα πάντα
εἰκῇ ἀποκλασθέντα· πολὺς δ' ἐξ οὐρανοῦ ὄμβρος
νυκτὸς ἐφερπούσης· παταγεῖ δ' εὐρεῖα θάλασσα   15
κοπτομένη πνοιαῖς τε καὶ ἀρρήκτοισι χαλάζαις.
ἀλλ' ἔμπης ὑμεῖς γε καὶ ἐκ βυθοῦ ἕλκετε νῆας

8 εἰσανιόντα **a**: ἐξανιόντα **m**

αὐτοῖσιν ναύτῃσιν ὀϊομένοις θανέεσθαι·
αἶψα δ' ἀπολήγουσ' ἄνεμοι, λιπαρὴ δὲ γαλήνη
ἂμ πέλαγος· νεφέλαι δὲ διέδραμον ἄλλυδις ἄλλαι·   20
ἐκ δ' Ἄρκτοι τ' ἐφάνησαν Ὄνων τ' ἀνὰ μέσσον
    ἀμαυρή
Φάτνη, σημαίνουσα τὰ πρὸς πλόον εὔδια πάντα.
ὦ ἄμφω θνητοῖσι βοηθόοι, ὦ φίλοι ἄμφω,
ἱππῆες κιθαρισταὶ ἀεθλητῆρες ἀοιδοί,
Κάστορος ἢ πρώτου Πολυδεύκεος ἄρξομ' ἀείδειν;   25
ἀμφοτέρους ὑμνέων Πολυδεύκεα πρῶτον ἀείσω.

ἡ μὲν ἄρα προφυγοῦσα πέτρας εἰς ἓν ξυνιούσας
Ἀργὼ καὶ νιφόεντος ἀταρτηρὸν στόμα Πόντου,
Βέβρυκας εἰσαφίκανε θεῶν φίλα τέκνα φέρουσα.
ἔνθα μιᾶς πολλοὶ κατὰ κλίμακος ἀμφοτέρων ἔξ   30
τοίχων ἄνδρες ἔβαινον Ἰησονίης ἀπὸ νηός·
ἐκβάντες δ' ἐπὶ θῖνα βαθὺν καὶ ὑπήνεμον ἀκτήν
εὐνάς τ' ἐστόρνυντο πυρεῖά τε χερσὶν ἐνώμων.
Κάστωρ δ' αἰολόπωλος ὅ τ' οἰνωπὸς Πολυδεύκης
ἄμφω ἐρημάζεσκον ἀποπλαγχθέντες ἑταίρων,   35
παντοίην ἐν ὄρει θηεύμενοι ἄγριον ὕλην.
εὗρον δ' ἀέναον κρήνην ὑπὸ λισσάδι πέτρῃ
ὕδατι πεπληθυῖαν ἀκηράτῳ· αἱ δ' ὑπένερθε
λάλλαι κρυστάλλῳ ἠδ' ἀργύρῳ ἰνδάλλοντο
ἐκ βυθοῦ· ὑψηλαὶ δὲ πεφύκεσαν ἀγχόθι πεῦκαι   40
λεῦκαί τε πλάτανοί τε καὶ ἀκρόκομοι κυπάρισσοι
ἄνθεά τ' εὐώδη, λασίαις φίλα ἔργα μελίσσαις,
ὅσσ' ἔαρος λήγοντος ἐπιβρύει ἂν λειμῶνας.
ἔνθα δ' ἀνὴρ ὑπέροπλος ἐνήμενος ἐνδιάασκε,
δεινὸς ἰδεῖν, σκληρῇσι τεθλασμένος οὔατα πυγμαῖς·   45
στήθεα δ' ἐσφαίρωτο πελώρια καὶ πλατὺ νῶτον

39 λάλλαι z: ἄλλαι m   45 τεθραυμένος a

σαρκὶ σιδηρείῃ, σφυρήλατος οἷα κολοσσός·
ἐν δὲ μύες στερεοῖσι βραχίοσιν ἄκρον ὑπ' ὦμον
ἔστασαν ἠΰτε πέτροι ὀλοίτροχοι οὕστε κυλίνδων
χειμάρρους ποταμὸς μεγάλαις περιέξεσε δίναις·   50
αὐτὰρ ὑπὲρ νώτοιο καὶ αὐχένος ᾐωρεῖτο
ἄκρων δέρμα λέοντος ἀφημμένον ἐκ ποδεώνων.
τὸν πρότερος προσέειπεν ἀεθλοφόρος Πολυδεύκης.

ΠΟΛΥΔΕΥΚΗΣ

χαῖρε, ξεῖν', ὅτις ἐσσί. τίνες βροτοὶ ὧν ὅδε
    χῶρος;

ΑΜΥΚΟΣ

χαίρω πῶς, ὅτε τ' ἄνδρας ὁρῶ τοὺς μὴ πρὶν
    ὄπωπα;   55
ΠΟ. θάρσει· μήτ' ἀδίκους μήτ' ἐξ ἀδίκων φάθι
    λεύσσειν.
ΑΜ. θαρσέω, κοὐκ ἐκ σεῦ με διδάσκεσθαι τόδ' ἔοικεν.
ΠΟ. ἄγριος εἶ, πρὸς πάντα παλίγκοτος ἠδ' ὑπερόπτης;
ΑΜ. τοιόσδ' οἷον ὁρᾷς· τῆς σῆς γε μὲν οὐκ ἐπιβαίνω.
ΠΟ. ἔλθοις, καὶ ξενίων κε τυχὼν πάλιν οἴκαδ'
    ἱκάνοις.   60
ΑΜ. μήτε σύ με ξείνιζε, τά τ' ἐξ ἐμεῦ οὐκ ἐν
    ἑτοίμῳ.
ΠΟ. δαιμόνι', οὐδ' ἂν τοῦδε πιεῖν ὕδατος σύγε δοίης;
ΑΜ. γνώσεαι εἴ σευ δίψος ἀνειμένα χείλεα τέρσει.
ΠΟ. ἄργυρος ἢ τίς ὁ μισθός — ἐρεῖς; — ᾧ κέν σε
    πίθοιμεν;
ΑΜ. εἰς ἑνὶ χεῖρας ἄειρον ἐναντίος ἀνδρὶ καταστάς. 65
ΠΟ. πυγμάχος ἢ καὶ ποσσὶ θένων σκέλος ὄμμα τ'
    ὀρύσσων;

66 ὄμμα τ' ὀρύσσων z: ὄμματα δ' ὀρθός vel -θά m

ΑΜ. πὺξ διατεινάμενος σφετέρης μή φείδεο τέχνης.
ΠΟ. τίς γάρ, ὅτῳ χεῖρας καὶ ἐμοὺς συνερείσω
     ἱμάντας;
ΑΜ. ἐγγὺς ὁρᾷς· οὐ γύννις ἐὼν κεκλήσεθ᾽ ὁ πύκτης.
ΠΟ. ἦ καὶ ἄεθλον ἑτοῖμον ἐφ᾽ ᾧ δηρισόμεθ᾽ ἄμφω; 70
ΑΜ. σὸς μὲν ἐγώ, σὺ δ᾽ ἐμὸς κεκλήσεαι, αἴ κε
     κρατήσω.
ΠΟ. ὀρνίθων φοινικολόφων τοιοίδε κυδοιμοί.
ΑΜ. εἴτ᾽ οὖν ὀρνίθεσσιν ἐοικότες εἴτε λέουσι
     γινόμεθ᾽, οὐκ ἄλλῳ κε μαχεσσαίμεσθ᾽ ἐπ᾽ ἀέθλῳ.

ἦ ῥ᾽ Ἄμυκος καὶ κόχλον ἑλὼν μυκήσατο κοῖλον. 75
οἱ δὲ θοῶς συνάγερθεν ὑπὸ σκιερὰς πλατανίστους
κόχλου φυσηθέντος ἀεὶ Βέβρυκες κομόωντες.
ὣς δ᾽ αὔτως ἥρωας ἰὼν ἐκαλέσσατο πάντας
Μαγνήσσης ἀπὸ νηὸς ὑπείροχος ἐν δαὶ Κάστωρ.
οἱ δ᾽ ἐπεὶ οὖν σπείραισιν ἐκαρτύναντο βοείαις   80
χεῖρας καὶ περὶ γυῖα μακροὺς εἵλιξαν ἱμάντας,
ἐς μέσσον σύναγον φόνον ἀλλήλοισι πνέοντες.
ἔνθα πολύς σφισι μόχθος ἐπειγομένοισιν ἐτύχθη
ὁππότερος κατὰ νῶτα λάβοι φάος ἠελίοιο.
ἰδρείῃ μέγαν ἄνδρα παρήλυθες, ὦ Πολύδευκες,   85
βάλλετο δ᾽ ἀκτίνεσσιν ἅπαν Ἀμύκοιο πρόσωπον.
αὐτὰρ ὅγ᾽ ἐν θυμῷ κεχολωμένος ἵετο πρόσσω,
χερσὶ τιτυσκόμενος. τοῦ δ᾽ ἄκρον τύψε γένειον
Τυνδαρίδης ἐπιόντος· ὀρίνθη δὲ πλέον ἢ πρίν,
σὺν δὲ μάχην ἐτάραξε, πολὺς δ᾽ ἐπέκειτο νενευκώς   90
ἐς γαῖαν. Βέβρυκες δ᾽ ἐπαύτεον, οἱ δ᾽ ἑτέρωθεν
ἥρωες κρατερὸν Πολυδεύκεα θαρσύνεσκον,
δειδιότες μή πως μιν ἐπιβρίσας δαμάσειε
χώρῳ ἐνὶ στεινῷ Τιτυῷ ἐναλίγκιος ἀνήρ.

88 ἔτυψε μέτωπον m

ἤτοι ὅγ' ἔνθα καὶ ἔνθα παριστάμενος Διὸς υἱός 95
ἀμφοτέρῃσιν ἄμυσσεν ἀμοιβαδίς, ἔσχεθε δ' ὁρμῆς
παῖδα Ποσειδάωνος ὑπερφίαλόν περ ἐόντα.
ἔστη δὲ πληγαῖς μεθύων, ἐκ δ' ἔπτυσεν αἷμα
φοίνιον· οἱ δ' ἄμα πάντες ἀριστῆες κελάδησαν,
ὡς ἴδον ἕλκεα λυγρὰ περὶ στόμα τε γναθμούς τε· 100
ὄμματα δ' οἰδήσαντος ἀπεστείνωτο προσώπου.
τὸν μὲν ἄναξ ἐτάρασσεν ἐτώσια χερσὶ προδεικνύς
πάντοθεν· ἀλλ' ὅτε δή μιν ἀμηχανέοντ' ἐνόησε,
μέσσης ῥινὸς ὕπερθε κατ' ὀφρύος ἤλασε πυγμῇ,
πᾶν δ' ἀπέσυρε μέτωπον ἐς ὀστέον. αὐτὰρ ὁ
πληγείς 105
ὕπτιος ἐν φύλλοισι τεθηλόσιν ἐξετανύσθη.
ἔνθα μάχη δριμεῖα πάλιν γένετ' ὀρθωθέντος,
ἀλλήλους δ' ὄλεκον στερεοῖς θείνοντες ἱμᾶσιν.
ἀλλ' ὁ μὲν ἐς στῆθός τε καὶ ἔξω χεῖρας ἐνώμα
αὐχένος ἀρχηγὸς Βεβρύκων· ὁ δ' ἀεικέσι
πληγαῖς 110
πᾶν συνέφυρε πρόσωπον ἀνίκητος Πολυδεύκης.
σάρκες δ' ᾧ μὲν ἱδρῶτι συνίζανον, ἐκ μεγάλου δέ
αἶψ' ὀλίγος γένετ' ἀνδρός· ὁ δ' αἰεὶ πάσσονα γυῖα
ἁπτομένου φορέεσκε πόνου καὶ χροιῇ ἀμείνω.
πῶς γὰρ δὴ Διὸς υἱὸς ἀδηφάγον ἄνδρα
καθεῖλεν; 115
εἰπέ, θεά, σὺ γὰρ οἶσθα· ἐγὼ δ' ἑτέρων ὑποφήτης
φθέγξομαι ὅσσ' ἐθέλεις σὺ καὶ ὅπως τοι φίλον αὐτῇ.
ἤτοι ὅγε ῥέξαι τι λιλαιόμενος μέγα ἔργον
σκαιῇ μὲν σκαιὴν Πολυδεύκεος ἔλλαβε χεῖρα,
δοχμὸς ἀπὸ προβολῆς κλινθείς, ἑτέρῳ δ' ἐπιβαίνων 120
δεξιτερῆς ἤνεγκεν ἀπὸ λαγόνος πλατὺ γυῖον.
καί κε τυχὼν ἔβλαψεν Ἀμυκλαίων βασιλῆα,

112 ᾧ z: οἷ m: αἶ m   114 αὐξομένου z   120 ἑτέρῳ z: ἑτέρῃ m

ἀλλ' ὅγ' ὑπεξανέδυ κεφαλῇ, στιβαρῇ δ' ἅμα χειρί
πλῆξεν ὑπὸ σκαιὸν κρόταφον καὶ ἐπέμπεσεν ὤμῳ·
ἐκ δ' ἐχύθη μέλαν αἷμα θοῶς κροτάφοιο
χανόντος.   125
λαιῇ δὲ στόμα κόψε, πυκνοὶ δ' ἀράβησαν ὀδόντες·
αἰεὶ δ' ὀξυτέρῳ πιτύλῳ δηλεῖτο πρόσωπον
μέχρι συνηλοίησε παρήϊα. πᾶς δ' ἐπὶ γαίῃ
κεῖτ' ἀλλοφρονέων καὶ ἀνέσχεθε νεῖκος ἀπαυδῶν
ἀμφοτέρας ἅμα χεῖρας, ἐπεὶ θανάτου σχεδὸν
ἦεν.   130
τὸν μὲν ἄρα κρατέων περ ἀτάσθαλον οὐδὲν ἔρεξας,
ὦ πύκτη Πολύδευκες· ὄμοσσε δέ τοι μέγαν ὅρκον,
ὃν πατέρ' ἐκ πόντοιο Ποσειδάωνα κικλήσκων,
μήποτ' ἔτι ξείνοισιν ἑκὼν ἀνιηρὸς ἔσεσθαι.

     καὶ σὺ μὲν ὕμνησαί μοι, ἄναξ· σὲ δέ, Κάστορ,
          ἀείσω,   135
Τυνδαρίδη ταχύπωλε, δορυσσόε, χαλκεοθώρηξ.

     τὼ μὲν ἀναρπάξαντε δύω φερέτην Διὸς υἱώ
δοιὰς Λευκίπποιο κόρας· δισσὼ δ' ἄρα τώγε
ἐσσυμένως ἐδίωκον ἀδελφεὼ υἷ' Ἀφαρῆος,
γαμβρὼ μελλογάμω, Λυγκεὺς καὶ ὁ καρτερὸς
          Ἴδας.   140
ἀλλ' ὅτε τύμβον ἵκανον ἀποφθιμένου Ἀφαρῆος,
ἐκ δίφρων ἅμα πάντες ἐπ' ἀλλήλοισιν ὄρουσαν
ἔγχεσι καὶ κοίλοισι βαρυνόμενοι σακέεσσι.
Λυγκεὺς δ' ἄρ μετέειπεν, ὑπὲκ κόρυθος μέγ' ἀΰσας,
'δαιμόνιοι, τί μάχης ἱμείρετε; πῶς δ' ἐπὶ
          νύμφαις   145
ἀλλοτρίαις χαλεποί, γυμναὶ δ' ἐν χερσὶ μάχαιραι;
ἡμῖν τοι Λεύκιππος ἑὰς ἔδνωσε θύγατρας
τάσδε πολὺ προτέροις· ἡμῖν γάμος οὗτος ἐν ὅρκῳ.

ὑμεῖς δ᾽ οὐ κατὰ κόσμον ἐπ᾽ ἀλλοτρίοισι λέχεσσι
βουσὶ καὶ ἡμιόνοισι καὶ ἄλλοισι κτεάτεσσιν 150
ἄνδρα παρετρέψασθε, γάμον δ᾽ ἐκλέψατε δώροις.
ἦ μὴν πολλάκις ὔμμιν ἐνώπιον ἀμφοτέροισιν
αὐτὸς ἐγὼ τάδ᾽ ἔειπα καὶ οὐ πολύμυθος ἐὼν περ·
"οὐχ οὕτω, φίλοι ἄνδρες, ἀριστήεσσιν ἔοικε
μνηστεύειν ἀλόχους αἷς νυμφίοι ἤδη ἑτοῖμοι. 155
πολλή τοι Σπάρτη, πολλὴ δ᾽ ἱππήλατος Ἦλις
Ἀρκαδίη τ᾽ εὔμηλος Ἀχαιῶν τε πτολίεθρα
Μεσσήνη τε καὶ Ἄργος ἅπασά τε Σισυφὶς ἀκτή·
ἔνθα κόραι τοκέεσσιν ὑπὸ σφετέροισι τρέφονται
μυρίαι οὔτε φυῆς ἐπιδευέες οὔτε νόοιο, 160
τάων εὐμαρὲς ὔμμιν ὀπυιέμεν ἅς κ᾽ ἐθέλητε·
ὡς ἀγαθοῖς πολέες βούλοιντό κε πενθεροὶ εἶναι,
ὑμεῖς δ᾽ ἐν πάντεσσι διάκριτοι ἡρώεσσι,
καὶ πατέρες καὶ ἄνωθεν ἅπαν πατρώιον αἷμα.
ἀλλά, φίλοι, τοῦτον μὲν ἐάσατε πρὸς τέλος
    ἐλθεῖν 165
ἄμμι γάμον· σφῶν δ᾽ ἄλλον ἐπιφραζώμεθα πάντες."
ἴσκον τοιάδε πολλά, τὰ δ᾽ εἰς ὑγρὸν ᾤχετο κῦμα
πνοιὴ ἔχουσ᾽ ἀνέμοιο, χάρις δ᾽ οὐχ ἕσπετο μύθοις·
σφὼ γὰρ ἀκηλήτω καὶ ἀπηνέες. ἀλλ᾽ ἔτι καὶ νῦν
πείθεσθ᾽· ἄμφω δ᾽ ἄμμιν ἀνεψιὼ ἐκ πατρός
    ἐστον.' 170

.   .   .   .

(ΚΑ.) 'εἰ δ᾽ ὑμῖν κραδίη πόλεμον ποθεῖ, αἵματι δὲ χρή
νεῖκος ἀναρρήξαντας ὁμοίιον ἔγχεα λοῦσαι,
Ἴδας μὲν καὶ ὅμαιμος ἐμός, κρατερὸς Πολυδεύκης,
χεῖρας ἐρωήσουσιν ἀποσχομένω ὑσμίνης·
νῶϊ δ᾽, ἐγὼ Λυγκεύς τε, διακρινώμεθ᾽ Ἄρηι, 175

164 μητρώϊον m   post 170 lac. stat. z   175 Λυγκεὺς
m: Κάστωρ m

ὁπλοτέρω γεγαῶτε. γονεῦσι δὲ μὴ πολὺ πένθος
ἡμετέροισι λίπωμεν. ἅλις νέκυς ἐξ ἑνὸς οἴκου
εἶς· ἀτὰρ ὧλλοι πάντας ἐϋφρανέουσιν ἑταίρους,
νυμφίοι ἀντὶ νεκρῶν, ὑμεναιώσουσι δὲ κούρας
τάσδ'. ὀλίγῳ τοι ἔοικε κακῷ μέγα νεῖκος
    ἀναιρεῖν.'   180
εἶπε, τὰ δ' οὐκ ἄρ' ἔμελλε θεὸς μεταμώνια θήσειν.
τὼ μὲν γὰρ ποτὶ γαῖαν ἀπ' ὤμων τεύχε' ἔθεντο,
ὢ γενεῇ προφέρεσκον· ὁ δ' εἰς μέσον ἤλυθε Λυγκεύς
σείων καρτερὸν ἔγχος ὑπ' ἀσπίδος ἄντυγα πρώτην·
ὣς δ' αὔτως ἄκρας ἐτινάξατο δούρατος ἀκμάς   185
Κάστωρ· ἀμφοτέροις δὲ λόφων ἐπένευον ἔθειραι.
ἔγχεσι μὲν πρώτιστα τιτυσκόμενοι πόνον εἶχον
ἀλλήλων, εἴ που τι χροὸς γυμνωθὲν ἴδοιεν·
ἀλλ' ἤτοι τὰ μὲν ἄκρα πάρος τινὰ δηλήσασθαι
δοῦρ' ἐάγη σακέεσσιν ἐνὶ δεινοῖσι παγέντα.   190
τὼ δ' ἄορ ἐκ κολεοῖο ἐρυσσαμένω φόνον αὖτις
τεῦχον ἐπ' ἀλλήλοισι, μάχης δ' οὐ γίνετ' ἐρωή.
πολλὰ μὲν εἰς σάκος εὐρὺ καὶ ἱππόκομον
    τρυφάλειαν
Κάστωρ, πολλὰ δ' ἔνυξεν ἀκριβὴς ὄμμασι Λυγκεύς
τοῖο σάκος, φοίνικα δ' ὅσον λόφον ἵκετ'
    ἀκωκή.   195
τοῦ μὲν ἄκρην ἐκόλουσεν ἐπὶ σκαιὸν γόνυ χεῖρα
φάσγανον ὀξὺ φέροντος ὑπεξαναβὰς ποδὶ Κάστωρ
σκαιῷ· ὁ δὲ πληγεὶς ξίφος ἔκβαλεν, αἶψα δὲ
    φεύγειν
ὡρμήθη ποτὶ σῆμα πατρός, τόθι καρτερὸς Ἴδας
κεκλιμένος θηεῖτο μάχην ἐμφύλιον ἀνδρῶν.   200
ἀλλὰ μεταΐξας πλατὺ φάσγανον ὦσε διαπρό
Τυνδαρίδης λαγόνος τε καὶ ὀμφαλοῦ· ἔγκατα δ'
    εἴσω

χαλκὸς ἄφαρ διέχευεν, ὁ δ' ἐς στόμα κεῖτο
νενευκώς
Λυγκεύς, κὰδ δ' ἄρα οἱ βλεφάρων βαρὺς ἔδραμεν
ὕπνος.
οὐ μὰν οὐδὲ τὸν ἄλλον ἐφ' ἑστίῃ εἶδε
πατρώῃ   205
παίδων Λαοκόωσα φίλον γάμον ἐκτελέσαντα.
ἢ γὰρ ὅγε στήλην Ἀφαρηῖου ἐξανέχουσαν
τύμβου ἀναρρήξας ταχέως Μεσσήνιος Ἴδας
μέλλε κασιγνήτοιο βαλεῖν σφετέροιο φονῆα·
ἀλλὰ Ζεὺς ἐπάμυνε, χερῶν δέ οἱ ἔκβαλε
τυκτήν   210
μάρμαρον, αὐτὸν δὲ φλογέῳ συνέφλεξε κεραυνῷ.

οὕτω Τυνδαρίδαις πολεμιζέμεν οὐκ ἐν ἐλαφρῷ·
αὐτοί τε κρατέουσι καὶ ἐκ κρατέοντος ἔφυσαν.
χαίρετε, Λήδας τέκνα, καὶ ἡμετέροις κλέος
ὕμνοις
ἐσθλὸν ἀεὶ πέμποιτε. φίλοι δέ τε πάντες
ἀοιδοί   215
Τυνδαρίδαις Ἑλένῃ τε καὶ ἄλλοις ἡρώεσσιν
Ἴλιον οἳ διέπερσαν ἀρήγοντες Μενελάῳ.
ὑμῖν κῦδος, ἄνακτες, ἐμήσατο Χῖος ἀοιδός,
ὑμνήσας Πριάμοιο πόλιν καὶ νῆας Ἀχαιῶν
Ἰλιάδας τε μάχας Ἀχιλῆά τε πύργον ἀϋτῆς· 220
ὑμῖν αὖ καὶ ἐγὼ λιγεῶν μειλίγματα Μουσέων,
οἷ' αὐταὶ παρέχουσι καὶ ὡς ἐμὸς οἶκος ὑπάρχει,
τοῖα φέρω. γεράων δὲ θεοῖς κάλλιστον ἀοιδαί.

XXIV

Ἡρακλέα δεκάμηνον ἐόντα ποχ' ἁ Μιδεᾶτις
Ἀλκμήνα καὶ νυκτὶ νεώτερον Ἰφικλῆα,
ἀμφοτέρους λούσασα καὶ ἐμπλήσασα γάλακτος,
χαλκείαν κατέθηκεν ἐς ἀσπίδα τὰν Πτερελάου
Ἀμφιτρύων καλὸν ὅπλον ἀπεσκύλευσε πεσόντος.   5
ἁπτομένα δὲ γυνὰ κεφαλᾶς μυθήσατο παίδων·
'εὕδετ', ἐμὰ βρέφεα, γλυκερὸν καὶ ἐγέρσιμον ὕπνον·
εὕδετ', ἐμὰ ψυχά, δύ' ἀδελφεοί, εὔσοα τέκνα·
ὄλβιοι εὐνάζοισθε καὶ ὄλβιοι ἀῶ ἵκοισθε.'
ὣς φαμένα δίνασε σάκος μέγα· τοὺς δ' ἕλεν ὕπνος.   10
ἆμος δὲ στρέφεται μεσονύκτιον ἐς δύσιν Ἄρκτος
Ὠρίωνα κατ' αὐτόν, ὁ δ' ἀμφαίνει μέγαν ὦμον,
τᾶμος ἄρ' αἰνὰ πέλωρα δύω πολυμήχανος Ἥρα,
κυανέαις φρίσσοντας ὑπὸ σπείραισι δράκοντας,
ὦρσεν ἐπὶ πλατὺν οὐδόν, ὅθι σταθμὰ κοῖλα θυράων   15
οἴκου, ἀπειλήσασα φαγεῖν βρέφος Ἡρακλῆα.
τὼ δ' ἐξειλυσθέντες ἐπὶ χθονὶ γαστέρας ἄμφω
αἱμοβόρους ἐκύλιον· ἀπ' ὀφθαλμῶν δὲ κακὸν πῦρ
ἐρχομένοις λάμπεσκε, βαρὺν δ' ἐξέπτυον ἰόν.
ἀλλ' ὅτε δὴ παίδων λιχμώμενοι ἐγγύθεν ἦνθον,   20
καὶ τότ' ἄρ' ἐξέγροντο, Διὸς νοέοντος ἅπαντα,
Ἀλκμήνας φίλα τέκνα, φάος δ' ἀνὰ οἶκον ἐτύχθη.
ἤτοι ὅγ' εὐθὺς ἄϋσεν, ὅπως κακὰ θηρί' ἀνέγνω
κοίλου ὑπὲρ σάκεος καὶ ἀναιδέας εἶδεν ὀδόντας,
Ἰφικλέης, οὔλαν δὲ ποσὶν διελάκτισε χλαῖναν   25
φευγέμεν ὁρμαίνων· ὁ δ' ἐναντίος ἵετο χερσίν
Ἡρακλέης, ἄμφω δὲ βαρεῖ ἐνεδήσατο δεσμῷ,
δραξάμενος φάρυγος, τόθι φάρμακα λυγρὰ τέτυκται
οὐλομένοις ὀφίεσσι, τὰ καὶ θεοὶ ἐχθαίροντι.

τὼ δ' αὖτε σπείραισιν ἑλισσέσθην περὶ παῖδα 30
ὀψίγονον, γαλαθηνὸν ὑπὸ τροφῷ, αἰὲν ἄδακρυν·
ἂψ δὲ πάλιν διέλυον, ἐπεὶ μογέοιεν, ἀκάνθας
δεσμοῦ ἀναγκαίου πειρώμενοι ἔκλυσιν εὑρεῖν.
'Αλκμήνα δ' ἄκουσε βοᾶς καὶ ἐπέγρετο πράτα·
'ἄνσταθ', 'Αμφιτρύων· ἐμὲ γὰρ δέος ἴσχει ὀκνηρόν· 35
ἄνστα, μηδὲ πόδεσσι τεοῖς ὑπὸ σάνδαλα θείης.
οὐκ ἀίεις, παίδων ὁ νεώτερος ὅσσον ἀϋτεῖ;
ἢ οὐ νοέεις ὅτι νυκτὸς ἀωρί που, οἱ δέ τε τοῖχοι
πάντες ἀριφραδέες καθαρᾶς ἄτερ ἠριγενείας;
ἔστι τί μοι κατὰ δῶμα νεώτερον, ἔστι, φίλ'
      ἀνδρῶν.' 40
ὡς φάθ', ὁ δ' ἐξ εὐνᾶς ἀλόχῳ κατέβαινε πιθήσας.
δαιδάλεον δ' ὥρμασε μετὰ ξίφος, ὅ οἱ ὕπερθεν
κλιντῆρος κεδρίνου περὶ πασσάλῳ αἰὲν ἄωρτο.
ἤτοι ὅγ' ὠριγνᾶτο νεοκλώστου τελαμῶνος,
κουφίζων ἑτέρᾳ κολεόν, μέγα λώτινον ἔργον. 45
ἀμφιλαφὴς δ' ἄρα παστὰς ἐνεπλήσθη πάλιν ὄρφνας.
δμῶας δὴ τότ' ἄϋσεν ὕπνον βαρὺν ἐκφυσῶντας·
'οἴσετε πῦρ ὅτι θᾶσσον ἀπ' ἐσχαρεῶνος ἑλόντες,
δμῶες ἐμοί, στιβαροὺς δὲ θυρᾶν ἀνακόψατ' ὀχῆας.'
'ἄνστατε, δμῶες ταλασίφρονες· αὐτὸς ἀϋτεῖ', 50
ἦ ῥα γυνὰ Φοίνισσα μύλαις ἔπι κοῖτον ἔχουσα·
οἱ δ' αἶψα προγένοντο λύχνοις ἅμα δαιομένοισι
δμῶες· ἐνεπλήσθη δὲ δόμος σπεύδοντος ἑκάστου.
ἤτοι ἄρ' ὡς εἶδονθ' ὑποτίτθιον Ἡρακλῆα
θῆρε δύω χείρεσσιν ἀπρὶξ ἀπαλαῖσιν ἔχοντα, 55
ἐκπλήγδην ἰάχησαν· ὁ δ' ἐς πατέρ' 'Αμφιτρύωνα
ἑρπετὰ δεικανάασκεν, ἐπάλλετο δ' ὑψόθι χαίρων
κουροσύνᾳ, γελάσας δὲ πάρος κατέθηκε ποδοῖιν
πατρὸς ἑοῦ θανάτῳ κεκαρωμένα δεινὰ πέλωρα.

36 ante 35 **a**　　39 ἅπερ z: δ' α[**a**　　58 γηθοσύνᾳ **a**

Ἀλκμήνα μὲν ἔπειτα ποτὶ σφέτερον βάλε κόλπον   60
ξηρὸν ὑπαὶ δείους ἀκράχολον Ἰφικλῆα·
Ἀμφιτρύων δὲ τὸν ἄλλον ὑπ' ἀμνείαν θέτο χλαῖναν
παῖδα, πάλιν δ' ἐς λέκτρον ἰὼν ἐμνάσατο κοίτου.
  ὄρνιθες τρίτον ἄρτι τὸν ἔσχατον ὄρθρον ἄειδον,
Τειρεσίαν τόκα μάντιν ἀλαθέα πάντα λέγοντα   65
Ἀλκμήνα καλέσασα χρέος κατέλεξε νεοχμόν,
καί μιν ὑποκρίνεσθαι ὅπως τελέεσθαι ἔμελλεν
ἠνώγει· 'μηδ' εἴ τι θεοὶ νοέοντι πονηρόν,
αἰδόμενός με κρύπτε· καὶ ὡς οὐκ ἔστιν ἀλύξαι
ἀνθρώποις ὅ τι Μοῖρα κατὰ κλωστῆρος ἐπείγει.   70
ἀλλ' Εὐηρείδα, μάλα τοι φρονέοντα διδάσκω.'
τόσσ' ἔλεγεν βασίλεια· ὁ δ' ἀνταμείβετο τοίοις·
'θάρσει, ἀριστοτόκεια γύναι, Περσήιον αἷμα,
θάρσει· μελλόντων δὲ τὸ λώιον ἐν φρεσὶ θέσθαι.
ναὶ γὰρ ἐμῶν γλυκὺ φέγγος ἀποιχόμενον πάλαι ὄσσων,   75
πολλαὶ Ἀχαιιάδων μαλακὸν περὶ γούνατι νῆμα
χειρὶ κατατρίψουσιν ἀκρέσπερον ἀείδοισαι
Ἀλκμήναν ὀνομαστί, σέβας δ' ἔσῃ Ἀργείαισι.
τοῖος ἀνὴρ ὅδε μέλλει ἐς οὐρανὸν ἄστρα φέροντα
ἀμβαίνειν τεὸς υἱός, ἀπὸ στέρνων πλατὺς ἥρως,   80
οὗ καὶ θηρία πάντα καὶ ἀνέρες ἥσσονες ἄλλοι.
δώδεκά οἱ τελέσαντι πεπρωμένον ἐν Διὸς οἰκεῖν
μόχθους, θνητὰ δὲ πάντα πυρὰ Τραχίνιος ἕξει·
γαμβρὸς δ' ἀθανάτων κεκλήσεται οἳ τάδ' ἐπῶρσαν
κνώδαλα φωλεύοντα βρέφος διαδηλήσασθαι.   85
[ἔσται δὴ τοῦτ' ἆμαρ ὁπηνίκα νεβρὸν ἐν εὐνᾷ
καρχαρόδων σίνεσθαι ἰδὼν λύκος οὐκ ἐθελήσει.]
ἀλλά, γύναι, πῦρ μέν τοι ὑπὸ σποδῷ εὔτυκον ἔστω,
κάγκανα δ' ἀσπαλάθου ξύλ' ἑτοιμάσατ' ἢ παλιούρου

66 τέρας a   71 ἀλλ' z: μάντι am   72 τὰν δ' Εὐηρ[είτ]ας
(sic 71 a) τοιῷδ' ἀπαμ[είβετο μύθῳ a   86f. secl. z

ἢ βάτου ἢ ἀνέμῳ δεδονημένον αὖον ἄχερδον·   90
καῖε δὲ τώδ' ἀγρίαισιν ἐπὶ σχίζαισι δράκοντε
νυκτὶ μέσᾳ, ὅκα παῖδα κανεῖν τεὸν ἤθελον αὐτοί.
ἦρι δὲ συλλέξασα κόνιν πυρὸς ἀμφιπόλων τις
ῥιψάτω, εὖ μάλα πᾶσαν ὑπὲρ ποταμοῖο φέρουσα
ῥωγάδας ἐς πέτρας, ὑπερούριον, ἂψ δὲ νεέσθω   95
ἄστρεπτος. καθαρῷ δὲ πυρώσατε δῶμα θεείῳ
πρᾶτον, ἔπειτα δ' ἅλεσσι μεμιγμένον, ὡς νενόμισται,
θαλλῷ ἐπιρραίνειν ἐστεμμένῳ ἀβλαβὲς ὕδωρ·
Ζηνὶ δ' ἐπιρρέξαι καθυπερτέρῳ ἄρσενα χοῖρον,
δυσμενέων αἰεὶ καθυπέρτεροι ὡς τελέθοιτε.'   100
φῆ, καὶ ἐρωήσας ἐλεφάντινον ᾤχετο δίφρον
Τειρεσίας πολλοῖσι βαρύς περ ἐὼν ἐνιαυτοῖς.
    Ἡρακλέης δ' ὑπὸ ματρὶ νέον φυτὸν ὣς ἐν ἀλωᾷ
ἐτρέφετ', Ἀργείου κεκλημένος Ἀμφιτρύωνος.
γράμματα μὲν τὸν παῖδα γέρων Λίνος ἐξεδίδαξεν,   105
υἱὸς Ἀπόλλωνος μελεδωνεὺς ἄγρυπνος ἥρως·
τόξον δ' ἐντανύσαι καὶ ἐπὶ σκοπὸν εἶναι ὀϊστὸν
Εὔρυτος ἐκ πατέρων μεγάλαις ἀφνειὸς ἀρούραις.
αὐτὰρ ἀοιδὸν ἔθηκε καὶ ἄμφω χεῖρας ἔπλασσεν
πυξίνᾳ ἐν φόρμιγγι Φιλαμμονίδας Εὔμολπος.   110
ὅσσα δ' ἀπὸ σκελέων ἑδροστρόφοι Ἀργόθεν ἄνδρες
ἀλλάλους σφάλλοντι παλαίσμασιν, ὅσσα τε πύκται
δεινοὶ ἐν ἱμάντεσσιν ἅ τ' ἐς γαῖαν προπεσόντες
πάμμαχοι ἐξεύροντο σοφίσματα σύμφορα τέχνᾳ,
πάντ' ἔμαθ' Ἑρμείαο διδασκόμενος παρὰ παιδί   115
Ἁρπαλύκῳ Πανοπῆϊ, τὸν οὐδ' ἂν τηλόθε λεύσσων
θαρσαλέως τις ἔμεινεν ἀεθλεύοντ' ἐν ἀγῶνι,
τοῖον ἐπισκύνιον βλοσυρῷ ἐπέκειτο προσώπῳ.
ἵππους δ' ἐξελάσασθαι ὑφ' ἅρματι καὶ περὶ νύσσαν
ἀσφαλέως κάμπτοντα τροχοῦ σύριγγα φυλάξαι   120

114 σοφίσματα z: παλαίσματα m

Ἀμφιτρύων ὃν παῖδα φίλα φρονέων ἐδίδαξεν
αὐτός, ἐπεὶ μάλα πολλὰ θοῶν ἐξήρατ' ἀγώνων
Ἄργει ἐν ἱπποβότῳ κειμήλια, καί οἱ ἀαγεῖς
δίφροι ἐφ' ὧν ἐπέβαινε χρόνῳ διέλυσαν ἱμάντας.
δούρατι δὲ προβολαίῳ ὑπ' ἀσπίδι ὦμον ἔχοντα   125
ἀνδρὸς ὀρέξασθαι ξιφέων τ' ἀνέχεσθαι ἀμυχμόν,
κοσμῆσαί τε φάλαγγα λόχον τ' ἀναμετρήσασθαι
δυσμενέων ἐπιόντα, καὶ ἱππήεσσι κελεῦσαι,
Κάστωρ Ἱππαλίδας δέδαεν, φυγὰς Ἄργεος ἐνθών,
οὗ ποκα κλᾶρον ἄπαντα καὶ οἰνόπεδον μέγα Τυδεύς   130
ναῖε παρ' Ἀδρήστοιο λαβὼν ἱππήλατον Ἄργος·
Κάστορι δ' οὔτις ὁμοῖος ἐν ἡμιθέοις πολεμιστής
ἄλλος ἔην πρὶν γῆρας ἀποτρῖψαι νεότητα.

    ὧδε μὲν Ἡρακλῆα φίλα παιδεύσατο μάτηρ.
εὐνὰ δ' ἧς τῷ παιδὶ τετυγμένα ἀγχόθι πατρός   135
δέρμα λεόντειον μάλα οἱ κεχαρισμένον αὐτῷ,
δεῖπνον δὲ κρέα τ' ὀπτὰ καὶ ἐν κανέῳ μέγας ἄρτος
Δωρικός· ἀσφαλέως κε φυτοσκάφον ἄνδρα κορέσσαι·
αὐτὰρ ἐπ' ἄματι τυννὸν ἄνευ πυρὸς αἴνυτο δόρπον.
εἵματα δ' οὐκ ἀσκητὰ μέσας ὑπὲρ ἔννυτο κνάμας.   140

    .   .   .

125 ὦμον z: νῶτον am

XXVI

Ἰνὼ κΑὐτονόα χὰ μαλοπάραυος Ἀγαύα
τρεῖς θιάσως ἐς ὄρος τρεῖς ἄγαγον αὐταὶ ἐοῖσαι.
χαὶ μὲν ἀμερξάμεναι λασίας δρυὸς ἄγρια φύλλα,
κισσόν τε ζώοντα καὶ ἀσφόδελον τὸν ὑπὲρ γᾶς,
ἐν καθαρῷ λειμῶνι κάμον δυοκαίδεκα βωμώς,   5
τὼς τρεῖς τᾷ Σεμέλᾳ, τὼς ἐννέα τῷ Διονύσῳ.
ἱερὰ δ᾽ ἐκ κίστας πεπαναμένα χερσὶν ἑλοῖσαι
εὐφάμως κατέθεντο νεοδρέπτων ἐπὶ βωμῶν,
ὡς ἐδίδαξ᾽, ὡς αὐτὸς ἐθυμάρει Διόνυσος.
Πενθεὺς δ᾽ ἀλιβάτω πέτρας ἄπο πάντ᾽ ἐθεώρει,   10
σχῖνον ἐς ἀρχαίαν καταδύς, ἐπιχώριον ἔρνος.
Αὐτονόα πράτα νιν ἀνέκραγε δεινὸν ἰδοῖσα,
σὺν δ᾽ ἐτάραξε ποσὶν μανιώδεος ὄργια Βάκχω,
ἐξαπίνας ἐπιοῖσα, τά τ᾽ οὐχ ὁρέοντι βέβαλοι.
μαίνετο μὲν τ᾽ αὐτά, μαίνοντο δ᾽ ἄρ᾽ εὐθὺ καὶ ἄλλαι. 15
Πενθεὺς μὲν φεῦγεν πεφοβημένος, αἱ δ᾽ ἐδίωκον,
πέπλως ἐκ ζωστῆρος ἐς ἰγνύαν ἐρύσαισαι.
Πενθεὺς μὲν τόδ᾽ ἔειπε· 'τίνος κέχρησθε, γυναῖκες;'
Αὐτονόα τόδ᾽ ἔειπε· 'τάχα γνώσῃ πρὶν ἀκοῦσαι.'
μάτηρ μὲν κεφαλὰν μυκήσατο παιδὸς ἑλοῖσα,   20
ὅσσον περ τοκάδος τελέθει μύκημα λεαίνας·
Ἰνὼ δ᾽ ἐξέρρηξε σὺν ὠμοπλάτᾳ μέγαν ὦμον,
λὰξ ἐπὶ γαστέρα βᾶσα, καὶ Αὐτονόας ῥυθμὸς ωὑτός·
αἱ δ᾽ ἄλλαι τὰ περισσὰ κρεανομέοντο γυναῖκες,
ἐς Θήβας δ᾽ ἀφίκοντο πεφυρμέναι αἵματι πᾶσαι,   25
ἐξ ὄρεος πένθημα καὶ οὐ Πενθῆα φέροισαι.
    οὐκ ἀλέγω· μηδ᾽ ἄλλος ἀπεχθομένω Διονύσῳ
φροντίζοι, μηδ᾽ εἰ χαλεπώτερα τῶνδε μογήσαι,

13 ἱερὰ a   19 om a   27 μηδ᾽ ὅστις ἀπεχθόμενος a

εἴη δ' ἐνναετὴς ἢ καὶ δεκάτω ἐπιβαίνοι·
αὐτὸς δ' εὐαγέοιμι καὶ εὐαγέεσσιν ἄδοιμι.   30
ἐκ Διὸς αἰγιόχω τιμὰν ἔχει αἰετὸς οὕτως.
εὐσεβέων παίδεσσι τὰ λώϊα, δυσσεβέων δ' οὔ.

   χαίροι μὲν Διόνυσος, ὃν ἐν Δρακάνω νιφόεντι
Ζεὺς ὕπατος μεγάλαν ἐπιγουνίδα κάτθετο λύσας·
χαίροι δ' εὐειδὴς Σεμέλα καὶ ἀδελφεαὶ αὐτᾶς,   35
Καδμεῖαι πολλαῖς μεμελημέναι ἡρωίναις,
αἳ τόδε ἔργον ἔρεξαν ὀρίναντος Διονύσω
οὐκ ἐπιμωματόν. μηδεὶς τὰ θεῶν ὀνόσαιτο.

29 ἐπιβαίην a

XXVIII

   γλαύκας, ὦ φιλέριθ' ἀλακάτα, δῶρον Ἀθανάας
γύναιξιν νόος οἰκωφελίας αἷσιν ἐπάβολος,
θέρσεισ' ἄμμιν ὑμάρτη πόλιν ἐς Νήλεος ἀγλάαν,
ὄππα Κύπριδος ἶρον καλάμω χλῶρον ὑπ' ἀπάλω.
τυίδε γὰρ πλόον εὐάνεμον αἰτήμεθα πὰρ Δίος   5
ὄππως ξέννον ἔμον τέρψομ' ἴδων κἀντιφιληθέω,
Νικίαν, Χαρίτων ἰμεροφώνων ἴερον φύτον,
καὶ σὲ τὰν ἐλέφαντος πολυμόχθω γεγενημέναν
δῶρον Νικίας εἰς ἀλόχω χέρρας ὀπάσσομεν,
σὺν τᾷ πόλλα μὲν ἔργ' ἐκτελέσεις ἀνδρείοις πέπλοις, 10
πόλλα δ' οἷα γύναικες φορέοισ' ὑδάτινα βράκη.
δὶς γὰρ μάτερες ἄρνων μαλάκοις ἐν βοτάνᾳ πόκοις
πέξαιντ' αὐτοέτει, Θευγένιδός γ' ἔννεκ' ἐΰσφύρω·
οὕτως ἀνυσίεργος, φιλέει δ' ὅσσα σαόφρονες.
οὐ γὰρ εἰς ἀκίρας οὐδ' ἐς ἀέργω κεν ἐβολλόμαν   15
ὄπασσαί σε δόμοις, ἀμμετέρας ἔσσαν ἀπὺ χθόνος.

καὶ γάρ τοι πάτρις ἃν ὢξ Ἐφύρας κτίσσε ποτ'
   Ἀρχίας,
νάσω Τρινακρίας μύελον, ἀνδρῶν δοκίμων πόλιν.
νῦν μὰν οἶκον ἔχοισ' ἄνερος ὃς πόλλ' ἐδάη σόφα
ἀνθρώποισι νόσοις φάρμακα λύγραις ἀπαλάλκεμεν,   20
οἰκήσεις κατὰ Μίλλατον ἐράνναν πεδ' Ἰαόνων,
ὡς εὐαλάκατος Θεύγενις ἐν δαμότισιν πέλη,
καί οἱ μνᾶστιν ἄει τὼ φιλαοίδω παρέχῃς ξένω.
κῆνο γάρ τις ἔρει τὦπος ἴδων σ'· 'ἦ μεγάλα χάρις
δώρῳ σὺν ὀλίγῳ· πάντα δὲ τίματα τὰ πὰρ φίλων'.   25

EPIGRAMS

4

τήναν τὰν λαύρην τόθι ταὶ δρύες, αἰπόλε, κάμψας
   σύκινον εὑρήσεις ἀρτιγλυφὲς ξόανον
τρισκελὲς αὐτόφλοιον ἀνούατον, ἀλλὰ φάλητι
   παιδογόνῳ δυνατὸν Κύπριδος ἔργα τελεῖν.
σακὸς δ' εὐίερος περιδέδρομεν, ἀέναον δέ   5
   ῥεῖθρον ἀπὸ σπιλάδων πάντοσε τηλεθάει
δάφναις καὶ μύρτοισι καὶ εὐώδει κυπαρίσσῳ,
   ἔνθα πέριξ κέχυται βοτρυόπαις ἕλικι
ἄμπελος, εἰαρινοὶ δὲ λιγυφθόγγοισιν ἀοιδαῖς
   κόσσυφοι ἀχεῦσιν ποικιλότραυλα μέλη,   10
ξουθαὶ δ' ἀδονίδες μινυρίσμασιν ἀνταχεῦσι
   μέλπουσαι στόμασιν τὰν μελίγαρυν ὄπα.
ἕζεο δὴ τηνεὶ καὶ τῷ χαρίεντι Πριήπῳ
   εὔχε' ἀποστέρξαι τοὺς Δάφνιδός με πόθους,

3 ἀσκελὲς z   5 κᾶπος m

κευθὺς ἐπιρρέξειν χίμαρον καλόν. ἢν δ' ἀνανεύσῃ,   15
   τοῦδε τυχὼν ἐθέλω τρισσὰ θύη τελέσαι·
ῥέξω γὰρ δαμάλαν, λάσιον τράγον, ἄρνα τὸν ἴσχω
   σακίταν. ἀΐοι δ' εὐμενέως ὁ θεός.

17

θᾶσαι τὸν ἀνδριάντα τοῦτον, ὦ ξένε,
   σπουδᾷ, καὶ λέγ' ἐπὴν ἐς οἶκον ἔνθῃς·
' 'Ανακρέοντος εἰκόν' εἶδον ἐν Τέῳ
   τῶν πρόσθ' εἴ τι περισσὸν ᾠδοποιῶν.'
προσθεὶς δὲ χὤτι τοῖς νέοισιν ἅδετο   5
   ἐρεῖς ἀτρεκέως ὅλον τὸν ἄνδρα.

18

ἅ τε φωνὰ Δώριος χὠνὴρ ὁ τὰν κωμῳδίαν
   εὑρὼν 'Επίχαρμος.
ὦ Βάκχε, χάλκεόν νιν ἀντ' ἀλαθινοῦ
   τὶν ὧδ' ἀνέθηκαν
τοὶ Συρακούσαις ἐνίδρυνται, πελωρίστᾳ πόλει,   5
   οἷ' ἄνδρα πολίταν.
σοφῶν ἔοικε ῥημάτων μεμναμένους
   τελεῖν ἐπίχειρα·
πολλὰ γὰρ ποττὰν ζόαν τοῖς παισὶν εἶπε χρήσιμα.
   μεγάλα χάρις αὐτῷ.   10

19

ὁ μουσοποιὸς ἐνθάδ' 'Ιππῶναξ κεῖται.
εἰ μὲν πονηρός, μὴ προσέρχευ τῷ τύμβῳ·
εἰ δ' ἐσσὶ κρήγυός τε καὶ παρὰ χρηστῶν,
θαρσέων καθίζευ, κἢν θέλῃς ἀπόβριξον.

18.7 σοφῶν ἔοικε z: σωρὸν (γὰρ) εἶχε **m**   χρημάτων **m**

21

Ἀρχίλοχον καὶ στᾶθι καὶ εἴσιδε τὸν πάλαι ποιητάν
τὸν τῶν ἰάμβων, οὗ τὸ μυρίον κλέος
διῆλθε κἠπὶ νύκτα καὶ ποτ' ἀῶ.
ἦ ῥά νιν αἱ Μοῖσαι καὶ ὁ Δάλιος ἠγάπευν Ἀπόλλων,
ὡς ἐμμελής τ' ἐγένετο κἠπιδέξιος   5
ἔπεά τε ποιεῖν πρὸς λύραν τ' ἀείδειν.

22

τὸν τοῦ Ζανὸς ὅδ' ὑμὶν υἱὸν ὡνήρ
τὸν λεοντομάχαν, τὸν ὀξύχειρα,
πρᾶτος τῶν ἐπάνωθε μουσοποιῶν
Πείσανδρος συνέγραψεν οὐκ Καμίρου,
χὥσσους ἐξεπόνασεν εἷπ' ἀέθλους.   5
τοῦτον δ' αὐτὸν ὁ δᾶμος, ὡς σάφ' εἰδῆς,
ἔστασ' ἐνθάδε χάλκεον ποήσας
πολλοῖς μησὶν ὄπισθε κἠνιαυτοῖς.

Commentary

POEM I

The poem is dramatic in form, but in effect an inconspicuous dramatic frame encloses a long description and a long narrative. A goatherd (unnamed) and a shepherd (Thyrsis [19, 65]) receive elaborate compliments from each other, the goatherd on his piping and the shepherd on his singing. The goatherd asks Thyrsis to sing 'the pains of Daphnis' (19) and offers him as a reward a richly carved wooden bowl; this bowl is described at length (27–56). Thyrsis sings the story of the death of Daphnis (64–145) and duly receives the bowl.

All parts of the poem except the description of the bowl abound in the repetitive and symmetrical patterns characteristic of bucolic poetry (**F2**). The richness and generosity of nature are also stressed (6, 8 f., 12 f., 21 ff., 25 f., 46, 58), as in the bucolic world at its most idealized, with a seasoning of down-to-earth rusticity (87 f., 151 f.).

Daphnis dies in eastern Sicily (68 f., 117 f.), and Thyrsis himself comes from the same region (65). But the goatherd's mention of the figs which come from a particular Attic deme (147) argues greater knowledge of the world than one might expect in a Sicilian goatherd, and the 'ferryman' from whom he got the bowl is either 'Kalydonian' or 'Kalydnian' (57 n). Theokritos could make this ferryman what nationality he liked; and, whichever is the right reading, it takes us far from Sicily. If 'Kalydnian' is right, there is a strong probability that the poem was written after Theokritos had come to Kos (**C2**). There is no indication whether we are to regard Thyrsis and the goatherd as belonging, like Daphnis himself, to the legendary past (**G3**).

1 f. ἀδύ . . . μελίσδεται: Lit., 'something pleasant the whispering that pine-tree . . . makes music', i.e. 'sweet is the whispered music which that pine-tree makes'. **καί . . . καί** is superimposed on ἀδύ . . . ἀδὺ δέ, thus:

ἀδύ τι   καὶ ἁ πίτυς   μελίσδεται
ἀδὺ δὲ   καὶ τὺ   συρίσδες

3. συρίσδες: E9(c).5. **Πᾶνα**: G5. **ἆθλον**: It comes naturally to a Greek to put a compliment in terms of competition for prizes; and the context being what it is, Thyrsis thinks of a he-goat, she-goat and kid as prizes.

6. ἔστε κ' ἀμέλξῃς: 'Until you have milked her', i.e. as long as she has not yet grown up to bear a kid herself.

7 f. ἅδιον . . . ὕδωρ: Lit., 'sweeter . . . ⟨is⟩ your song than that . . . water is poured down', i.e. '. . . than the sound of that water which . . .'.

11. τὺ δέ: In sentences of the form 'if *p*, *x*; but if *q*, *y*', δέ, which in clause *q* has a connective force, can be repeated in clause *y* (most commonly with a demonstrative or personal pronoun) without such force.

12. τεῖδε: This invitation to a spot lovingly described is outdone in 21 ff.; cf. v.31 ff., 45 ff., 55 ff., XI.42 ff.

13. ὡς: 'Where', as in v.101, 103; cf. ὧδε = 'here', v.33 al.

14. συρίσδεν: E10(d).

15. οὐ θέμις: i.e. contrary to what is accepted as the rules — sometimes ritual, sometimes moral — which the gods require humans to obey. **τὸ μεσάμβρινον**: During the summer in the Mediterranean people rise early, work late, and rest in the heat of the day (cf. VII.20 f.); their gods do likewise, and resent disturbance.

18. ποτὶ ῥινί: In Herodas 6.37 one woman implores another μὴ δή . . . τὴν χολὴν ἐπὶ ῥινός / ἔχ' εὐθύς, i.e. 'don't lose your temper'. (When Odysseus saw his father weeping [*Od.* xxiv.318 f.] 'bitter strength struck forward along his nostrils', but a sob would be more appropriate to that context than anger).

19 ff. ἀλλά . . . ἐσδώμεθα: 'But, *since* you . . . , let us . . .'.
Δάφνιδος: G3. **ἀείδες**: Cf. 3 n. **βουκολικᾶς**: G.2. **ἐπὶ τὸ πλέον ἵκεο**: Lit., 'came to the ⟨point⟩ in excess ⟨of others⟩

of bucolic song', i.e. 'have attained distinction' (or 'mastery') 'in . . .'. Cf. III.47.

21. Πριήπω: G5.

24. Λιβύαθε: Libya was traditionally famous for its flocks (*Od.* iv.85 f., 'Libya, where the lambs grow horns at once'; cf. III.5); which is not the same as saying that its flocks were good in Theokritos's time.

25. ἐς τρίς: =τρίς; cf. II.43.

26. ποταμέλγεται: The point of ποτ- is 'in addition'; even after her two kids are fed, her owner can still get two pails of milk from her.

27. κισσύβιον: In *Od.* ix.346 Odysseus offers the Cyclops a κισσύβιον full of wine, and in *Od.* xvi.52 Eumaios mixes wine in a κισσύβιον; in *Od.* xiv.112 he hands Odysseus a σκύφος full of wine; these passages suggest that a κισσύβιον is larger and deeper than a σκύφος. But below (143) Thyrsis uses the word σκύφος of the κισσύβιον which the goatherd offers him, and he proposes (143 f., cf. 151) to milk the goat into it. In the Classical period κισσύβιον seems to have been interpreted as a deep bowl of ivy-wood, primarily for milk; so in Eur. fr. 146.1 a shepherd has an ivy-wood bowl (κίσσινον σκύφος) of milk, and Euripides' Cyclops (*Cy.* 390) drinks from a vast σκύφος κισσοῦ. Neither Euripides nor anyone since who has repeated this interpretation can have given much thought to the practical problem of making a capacious vessel out of ivy-wood (though Nikandros [fr. 1] was not satisfied, and offered a more recherché explanation). If the word κισσύβιον has anything at all to do with ivy, it may refer to a common decorative motif (29 f.). **κηρῷ:** To reduce permeability in a wooden vessel.

29–63. The long description of the carving on the bowl is a major component of this poem, such as we do not find in the other bucolic poems. Descriptions of this kind have a distinguished ancestry in Greek poetry, beginning with the shield of Achilles in *Il.* xviii.478 ff. and the shield of Herakles in the Hesiodic poem named after it, 139 ff.; cf. Epicharmos fr. 79, and also Eur. *Ion* 184 ff., where the chorus of Athenian women admires the sculptures of Delphi. Theokritos avoids the monotonous catalogue-technique of the epic exemplars (ἐν δέ ... τέτυκτο, ἐν δ' ἔσαν, etc.), and the subjects chosen by an artist as appropriate to a countryman's bowl are naturally different from those on a warlike hero's shield, where even the peaceful scenes — weddings, festivities, reapers, wine-treaders, litigation — are on a grander scale than the highly particularized vignettes on Theokritos's bowl. In the Hellenistic age we find Jason's robe described by Apollonios (i.730 ff.), and Europa's basket in Moschos, *Europa* 43 ff. The women in Herodas 4.27 ff., 57 ff., admire the dedications in a sanctuary of Asklepios; and many epigrams are ostensibly inspired by striking works of art.

We appear to be told that three scenes (32 ff., 39 ff., 45 ff.) are carved *inside* (ἔντοσθεν, 32) the vessel; the outside, therefore, is either blank below the rim (29) and between the handles (28) or decorated solely with an akanthos-motif (55). This is an odd bit of work, extraordinarily difficult to execute (the vessel is deep [27]) and very disagreeable to use for milk; even Greek standards of hygiene and washing-up might have been affronted by it. Either, therefore, ἔντοσθεν means 'within the area bounded by the rim', i.e. '*below*' (cf. Thuc. i.16, 'within the River Halys' = 'west of the Halys'), or Theokritos visualized the akanthos (which he has not yet mentioned) as round the base of the vessel, so that ἔντοσθεν means '*between* ⟨the rim-pattern and the base-pattern⟩' (A. M. Dale, *CR* N.s. ii [1952], 129 ff.). Either translation makes the description methodical: rim, main surface, base. If we object that 'inside' (32) and 'everywhere' (55) are misleading, we should reflect that Theokritos was describing a type of design familiar to him and to his readers, and could hardly foresee our perplexity. The fact that there are three scenes on a two-handled cup is a further oddity, if we are to imagine the handles as set low. We do however possess Hellenistic and Roman metal vessels which have on their exterior a continuous frieze of moulded figures or even a trio of scenes (S. Nicosia, *Teocrito e l'Arte*

Figurata [Palermo, 1968], 30); the most striking examples are pails or single-handled cups, but there is no reason why the same type of exterior should not be designed for the very high setting of a pair of handles. It is no doubt a metal vessel of which Theokritos has a mental picture; but he has put together a summary description of a rustic wooden vessel and a very full description of a much more elaborate and expensive metal cup (Nicosia, 27 f.).

30 f. ἐλιχρύσῳ . . . κροκόεντι: ἐλίχρυσος is not always the grey-leafed, yellow-flowered 'helichrysum', but (according to the Suda) also the ivy-flower. κεκονιμένος, lit, 'dusted', is here presumably 'spotted', since in Greek ivy-motifs the flowers or fruit are represented as clusters of round spots alternating with the leaves. Lit., 'and the ⟨ivy-⟩tendril is wound along it' (*sc.* the ivy) seems odd, but (if the text is sound) must mean that the κισσός is thought of as the pattern of leaves. For ἕλιξ cf. Ar. *Thesm.* 999 f. κισσὸς εὐπέταλος ἕλικι θάλλει.

32. γυνά . . .τέτυκται: Lit., 'a woman is depicted ⟨as⟩ a-sort-of . . .', i.e. 'the woman depicted there is, one might say, . . .'. Punctuation before the postpositive τι, making τι θεῶν δαίδαλμα a phrase in apposition, is to be avoided. **θεῶν:** Cf. xv.79.

33 ff. The alternation of the suitors' contest and of the woman's inclination cannot be shown in a carving, but in interpreting the static scene, as well as in the inference to the woman's state of mind, Theokritos is following (and exaggerating) Homeric precedent: on the shield of Achilles litigants speak in turn (*Il.* xviii.506) and ploughmen stop for refreshment and then resume their ploughing (*ibid.* 544 ff.).

36. γέλαισα: < *γέλα-νσα, Attic γελῶσα (< *γελά-ουσα); cf. Ε10(*e*).

38. ἐτώσια μοχθίζοντι: Cf. vii.48.

39. τοῖς δὲ μέτα: 'And with them'; cf. 91. **τέτυκται:** The subject of a singular verb can often be a pair of singulars.

41. κάμνοντι . . . ἐοικώς: The phrase owes something to the description of the fisherman on the shield of Herakles

(Hes. *Sc.* 212 ff.), ἀπορρίψοντι ἐοικώς. **τὸ κάρτερον**: =καρτερῶς; cf. III.3, 18, Herodas 1.54 πλουτέων τὸ καλόν.

42. =φαίης κέν νιν ἐλλοπιεύειν ὅσον σθένος ἐστὶ τῶν γυίων: cf. (e.g.) *Il.* iii.220 φαίης κεν ζάκοτόν τε τιν' ἔμμεναι κτλ. We would say, 'with all the strength . . .'; cf. Ap. Rh. ii.591 ἐμβαλέειν κώπῃσιν ὅσον σθένος.

45. τυτθὸν δ' ὅσσον ἄπωθεν: Lit., '⟨it is⟩ a small amount, how much distant . . .', i.e. 'and close by . . .'. Cf. Hdt. iv.194 οἱ δέ σφι ἄφθονοι ὅσοι ἐν τοῖς ὄρεσι γίνονται.

46. καλόν: Cf. 34.

48. δύ' ἀλώπεκες ἁ μέν . . . ἁ δέ: Not exactly, '⟨there are⟩ two foxes; one . . . and the other . . .', but 'one of two foxes . . . , and the other . . .'. Cf. *Od.* vii.129 δύω κρῆναι ἡ μέν τε . . . σκίδναται, ἡ δέ . . . ἵησι.

49. τὰν τρώξιμον: Ellipse of a noun is common (cf. v.61 τὰν σαυτῶ πατέων, sc. ὁδόν), and there are some expressions (e.g. διὰ κενῆς) in which we cannot be sure what the noun would be if it were there; here probably σταφυλή, 'clusters of grapes' (collective singular, as in documents of the period).

50 f. οὐ πρίν . . . καθίξῃ: For the element of interpretation in the description of the scene cf. 33 n. '. . . that she won't give up' (or 'leave him alone'; either is possible) 'until . . .', and then comes the difficulty. 'Until she has caused him to sit breakfasted on dry ⟨food⟩' — having stolen his figs, cheese, or whatever he had to go with his bread? If ἀκράτιστον is what Theokritos wrote, it must mean 'having breakfasted' (ἀκρᾱτίζεσθαι = 'have breakfast'). No other such relationship between (positive) -ιστος and (middle) -ίζεσθαι is known, but it may be that the adjective was brought into existence by its purely formal resemblance to the numerous adjectives in -τος (including -ιστος) which begin with negative ἀ- (e.g. Ar. *Wasps* 752 τίς ἀψήφιστος, 'Who hasn't voted?'). Σ may have known of a variant ἀκρατισμόν (or -μῶ), 'breakfast', but no one has found it easy to say what ἐπὶ ξηροῖσι καθίξῃ means if its object is the boy's breakfast. **φατί**: 'Thinks'; in φάναι and φάσθαι the distinction between speaking one's thoughts aloud and thinking them silently is not important. Cf. II.130.

52. ἀκριδοθήκαν: 'Grasshopper-cage', made by treating asphodel-stems and rushes as weft and warp; σχοίνῳ is collective (cf. 49 n.), not '*a* rush' (ctr. Hdt. IV.190 ἀνθερίκων ἐνειρμένων περὶ σχοίνους). The variant ἀκριδοθήραν, 'grasshopper-trap', is unattractive; the easiest way to catch grasshoppers is simply to walk into the grass and pounce on them (catching cicadas [cf. V.111 n.] is a different matter). Admittedly γαλεάγρα, 'weasel-trap', comes to mean also 'weasel-cage', but one *can* bait a cage-like trap for weasels and similar creatures. ἀκρίδες could be held in captivity for long periods; Leonidas (*HE*) 21, Mnasalkes (*HE*) 12, 13, Nikias (*HE*) 14 are epitaphs on pet ἀκρίδες.

55. παντᾷ: 'Everywhere', 'this way and that', round the base.

56. αἰπολικὸν θάημα: Lit., 'a spectacle characteristic of goatherds'; Theokritos is making the point that his idealised pastoral world has much to teach us in the craft of carving, as in poetry (**G8**). There was an ancient variant αἰολικόν, 'Aeolian', but if Theokritos wrote that we do not know what he had in mind. Σ (followed by Hesychios) says (guessing?) that αἰολικός can = αἰόλος.

57. πορθμῆϊ Καλυδνίῳ: This associates the scene with Kos, since the island of Kalydna (Kalymos) lies north-west from Kos. The variant πορθμεῖ Καλυδωνίῳ dissociates the ferryman from any of Theokritos's favoured localities, since Kalydon lies at the western end of the Corinthian Gulf. It would, however, be wrong to suppose that a πορθμεύς is necessarily a 'ferryman' operating across a narrow expanse of water; in Hdt. i.24.3 the crew of a ship hired to take Arion from South Italy to Corinth are πορθμεῖς.

58. ὦνον: '⟨As the⟩ price of it I gave . . .' or 'For it I gave . . . ⟨as the⟩ price . . .'.

59. ποτὶ χεῖλος ἐμὸν θίγεν: Since in the few examples found elsewhere προσθιγγάνειν takes a genitive, it can be argued that χεῖλος ἐμόν is the subject of ποτί + θίγεν; but this seems unnatural.

61. τόν . . . ὕμνον: '*That* . . . song'; the goatherd has heard it, or songs on the same subject, from Thyrsis before (19).

62 f. τὰν γάρ ... φυλαξεῖς: The point is similar to 'you can't take it with you' (XVI.40 ff., 59) or 'gather ye rosebuds while ye may'.

63. ἐκλελαθόντα: Cf. *Il.* ii. 599 f., where the Muses ἐκλέλαθον the lyre-playing of Thamyris, i.e. made him forget how to do it.

64–145. The song of Thyrsis is formally characterized by three successive refrains, 'lead the way (ἄρχετε), beloved Muses, lead the way in bucolic song', 'lead, Muses, lead again in bucolic song', and 'come to an end (λήγετε), Muses, now come to an end of bucolic song'. The manuscript tradition is far from unanimous on the points at which we pass from the first refrain to the second and from the second to the third, and the content of the story does not make it easy to decide. Since the song begins, but does not end, with a refrain, it seems that the refrain is felt as an introduction to the verse which follows it, not as rounding off those which have preceded it; and this fact suggests that 94 is the right place for the introduction of the second refrain, introducing the entry of Aphrodite. We might also suspect that the third refrain began at 114, immediately before Daphnis begins his farewells. (Note that the use of refrains in II is quite different; and on refrains in general, cf. **F3**).

The song describes the death of Daphnis; *why* he dies, emerges little by little, but never emerges fully; and *how* he dies at the end is veiled in a curious ambiguity. We are told (66, 82) that he 'wasted away', a term applicable to disease, hunger, jealousy (V.12) or unsatisfied love (II.29, 83). Hermes, the first to visit him, assumes (77 f.) that the trouble is unsatisfied love. One might think, *unrequited* love; but Priapos strikes a new note by revealing that 'the girl' is searching for Daphnis everywhere (82 ff.) and that Daphnis yearns to be 'dancing with the girls' although this is impossible for him (85 ff.). Why is it impossible, and why does Daphnis flee from a girl who seeks him? Hardly (as suggested by E. A. Schmidt, *Hermes* xcvi [1968], 539 ff.) because he is so much in love that he does not know what he is doing. We may suspect that he has been punished for some offence against a god and has become impotent; in which case there is no point in the encouragement offered by Priapos, unless the reader is expected to know what Priapos and Hermes do not. Or he has been threatened by a god with punishment if he has sexual relations with the girl mentioned in 82, or with any girl; again, if that is so, Hermes and Priapos do not know it. Or he has boasted (cf. Hippolytos) that he is immune from Eros, has perhaps even taken a vow of chastity, and fears terrible punishment if he breaks his oath. We may hope for some enlightenment later in the song, but we should pause for a moment to put ourselves into the position of a reader, well educated in poetry and mythology, in Theokritos's own time. The poet writes as if he presupposed *some* knowledge of *some* story about Daphnis, as in VII.73 ff., where it is said that Daphnis 'fell in love with Xenea' (who she was, is explained neither there nor anywhere else in Theokritos), 'and the oak-trees sang his dirge while he wasted away like the snow on the mountains'; but this is not quite the same as saying that the poet really expects the reader to know (cf. G3, H1[d]). According to the Daphnis legend attributed by a late writer to Timaios, a Sicilian and an older contemporary of Theokritos, a nymph fell in love with Daphnis (who led a solitary life in the wilds) and threatened that if he ever had intercourse with a mortal woman she would blind him; a king's daughter made him drunk and seduced him, whereupon the nymph carried out her threat. Diodoros iv.84.4, pretty certainly based on Timaios (Diodoros's usual source for the legends and history of the Greeks of the West), adds the detail that Daphnis was a companion of Artemis; and this reminds us of Hippolytos, whose devotion to Artemis manifested itself in his chaste hostility to Aphrodite. The story told by Aelian, which he may have regarded as going back, at least in part, to Stesichoros (cf. G9), is slightly different in suggesting that Daphnis's misfortune was not indiscriminate chastity (as in the case of Hippolytos) but a vow of fidelity to the nymph.

So far there is an obvious general affinity of Theokritos's
story with earlier stories, but no obvious identity with any
one earlier story. The words of Aphrodite (97 f.) take us
further, because they make it plain that Daphnis has
himself vowed to resist Love; so does his reply (103); and if
we take his scornful references to Aphrodite's own love-
affairs (105 ff.) in conjunction with Priapos's implication
(91) that Daphnis is in some way unable to 'dance with the
girls', it seems that Daphnis is the stubborn victim of his
own boast that he could easily resist all sexual temptation.

But what does he die of? People who 'waste away' through
unrequited love or through resistance to a consuming
passion may end by hanging themselves or throwing them-
selves down cliffs or into rivers (in despair or preoccupation),
but they do not as a rule simply die of their physical
condition. Daphnis, on the other hand, is quite sure that he
is dying (103, 115 ff., 130, 135), and he is right. The words
describing the moment of his death are (140 f.) 'Daphnis
went to the stream, and the eddy washed him who was dear
to the Muses . . .'. If this means that he went to Acheron,
the river which the souls of the dead cross, the concept is
traditional and the language in part also traditional (cf.
Alkaios fr. 38.8 δινάεντ' 'Αχέροντ' ἐπέραισε, Ap. Rh. i.646 f.
ἀποιχομένου [sc. εἰς] 'Αχέροντος δίνας, ii.355 δινήεις τ' 'Αχέρων),
but 'the stream' = 'Acheron' is uniquely allusive. It has been
argued (R. M. Ogilvie, *JHS* lxxxii [1962], 106 ff.) that
Daphnis in fact was drowned (in the 'stream of Anapos'
mentioned at the beginning of the song [68]), i.e. that he
drowned himself under the supernatural impulse of the
nymph who demanded his fidelity. The chief objection to
this interpretation is that we are given a strong impression
in the preceding words (138 f., 'Aphrodite wanted to raise
him up') that Daphnis had become too weak to move;
a further objection is that 66 ff., 'Where were you, Nymphs
. . .?', implying 'If only you had been there, you could
have saved him', and 141, 'him who was not displeasing
to the Nymphs', are peculiarly misleading if in fact a
nymph encompassed Daphnis's death. Despite all the diffi-

culties, it seems to me that Theokritos intends us to envisage Daphnis as starving himself to death, and does not intend us to recall or infer any more of the story than the song itself progressively reveals. Σ is unable to point to any other writer's version of the Daphnis legend which exactly fits this song.

65. καὶ Θύρσιδος ἀδέα φωνά: Not 'and it' (*sc.* the voice singing) 'is the sweet voice of Thyrsis', but 'and the voice of Thyrsis is sweet'. Cf. Theognis 22 f. 'and everyone will say, "The verses are by Theognis of Megara, and ⟨he is⟩ famous throughout mankind"'. For ἀδέα = ἡδεῖα cf. III.20 ἀδέα τέρψις, the Homeric ὠκέα Ἶρις and Epicharmos 63.2 ἀδέαι δ' ἐν τῷ θέρει.

66. πᾷ ποκ' ἄρ' ἦσθ': (ἦσθ' = ἦστε = ἦτε). The point is 'Why did you not save him?' And since deities, though they can hear an appeal from afar (123 ff. n.), cannot be in two places at once, Thyrsis assumes that they failed to save Daphnis because they were somewhere else — rather as Poseidon's absence among the Ethiopians enables the gods in *Od.* i.22 ff. to consider Odysseus's fortunes favourably. Whereas the Greeks usually regard nymphs as extremely localized minor divinities, Theokritos here elevates them to the status of goddesses who can roam the world; cf. VII.148 n.

67. Πηνειῶ ... Πίνδω: Theokritos looks away from Sicily to remote parts of Greece; the Pindos range occupies the centre of northern Greece, including the innermost parts of Thessaly, and the river Peneios rises in the northern part of the range, flowing into the sea south of Mt. Olympos.

68. 'Ανάπω: The Anapos flows into the great harbour of Syracuse.

69. "Ακιδος: The Akis flows into the sea on the east coast of Sicily, south of Mt. Etna.

72. λέων: Sicilian lions, even in antiquity, do not belong to the real world, but the lion is as familiar in fables as in Homeric similes; cf. Leonidas (*HE*) 49, 53, on lions and herdsmen. **θανόντα:** 'Dead', not 'dying'; this couplet makes it clear that Daphnis's 'wasting away' ended in death, and after thus looking ahead we return in 74 to the scene preceding his death.

78. ἔρασαι: For -ρᾱ- cf. II.149 Δέλφις ἔρᾱται: outside Theokritos we find ἐρῶ (< ἐράω), ἔρᾰμαι and ἐρῶμαι (< ἐράομαι), but never ἔρᾱμαι; in Sappho fr. 16.3 f. ὅττω τις ἔρᾱται the verb is almost certainly subjunctive, but Theokritos may have thought it was indicative.

82. ἀ δέ τυ κώρα: The insertion of an enclitic pronoun object between article and noun is normal in Ionic with οἱ, σφι, etc., but otherwise rare.

85. ζάτεισ': Eιο(e), and cf. 36 n. It is a common and effective device in epic to introduce a new and important element at the beginning of a line, with a pause immediately following, e.g. *Od.* i.7 f. ὄλοντο | νήπιοι, οἳ κτλ. Here the effect is greatly strengthened by the interposition of the refrain. **δύσερως**: One uses this word of a person whose relationship to ἔρως evokes an adverse emotional or intellectual reaction in oneself, and the reaction may be one of pity, resentment, revulsion or fear (selfish or disinterested); in VI.7 Galateia calls Polyphemos δύσερως because he is backward in responding to her advances. **τις**: It is not always possible to be sure what tone is imparted by τις, any more than we could say with confidence whether 'You're a difficult sort of person' or 'You're one of those difficult people' is more or less discourteous than 'You're difficult'.

86. ἔοικας: What follows is an elaborate 'likeness' (εἰκών, εἰκάζειν), a common form of Greek wit, often exploited by Aristophanes (e.g. *Birds* 803 ff.). It has a certain affinity with the riddle-form, 'Why is X like Y? Because . . .'.

87 ff.: F2.

92 f. τόν . . . ἔρωτα: This at last confirms that Daphnis *is* in love; hitherto we have only had the assumptions of Hermes and Priapos to go on.

95. ἀδεῖα: The sense we want is not 'smiling agreeably' but 'laughing with enjoyment'; Homer's Greeks often ἡδὺ γέλασσαν at the discomfiture of others (e.g. *Il.* ii.270), and Aphrodite in *H. Hom.* 5.49 boasts of her powers ἡδὺ γελοιήσασα. This means that ἀδεῖα must be a neuter plural; cf. Hes. *Sc.* 348 ὀξεῖα χρέμισαν.

96. λάθρη . . . ἀνέχοισα: For the connective μέν — 'that is to say' — cf. Ap. Rh. i.90 Αἰακίδαι μετεκίαθον, οὐ μὲν ἄμ' ἄμφω, κτλ. If we laugh λάθρη, others do not see that we are laughing. Aphrodite therefore comes to Daphnis with a straight face (as Klytaimestra in Aisch. *Cho.* 738 'hides laughter inside her eyes') and keeps to herself the emotions of pleasure and malice which incline her to laughter. She 'holds up' grief (cf. Kallim. *H.* 6.80 βαρύθυμος . . . δακρύοισα) as one raises a sign for others to see (cf. Thuc. iv.111.2 τὸ σημεῖον τοῦ πυρός . . . ἀνέσχον). This is the interpretation of G. Zuntz, *CQ* N.S. x (1960), 37 ff., and it is in keeping with Aphrodite's pretended mood of sympathy that she should use the highly derogatory word ἀργαλέος of Love in 98. Daphnis sees through her, as his angry words show.

97 f. In the Hellenistic poets (XIX, and especially Ap. Rh. iii) Eros is the son of Aphrodite; he is not so in earlier literature (with the possible exception of Sappho, on whom the evidence [fr. 198] is conflicting), but at times her minister, more commonly an independent but kindred power. The province of Aphrodite is love in the sense which it bears in our expression 'make love', and τὰ ἀφροδίσια is a common term for heterosexual or homosexual intercourse, including marital intercourse. Eros is the personification of love in the sense which it bears in our expressions 'fall in love' and 'be in love'. The distinction is blurred by all the speakers in Plato's *Symposium* except Aristophanes, and was no doubt commonly blurred by the Greeks; Prodikos (DK) fr. B7 defined ἔρως as 'desire doubled'.

100 f. Κύπρι . . . ἀπεχθής: The 'rising trikolon', in which the second element is longer than the first and the third longer than the second, is a recurrent phenomenon in Greek poetry, first in *Il.* i.145 ἢ Αἴας ἢ Ἰδομενεὺς ἢ δῖος Ὀδυσσεύς. Cf. 115.

102. The point is not 'Do you think I'm as good as dead?', because he is, and he knows it, but 'Do you think I'm *beaten*?' The next line declares that he is not. γάρ means 'No' (with reference to 98), ⟨you are wrong in thinking . . .⟩. Cf. the peroration of Philip V of Macedon in Livy xxxix.

26.9: *elatus deinde ira adiecit, nondum omnium dierum solem occidisse* — an utterance which (*minaciter dictum*) caused a stir.

103. He will be a 'pain' to Love because he will not have conceded victory by accepting the natural consequence of falling in love. The notion of maintaining enmity even after death goes back to *Od.* xi.541 ff., where the ghost of Ajax will not speak to Odysseus; cf. also the threat of Chalkiope in Ap. Rh. iii.703 f. ἦ σοί γε . . . εἴην ἐξ 'Αΐδεω στυγερὴ μετόπισθεν 'Ερινύς, and Leonidas (*HE*) 58.5 f. **κἠν 'Αΐδα:** 'Even in ⟨the house⟩ of Hades'; Hades is a person, not a place. ἐν and εἰς often take a genitive (e.g. VII.131, XXIV.82), as in the English 'to Joe's', 'to my brother's', etc.

105 f. οὐ λέγεται . . . ποτ' 'Αγχίσαν: The 'cowherd' is the Trojan Anchises (hence the reference to Mt. Ida), by whom Aphrodite became the mother of Aineias; the story is told in the Homeric Hymn to Aphrodite. Daphnis leaves unspoken the infinitive dependent on λέγεται, as if he had in mind a coarse word for sexual intercourse but disdained to utter it. Omission of the verb (though not for reasons of propriety) is common in proverbs.

106 f. τηνεί . . . μέλισσαι: The manuscripts have τηνεί δρύες, ὧδε κύπειρος, / ὧδε κτλ., i.e. '*there* (sc. on Ida) there are oaks, ⟨but⟩ *here* there is galingale, *here* bees . . .', as in v.45 f., 'I won't come over there; *there* (τουτεί) there are oaks, *here* (ὧδε) galingale, *here* (ὧδε) bees . . .'. But a Latin translation of a lost work of Plutarch shows that Plutarch used a text which meant '. . . *and* galingale, *and* bees . . .'; hence Meineke's emendation to ἠδὲ κύπειρος, / αἰ δὲ κτλ. It would in any case be hard to see any point, in this context, in drawing a distinction between Ida and Daphnis's own locality; and the corruption can be explained as deliberate assimilation to v.45 f. Daphnis appears to be praising Ida (in terms characteristic of bucolic poetry) as a way of saying 'Why don't you leave me alone? You'd like Ida much better'. But the third element, the bees, suddenly introduces a malicious point, in Plutarch's view: there was a traditional belief that bees sting adulterers.

109 f. ὡραῖος . . . διώκει: Adonis, with whom Aphrodite

was in love, was killed by a boar; cf. xv.100–144. Daphnis calls him ὡραῖος (i.e. at the stage of life which is most desirable sexually [150 n.]) because (ἐπεί), in addition to herding flocks and killing hares, he 'chases beasts of all kinds', an occupation typical of healthy young men (ctr. v.107 n.). Daphnis speaks with malevolent 'innocence', to hurt Aphrodite, as if Adonis had not yet met his death in the course of hunting beasts.

112 f. αὖτις . . . μάχευ μοι: The third insult refers to the encounter of Aphrodite with Diomedes when she intervened in the fighting at Troy; he wounded her, and she fled wailing from the field, pursued by his taunts (*Il.* v.318 ff.). **ὅπως:** ὅπως with the future commonly means 'Mind you . . . !', but here rather 'Why don't you . . .?' **ἀλλά:** 'Come', 'come on!'

115 ff. Cf. the long farewell of the abducted Philoktetes to his familiar island scenery in Soph. *Phil.* 936 ff.; there, as here, a 'rising trikolon' (cf. 100 f. n.).

117 f. χαῖρ' . . . ὕδωρ: The references accord with those of 68 f. Arethusa is the perpetual spring which rises in the city of Syracuse. The name 'Thybris' is associated with Sicily in several late references, but both its location and its nature are obscure to us; here ('down Thybris', 'down from Thybris') it sounds like a valley or a mountainside.

123 ff. ὦ Πάν . . . ἀγητόν: Greek invocation often takes the form 'Whether you are in . . . or at . . . . , *come* . . .!' Cf. Orestes' cry to Athena, Aisch. *Eum.* 292 ff. 'Whether she is in Libya or on the Phlegraean plain . . . may she come . . .!' (cf. also 66 n. above). Pan is naturally the deity to whom Daphnis feels himself closest (**95**). **Λυκαίω:** Lykaion was a mountain of Arkadia, a region traditionally associated with Pan, 'ruler of Arkadia' in Pindar fr. 95.1 and twin brother of Arkas in Epimenides (DK) B 16. **τύγ':** Although γε commonly emphasizes a pronoun, it is wholly unemphatic when it accompanies a pronoun inserted with the second member of a disjunction, as here (εἴτε . . . εἴτε τύ γε); cf. Theognis 559 f. ὥστε σε μήτε . . . ἀφνεὸν . . . γενέσθαι μήτε σέ γ' ἐς . . . χρημοσύνην ἐλάσαι. **Μαίναλον:** Mainalos too

is an Arkadian city; and the nearby mountain Mainalion
was above all the place of Pan (cf. Kallim. *H.* 3.88 f.,
where it is the scene of Pan's hunting), 'where the local
people say you can hear him piping' (Paus. viii.36.8).
Σικελάν: 'Sicilian', applying to the whole island, not (as
commonly in earlier writers), 'Sikel', applying to one
particular (non-Greek) people. Ἑλίκας . . . Λυκαονίδαο:
Helike was daughter of Lykaon; and Arkas was the son of
Kallisto, a daughter of Lykaon. Since Paus. viii.35.8
describes a 'tomb of Kallisto' as a high barrow covered with
trees, and .(36.8) that of Arkas as being on Mainalion, it
seems that Theokritos is identifying Kallisto with Helike.

128 f. πακτοῖο . . . σύριγγα: A syrinx is made by glueing
reeds together with wax, binding them round, and stopping
the pipes with wax to give different notes. Lit., 'honey-
breathing from put-together wax' may refer to smell (cf.
28, 149), not sound, for the wax stoppings on which the
music of the syrinx depends are πηκτός only in the sense that
any cold wax can be called so.

129. καλόν . . . ἑλίκταν: Lit., 'well wound about the lip',
a reference to the binding round the mouth-end of the syrinx.

130. ἐς Ἄιδαν: D2(*b*).

132 ff. The effect of a catalogue is alleviated by unsys-
tematic order: 'May A and B and C happen, may every-
thing be reversed, and may D happen, since Daphnis is
dying, and may E and F happen' instead of 'May A and B
and C and D and E and F happen . . .'. (cf. Ar. *Frogs* 613 f.
'if I ever came here, I'm willing to be executed, or ⟨if⟩ I
ever stole . . .). The idea that the order of nature will be
reversed because something unnatural has happened is
traditional; cf. Archil. (D³) fr. 74.6, 'Let no one now be
amazed even if beasts and dolphins change places', Hdt.
v.92.*a*.1, 'Earth and sky, men and fish, will change places
now that you Spartans are preparing to establish a tyranny'.
A *wish* that the order of nature may be reversed is not
significantly different. (Note, however, that in Verg. *Ecl.*
3. 88–91 the point *is* quite different). Why Daphnis should
regard his own death in this extravagant light (he is *not*

saying simply that all nature should become ugly with mourning) is not altogether clear. Possibly Sicilian folklore and local cults commonly treated him as an immortal spirit manifested in the lives of wild flora and fauna, and Theokritos has taken this concept for granted.

136. κἠξ ὀρέων: The little scops owl of the Mediterranean lives close to man, the nightingale in lowland woods. That either of them should move to the mountains is not a very striking reversal of nature, compared with what has gone before, but I think we must accept that to Theokritos, for some personal reasons not known to us, it seemed so. **γαρύσαιντο**: We should expect 'outdo' or 'surpass'; even 'cry in competition with . . .' (cf. v.29, vii.47) would fall short of a reversal of nature, since in a sense the scops owl *does* 'compete with' the nightingale. Unless the text is corrupt, it seems that to Theokritos γηρύομαί σοι implies that you listen to me with silent admiration and respect; the reversal of nature will then be that the nightingale falls silent to listen to the owl's cries.

138 f. τὸν δ' ... ἀνορθῶσαι: If he dies, it is a hollow victory for Aphrodite, for he will have kept his vow; that is why she wants to save his life, hoping that he may yet surrender.

139. λίνα: The idea that a thread spun by the Fates is coexistent with each human life is Homeric (e.g. *Il.* xx.127 f.) and recurrent. **λελοίπει**: Cf. *Od.* xiv.213 νῦν δ' ἤδη πάντα λέλοιπεν, 'but by now everything has run out'.

140. ἐκ Μοιρᾶν: ἐκ indicates, as it were, the supernatural authority by which an event happens; cf. ii.40 ['30'].

ἔβα ῥόον: Cf. p. 85. There is no parallel for the interpretation 'went ⟨down⟩stream' = 'perished'; Eur. *Herc. Fur.* 650 f. κατὰ κυμάτων ἔρροι (*sc.* τὸ γῆρας) is not close enough. **ἔκλυσε**: 'Washed', not 'engulfed' (cf. 27 and the harbour, κλυζομένῳ ἴκελος, depicted on the shield of Herakles, Hes. *Sc.* 209); the souls of the dead were not submerged in Acheron, but waited at the water's edge to be ferried across (xvii.46 ff., Aisch. *Sept.* 854 ff.).

141. For the form of the line cf. xiii.7, xv.86.

144. σπείσω: The pouring of a libation is one of the commonest ways in which a Greek symbolically shares what he has with his gods.

144 f. ὦ χαίρετε ... ᾀσῶ: This cry, which does not accompany the libation (for Thyrsis does not get the bowl until 149, let alone milk the goat), gives the song an ending rather like that of a traditional hymn; both the Homeric hymns and those of Kallimachos end by addressing the god with χαῖρε, and cf. xxii.214. It adds a promise implying a prayer such as we find in an Athenian dedication (*IG* i².650), 'May you rejoice in the statue and grant him to dedicate another' or in Aigisthos's prayer (Eur. *El.* 805), '⟨I pray that I may⟩ often sacrifice ⟨to you⟩'. Cf. vii.155 f. n., xv. 149.

146. μέλιτος: A mouth *full* of honey sounds rather sickening; cf. the excessive physiological realism of iii.54. For the application of the metaphors 'honey' and 'nectar' to song and poetry cf. vii.82 n.

147. ἀπ' Αἰγίλω: The phrase serves as an adjective qualifying ἰσχάδα. The figs of the Attic deme Aigilia were famous; Aigilos, the eponymous hero of the deme, is treated here virtually as a place-name.

148. τέττιγος: The cicada is the singer *par excellence*; Sokrates in Pl. *Phdr.* 259B ff. tells a story that cicadas were once upon a time men who took such delight in singing that the Muses turned them into creatures who would do nothing else.

150. Ὡρᾶν: The 'Hours' are the personification of those stages in the life of creatures and plants which attract us by their beauty (Pi. *Nem.* 8.1 addresses Ὥρα as 'herald of Aphrodite'); they can therefore be regarded as the supernatural powers who actually *confer* beauty of this kind (cf. p. 217). The 'spring of the Hours' is probably an invention of Theokritos.

151. Κισσαίθα: A good name for a goat, since goats differ from other animals in their appetite for ivy (κισσός). **αἱ δὲ χίμαιραι**: The article is not uncommon in peremptory orders; cf. iv.45 f. and Ar. *Frogs* 521 ὁ παῖς ἀκολούθει δεῦρο τὰ σκεύη φέρων.

POEM II

A girl, Simaitha by name (101; as in **Old Comedy**, we get to know the character long before we are told the name), is trying by means of magic to recapture the love of a young man (Delphis; 21, etc.) who has apparently grown tired of her. She is accompanied by a slave (Thestylis; 1), who has no speaking part in the poem. Her spells are addressed to Hekate, and the magic is performed by moonlight; when she has sent off Thestylis to put some magical material on Delphis's house (64) she tells the Moon the whole story of her love-affair.

The poem is a dramatic monologue, but not exactly a soliloquy, for it is addressed to the supernatural powers which Simaitha invokes. The first part of is it enlivened by the direction of orders and abuse at the slave; the slave's departure is a dramatic contrivance which opens the way for Simaitha's exposure of her innermost thoughts and feelings to the Moon. The casting of the spells is begun, ended and punctuated by a refrain, 'Magic wheel, bring that man to my house!', by which the first part of the poem is divided into quatrains (cf. 61 n.). The use of refrains, though not unknown in ancient magic, is not specially characteristic of it, and it is probable that its use by Theokritos here is the artistic equivalent, already favoured in his bucolic poetry, of the monotonous repetitions of words and phrases which actually characterize magical spells (**F3**). The story which Simaitha tells to the Moon is also divided into sets of five verses by a different refrain, 'Mark, mistress Moon, whence came my love!' This refrain reflects the formal influence of the spell on the narrative, and it is interesting that at the emotional climax (138-143), whereafter the story descends into darkness and melancholy, the refrain is dropped.

The strength of Simaitha's emotion is reflected in the adjectives which intrude into, and colour, her factual statements: 4 τάλας, 6 ἀνάρσιος, 35 ['40'] τάλαιναν, 83 δειλαίας,

66 τάλαιναν; 72 ἁ μεγάλοιτος, 112 ὡστοργος, 138 ἁ ταχυπειθής. As in the bucolic poems, much of the vocabulary is prosaic and the sentence-structure simple, but permeated with epicisms (e.g. 20 τέτυγμαι, and cf. 29 ['34'] and 124 nn.). Since nearly all that Simaitha says is addressed to goddesses, and part of it serves a magical purpose, the intrusion of poetic language, characteristic of ritual utterance, is much less incongruous than in the conversation of herdsmen. The elaborate imagery of Simaitha's farewell to the Moon (165 f.) reminds us of hymns; so do the rhetorical questions at the beginning of her narrative (64 f.), with which we may compare xxii.23 ff. and *H. Hom.* 3. 207 ff., 'How shall I hymn you? Shall I sing of your triumphs in love? . . . Or of how you went to seek an oracle . . . ?' Highly poetic language also intrudes in 147 f., 'today, when her horses were bearing rosy Dawn . . .' (= 'this morning'), where the immediate context is domestic. So too the simile of 108 f. is elaborated somewhat beyond the limits of ordinary usage. Except perhaps in 19 f. (v.n.) Theokritos has not succumbed to the temptation to satirise or patronise the girl or to put any obstacle in the way of our recognising that the emotional predicament of a suburban Medeia does not differ in nature from that of a princess of Kolchis (a fact which Euripides would have recognised too).

Nothing in the poem indicates unambiguously Simaitha's status and how she makes a living. Her name (σιμός = 'snub-nosed', and for -αίθα cf. the she-goats of 1.151 and v.102) suggests a hetaira, a girl living in an alien city and hoping to become the mistress of an attractive and well-to-do citizen or metic. The fact that she seems to be unencumbered by parents or guardians (100 ff., 118 ff.) points in the same direction. On the other hand, she seems to have been a virgin when she met Delphis (41), and there is nothing commercial in their relations. She talks to Thestylis as to a slave whom she owns (20), and Thestylis's slave status is confirmed in 94. Among the women who figure as her friends one, the 'Thracian nurse of Theumaridas' (70) is presumably a slave; 'Anaxo, daughter of Eubulos' (66) is surely not so, for she went as 'basket-bearer', normally a function of girls of honourable citizen families, to take part in a cult of Artemis; and the status of 'the mother of Philisto, our flute-girl, and of Melixo' (146) turns on a point which admits of no clear answer, the meaning of 'our'. Problems of this kind arise for us largely because most extant Greek literature presents us with well-to-do households — even the earthy heroes of Aristophanes are prosperous by the standards of the average citizen — and we are inclined to forget that towards the bottom end of the social scale the bourgeois pattern of respectability could not always be maintained, so that social distinctions between slave and free, at least on the level of personal relations, must have become blurred (cf. p. 128). Perhaps we are meant to imagine that Simaitha's father was abroad, that her mother was dead, and that no officious uncle was to hand; and perhaps situations of this kind were sufficiently familiar to Theokritos to need no explanation.

The modern reader wonders whether Simaitha is pregnant — he must, indeed, wonder why, after making love so often (155), she does not say that she is pregnant and worry about this. Possibly Greek contraceptive and abortifacient techniques were more advanced than we know; more probably, since Greek society regarded infanticide by exposure as respectable and was so constructed that an unmarried mother did not face the same economic problems as nowadays, the risk of pregnancy is nothing like as important, even to Simaitha herself, as we might have expected. But maybe Simaitha's apparent indifference to pregnancy is attributable to the fact that Theokritos, like most Greek writers, was male.

Delphis comes from Myndos in Karia (29, 96), and this fact suggests Kos as a likely scene for the poem; curiously enough, the name (exceedingly uncommon) is known from a Koan family in the third century B.C. The reference in 115 to a runner named Philinos is relevant both to the scene and to the date, for Philinos of Kos was a notable athlete who won Olympic victories in 264 and 260 and many other international victories which are undatable. Theokritos

may well have had this man in mind, for although 'Philinos'
is a very common name, 115 (cf. n.) has a particular point
if the reader recognises Philinos as a famous athlete.

According to Σ the poem borrows Thestylis and her
mission to Delphis's house from a mime of Sophron entitled
'The women who claim to drive out the goddess', *sc.* by
exorcism. We have a papyrus fragment of Sophron ([ed.]
D. L. Page, *Select Literary Papyri*, 328 ff.) which portrays in
dramatic dialogue the preparations for a magical ceremony;
it may be, but is not necessarily, a fragment of 'The
women . . .'. The purpose of exorcism is, of course, very
different from Simaitha's, but Theokritos may have been
the first after Sophron to offer a detailed literary portrayal
of a magical procedure.

There are certain points of contact, which may or may
not be fortuitous, between Theokritos's poem and the
passage of Ap. Rh. (iii.744–824) in which Medeia, who fell
in love with Jason at first sight (as Simaitha did with
Delphis), contemplates, in tumultuous emotion, whether
to use her chest of magical materials and her knowledge of
magical procedures to help Jason or to end her own life.
In particular, Simaitha's words (30 ff. = '35' ff.)

> ταὶ κύνες ἄμμιν ἀνὰ πτόλιν ὡρύονται·   30
> ἁ θεὸς ἐν τριόδοισι . . .
>
> ἠνίδε σιγῇ μὲν πόντος, σιγῶντι δ' ἀῆται,   33
> ἁ δ' ἐμὰ οὐ σιγῇ στέρνων ἔντοσθεν ἀνία . . .

have resemblances to Ap. Rh. iii

> νὺξ μὲν ἔπειτ' ἐπὶ γαῖαν ἄγεν κνέφας . . .   744
> οὐδὲ κυνῶν ὑλακὴ ἔτ' ἀνὰ πτόλιν, οὐ θρόος ἦεν   749
> ἠχήεις, σιγὴ δὲ μελαινομένην ἔχεν ὄρφνην
> ἀλλὰ μάλ' οὐ Μήδειαν ἐπὶ γλυκερὸς λάβεν ὕπνος . . .
> πύκνα δέ οἱ κραδίη στέρνων ἔντοσθεν ἔθυιεν . . .   755
>   ἔνδοθι δ' αἰεὶ   761
> τεῖρ' ὀδύνη . . .
> ἔνθ' ἀλεγεινότατον δύνει ἄχος, ὁππότ' ἀνίας   764
>   . . . ἐνισκίμψωσιν ἔρωτες.

The bulk of our evidence for Greek magic comes from
Roman, often late Roman, times (Verg. *Ecl.* 8.64 ff. owes
much to Theokritos, but contains also much that is not
Theokritean). We have, however, glimpses of it in the
archaic and classical periods, and some of what Simaitha
says and does can also be paralleled from Oriental sources.
In the poem, as commonly, strictly magical procedures are
blended with what should rather be called religious pro-
cedures; in the former, symbolic acts necessarily (if correctly
performed) effect the desired result through a supernatural
mechanism which exists in parallel with the mechanisms of
the physical world, whereas in the latter one must pray to
deities for the result and hope that they, as persons with
free will, will grant one's prayer. (For a general survey of
the evidence, cf. J. E. Lowe, *Magic in Greek and Roman
Literature* [Oxford, 1929]).

1. Simaitha 'ties down' Delphis ($\kappa\alpha\tau\alpha\delta\dot\eta\sigma o\mu\alpha\iota$ 10, 158);
this is a technical term often found in curses (some of them
from the subliterate stratum of society) inscribed on pot-
sherds from the classical period onwards.

2. Bay and red wool (1 f.) are designed to protect
Simaitha herself against the rather unpredictable powers
which she conjures up. In the Sophron fragment the com-
pany is told to put bay behind the ears before the ritual
begins, and the 'superstitious man' in Theophrastus (*Char.*
16.2) puts it in his mouth to avert evil. Red wool or threads
serve a similar purpose in Roman and Oriental magic.
Again, Simaitha tells Thestylis to 'make the bronze sound'
(31 = '36') when Hekate approaches, a worldwide protection
against evil spirits.

3. A number of substances are burned as symbols of the
condition to which Simaitha wishes to reduce Delphis:
barley flour (18), the sprinkling of which is accompanied
by the words, 'I am sprinkling ⟨on the fire⟩ the bones of
Delphis' (21); bay (23 f.), that Delphis too may be totally
consumed by love (26); and wax (38 = '28'), that Delphis
may similarly 'melt' ($\tau\dot\alpha\kappa o\iota\tau o$ 39 = '29'; the word is com-
monly used of consuming desire [1.82]). The melting of wax

dolls, accompanied by an imprecation, is prescribed for a certain oath in a state inscription of Kyrene, and we should also recall *Il.* iii.299 ff., where a libation accompanying a truce is poured with the words, 'Whichever side transgresses this oath, may their brains be poured on the ground like this wine!' How far the burning of bran (28 = '33') is symbolic is uncertain.

4. Slightly different in character, because not wholly symbolic, is the burning of a wisp from Delphis's cloak (53 f.). Cf. Eur. *Hipp.* 513 ff., where the Nurse tells Phaidra that she needs hair from Hippolytos, or fabric from his clothes, for her pretended spell.

5. Slightly different again is the concoction entrusted to Thestylis in 59 ff., for although she must say 'I knead the bones of Delphis' as she mixes the ingredients she must also mix them at a special place, Delphis's own doorway.

6. Simaitha speaks of pounding up a lizard and taking Delphis an 'evil drink' (58). Although her resentment sometimes gains the upper hand over her desire (cf. 159 f.), she probably intends the lizard-drink as a love-potion. We may recall that in Antiphon i.9 a woman accused of trying to poison her husband said that she was only trying to secure his affection by a potion.

7. Simaitha accompanies her ritual by rotating a wryneck (ἴυγξ) on a four-spoked wheel, to draw (ἕλκε) Delphis to her house. This love-magic was known to Pindar, who ascribes its invention to Aphrodite herself (*Pyth.* 4.213 ff.), and he uses ἴυγγι ἕλκομαι metaphorically in *Nem.* 4.35. Anon. (*HE*) 35 is a dedication of an ἴυγξ to Aphrodite.

8. Simaitha also whirls a bullroarer (ῥόμβος, 40 = '30') as a symbolic act (χὼς δινεῖθ' ὅδε ῥόμβος ... ὣς τῆνος δινοῖθ' κτλ.). Eur. *Hel.* 1362 f. includes 'the vibration of the bullroarer whirled round in the air' among the exotic rituals of the Mother-goddess, and the object is mentioned in a late magical document.

9. The ritual is, as normally in magic, whispered or spoken in a low tone (11, 62). Cf. the prayers which the

Athenians tell Oidipous to mutter to the dreaded Semnai Theai (Soph. *Oed. Col.* 489).

10. Simaitha uses the formula (44 f.) 'whether woman or man . . . , may he forget . . .'; such 'whether/whether' formulae are known from magical documents.

11. She cries the formula three times and pours a triple libation (43). Three is a number constantly found in religious as well as in magical ceremonies; the superstitious man (Theophr. *Char.* 16.3) throws three stones across the road when he encounters a weasel.

Simaitha says at an early stage (10 ff.) that she will utter her spells 'Moon . . . , to you, and to Hekate of the under-world (χθονία)'. Accordingly she invokes Hekate by name (14) and the Moon throughout the second half of the poem: 79, 142, the refrain from 69 onwards, and at the close (163 ff.). The goddess who is 'at the crossroads' in 36 must be Hekate, called εἰνοδία in Eur. *Hel.* 570 (in connection with her power to send ghosts to trouble men) and γῆς τριόδους ναίουσ᾽ ἱεράς in Soph. fr. 492. 'Mistress' (πότνια 43) is presumably Hekate, addressed in the course of the spells, and δέσποινα (162) the Moon (as πότνια in 164 must be). Simaitha thus treats Hekate and the Moon — formally, at least — as separate deities, and that is normal in the period before Theokritos. When we first meet Hekate in Greek literature (Hes. *Theog.* 411 ff.) she has no con-nection with the Moon, nor has she the sinister associations with darkness, magic, ghosts, corpses and the underworld which she acquired by the fifth century B.C. Nevertheless the identification was early, for it seems to be implied by the pairing of Hekate with the Sun in the *H. Hom.* 2.25 f., a pairing which recurs in Soph. fr. 492. Her association with magic is evident in Medeia's special devotion to her (Eur. *Med.* 395 ff.), which, of course, is prominent in Apollonios, e.g. iii.529 f. (Medeia taught τεχνήσασθαι φάρμακα by Hekate), 828 ff. (Jason meets Medeia at the temple of Hekate to receive instructions), and 1194 ff. (Jason invokes the help of Hekate by a sacrifice at night and the goddess appears in frightening guise, 'dogs of the underworld barking shrilly around her').

A complication is introduced at 33, where Simaitha addresses Hekate as 'Artemis'. The identification is hinted at in Aisch. *Supp.* 676 (῞Αρτεμιν ἑκάταν, i.e. '. . . who ⟨shoots from⟩ afar', cf. the Homeric ἕκατος = ἑκατηβόλος as an epithet of Apollo) and was made explicit in some local cults. Identification of Artemis with the moon, normal in Hellenistic times, is only rarely foreshadowed in classical literature; the interpretation of Aisch. fr. 170 is controversial, and Eur. *Iph. Aul.* 1570 f., although unambiguous, is probably a post-Euripidean interpolation. The religious attitude underlying the facility with which Greeks identify and multiply divine names and functions (the distinction, e.g., between two different Aphrodites is the converse of combining Artemis and Hekate) is elusive. Syncretism of a very wide range of local cults has a bearing on it, but, what is more important, the essence of Greek religion is not the acceptance of propositions *about* gods but the performance of ritual acts and utterances addressed *to* gods, and different acts can require different names. Thus, although 'Ares' and 'Enyalios' can fairly be described as two names for the same god or as respectively 'name' and 'epithet' of that god (e.g. *Il.* xvii.210 f.), Ar. *Peace* 457 treats a prayer to Ares and a prayer to Enyalios as different religious acts.

3. ὡς . . . καταδήσομαι: The meaning may be not 'since I am going to . . .' but 'to enable me to . . .'. Cf. Hdt. iii.159.2 ὡς δ' ἕξουσι γυναῖκας οἱ Βαβυλώνιοι . . . τάδε Δαρεῖος προϊδὼν ἐποίησε κτλ.

4. δωδεκαταῖος: Lit., 'who ⟨is⟩ for me a twelfth-day-person from which' (i.e. 'since') 'he . . . does not even come to ⟨me⟩'. Many expressions of time which are adverbial phrases in English are adjectives in Greek, e.g. τριταῖοι ἀφίκοντο, 'they arrived on the third day'.

5. ἔγνω: The aorist ἔγνων, 'I came to know', is commonly used where English idiom would lead us to expect γιγνώσκω.
ζοοί: As in Tragedy, when a woman uses 'we' for 'I' the

adjectives or participles referring to the subject are masculine in form.

7. Ἔρως ... ᾿Αφροδίτα: Cf. 1.97 f. n.

8. Τιμαγήτοιο: Cf. 80, 97 f. Gymnasia and wrestling-schools were often private, and in such cases were identified by the owner's name. We do not know whether Timagetos was a real person.

11. φαῖνε: Used intransitively of heavenly bodies, 'shine'. **δαῖμον**: When a Greek wished to distinguish between superior and inferior orders of supernatural beings he would denote the former by θεοί and the latter by δαίμονες (e.g. Hes. *Op.* 121 f., Pl. *Ap.* 27c ff., *Smp.* 202E f.), but at the same time the poets freely treated θεός and δαίμων as synonyms (e.g. *Il.* i.222, where Athena returns to Olympos μετὰ δαίμονας ἄλλους).

12. καὶ σκύλακες: The implication of καί is not that dogs are braver than people, but that they proverbially lack shame, reverence or discretion; their special reason for fearing Hekate is that they are sacrificed to her (Sophron fr. 8; Ar. fr. 204, 'have you bought a little white dog for the goddess at the crossroads?').

13. αἷμα: One does not normally find blood in cemeteries, and the reference may be to the exposed bodies of male-factors (cf. Pl. *Rep.* 439E); but Ap. Rh. iv.60 ff. οὐ γὰρ ἄϊδρις / ἦεν (sc. Medea) ὁδῶν, θαμὰ καὶ πρὶν ἀλωμένη ἀμφί τε νεκρούς / ἀμφὶ δὲ δυσπαλέας ῥίζας χθονός hint at the exhumation of fresh corpses.

14. δασπλῆτι: An epithet of a Fury in *Od.* xv.234; cf. Simon. (*PMG*) 522.1 δασπλῆτα χάρυβδιν.

15. f. χερείονα ... Περιμήδας: i.e. 'as powerful as those of . . .'; 'not worse than' is the usual Greek way of saying 'as good as'. It is natural that Kirke and Medeia should be treated by poets as supreme sorceresses. As for Perimede, it is possible that Theokritos slightly misremembered a Homeric name, for *Il.* xi.740 mentions an Agamede who is ξανθή, a great magician (she is also a granddaughter of the Sun, and Σ on *Il.* identifies her with Medeia herself). If so, he set a precedent (Perimede appears again in Propertius) and a

problem; one ancient commentator identified Perimede
with Polydamna, the Egyptian from whom (*Od.* iv.228)
Helen obtained the delightful drug which she put in
Telemachos's wine. Cf. however, XIII.116 for a similar
variation in names.

18. ἀλλ': 'Come on', 'get on!'

19 f. δειλαία . . . τέτυγμαι: In humorous and ostensibly
realistic literature masters and mistresses often abuse their
slaves for slowness and stupidity; Praxinoa in XV nags
mercilessly, and so does the woman in Herodas 4.41 ff. An
early example in the same genre, handled with a lighter
touch, is the bullying of Peisetairos's slave in Ar. *Birds*
1323 ff., and cf. *Lys.* 184.

23. ἐπὶ Δέλφιδι: ἐπί is, as often, untranslatable by any
one English preposition; it suggests here 'in order to
affect . . .', 'in order to get . . .' and 'with my mind upon . . .'.

In some medieval manuscripts 38–42 come at this point;
hence the conventional numbering (here in quotation
marks), which was established before the discovery of the
ancient fragments which vindicate the other order.

29. ('33') κινήσαις: As it stands, at first sight a wish:
'*May* you move . . .' But the continuation καὶ εἴ τι περ κτλ.
shows that Simaitha's point is : 'You *can* move anything;
therefore move Delphis'. The verb must thus be a potential
optative without ἄν; this is Homeric (e.g. *Il.* x.556 f. ῥεῖα
θεός γ' ἐθέλων καὶ ἀμείνονας . . . ἵππους δωρήσαιτο) and sporadic
in classical and Hellenistic poetry. Prayers commonly
remind a god of his powers; cf. Glaukos's prayer to Apollo
in *Il.* xvi.514 ff., 'Hear me, Lord . . . for you can hear any-
where a man in distress'.

30. ('35') κύνες: Cf. 12 n., p. 97 and Ap. Rh. iii.1040.

36. ('41'): She is no longer a virgin (143), but Delphis has
not made her his wife (γυναικός: cf. 132 n.); hence her
socially dishonoured (κακάν) position.

40. ('30') ἐξ Ἀφροδίτας: Aphrodite is, as it were, the
supernatural authority for the effect of the bullroarer; cf.
1.140 n.

44. εἴτε καὶ ἀνήρ: Simaitha takes it for granted, as indeed

she must, that Delphis's love-affair may be homosexual
(cf. 150), for the average Greek regarded homosexual desire
as natural and inevitable and could be attracted indifferently
to a pretty girl or a handsome youth. A homosexual affair
did not imply, as it would usually imply in a modern culture,
an exclusively or even predominantly homosexual orienta-
tion of the personality; it was a prolongation into adult life
of the homosexual play characteristic of the early 'teens in a
society which strictly segregates the sexes. Cf. K. J. Dover,
Bull. Inst. Class. Stud. xi (1964), 31 ff., and G. Devereux,
Symbolae Osloenses xlii (1967), 69 ff.

45. τόσσον ἔχοι λάθας: Since desire (150, XVI.65) and
fear (XXV.220) can ἔχειν a person, probably 'may so great
a forgetfulness possess ⟨him⟩'. For τόσσον with a genitive
cf. *Od.* xxi.402 τοσσοῦτον ὀνήσιος, 'so much prosperity'.

45 f. Θησέα . . . 'Αριάδνας: When Ariadne had enabled
Theseus to kill the Minotaur, they fled from Crete together,
but Theseus deserted Ariadne on the way to Athens (Hes.
frr. 147, 298). In later antiquity the place of her desertion
was Naxos; but *Od.* xi.324 f., alluding to a different version
of the myth, represents Ariadne as killed by Artemis on the
island Dia, and Kallimachos fr. 601 treats Dia as an old
name for Naxos.

48 ff. On the simile with 'so . . .' but no 'as . . .' cf.
XIII.62 f., XIV.39 ff.

τῷ δ' ἔπι: The analogy of x.31 ('the goat pursues cytisus,
the wolf the goat . . . ἐγὼ δ' ἐπὶ τὶν μεμάνημαι': cf. ἐπί in 23
and 40 above) suggests that the horses go mad not in con-
sequence of eating the plant hippomanes but in their
anxiety to find it.

55. ἀνιαρέ: Eros is 'cruel' and 'painful' to the Greeks
not only as responsible for the obsession and debility pro-
duced by unrequited love, but also because even when love
is mutual and physical satisfaction constantly achieved
there is often a residue of uneasy, unappeasable desire which
makes the lover feel that he is not master of himself but
victim of a relentless external power. Hence in Ar. *Eccl.*
952 ff. the youth and the girl who is on the point of letting

him into her house sing of their imminent union as a
(temporary) *release from* Eros: 'Let me go, Eros, I beseech
you!' Cf. the outburst against Eros in Ap. Rh. iv.445 ff.

55 f. τί μευ . . . πέπωκας: i.e. τί ἐμφὺς ὡς λιμνᾶτις βδέλλα
ἅπαν τὸ μέλαν μευ αἷμα ἐκ τῆς χροᾶς ἐκπέπωκας;

59 f. ὑπόμαξον . . . καθυπέρτερον: 'Knead them sur-
reptitiously (ὑπο-) above his threshold'; φλιά can, in late
Greek, mean 'threshold' as well as 'lintel' and 'doorpost',
and Thestylis is hardly to be imagined as taking a step-
ladder with her. The point of kneading the material above
the threshold appears in 62; the place is magically signi-
ficant, and magical material to turn away evil was commonly
buried under the threshold (cf. M. B. Ogle, *Am. Journ. Phil.*
xxxii [1911], 251 ff.)

60. ἅς ἔτι καὶ νύξ: νύξ is a modern emendation; the
transmitted text (ancient as well as medieval) has νῦν, which
makes no grammatical sense unless some clause is to inter-
vene before 62. Most manuscripts give us such a clause:
ἐκ θυμῶ δέδεμαι· ὁ δέ μευ λόγον οὐδένα ποιεῖ, but this is not in
the ancient text; it turns 58–62 into the only five-line
passage during the magical rites, and it is a pointless utter-
ance in the context, for it represents Simaitha as envisaging
a time, quite soon, when she will no longer be in love with
Delphis. There is little doubt that the line is patchwork
(ὁ δέ μευ κτλ. ~III.33 τὸ δέ μευ λόγον οὐδένα ποιῇ) constructed
after the corruption of νύξ to νῦν.

66. ἁ τωὐβούλοιο: sc. θυγάτηρ, not γυνή, for a κανηφόρος
in a religious procession would normally be an unmarried
girl (cf. Ar. *Ach.* 253 ff., *Lys.* 646). **ἄμμιν**: The dative
indicates simply that Simaitha, through friendship and
neighbourhood and interest, was affected by Anaxo's going.

68. ἐν δέ: 'And among them . . .'.

70. ἁ μακαρῖτις: 'Now dead'; μακαρίτης (fem. -ῖτις),
suggesting 'citizen of the land of the blessed', was the
normal, polite way of referring to the dead; cf. Ar. fr. 488.
10 πᾶς γὰρ λέγει τις· 'ὁ μακαρίτης οἴχεται'. The notion that the
dead could normally expect to go to a kind of heaven
(or, if wicked, to a kind of hell) gradually replaced the

archaic notion that only the most exceptional heroes received special treatment in the after-life, and it becomes clear in the epitaphs of the Hellenistic age. Cf. p. 216.

74. τὰν Κλεαρίστας: Greeks commonly lent one another clothes for festive occasions; cf. Ar. *Lys.* 1189 ff., where the women sing, 'All the dresses and ornaments I have, I never grudge them . . . when someone's daughter is a basket-bearer'.

76. τὰ Λύκωνος: Whether fields or house or some other property, we cannot tell; v.112 f. τὰ Μίκωνος = 'Mikon's ⟨vineyard⟩', Ar. *Wasps* 1432 εἰς τὰ Πιττάκου = 'to Pittakos's ⟨surgery⟩', Herodas 5.52 f. μὴ παρὰ τὰ Μικκάλης αὐτὸν / ἄγε = 'don't take him via Mikkale's'.

77. εἶδον: Since the women of respectable families were secluded as far as was practicable, but appeared in public at festivals, festivals were the occasions on which (at any rate in fiction) love-affairs began. In Herodas 1.56 f. a young man falls in love with another man's wife 'at ⟨the festival commemorating⟩ the Descent of Mise'; cf. Dioskorides (*HE*) 3 on seeing a girl at the Adonia.

78. ξανθοτέρα: Although vase-painters normally depict people and deities as black-haired (including Apollo, despite his epithet 'golden-haired' in some passages of poetry) — there are exceptions on white-ground vases, where the painter's range of colours is not restricted, and a few exceptions elsewhere (e.g. a Ganymede with flaming red hair). The comparison with helichryse here shows that Delphis and his friend had incipient beards of a golden yellow. This is not to say that ξανθός means 'golden' or 'flaxen' in every passage of Greek in which it is applied to hair.

80. ὡς: Not 'as if . . .' but 'as they would be, because . . .' **ἀπό**: With λιπόντων.

82. Demonstrative ὥς is common in Homer, and one particular usage of it was widely imitated in Hellenistic poetry (cf. III.42, IV.39, XV.25): *Il.* xiv.293 ὡς ἴδεν, ὥς μιν ἔρως . . . ἀμφεκάλυψεν, *Il.* xix.16 ὡς εἶδ', ὥς μιν μᾶλλον ἔδυ χόλος.

83. δειλαίας: One might have expected δειλαίᾳ in agreement with μοι, but cf. vii.25 f. ὥς τοι ποσὶ νισσομένοιο / πᾶσα λίθος . . . ἀείδει — and, indeed, 78 ff. above τοῖς δέ . . . ὡς ἀπό . . . λιπόντων.

89. αὐτά: '⟨By⟩ themselves', i.e. 'alone', as commonly; cf. the Scots idiom 'He lived himself', etc.

91. ἔλιπον: 'Passed over', i.e. 'failed to visit'. **ἐπᾷδεν**: Simaitha's search for old women who cast spells is not a manifestation of any special propensity to magic on her part, for common Greek practice (taken for granted by the Platonic Sokrates, e.g. *Rep.* 427b) looked upon spells (ἐπῳδαί) and amulets in the same light as medicines. Cf. G. Lanata, *Medicina, Magica e Religione Popolare in Grecia* (Rome, 1967).

92. ἐλαφρόν: Either, lit., 'it was in no way light', or (as Σ took it) 'there was nothing which alleviated ⟨my love⟩'; the fact that in xi.3 Theokritos calls a remedy κοῦφον . . . καὶ ἀδύ suggests that Σ may have been right.

94. Hitherto she had concealed the true cause of her illness, like Euripides' Phaidra.

95. εἰ δ' ἄγε: An epic expression, e.g. *Od.* i.271 εἰ δ' ἄγε νῦν ξυνίει κτλ. **μοι**: An enclitic pronoun can occasionally be preceded by a vocative; cf. Eur. *Hipp.* 1445 λαβοῦ πάτερ μου.

100. μόνον: With ἐόντα, 'that he is alone'.

101. ὅτι: Unlike English, Greek commonly inserts ὅτι or ὡς before directly quoted words. **Σιμαίθα τυ καλεῖ**: It was unthinkable that Simaitha should go to, or near, the wrestling-school herself; slaves, upon whose loyalty and discretion much depended, had to serve as intermediaries in affairs of this kind. Cf. also xi.26, 68 n. καλεῖν is the word normally used of inviting guests.

104. ἄρτι: It looks as if ὡς ἐνόησα ἄρτι means ἐπειδὴ τάχιστα ἐνόησα, 'as soon as I was aware . . .'. Cf. Aratos 606 ἦμος . . . ἄρτι γένηται.

105. For the dramatic effect of the break made by the refrain cf. 1.85 n.

107. ἱδρώς: Apollonios's Medeia, who blushes readily (iii.297 f., 963), does not sweat; Simaitha, who does not blush, streams with cold sweat like Sappho in the famous poem φαίνεταί μοι κῆνος κτλ. (fr. 31). Sappho describes, with almost clinical precision, the symptoms of an anxiety state caused, in her case, by homosexual jealousy. It is uncertain whether Theokritos entered the realm of psychopathology deliberately or drew unthinkingly on Sappho or descriptions based on hers (Theognis 1017 raises the same question). Cf. G. Devereux, *CQ* N.S. xx (1970), 17 ff.

109. κνυζεῦνται: The general rule that a neuter plural subject takes a singular verb admits of many exceptions; these are not always explicable, but one of the commonest types is that in which the subject, as here, denotes human beings.

114 ff. Of course we do not have to believe that Delphis has ever noticed or heard of Simaitha before; but she does not question his veracity.

114. τόσσον . . . ὅσον: 'By no more than . . .'; in English 'as much as . . .' normally implies a large amount, but in Greek it may just as well imply a small amount.

115. Φιλῖνον: Delphis contrives an artful boast under the disguise of modesty; Philinos of Kos was one of the greatest athletes of his day (cf. p. 96).

116. ἢ 'μέ παρῆμεν: For ἤ=πρὶν (ἤ) after φθάνειν (114 ἔφθασας) cf. *Od.* xi.58 ἔφθης πεζὸς ἰὼν ἢ ἐγὼ σὺν νηΐ, 'you got here on foot before I did by ship'.

119. ἢ τρίτος . . . φίλος: 'With two or three friends'; cf. Plu. *Pel.* 13.7 δωδέκατος κατελθών, 'returning home with eleven friends', and the classical expressions with αὐτός, e.g. δέκατος αὐτός, 'with nine colleagues'.

120. μᾶλα . . . Διωνύσοιο: Apples are offered as a love-token (cf. III.10, XI.10); the meaning of 'apples of Dionysos' is obscure; Philitas ([*Coll. Alex.*] fr. 18) said that Aphrodite gave Hippomenes 'apples of Dionysos' wherewith to captivate Atalanta. According to Neoptolemos of Parion, Dionysos 'invented' apple-growing, as he did vine-growing (Ath. 82D). **ἐν κόλποισι**: A Greek had no pockets, and so had to carry things in his hand or mouth, in a bag, or (as here) inside the upper part of the clothing, where the belt prevented them from slipping down. So the greedy Alkmeon in the treasury of Kroisos (Hdt. vi.125.4) filled his κόλπος with gold.

121. λεύκαν . . . ἔρνος: Σ and Paus. v.14.2 (from Eratosthenes? Cf. *FGrHist* 241 fr. 6) record an Elean legend that Herakles introduced the white poplar into Greece.

124. φίλα: The words which follow suggest that the meaning is 'agreeable to both of us', since he is reckoned handsome as well as a good runner (a common epic sense of ἐλαφρός).

126. εὗδον τ' εἴ κε . . . ἐφίλησα: = εὗδον τ' ἄν εἰ . . . ἐφίλησα: the modal particle with εὗδον is understood from the preceding sentence (cf. *Od.* xv.452 f. τόν κεν ἄγοιμι . . . ὁ δέ . . . ἄλφοι) and its insertion with εἰ is peculiarly epic (e.g. *Il.* xxiii. 526 εἰ δέ κε . . . γένετο δρόμος, τῷ κέν μιν παρέλασσε). Delphis means: 'I would have been content, gone home to bed, and gone to sleep'. He deploys the well-known technique, 'Just one kiss, honestly, that's all!' to make a good impression at no cost to himself, for the initiative has in fact come from Simaitha and he does not have to pretend now (133 f.) that a kiss will content him.

127 f. εἰ δ' . . . ἐθ' ὑμέας: Delphis and his friends would have come, he claims, as a κῶμος, garlanded and carrying torches (and a bit drunk), willing to ask for admission but ready, if not admitted, to hack and burn down the door. Cf. Kallim. *Epigr.* 42, where a lover ἐπικωμάζει, 'driven by wine and Eros', and kisses the doorpost of his beloved. In Herodas 2.33 ff., 63 ff., the owner of the prostitute Myrtale complains that his adversary set fire to his house at night and tried to carry off the girl by force.

130. ἔφαν: Almost 'I have realized' (cf. 5 n., 1.51 n.).

131. δευτέρα: Aphrodite has heard his prayers and has inclined Simaitha favourably towards him; Simaitha has implemented the goddess's decision.

132. ὦ γύναι: Evidently complimentary, as in III.9, perhaps because, although it implies 'not a virgin' it is the normal address of husband to wife and implies a promise of marriage.

133. Λιπαραίω: The 'islands of Aiolos', which include Lipara, include also Hiera, which was an active volcano; 'the people there say that Hephaistos forges on Hiera' (Thuc. iii.88.2f.).

136. μανίαις: Cf. xi.11. **παρθένον**: This passage may have been in the mind of Anon. (*HE*) 35.1 f., where an ἴυγξ which has the power to ἕλκειν . . . ἐκ θαλάμων παῖδας is dedicated to Aphrodite.

137. ἐφόβησ': Usually 'frighten', a surprising word to use of Eros; but it must denote driving to action under an irrational external impulse. Cf. xiii.48; and in Bacchylides 11.43 the word is used of Hera when she inspired the daughters of Proitos to utter impious boasts. **ἔτι**: With θερμά.

142. ὡς καί τοι . . . θρυλέοιμι: Cf. Dem. xlii.7 τέλος δέ, ἵνα μὴ μακρολογῶ κτλ., 'Eventually, to cut a long story short, . . .'. **φίλα . . . Σελάνα**: This splitting of a vocative expression is highly unusual; in (e.g.) Kallim. *H*. 5.4 ὦ ξανθαὶ σοῦσθε Πελασγιάδες, the fact that the intervening word is an imperative, which can be introduced by ὦ in its own right, makes all the difference. But cf. the splitting of an oath in 118 above.

143. ἐς πόθον: πόθος is usually a state of longing and desire (as in 164), but here 'came to desire' must mean 'attained what we desired'; ctr. Anaxilas (*CAF*) fr. 21.5 f. ἑταίρας δ' εἰς ἔρωτα . . . ἐληλυθώς, '. . . having fallen in love with . . .'.

144. μέσφα τό γ' ἐχθές: But he has not come to see her for eleven days (4, 157). Presumably his absence was not in itself suspicious — there may have been many good reasons to explain his presumed absence from the city — but it became so when she heard today that yesterday, at any rate, he was in the city but was apparently in love with someone else.

145 f. ἅ τε Φιλίστας . . . ἅ τε Μελιξοῦς: For the repetition of the article with the same reference cf. Dem. xix.280 Θρασυβούλου τοῦ δημοτικοῦ καὶ τοῦ . . . καταγαγόντος τὸν δῆμον.

149. ἔραται: Cf. 1.78 n.

150. ἀνδρός: Cf. 44 n.

151. ἴδμεν: =Att. ἴσμεν.

151 f. αἰέν . . . ἐπεχεῖτο: Lit. 'continually he caused-to-be-poured-for-himself of unmixed ⟨wine⟩ of Love', i.e. 'he kept on telling the wine-pourer to give him a cup of wine unmixed with water, as a toast of the kind one drinks when in love with someone'. Cf. Alexis (*CAF*) fr. 111.1 f. φιλίας κυάθους ('measures') τοὺς τῶν παρόντων ('present company') τέτταρας, / τοὺς τρεῖς δ' ἔρωτος . . . ὕστερον: cf. also XIV.18 n. **οἱ**: The person with whom Delphis is in love; and τῆνα = 'that ⟨person's⟩'.

154. ἀλαθής: 'Truthful'.

155. καὶ τρὶς καὶ τετράκις: *sc*. daily.

156. καὶ παρ' ἐμὶν ἐτίθει: A silent pledge of return is often more tasteful than verbal assurances. **τὰν Δωρίδα . . . ὄλπαν**: If Kleitarchos *ap*. Ath. 495c was right in saying that what the Athenians called λήκυθος was called ὄλπᾱ at Corinth and certain other places, Theokritos's point may be not 'the Dorian ⟨type of⟩ oil-bottle' but 'what Dorians call ὄλπα'.

157. δωδεκαταῖος: Cf. 4 n.

159. καταδήσομαι: i.e. 'the binding-spell which I *have* performed *will* take effect'.

160. τὰν Ἀΐδαο . . . ἀραξεῖ: i.e. if he won't knock on my door (6), he will knock on the door of Death. Cf. 58 n. **ναὶ Μοίρας**: In the Doric dialects positive and negative oaths are commonly introduced by ναί (not ναὶ μά or νή) and οὐ (not οὐ μά) respectively; cf. IV.17, VII.39.

162. Ἀσσυρίω: The kingdom of Assyria, on the upper Tigris and Euphrates, perished at the end of the seventh century B.C.; but the term 'Assyrians' was applied by the Greeks to a people of the Black Sea coast of Asia Minor (Ap. Rh. ii.946) and sometimes to the inhabitants of Syria. Eastern peoples were credited with potent magic and rare drugs, as (correctly) with astrology, spices and perfumes.

164. ὥσπερ ὑπέσταν: Cf. Eur. *Tro*. 414 f. τῆσδ' ἔρωτ'

ἐξαίρετον / μαινάδος (sc. Kassandra) ὑπέστη (sc. Agamemnon).
Simaitha's point is: 'it was I, not you, mistress Moon, who
fell in love; and I who will endure it, while you depart'.

166. ἄντυγα: Originally 'chariot-rail', but sometimes
interpreted as 'chariot' by classical writers, e.g. Eur. *Hipp.*
1231, where the supernatural bull which terrifies Hip-
polytos's horses ἄντυγι ξυνείπετο. The idea that Night, like
the Dawn and the Sun, rides in a horse-drawn chariot is
found in Eur. fr. 114.

POEM III

An unnamed goatherd goes to serenade Amaryllis, the girl
with whom he is in love, and who has at least given him
a little encouragement (11; cf. also 36~vi.15). The formal
serenade itself, which honours the power of Love by
citing examples from legend, is brief (40–51). It is pre-
ceded (6–39) by a much longer passage in which appeals
to Amaryllis (who does not appear) are blended with the
expression of the goatherd's own thoughts and feelings;
and it is followed by a similar despairing utterance
(52–54). The poem as a whole, which could have been
introduced by a narrative, e.g. 'Once a goatherd went
to serenade Amaryllis, and this is what he sang' (cf. vi.3 ff.,
xi.17 f.), is presented as a dramatic monologue from the
first. Tityros, who has no speaking part, is addressed in 2 f.,
and the scene changes between 5 and 6.

The poem transfers features of the urban κῶμος (note
κωμάσδω 1, and cf. ii.127 f. n.) to a setting of primitive
rusticity. Amaryllis lives in a cave, and the goatherd comes
alone to her 'door'. He brings her apples (10; cf. ii.120) and
a wreath (21 ff., v.n.; cf. ii.153). Since she gives no sign of
acknowledging his presence, he becomes a lonely, rejected
suitor singing what Plutarch (*Amatorius* 753B) calls
παρακλαυσίθυρον, 'a song sung at a closed door', and proclaim-
ing his intention of lying down to die on the spot (53).

By contrast with his attitude in other bucolic poems, the poet's tone is one of patronising humour.

3. τὸ καλόν: Cf. 1.41 n.

5. Λιβυκόν: Cf. 1.24 n. κνάκωνα: Cf. VII.15 f. τράγοιο / κνακὸν δέρμα.

7. παρκύπτοισα: The word is used in comedy (e.g. Ar. *Peace* 981 ff., *Eccl.* 884) of a coquettish woman peeping at a man through a door or window. καλεῖς: Cf. II.101 n.

8. σιμός: 'Snub-nosed', and therefore ugly by Greek standards; the vase-painters give snub noses to satyrs and Egyptians. ἐγγύθεν: 'At close quarters'; cf. Moschos, *Europa* 155, where Zeus, in the form of a bull, says to Europa, 'I am Zeus, though ἐγγύθεν I look like a bull'.

9. νύμφα: Amaryllis is not a supernatural 'nymph' but a human girl, whom the goatherd addresses as 'bride'; cf. II.137, 132 n.

10. μᾶλα: Cf. II.120 n.

12. θᾶσαι μάν: Cf. Sophron fr. 26 ἴδε . . . , ἴδε φίλα· θᾶσαι μάν ('just look!'), how red they are.' His failure to entice Amaryllis out leads to the woebegone words which follow, lit. '⟨my⟩ trouble ⟨is⟩ to me heart-paining'; to make θυμαλγὲς ἐμὸν ἄχος (ἐμόν is the medieval text, and metrically possible [D4(a)]) object of θᾶσαι μάν dissociates the passage from its precedent in Sophron, and 'look at my heart-paining trouble' does not sound quite right.

12 ff. αἴθε γενοίμαν . . . πυκάσδει: The conceit is akin to the traditional one of the skolia *PMG* 900 f., 'If only I could be a lyre . . . carried by handsome boys . . .' and 'If only I could be a golden ornament . . . worn by a lovely woman' (also an ancient Eastern conceit; cf. M. L. West, *Harv. Stud.* lxxiii [1968], 132). Cf. Rhianos (*HE*) 10, in which the poet wishes he were a bird caught in the hand of Dexionikos. The botanical detail which Theokritos puts in is characteristic of him. ἁ βομβεῦσα μέλισσα: Probably not generic, but '*that* buzzing bee'; the sight of a bee nosing its way into the cave gives the speaker the idea.

15. νῦν: i.e. now at last (*sc.* and never fully before). ἔγνων: Cf. 11.5 n. βαρύς: Cf. 11.55 n.

15 f. ἦ ῥα λεαίνας . . . μάτηρ: Cf. Patroklos's reproach to Achilles, *Il.* xvi.33 ff., 'Peleus was not your father, nor Thetis your mother . . .; it was the grey sea that generated you, and the rough rocks, so cruel is your heart; Theognis 1231 σχέτλι' Ἔρως, μανίαι σε τιθηνήσαντο λαβοῦσαι ('suckled', 'nursed'). The lack of any accepted genealogy of Eros (cf. XIII.2 n.) gives the conceit an additional point.

17. Ap. Rh. iii.761 ff. describes the pangs of love as σμύχουσα διὰ χροὸς ἀμφί τ' ἀραιὰς / ἶνας καὶ κεφαλῆς ὑπὸ νείατον ἴνιον ἄχρις ('. . . under the bottom of the occipital bone, right through').

18. τὸ καλόν: Cf. 3; but here the construction is also related to expressions such as ὀξὺ βλέπειν. τὸ πᾶν λίθος: λίθος is used of anyone lacking awareness, sensibility or compassion; cf. Telemachos to Penelope, *Od.* xxiii.103, 'Your heart is always harder than stone (στερεωτέρη . . . λίθοιο)', Aisch. *Pr.* 242, 'Iron-hearted and wrought of rock (ἐκ πέτρας) ⟨would be⟩ he who is not distressed by your sufferings', Anon. (*HE*) 13.3 f., 'If you saw him and were not overcome by the flame of desire, you must be either a god or a stone'. It is, however, surprising to find a reproach sandwiched between two compliments to Amaryllis's beauty, and Σ suggested that λίθος here means 'white marble'; but it is hard to see how Theokritos's audience would have understood this (in VI.38 we have 'whiter than Parian stone', which makes all the difference). There is a variant λίπος, 'fat', 'oil'; λιπαρός, 'shining ⟨as if oiled⟩', is a high compliment, e.g. Bacchyl. 5.169, 'Is there a daughter of Oineus . . . like you in bodily beauty? Gladly would I make her my splendid (λιπαράν) wife!', and Delphis in 11.102 (not fresh from wrestling) is λιπαρόχρως.

20. κενεοῖσι: 'Empty', i.e. not progressing to sexual intercourse. ἀδέα: Cf. 1.65 n.

21. τῖλαί με . . . λεπτά: Probably = κατατῖλαι αὐτίκα λεπτά, i.e. 'pluck it straightway into little pieces'; for the position of κατὰ cf. διά in Ap. Rh. i.9 χειμερίοιο ῥέεθρα κιὼν διὰ ποσσὶν

'Αναύρου, 'going on foot through the stream of the torrential Anauros', and for λεπτά cf. *Od.* xii.173 f. κηροῖο μέγαν τροχόν ... τυτθὰ διατμήξας, 'cutting up the big disk of wax into little bits'. Another possibility is that καταυτίκα (not otherwise attested) = αὐτίκα

22. κισσοῖο: '⟨— and it is⟩ of ivy ⟨ — ⟩'; cf. Thuc. vi.100.1, 'and the Syracusan conduits, which had been led underground ποτοῦ ὕδατος' (lit., 'of drinkable water') 'they destroyed', Ap. Rh. ii.34 καλαύροπα ('shepherd's crook') . . . τὴν θορέεσκεν ὀριτρεφεός κοτίνοιο ('wild olive'.) **φυλάσσω:** 'Keep' cf. II.120; he may be wearing the garland himself, to judge from VII.64; and XV.113 suggests that φυλάσσω conveys the idea 'I have made and still have'. But one can also make a garland for one's girl; cf. Meleagros (*HE*) 46 on the ingredients of the garland he is making for Heliodora.

23. ἀμπλέξας: i.e. entwining ivy with the other plants named.

26. τὼς θύννως σκοπιάζεται: Looking out for shoals of tunny was important in the ancient as in the modern Mediterranean. Ar. *Knights* 313 compares Kleon, watching the tribute from the allies coming across the sea to Athens, to a man standing on the rocks θυννοσκοπῶν, 'watching for tunny'. **ὁ γριπεύς:** For the association of fishermen with the bucolic scene cf. 1.39 ff. and XXI.

27. τό γε μὰν τεὸν ἁδύ τέτυκται: 'At any rate your pleasure is done'; cf. Eur. *Hec.* 120 f. ἦν ὁ τὸ μὲν σὸν σπεύδων ἀγαθόν . . . 'Αγαμέμνων, 'and it was Agamemnon who was anxious for your good'. A different analysis is favoured by Σ: 'at any rate so far as you are concerned, it (*sc.* my death) is done ⟨as something⟩ pleasant ⟨for you⟩'; cf. Pl. *Prt.* 338c τό γ' ἐμὸν οὐδέν μοι διαφέρει, 'so far as I'm concerned it makes no difference'. If Theokritos really wrote γε μάν, he was using it in one of the senses of γε μέν (which in fact he may have written), e.g. Hes. *Sc.* 259 f. οὔ τι πέλεν μεγάλη θεός, ἀλλ' ἄρα ἥ γε / τῶν γε μὲν ἀλλάων προφερής τ' ἦν. For the neurotic sentiment, 'You'll be *glad* if I'm dead!' cf. 52 ff. As for τέτυκται in statements about the future, it is always possible to substitute present or perfect tenses for dramatic effect; cf. Thuc. vi.91.3 καὶ εἰ αὕτη ἡ πόλις ληφθήσεται, ἔχεται καὶ ἡ πᾶσα Σικελία.

28. μεμναμένῳ: 'When I was thinking ⟨of you and wondering⟩ whether . . .'. Cf. Ap. Rh. iii.534 μνησάμεθ' εἴ κε δύναιτο κτλ.; and in general εἰ often means 'to see if . . .', 'asking oneself whether . . .', etc.

29 f. οὐδὲ τὸ τηλέφιλον . . . ἐξεμαράνθη: Lit., 'and not even did the smack make the love-in-absence' (obviously some kind of flower or leaf) 'stick to me' (or '. . . make the love-in-absence stick ⟨me⟩ to itself'), 'but it simply withered off in contact with my smooth forearm'. Clearly this was a kind of 'she loves me, she loves me not' divination in which a man smacked a petal or leaf on to the hairless underside of his arm and got his answer from whether it remained stuck to him when the arm was held normally (all the air between it and the flesh having been expelled; ἀπαλῷ is not a merely ornamental epithet) or curled and fell off. It was later believed (by Σ, among others) that the sound made by the smack was crucial. Pollux ix.127 gives an account of the procedure irreconcilable with what Theokritos says here.

31. κοσκινόμαντις: Old women who divined by sieves and told herdsmen how to cure sick animals are mentioned by Philostratos *Vit. Ap.* vi.11; we do not know how they used the sieves.

32. ποιολογεῦσα παραιβάτις: 'Collecting' (i.e. cutting) 'grass beside me'. In Ap. Rh. i.754 Hippodameia is παραιβάτις to Pelops because she rides beside him in his chariot. Theokritos's choice of words rather suggests that we should imagine the goatherd and the old woman as employed, as part of a team, to cut an area of grass, keeping roughly level in their cutting, like the reapers in x.3. **οὔνεκ':** 'That . . .'.

33. τὶν ὅλος ἔγκειμαι: Lit., 'I have been entire⟨ly⟩ put in you', as we might say 'I am wrapped up in you'; cf. Eur. *Ion.* 181 f. οἷς δ' ἔγκειμαι μόχθοις, Φοίβῳ δουλεύσω,

35. μελανόχρως: 'Dark-skinned', 'swarthy', not 'black-

skinned'; cf. x.26 ff., and Ar. *Thesm.* 31 μῶν ὁ μέλας, ὁ
καρτερός; 'Why, do you mean the dark, strong man?'

37. ἄλλεται: According to the Hellenistic writer
Melampous a twitching of the right eye means that one will
triumph over one's enemies; not an appropriate idea here,
but no doubt interpretations of this kind of omen differed
from place to place. Cf. the modern idea that burning ears
mean that one is being talked about. **ἰδησῶ:** No other instance
of this future of ὁρῶ is known; εἰδήσω is not uncommon, and
ἰδήσω (then with the Doric future stem [**E10** (*f*)], ἰδησῶ) seems
to be derived from the relation between the augmented aorist
indicative εἶδον and the aorist oblique moods ἴδω, ἴδοιμι etc.

38. ποτὶ τὰν πίτυν: With ἀποκλινθείς.

39. ποτίδοι: 'Look on (*sc.* deliberately, in sympathy)',
as the following words show, not 'catch sight of'. **ἀδαμαντίνα:**
The insensitive or unsusceptible person is regarded as made
not only of stone (18 n.) but also of iron or adamant; this
is Homeric (σιδήρεος θυμός), and cf. Hes. *Theog.* 239 ἀδάμαντος
ἐνὶ φρεσὶ θυμόν and Pl. *Rep.* 360B, 'No one could be so
ἀδαμάντινος as to abide by justice . . . if he could do as he
pleased'.

40–51. On the citation of legendary *exempla* cf. **F6**; the
present example is of 'catalogue' type, achieving much the
same effect as (e.g.) Tyrtaios (D³) fr. 9.3 ff. Hippomenes
and Melampous are analogous to the goatherd himself
because they earned a bride (Melampous vicariously, cf.
43 ff. n.) by the gifts which they were able to offer. Adonis,
Endymion and Iasion are analogous in that they are here
regarded (perhaps by assimilation to the legend of Anchises
[1.105 f.]) all as herdsmen beloved by goddesses: cf. xx.37,
'Was not Endymion a herdsman?' and, on Iasion, Nonnos
Dion. xlviii.667 f., 676 ff. (other versions gave Endymion
and Iasion a higher status, but this is not necessarily in-
compatible with their working as herdsmen [**G8**(*c*)]).
The Moon fell in love with Endymion, and although he
was granted eternal life and youth, it was at the price of
eternal sleep (Apollodoros i.56; cf. Sappho fr. 199). Accord-

ing to *Od.* v.125 ff. Demeter, 'yielding to ⟨the inclination of⟩ her heart', gave herself to Iasion (cf. Hes. *Theog.* 969 ff.), whereupon Zeus killed him with a thunderbolt. The goatherd's citation of mortals whose enjoyment of the love of goddesses was so brief and tragic (there are violent and sinister elements in some versions of the Endymion legend) suggests at first hearing an extravagant humility, as if Amaryllis were a goddess compared with himself, or a comically insensitive and ignorant choice of *exempla*. But part of his point is 'If even a goddess . . . , you need not be ashamed . . .' (cf. the well-worn argument [e.g. Ar. *Clouds* 1079 ff.], 'If even Zeus can't resist the temptation to commit adultery, how can I?'). Another part is suggested by Anchises' words in *H. Hom.* 5. 149 ff., 'Neither god nor man shall restrain me from lying with you now, at once . . . And then I would be willing . . . , when I have been in your bed, to enter the house of Hades'. In his self-pitying and self-destructive mood the goatherd thinks extinction a fair price to pay for brief attainment of his desire.

40 ff. Ἱππομένης . . . ἔρωτα: There are different versions of the Atalante myth. The most familiar to us is that in which the successful suitor (Hippomenes, in the version of Hesiod [frr. 72, 74]) beat her in running because he dropped golden apples (Aphrodite's gift to him) and she paused to pick them up. The story told by Philitas (*Coll. Alex.*) fr. 18 and perhaps implied here by Theokritos is a little different: that the apples proved an irresistible love-token (cf. ii.120 n.) ὡς ἴδεν κτλ: Cf. ii.82 n.

43 ff. τὰν ἀγέλαν . . . ' Ἀλφεσιβοίας: Melampous, brother of Bias, brought back from Mt. Othrys the cattle of Tyro, the mother of Neleus, because Bias was a suitor of Neleus's daughter Pero. Alphesiboia was one of the children of Bias and Pero. The story is told briefly and allusively (Melampous is called simply 'the seer') in *Od.* xi.281 ff., but was told in detail by Pherekydes (*FGrHist* 3) fr. 3.

46 ff. τὰν δὲ καλάν . . . τίθητι: Cf. i.109 f. n. **Κυθέρειαν:** Aphrodite, with whom the island of Kythera, off the southern tip of the Peloponnese, was associated in cult and

legend (Hes. *Theog.* 192 ff.) **οὐδὲ φθίμενόν νιν**: Neither
Bion's *Lament for Adonis* nor any other source suggests that
when Adonis died Aphrodite miraculously preserved his
corpse from decomposition (as, for example, the corpse of
Hektor was preserved for a time [*Il.* xxiii.184 ff.]) in order
to continue embracing him. But he was regarded as return-
ing to life on earth once a year, and the festival Adonia
celebrated this return before it turned to mourning for his
death; cf. p. 209. **ἄτερ**: = χωρίς. Theokritos perhaps envisages
the scene as Greek artists sometimes portray it, with
Aphrodite· cradling the head of the lifeless Adonis against
her breasts and crouching to support his shoulders.

47. **ἐπὶ πλέον**: Cf. Herodas 3.7 f. συμφορῆς δ' ἤδη | ὁρμᾷ 'πὶ
μέζον.

50. **φίλα γύναι**: Cf. 9, 11.132 n.

51. **ὅσ' οὐ πευσεῖσθε βέβαλοι**: βέβηλος, an opposite of
ἱερός, denotes 'not belonging to the gods' and then 'not
qualified for contact with the gods', i.e. uninitiated. Hence
in xxvi.14 sacred objects in the bacchants' worship of
Dionysos are called 'on which βέβηλοι do not look'. The
goatherd apostrophizes the 'uninitiated' in imitation of
ritual prohibitions such as θύρας ἐπίθεσθε. βέβηλοι (our
explicit information on this formula comes from late
sources, but there is a clear imitation of it in Pl. *Smp.* 218b);
Kallim. *H.* 6.3 is similar. There may well have been a
mystery-cult in which both Demeter and Iasion figured;
Demeter is certainly associated with mystery-cults (notably
that of Eleusis) and Iasion with the Samothracian cult
(Diod. v.49).

53. **χεισεῦμαι δὲ πεσών**: 'I *won't* lie down, though I've
fallen!' are the words of a man who refuses to admit defeat
(Ar. *Clouds* 126), 'I'll lie where I fall!' the words of a lover
admitting despair and accepting humiliation; so too in the
love-song of Ar. *Eccl.* 963, 'If you don't open the door, I'll
fall down and lie ⟨here⟩!' Cf. vii.122 f., Kallim. *Epigr.* 63,
Asklepiades (*HE*) 11, 42.

54. For the sentiment cf. 27, and for the metaphor 1.146 n.

POEM IV

This poem, wholly dramatic in form, portrays an amicable
and gossipy conversation between a cowherd, Korydon,
and a goatherd (39), Battos. The tone is — a little self-
consciously — rustic and earthy, with harsh teasing (3)
and sarcasm (7 ff.), malevolence towards people of another
locality (20 ff.), ready recourse to proverbial utterance
(42 f.), simple-minded laughter about a feat of strength
(33 f.) and a belly-laugh about an old lecher (58 ff.). The
goatherd's scale of values is illustrated by his words about
the death of Amaryllis (39) and by his attitude to Aigon's
participation in the Olympic games (7 ff.); but, of course,
as one would expect in Theokritos, he and Aigon are both
musicians (28 ff.). A sententious element, slightly reminiscent
of Hesiod's *Works and Days*, intrudes at 56 f. (cf. x.46 ff.).
The dramatic character of the conversation is emphasized by
its interruptions in 44 ff., where the calves have to be driven
away from the olive-shoots and Battos gets a thorn in his
foot (cf. v.147 ff.).

Several topographical details help to fix the scene of the
meeting. The cattle are pastured by the rivers Aisaros (17)
and Neaithos (24); these are both near Kroton, which lay
halfway along the eastern side of the 'toe' of Italy (cf. p.
127). This accords well with 32 f., 'I sing the praises of
Kroton . . . and the Lakinion that faces the dawn' (a
sanctuary on the promontory which stretches out eastwards
south of Kroton). We have no independent evidence on
'Latymnon' (19). A rough indication of dramatic date is
given by the reference (31) to the 'songs of Glauke', for
Hedylos, an epigrammatist contemporary with Theokritos,
refers in an epitaph on a piper ([*HE*] 10.7) to the music
of Glauke, and later anecdotes (Plin. *Nat. Hist.* x.51,
Aelian *Nat. An.* viii.11) associate Glauke with Ptolemy
Philadelphos. One interesting conclusion can be drawn
from this fact; not only is mention of Glauke by an Italiot

countryman unrealistic (cf. 1.147), but it is unlikely that
Theokritos himself would have heard of Glauke, or — what
is, perhaps, more important — would have wanted to
bring her into the Western setting of the poem, before he
had gone to Alexandria or Kos. Pyrrhos, also mentioned
in 31, was an Ionic poet, but we have no information on his
date.

Milon bears the name of a famous Krotonian athlete of
the sixth century B.C.; presumably Theokritos chose the
name as appropriate (perhaps as very common in South
Italy) but, to judge from the mention of Glauke, did not
intend us to locate the meeting of Battos and Korydon in
the remote past.

Kroton suffered continuously and severely in the first half
of the third century B.C., being defended, attacked, cap-
tured, and plundered at least three times; and Livy
(xxiv.3.1) comments on its consequent diminution and
desolation. There is no reason why this situation should be
reflected or hinted at in Theokritos; cf. **G4**.

3. ἀμέλγες: Cf. 1.3 and **E9**(c).5.

4. ἀλλ᾽: 'Why, no, . . .'. ὁ γέρων: Perhaps Aigon's father
as Σ observes; if so, the father will have handed over the
management of the family's property to his son, as is normal
Greek practice. ὑφίητι: sc. ταῖς βουσίν.

5. ὁ βούκολος: sc. Aigon; so too in 13 and 37.

6. ἐπ᾽ ᾽Αλφεόν: i.e. to the Olympic games; the Alpheos
is the river on which Olympia stands.

7. ἔλαιον: Treated here as a symbol of sport; cf. 11.79 f.
ἐν ὀφθαλμοῖσιν ὀπώπει: A Homeric expression (e.g.
Il. i.587 ἐν ὀφθαλμοῖσιν ἴδωμαι), but Theokritos here uses
it in the sense 'ever ⟨even⟩ set eyes on . . .', whereas
it meant (cf. similar phrases in classical Greek, 'hear with
the ears', 'say with the voice', etc.) 'see before one's very
eyes'.

8. βίην καὶ κάρτος: Cf. *Od.* vi.197 κάρτος τε βίη τε:
in such a phrase we should probably retain the epic η.

ἐρίσδειν: Lit., 'contend', i.e. 'rival', 'be a match for'.

9. ἁ μάτηρ: Battos is sarcastic, implying 'You can't take seriously what people *say*'. **Πολυδεύκεος**: Both the Dioskuroi, Kastor and Polydeukes, were associated with sport, and Polydeukes especially with boxing; cf. xxii.

10. σκαπάναν: Digging was part of a sportsman's training; cf. an anecdote in Ath. 518D on 'a sportsman digging (σκάπτοντι) at Kroton'. **μῆλα**: As his provisions, mutton on the hoof; cf. 34 n.

11. One would have expected the point to be: 'If Milon can talk Aigon into competing at Olympia, he could persuade even . . .', but then 'the wolves to go mad at once' gives the utterance a different orientation, for there is nothing incongruous about rabies in wolves. Battos must be taking up the implication of 10, and must mean: 'if Aigon has been persuaded by Milon to go off in pursuit of a useless ambition, taking twenty sheep, Milon *might as well* . . .'. Rabid wolves (on this meaning of λυττᾶν cf. Ar. *Lys.* 298 ὥσπερ κύων λυττῶσα τὠφθαλμὼ δάκνει) could destroy a flock, because they would lose their natural caution and would kill far more than they needed to eat.

13. ὡς: Exclamatory.

14. ἦ μάν: In Attic μέντοι would be used in such a case, with repetition of the previous speaker's words, 'They are indeed poor creatures' (cf. Denniston, *GP* 401).

15. αὐτά: Cf. ii.89 n.

16. μή: An exasperated or incredulous question, 'She doesn't . . . , does she?' Cf. v.74 μή τυ τις ἠρώτη, 'No one asked you, did they?' **ὁ τέττιξ**: This reflects a traditional belief about the cicada, 'whose food and drink are the dew' (Hes. *Sc.* 395).

17. οὐ Δᾶν: Cf. ii.160 n. **ὅκα μέν**: We realize, when we come to ἄλλοκα δέ in 19, that this must mean 'sometimes', not 'when . . .'; cf. i.36 f.

21. τοὶ τῶ Λαμπριάδα: Although the members of a deme, i.e. a local subdivision of the citizen body, *could* be called 'those of X', X being the eponymous hero of the deme or a hero worshipped in it, the expression is unusual (so is an -άδης name for an eponymous hero), and the distinction suggested by 'when the demesmen . . .' points rather to 'the sons of Lampriadas', who are imagined as providing the principal sacrifice at their deme's festival of Hera. There is no reason why Theokritos should expect us to know — no reason, indeed, why he should have known himself — anything about the internal organization and politics of an Italiot city; he is simply portraying in specific form a typical situation and a typical attitude on the part of his rustic. Battos wishes them a scraggy victim so that (a) Hera will be displeased with them, and (b) they will not get much of a dinner when they eat the victim themselves.

23. καὶ μάν: This corresponds to heavy stress on 'and' to give the sense 'and yet, you know, . . .'. Σ says Physkos was a mountain (hence 'the fields on the slopes of Physkos'?); we have no independent evidence, but should not too readily assume that Σ had none, for the easier interpretation would have been to take Physkos as a person (cf. II.76 n.).

24. φύοντι: The masculine and feminine nouns which follow help to determinate the plurality of the verb, despite the neuter plural subject which precedes it; cf. II.109 n. On grounds of sense emendation to φύονται is tempting, but the active φύειν does occasionally have the sense 'be produced', instead of 'produce', 'generate'; cf. Il. vi.149 γενεὴ ἡ μὲν φύει ἡ δ' ἀπολήγει.

26. καὶ ταὶ βόες: 'Your cattle too'? But the last fourteen lines have been about cattle, and there has been no mention of sheep since 16 f. 'Even your cattle' has no clear point. I suspect that καί looks forward to καὶ τύ in 27; cf. Soph. El. 1301 f. ὅπως καὶ σοὶ φίλον, καὶ τοὐμὸν ἔσται (Denniston, GP, 324).

27. ὅκα: 'Because . . . now . . .', a common meaning of ὅτε, as in English 'Now that . . .'.

28. ἐπάξω: On the variant ἐπάξᾱ cf. E7(b)4.

29. οὐ Νύμφας: Cf. II.160 n. Πῖσαν: The city (Πῑσᾱ in Pindar, Πῑσᾱ in Hellenistic poetry [e.g. Kallim. fr. 98]) was close to Olympia and is commonly treated by poets as synonymous with Olympia.

30. τις: Cf. 1.85 n.; Korydon is not claiming professional status. **μελίκτας**: Probably 'singer', in view of 32, and μέλισμα is 'song' in xiv.31. No one can sing and play a syrinx simultaneously, but passages of song can alternate with passages of piping, and this may be the meaning of καλᾷ σύριγγι μελίσδων in *Ep.* 2.1. On the other hand, μέλισμα and the active verb μελίζειν pretty clearly denote playing on an instrument in xx.28. The interpretation of Antipatros (*HE*) 16.3 f. is controversial.

32 f. If the text is sound, Korydon says 'I praise Kroton and . . .'; then, before coming to the second object, he quotes from a song (ch. xiv.30). 'A fair city is Zakynthos and . . .'; presumably this song went on to praise Kroton, on the lines 'fair is Zakynthos, and fair is . . . , but fairest of all is Kroton'. Cf. Pi. *Py.* 1.99 f., 'kind fortune is the best of prizes, and good repute the second best; and if a man has both . . .', and F. Dornseiff, *Pindars Stil* (Berlin, 1921), 97 ff. **ἅ τε Ζάκυνθος**: In this name ζ is treated by poets as if it were a single consonant sound (cf. *Od.* i.246 ὑλήεντι Ζακύνθῳ); the name could not otherwise be used in hexameters.

33. καὶ τὸ ποταῷον τὸ Λακίνιον: 'And the ⟨place, sanctuary⟩ to the east, the Lakinian ⟨place, etc.⟩'. The sanctuary of Hera Lakinia was situated on a promontory which jutted out south-eastwards from the territory of Kroton.

33 f. ὁ πύκτας Αἴγων: So far we have viewed Aigon only through the sceptical eyes of Battos; Korydon gives us a quite different picture, and the form of his words is intended as a corrective to Battos's scorn: 'that ⟨famous⟩ boxer — Aigon ⟨, I mean,⟩ — . . .'.

34. ὀγδώκοντα . . . μάζας: The gross appetite of boxers and of sportsmen generally was notorious; Euripides (fr. 282.5) called the sportsman 'slave of his jaws and subject of his belly', and Ath. 412E ff. offers a run of anecdotes about monstrous feats of gluttony by sportsmen.

35. τὸν ταῦρον: Among many tall stories told of sportsmen, Milon of Kroton (Aelian *Var. Hist.* xii.22) is said to have seized a bull by the foot and dragged it out of the herd.

36. τᾶς ὁπλᾶς: 'By the hoof'; cf. 11.138 ἐγὼ δέ νιν . . . χειρὸς ἐφαιλαμένα κτλ. **'Αμαρυλλίδι**: Cf. 111.6.

38. μόνας: i.e. others we may forget, but you never.

39. ὅσον . . . ἀπέσβης: Lit., 'as dear as ⟨my⟩ goats ⟨are⟩ to me, so ⟨dear⟩ were you extinguished', i.e. 'When you died, I was as sorry as I would have been if my goats had died'; Theokritos's herdsmen may use extravagant rhetoric (as in III) as means to an end, but they are not men to repine overmuch when finally defeated. The relation between relative and demonstrative ὅσ(σ)ον is modelled on that between relative and demonstrative ὥς; cf. 11.82 n. and xv. 25 n.

40. τῶ σκληρῶ μάλα δαίμονος: Cf. Antiphon iii.γ.4 τῇ σκληρότητι τοῦ δαίμονος ἀπιστῶν, 'Mistrusting the harshness of ⟨my⟩ ill-fortune'. Events are regarded as caused by supernatural powers, and when the individual contemplates the power which has determined events in his own life he often calls it his δαίμων. **λελόγχει**: Cf. the words of the ghost of Patroklos to Achilles in *Il.* xxiii.78 ff. κήρ (much the same as δαίμων in many epic contexts) . . . στυγερή, ἥ περ λάχε (*sc.* με) γεινόμενόν περ.

41. ἔσσετ': 'It' (or 'things') 'will be better' is not a normal Greek expression but is modelled on 'it will be better if . . .', where the 'if . . .' clause is felt to be the subject of 'will be', and on numerous expressions in which 'if . . .' is replaced by an equivalent, e.g. Hdt. iii.72.5 ὃς ἄν (='if anyone . . .') . . . , αὐτῷ οἱ ἄμεινον . . . ἔσται.

42. ἐλπίδες ἐν ζωοῖσιν: The point is 'While there's life there's hope'; then '⟨it is only⟩ the dead ⟨that⟩ have nothing to hope for'. The form is characteristic of maxims (cf. Hes. *Op.* 354 f., καὶ δόμεν ὅς κεν δῷ καὶ μὴ δόμεν ὅς κεν μὴ δῷ· / δώτῃ μέν τις ἔδωκεν, ἀδώτῃ δ' οὔ τις ἔδωκεν) and the thought is expressed at much greater length by Lycurg. *Leocr.* 60.

43. Cf. Herodas 7.46 κἢν ὑῇ Ζεύς, 'even in bad times'.

44. βάλλε: 'Drive' by blows and missiles.

45 f. ἁ Κυμαίθα . . . ὁ Λέπαργος: Cf. 1.151 n.

47. κακὸν τέλος αὐτίκα δωσῶν: This unusual expression suggests the English idiom '(come to) a bad end'; cf. Eur. fr. 32 κακῆς ⟨ἀπ'⟩ ἀρχῆς γίγνεται κακὸν τέλος and Men. *Perik.* 208 f. μέγα τι σοι κακὸν / δώσω. But beyond these we may recall both *Od.* xxiv.124 ἡμετέρου θανάτοιο κακὸν τέλος and *Il.* viii.166 πάρος τοι δαίμονα δώσω.

49. ὥς τυ πάταξα: 'So that I might ⟨have⟩ . . .' is normally expressed by a past tense of the indicative without a modal particle when it is part of what the speaker wishes had been true; cf. vii.86 f. αἴθ' . . . ὤφελες ἦμεν / ὥς τοι ἐγὼν ἐνόμευον κτλ.

51. ὥς: Exclamatory.

52. κακῶς . . . ὄλοιτο: The expression is tragic, not colloquial (unlike κακῶς ἀπόλοιο): cf. Eur. *Hel.* 162 f. κακῶς δ' ὄλοιτο μηδ' ἐπ' Εὐρώτα ῥοὰς / ἔλθοι.

54. τε: Apparently co-ordinating 'and I have it' with 'yes, yes, ⟨I see it⟩'; its postponement is comparatively rare, but cf. Men. *Perik.* 7 f. τεθραμμένης τῆς παιδός, . . ./ . . . , ἐραστοῦ γενομένου τε τοῦ σφοδροῦ / τούτου νεανίσκου κτλ. **ἅδε καὶ αὐτά**: 'Here is' (lit. 'this ⟨is⟩') 'the actual thorn itself'; the wording reflects the well-known gulf between finding the place, which is easy, and actually getting the thorn out.

57. κομόωντι: E9(c).

58. μ': This must = μοι: cf. vii.19 καί μ' ἀτρέμας εἶπε and *Il.* ix.673 εἴπ' ἄγε μ' ὦ κτλ. **τὸ γεροντίον**: Presumably the γέρων of 4. **μύλλει**: Cf. the English slang 'grind'.

59. τᾶς ποκ' ἐκνίσθη: Lit., 'of whom at one time he was scratched'; the verb (which is not slang; cf. Hdt. vi.62.1 τὸν δὲ Ἀρίστωνα ἔκνιζε ἄρα τῆς γυναικὸς ταύτης ἔρως) takes the genitive on the analogy of ἐρασθῆναι, 'fall in love with . . .'.

60. ὦ δείλαιε: Elsewhere abusive or strongly (self-)pitying, and its point here is presumably 'Fancy your not knowing!' Its use as a vocative is absent from Attic comedy.

61. ἐνήργει: Cf. English slang, 'on the job'.

62. ὤνθρωπε φιλοῖφα: An apostrophe to the old man. **γένος**: 'Your breed', 'your stock'.

62 f. ἢ Σατυρίσκοις . . . ἢ Πάνεσσι: Satyrs, both in literature and in vase-painting, are represented as sexually irrepressible, and in xxvii.3, 49, a girl addresses her ardent lover as Σατυρίσκε. Pan, as the goat-legged god of the wild, was credited with a similar nature; cf. our expressions 'ram' and 'old goat'. The pluralization of Pan (cf. Ἔρως and Ἔρωτες) was classical; cf. Ar. Ec. 1069 ὦ Πᾶνες.

63. ἐρίσδει: Cf. 8 n.

POEM V

In this poem, as in IV, two herdsmen meet — Komatas the goatherd and Lakon the shepherd (Lākon — not 'Lakonian', Lăkon) — but the spirit of their meeting is much harsher. There was rough teasing and sarcasm in the dialogue of Battos and Korydon, and more than a touch of crabbed rustic malice; but Komatas and Lakon accuse, revile and ridicule each other at first sight; even their homosexual enjoyment of each other in the past (by contrast with that of the lovers in Pl. *Phdr.* 256CD, who 'consider that they have exchanged the greatest of pledges') serves only as material for spiteful recrimination. Both fancy themselves as singers, and they agree (with difficulty, as one might expect) to compete in a singing-match. They call on a woodcutter, Morson, to act as judge; and after listening to fifteen couplets from Komatas and fourteen from Lakon, Morson stops the contest and declares Komatas the winner.

The location of the scene is indicated by the reference to Lakon and the owner of the goats as men of Sybaris (1, 73), to the owner of the sheep as a man of Thurioi (72), and to the river Krathis (16, 124); there are also a spring (126) and a lake (146) named after Sybaris. Sybaris, close to the river Krathis, some sixty miles north-west of Kroton (cf. p. 121) and a few miles from the sea, maintained only a feeble and intermittent existence after the destruction of the

original city in the late sixth century B.C., and when the
Athenians founded a colony in its territory in the mid-fifth
century the name of the colony, Thurioi, prevailed.
Nevertheless, a community calling itself 'Sybarites' sur-
vived on another site; it was later (when exactly, we do not
know) expropriated by the Bruttians (Diod. xii.22.1), and
we hear no more of it — except in this poem. If in fact there
were no 'Sybarites' in Theokritos's day, then either he has
got his facts wrong or he has located the meeting of Komatas
and Lakon at some indeterminate date in the past. It seems
unlikely that an educated Syracusan should not know
whether Sybaris, in some form, existed or not; but we do
not really have enough evidence to decide between the
alternatives. We do not even have grounds for deciding
whether mention of a river Haleis (123) and a spring
Himera (124) reflects genuine local knowledge or a readi-
ness to invent plausible names. Thurioi, like Kroton,
suffered from assault and pillage in the early third century
B.C.; cf. p. 122.

Neither of the two herdsmen owns the flocks which he is
guarding. Komatas calls Lakon (5) 'slave of Sibyrtas';
Lakon retorts with a sarcastic ὦ 'λεύθερε (8), calls Eumaras
'master' of Komatas (10), and refers to an occasion on
which Eumaras tied up Komatas and beat him (118) —
just as Philokleon in Ar. Wasps 449 f. speaks of tying up and
beating a slave whom he caught stealing grapes. So far, it
would seem that Komatas and Lakon are both slaves. On
the other hand, Komatas speaks of Lakon (1) as τὸν
ποιμένα . . . τὸν Συβαρίταν, and of his own 'master' equally
(73) as Συβαρίτας; an adjective of this kind carries an
implication of status, and is not a mere topographical
term. Lakon calls himself (15) 'son of Kalaithis'; and even
if this is not a man's name (cf. 'Olpis' in III.26, not to
mention Daphnis, Delphis and Thyrsis) but a woman's
(cf. 'Kylaithis' in Herodas 6.50), it need only imply that
Lakon is the illegitimate son of a freeborn woman. The
labourer Bukaios (x.57 f.) and the Cyclops-herdsman
Polyphemos (xi.26, 67 ff.) seem to live with their mothers,

and we hear nothing of their fathers. Moreover, by choosing the name 'Komatas' for the goatherd, who wins the singing-match, Theokritos tacitly invites us to regard him as embodying the virtues and accomplishments of the legendary, quasi-heroic goatherd Komatas (vii.78 f.), a person in the tradition of the poets and 'sons of kings' who pastured flocks (**G8**). It seems to me consistent with the tone of the poem if we regard the references to slavery in 5 and 10 as part of the mockery and abuse which the two herdsmen heap on each other, and if we imagine that Komatas and Lakon are in fact hired labourers, proud of their status as freemen but with little else to be proud of, and vulnerable to mockery of their precarious dependence on others. I do not think that Komatas's beating at the hands of Eumaras is a conclusive objection to this interpretation; a free citizen labourer beaten by his employer could in theory bring a serious charge to court, and he might win, if by some good fortune he could find respectable witnesses; but who would employ him after that, and how would he live? The status of hired labourers, for practical purposes (whatever the law might say) in the twilight zone between bond and free, would explain why Lakon is so touchy (74 f.) when Morson is told by Komatas that the sheep belong to Sibyrtas, not to Lakon himself. It should be remarked that in iii.1 f. and iv.1 f. the men who pasture the animals are not their owners, but there is no reason to think that Tityros in iii and Korydon in iv are slaves; indeed, it is hard to believe it of Korydon. If Theokritos took it for granted that his rustic characters were free men, and if he assumed that his readers too would take this for granted, it may well be (especially after τὸν Συβαρίταν in the very first line of the poem) that he expected us to understand the tone of 5–10.

2. μευ: Interposition of an enclitic possessive pronoun immediately after the article which belongs to the possessed noun is extremely rare, but cf. Herodas 6.41 τήν μευ γλάσσαν.

3. οὐκ ἀπὸ τᾶς κράνας: The negative and elliptical

question as a form of command is mainly colloquial; cf. Ar. *Ach.* 864 οὐκ ἀπὸ τῶν θυρῶν;

5. τὰν ποίαν: There is a broad distinction between ὁ ποῖος, which asks a genuine question, 'What kind of . . .?', and ποῖος by itself, which is scornful, 'What do you mean, . . .?' But the distinction becomes blurred when an apparently innocent question is meant, as here, to insult or annoy.

7. ποππύσδεν: E10(*d*).

8 f. τάν μοι . . . νάκος: Lakon answers 5 f., ignoring 6 f. Cf. 11, and Soph. *Trach.* 423~421. **τίν: ἔβα** means 'went off', and the point of the dative τίν is 'to your detriment'. **τὸ ποῖον:** Cf. 5 n. **Λάκων:** In referring to himself in the third person Lakon may be standing on his dignity (as in 14; cf. 1.103, and so commonly in all literary genres), or he may be rejecting the thought entertained (and allegation broadcast) by Komatas; cf. Aisch. *Sept.* 5 f., where Eteokles says, 'If a disaster befalls us, Eteokles alone will be blamed'.

10. 'For not even Eumaras . . . had one to sleep in'. Cf. *Od.* iii.349 f. ᾧ οὔτι χλαῖναι . . ./ . . . μαλακῶς . . . ἐνεύδειν. Presumably Lakon uses the past tense ἦς with reference to the occasion (yesterday, in fact) on which he is alleged to have stolen the goatskin.

11. Like Lakon in 8, Komatas answers the question of 8 f., ignoring 10.

13. τὰ λοίσθια: Cf. iv.3 n.

14. τὸν ἄκτιον: Pindar fr. 98 spoke of Pan as protector of fishermen (cf. iii.26 n.), and a Hellenistic writer, Philostephanos of Kyrene, said that there was a sanctuary of Pan by the river Krathis. **τέ:** = σέ (E10[*b*]).

15. ὁ Καλαιθίδος: If this is in fact a woman's name (cf. p. 128), there is a humorous point (the same kind of humour as in vi.22, v.n.) in making Lakon proudly use the same form of words as a hero naming a distinguished father. **ἤ:** 'Or, ⟨if I am swearing falsely⟩, . . .'. Cf. Herodas 7.31 f., 'I swear . . . that I tell the truth . . . , *or* may Kerdon' (the speaker himself) 'enjoy no prosperity'.

17. ταύτας: Cf. 11.160 n.

18. ἵλαοί τε καὶ εὐμενέες: Both words are used especially of propitious deities; so Sokrates in Pl. *Phdr.* 257A asks Eros to grant him blessings εὐμενὴς καὶ ἵλεως.

19. Κομάτας: Cf. 9 n.

20. αἴ τοι πιστεύσαιμι: Lakon is determined to have the ill-natured last word on this topic, but does not pursue it further. **τὰ Δαφνιδος ἄλγε':** Cf. 1.19 and **G3**.

21. θέμεν: (**E10**[*d*]), 'offer', as a prize for which they can compete; cf. English 'put down' a bet or a payment.

21 f. ἐστὶ μὲν οὐδὲν ἱερόν: Since one fears to touch or disturb what is ἱερόν, the point of the expression might be 'Come on, don't be afraid!' (Lit., 'it is not in any respect sacred', *not* 'nothing is sacred'). But this does not adequately explain μέν and ἀλλά, which point rather to 'If you're willing . . . , ⟨then⟩, *although* a kid's not much to make a fuss about, *all the same* I'll sing in competition . . .' (so *Σ*).

22. ἀλλά γε: This rare combination of particles (cf. Denniston, *GP*, 23) occurs in Gorgias (DK) fr. 11a.10, 14; possibly Theokritos meant ἀλλ' ἄγε, which is occasionally used with a future tense in epic, e.g. *Od.* xiii.397 ἀλλ' ἄγε σ' ἄγνωστον τεύξω.

23. ὗς ποτ' ' Ἀθαναίαν: Komatas slightly perverts the proverb, which was normally used of presumptuous attempts by the ignorant to teach the accomplished. **κεῖται:** ~ θέμεν (21).

24. ἔρειδε: Lit., 'push', but a lamb does not need much pushing, and in VII.104 the verb is little more than 'bring', 'put' or 'make . . . go'.

25. ἐξ ἴσω: 'Fair', 'equitable'.

26 f. Both indignant questions are indirect ways of saying, 'A kid is not as much worth winning as a lamb.' **παρεύσας:** (=παρεοίσας, Att. παρούσης) Cf. xi.75, and Antiphanes (*CAF*) fr. 227.7 οὐδεὶς κρέως παρόντος ἐσθίει θυμόν.

28. Komatas offers an answer to Lakon's rhetorical questions: '⟨Why,⟩ a man who . . .'. But whereas Lakon meant, 'Who would . . . , if he were free to choose?', Komatas means that the man who is defeated in a contest is

compelled to choose the inferior alternative (cf. 1.3 ff.).
Instead of saying simply, 'Who is defeated', he says 'Who is
confident that he'll win although he's no good', implying
'and will therefore lose'. πεποίθεις: Whereas we say,
'Trusts, like you, ...', Greek often says, '(sc. trusts) as you
trust'. Cf. Theognis 541 f., 'I fear that ὕβρις (sc. may
destroy) this city, ὕβρις which destroyed the centaurs'.

29. σφάξ ... ἐναντίον: Antitheses of this kind are drawn
from nature also in 1.132 ff. (the most elaborate example),
VII.41, 47; cf. also 23 above, 136 f. below and 1.148.
ἀλλὰ γάρ: ἀλλὰ X γάρ ..., Y ... means 'But, since X ...,
therefore Y ...'; cf. 1.19 ff. Sometimes, as here, the form
ἀλλὰ γὰρ X ..., Y ... is adopted (Denniston, GP, 99).

30. ἔρισδε: 'Begin the contest'.

31. οὐ γάρ τοι πυρὶ θάλπεαι: An otherwise unattested
expression obviously meaning 'You don't have to be in
such a hurry about it'. ἄδιον: Probably 'in greater comfort',
and not a reference to the quality of the singing.

33. ψυχρόν: The colder the better, in a Mediterranean
summer; cf. XI.47.

34. χἀ στιβὰς ἅδε: 'And our (natural) couch' (cf. VII.67)
'is this', i.e. is the grass which grows here, or 'Here is our
couch' (cf. IV.48, 54).

36. ὄμμασι τοῖς ὀρθοῖσι: Cf. Soph. Oed. Tyr. 1385
ὀρθοῖς ἔμελλον ὄμμασιν τούτους ὁρᾶν; 'Would I have been
able to look them in the face?' ὀρθοῖς (τοῖς) ὄμμασι is the
usual form of all expressions of this type (cf. ἄκραις ταῖς
χερσίν, 'with the fingertips', etc.); Theokritos either
intends a demonstrative article, '... look at me (sc. as you
are now looking at me) with those unwavering eyes of yours',
or he adopts an unusual way of treating a banal expression,
'with straight eyes' (sc. as opposed to other possible ways of
using the eyes) rather than 'with the eyes straight'.

37. ἔτ': With ἐόντα παῖδ'. ἴδ' ... ἕρπει: Lit., 'see to
what eventually favour comes'. χάρις denotes both the
affection which prompts kindness and the gratitude felt by
the recipient of kindness; cf. Aisch. Pr. 545, where the chorus
says to Prometheus, who has helped mankind but cannot

expect help from mankind in his own suffering, φέρε πῶς χάρις ἁ χάρις; Cf. also p. 217.

38. The point obviously is, 'It's a waste of time to teach ungrateful pupils; you might as well bring up wolf-cubs — to devour you in the end'. Dog-lovers may wonder what dogs are doing in this rustic maxim. The probable explanation is that Greek dogs, traditionally credited with shamelessness rather than affection (cf. II.12 n., xv.53), will eat anything, including their master's corpse; cf. the suitors' threat to Eumaios, *Od.* xxi.362 ff., 'Before long the dogs which you reared (οὓς ἔτρεφες) will eat you'. Hence a proverb θρέψαι κύνας ὥς τυ φάγωντι could be used when a dog bit or snarled or stole food. The same point could be made in the same circumstances by saying θρέψαι καὶ λυκιδεῖς, implying 'You might as well rear wolf-cubs as rear puppies, for all the good you get from them'. καί points a distinction between wolf-cubs and the dogs which (*a*) are the subject of the proverb as known in its other form to speaker and hearer, and (*b*) are present to speaker and hearer at the time of utterance. Theokritos has simply added the two sayings together.

39 f. καὶ πόκ' . . . μέμναμ': Lit., 'And when do I remember having learned . . . ?', i.e. 'I don't remember ever having learned . . .'. ἀνδρίον: Cf. Eupolis (*CAF*) fr. 316 μὴ φθονερὸν ἴσθ' ἀνδρίον.

41 f. Lakon, rising to the bait, gave Komatas the chance to bring out this triumphant vulgarity. It is a standing joke against modern herdsmen that they console their lonely hours by intercourse with their female animals, but of this there is no trace in Theokritos. His Greek herdsmen, accustomed from boyhood to regard homosexual relations, whether casual or emotionally intense, as quite reconcilable with enjoyment of the opposite sex (cf. 87, II.44 n.), prefer each other to animals (cf 116 f. n.). But Komatas contrives to represent his penetration of Lakon not as an experience agreeable to both of them but as a kind of victory of his own, by which he established dominance; Lakon had to put up with the discomfort, and is now implicitly compared (41 f.) to the she-goats dominated by the he-goat. (One may

compare a very ancient rock-cut inscription on Thera, pro-
claiming a similar 'victory', presumably a boast to posterity).

43. To wish that a man might not be buried deeply is
malevolent; it is tantamount to wishing that his body may be
dug up and eaten by dogs. Lakon cleverly combines this
curse with a slur on Komatas's virility.

44. ἀλλὰ γάρ: Here simply, 'But, anyway, . . .'; cf. Pl.
Phdr. 261C ἴσως. ἀλλὰ γὰρ τούτους ἐῶμεν, 'Maybe. Anyway, let's
leave *them*' (Denniston, *GP* 103). **καὶ ὕστατα βουκολιαξῇ**:
The idea, 'You will be so crushingly defeated that you will
never dare to compete again' is Homeric, though in Homer
the context is always grimmer, e.g. *Il.* i.231 f. (Achilles to
Agamemnon), 'You rule over nobodies; were that not so,
this would be your last outrage' (νῦν ὕστατα λωβήσαιο).

48. οὐδὲν ὁμοία: 'Not at all like . . .' normally implies in
English, 'less good', but in Greek it commonly implies,
'better'; cf. II.15 f. n.

52. ἢ τύ περ ὄσδεις: Not altogether gratuitous rudeness,
for Mediterranean country-folk who deal with goats and
goats' milk and cheese sometimes give off so powerful a
stench that it is difficult to stay in the same room with them.
But Theokritos's taste, to judge from vii.16, was different
from ours.

53 f., 58 f. It is not clear in what sense these very large
quantities of milk, oil and honey will be 'for the Nymphs'
and 'for Pan'. When an animal was sacrificed 'to' a god, the
sacrificers ate it, sensibly leaving the god only the inedible
residue (cf. 139 f.); and when milk and other liquids were
poured as an offering the quantity wasted was small.
Presumably the herdsmen will pour a little of the liquids as
libations and use the rest themselves.

55. αἱ δέ κε καὶ τὺ μόλῃς: 'But if *you* come ⟨here⟩',
contrasted with 51.

61. τὰν σαυτῶ: sc. ὁδόν, as (e.g.) in ταύτῃ, sc. τῇ ὁδῷ.
ἔχε: Cf. 1.68; but it is hard not to hear in Lakon's words
the tone of the English, 'You can *keep* . . .!'

63 f. τὸν ἄνδρα . . . τὸν δρυτόμον: The article has
demonstrative force, '*that* man, . . .'.

66. τὺ κάλει νιν: Because Lakon is nearer (65).

67. ὅστις: 'To decide who . . .'. Cf. III.28 n.

69. ἐν χάριτι: Cf. Pl. *Phd.* 115B ὅτι ἄν σοι . . . ἐν χάριτι μάλιστα ποιοῖμεν, i.e. '. . . to please you'. **τύ γα**: Cf. I.124 n.

70. Κομάτα: Cf. 9 n.

71. τὸ πλέον: 'The advantage', as in expressions such as πλέον ἔχειν.

74. μή: Cf. IV.16 n.

76. οὖτος: The nominative οὖτος serves, as often in Comedy, as a vocative in the sense of a peremptory or contemptuous or startled '*you*' in English.

78. εἶα λέγ᾽ εἴ τι λέγεις: Cf. Herodas 7.47, where a cobbler complains that his lazy slaves cry importunately φέρ᾽ εἰ φέρεις τι; how the present tense can come to mean 'whatever you have to . . .' appears from Men. *Epitr.* 339 λέγ᾽ ὃ λέγεις, 'Go on saying what you've begun to say'.

79. ζῶντ᾽: The idea is similar to 'You'll be the death of me!', said to one who beats about the bush; cf. Men. *Sam.* 527 (Austin) ἀλλ᾽ ἀποκτενεῖς πρὶν εἰπεῖν. **ὦ Παιάν**: Since Paian is invoked as a healing god and as an averter of evil, the exclamation is peculiarly appropriate after the suggestion, 'You'll be the death of our friend'. **ἦσθα**: Lakon speaks as if he has just realized Komatas's true character; so in Eur. *Ion* 184 f. the chorus of Athenian women, admiring the buildings at Delphi, says (lit.), 'Not at Athens alone *were* there palaces of the gods'.

80–137. The contest itself, cast in polished and elegant verse, is a literary portrayal of a custom which still exists in Europe (**G8**[*b*]), and it would be surprising if the whole idea was an invention of Theokritos's. Both singers have to compose extempore; the second has to 'cap' the utterance of the first and score off him by a superior boast (82, 86, 90, 98, 102, 106, 126, 130, 134), by mockery (110, 118, 122), or by saying something which makes a parallel point and is not inferior in succinctness and elegance (94, 114). Each singer tries to make the other lose his temper (120–123). It is not entirely clear at 138 whether we should imagine that

Lakon falters after Komatas has sung 136 f. or that Morson judges Komatas's last couplet unanswerable and therefore prevents Lakon from attempting to reply. Perhaps we are meant to remember that the written text of a song-contest presents us with only one aspect of the real thing; we have to imagine the musical quality of the delivery.

80 f. τὸν ἀοιδὸν Δάφνιν: G3.

82. καὶ γάρ: 'Yes, and . . . too . . .', as in 90 and 114.

83 Κάρνεα: The Karneia was an annual festival of Apollo celebrated in the Dorian states, including those of Sicily and the Dodecanese. **καὶ δή**: This combination of particles often serves as a verbal gesture towards what is spatially or temporally imminent.

84. τὰς λοιπάς . . . ἀμέλγω: 'The rest ⟨of the goats which⟩ I milk ⟨are⟩ goats which have borne twins'; cf. 1.25 f.

85. ἁ παῖς: 'My girl', first named in 88. **αὐτὸς ἀμέλγεις**: Cf. 11.89 n. The girl implies, 'Wouldn't you like me to come and help you?'

86. φεῦ φεῦ: Not always an expression of grief; cf. Ar. *Birds* 1724 ὦ φεῦ φεῦ τῆς ὥρας τοῦ κάλλους, where it expresses admiration for beauty. Cf. also οἴμοι in Ar. *Clouds* 773 οἴμ' ὡς ἥδομαι.

87. ἄναβον: Cf. 41, 11.44 nn. **μολύνει**: 'Defiles' might suggest that Lakon is ashamed of himself, but derogatory terms are sometimes used complacently of one's own sexual achievements, as also in pornography for stimulant effect.

88. μάλοισι: A man offered apples as a love-token to a girl (cf. 11.120 n.), but a girl could also flirt with a man by throwing apples at him; cf. vi.6 f., and Ar. *Clouds* μήλῳ βληθεὶς ὑπὸ πορνιδίου.

92. συμβλήτ': A combination of a masculine with a feminine subject commonly has a neuter plural predicate; cf. Xen. *Mem.* iii.7.5 αἰδῶ δὲ καὶ φόβον οὐχ ὁρᾷς ἔμφυτα . . . ὄντα;

93. ῥόδα: The point of the comparison is probably that the beauty of Lakon's boy is necessarily short-lived (cf. vii.120 f.), like the anemone, whereas Komatas's girl, like a rose, will still be beautiful when she is a mature woman. There may well be a double meaning in ῥόδα, for in

Pherekrates (*CAF*) fr. 108.29 it means the female genitals.

94. οὐδὲ γὰρ οὐδ': Cf. (e.g.) *Il.* v.22 οὐδὲ γὰρ οὐδέ κεν αὐτὸς ὑπέκφυγε κῆρα: Denniston, *GP* 197. **ἀκύλοις ὁρομαλίδες:** Lakon, unlike Komatas, does not seem to make a specific point out of the comparison. The dative is here substituted for πρός + accus., as in 137; cf. Aisch. fr. 38.1 as quoted in Ar. *Frogs* 1403, ἐφ' ἅρματος γὰρ ἅρμα καὶ νεκρῷ νεκρός.

95. ἀπὸ πρίνοιο: '⟨Coming as they do⟩ from holm-oak' or '⟨Being as it is⟩ of holm-oak'. Cf. xv.117 ὅσσα τ' ἀπό ... μέλιτος (*sc.* πονέονται), and for the placing of the expression cf. iii.22 στέφανον ... τόν ... κισσοῖο φυλάσσω.

97. καθελών: 'Catch'.

99. αὐτός: 'Of my own accord', 'unasked'.

101. ὡς: 'Where', as in 103; cf. 1.13.

102. οὐκ ἀπὸ τᾶς δρυός: Cf. 3 n. **οὗτος:** Cf. 76 n. **ὁ Κώναρος:** Cf. 1.151 n. **Κιναίθα:** Cf. the she-goat Kissaitha in 1.151 and the calf Kymaitha in iv.46.

103. βοσκησεῖσθε: The future tense in a positive command is very rare; conceivably Theokritos interpreted some Homeric aorist imperatives (e.g. ἄξετε, οἴσετε) as futures; more probably οὐκ ἀπὸ τᾶς δρυὸς (*sc.* ἄπιτε); ... βοσκησεῖσθε is modelled on {οὐ μή + future} + {ἀλλά + future} = 'Do not ..., but do ...'. **ὁ Φάλαρος:** A ram's name, 'white-headed', 'white-crested'; cf. viii.27 ὁ κύων ὁ φάλαρος.

105. Πραξιτέλους: We are not seriously to imagine Komatas as possessing a bowl made by the famous Praxiteles, nor do we need to take him as referring to the younger Praxiteles; it was no doubt a widespread habit to attribute heirlooms to famous artists of the past — like calling an inferior modern chair in eighteenth-century style 'a Chippendale'.

106. ἄγχει: This verb is used not only for strangling and throttling, which a human effects by using his hands or a rope, but also of the manner in which a carnivore seizes its prey or enemy by the back of the neck (biting through the spine, and carrying the dead prey with the same hold) or by the throat. The appropriate translation here is 'gets by the throat'.

107. τὰ θηρία πάντα διώκειν: Cf. 1.110, where the same expression is used of the ὡραῖος Adonis.

108. ἀκρίδες: A general term for many species of orthoptera (cf. 34, 1.52 n.); here, given the threat to the vines from ἀκρίδες which hop over a fence, immature locusts.

109. ἐντὶ γὰρ αὖαι: He gives the locusts a reason why it is not worth their while to come to his vineyard.

110. τοί: Cf. IV.45 n.

111. τὼς καλαμευτάς: The word means 'angler' in Archias (GPh) 28; here, however, men who catch cicadas (for food) on birdlime-covered reeds (κάλαμος: cf. δόναξ ∼ δονακεύειν), a practice referred to by Apollonides (GPh) 18 and Bianor (GPh) 12; cf. E. K. Borthwick, CQ N.s. xviii (1967), 110 ff.

112. τὰ Μίκωνος: Cf. II.76 n.

113. τὰ ποθέσπερα: Cf. IV.3 n.

116. ἦ οὐ μέμνασ': Cf. Zeus's threatening words to Hera, Il. xv.18 ἦ οὐ μέμνῃ ὅτε τ' ἐκρέμω ὑψόθεν . . .; and Achilles' to Aineias, Il. xx.188 ἦ οὐ μέμνῃ ὅτε πέρ σε . . . / σεῦα . . .;

117. εἶχεο: The evidence of literature and vase-painting suggests that not only in buggery but also in normal heterosexual intercourse it was common for both partners to stand, the man penetrating from behind and below, and the woman bending forward to grasp her own knees or a tree (Ar. Thesm. 488 f.) or pillar.

118. τοῦτο μὲν οὐ μέμναμ': On Lakon's indignation cf. 41 n. **ὄκα μάν ποκα:** As we can say in English, 'But I remember when . . . once . . .'.

119. ἴσαμι: =οἶδα, as in Epicharmos (fr. 254) and Pindar.

120. τις: 'Someone is . . .' instead of 'This man is . . .' or 'You are . . .' is a joke found also in Ar. Frogs 552 κακὸν ἥκει τινί, 'Someone's in for trouble', said by Xanthias when his master Dionysos is assailed by angry landladies.

121. Addressed to Morson, not to Lakon. Squills were regarded as having the magical power to avert evil (cf. VII.107 n.); the superstitious man in Theophrastos (Char. 16.14) purifies his house with them. Gathering a plant from over a grave is a magical procedure, and an old woman's grave is especially appropriate because of the association of old women with magic (cf. II.91 n.).

123. κυκλάμινον: Plin. *Nat. Hist.* xxv.115 mentions a belief that cyclamen averted hostile spells from one's house.

127. ἁ παῖς: The girl is evidently part of Lakon's household; fetching water was a girl's job.

128. κύτισόν τε: Named in a list of goats' fodder in Eupolis (*CAF*) fr. 14.3; not the genus of plants now called *cytisus*, which would poison even goats, but the genus *medicago*.

133. τῶν ὤτων καθελοῖσ': This was a common way of kissing small children, but naturally (like other comforting reminders of childhood) acceptable to adult lovers. **τὰν φάσσαν**: The article refers to the one present to Komatas's recollection as he sings, not to the one mentioned in 96.

135. οὐ θεμιτόν: θέμις (cf. I.15 n.) and τὸ θεμιτόν are not only rules which men can (if they are unwise) disobey, but also laws of nature and the order of the universe — including the aesthetic order which we import into the universe. It is this aesthetic order which would be violated if a jay, which makes a brash noise, competed against a nightingale (cf. I.131 ff.). Komatas of course implies that he is to Lakon as the nightingale is to the jay.

137. κύκνοισι: The mute swan (*Cygnus olor*), with which the Greeks were fairly familiar, does not sing, but the whooper swan (*Cygnus cygnus*), which migrates to the western Black Sea coastal regions in winter, has a blood-stirring cry admired by the gods (Ar. *Birds* 769 ff., where the swans sit on the banks of the river Hebros in Thrace). The Greeks also believed, undeterred by the absence of evidence, that swans produced a beautiful song when about to die (Pl. *Phd.* 84E ff.), and naturally the hoopoe could not compete with that unheard melody.

142. καχαξῶ: It is not the Greek way to be modest and considerate in victory or generous in defeat. Komatas voices extravagant pleasure at his triumph, and Lakon is left speechless with shame.

143. ὅττι ποκ' ἤδη: Cf. Isok. vi.29, 'Being beset with

many perils, we were at last (ἤδη ποτέ) compelled to make peace'. Since ποτε is a postpositive which gravitates readily to a place after the word which introduces the clause (cf. 19 οὔ τευ τὰν σύριγγα . . . ἔκλεψε), ὅττι + ἤδη ποκά > ὅττι ποκ' ἤδη.

144. ἐς ὠρανόν: Cf. Xen. *Cyr.* i.4.11, of wild deer: 'They leapt πρὸς τὸν οὐρανόν as if winged'. **ὔμμιν:** Shades of 'for your delight', 'with you' and ' — you'll see! — ' could all be discerned in this dative.

147. οὗτος: Cf. 76 n.

148 f. πρὶν ἢ ἐμέ . . . ἀμνόν: Sexual intercourse by human beings was forbidden in Greek sanctuaries (Hdt. ii.64.1), and it was also forbidden to enter a sanctuary after intercourse without washing (*ibid.*, Ar. *Lys.* 911 f.). With humorously exaggerated religious scruples Komatas humanizes his goats and affects to believe that his sacrifice to the Nymphs will be vitiated if his he-goat covers any she-goats.

149 f. ἀλλὰ γενοίμαν . . . ἀντὶ Κομάτα: Cf. 20. **πάλιν:** *sc.* ὀχεύει. The disloyal goatherd Melanthios suffered exemplary punishment when the suitors had been killed, *Od.* xxii.474 ff.: his nose, ears, hands and feet were cut off, and his genitals cut off and thrown to the dogs to eat.

POEM VI

The singing-contest which occupies the greater part of this poem (6–19, 21–40) is intermediate in character between the acrimonious contest of v and the non-competitive pairs of songs in vii and x, for although the singers, Daphnis ('the cowherd', as in 1.86; cf. **G3**) and Damoitas (whom we do not encounter elsewhere in Theokritos), are contending (ἔρισδεν 5), each amicably admits the excellence of the other (43 ff.). The frame (1–5, 20, 42–46) is not dramatic, but narrative; cf. vii, contrast v and x.

The theme of both songs is the love-affair between the Cyclops Polyphemos and the Nereid Galateia, which provides the material for xi also. In xi.7 Theokritos calls

Polyphemos his own countryman (ὁ παρ' ἀμῖν). The idea
that the strange beings encountered by Odysseus in his
wanderings should be located in Sicily can be traced back
to Hesiod, who mentioned Ortygia, Etna (?) and the
Laistrygones in the same context (fr. 150.25 f.); Thuc.
vi.2.1 takes the location for granted; and the scene of
Euripides' satyr-play *Cyclops* is by Mt. Etna.

There is an element of grotesque humour in Euripides,
play, which no doubt reflects the attitude of his day towards
the Cyclops. About 400 B.C. Philoxenos of Kythera wrote a
dithyramb in which he portrayed Polyphemos in love with
Galateia (*PMG* 815–824), and this had considerable
influence on Attic Comedy; we hear of two plays called
Galateia and one called *Cyclops* during the fourth century.
Theokritos is thus using in both VI and XI a myth very well
established by his own time. It is possible that Hermesianax
(*Coll. Alex.*) fr. 1, 'Looking towards the sea, while his one
eyeball burned' has the same reference.

Daphnis sings as if addressing Polyphemos directly,
telling him that Galateia tries desperately to flirt with him
while Polyphemos fails to respond; Damoitas sings as if he
were Polyphemos, answering the first song. We are not
required to imagine that the situation portrayed in Daphnis's
song was true at the time of singing, or that Polyphemos
himself would have expressed the sentiments which Damoi-
tas puts into his mouth. The singers create an imaginary
situation, and Damoitas assumes a personality other than
his own — just as a dramatist does in composing dialogue
for his characters, and as the lyric poets did perhaps more
often than is commonly realized (cf. *Entretiens de la Fon-
dation Hardt* x [1963], 200–212).

The poem is addressed to Aratos (2), as XI and XIII are to
Nikias. Aratos appears also in VII.98 ff. as a friend of
'Simichidas', the narrator of VII. Identification of this man
with the famous poet Aratos is not entirely precluded by the
fact that the first syllable of the name of Theokritos's friend
is ἄ (VI.2, VII.102, 122) whereas the first syllable of the poet's
name is α in Kallim. *Ep.* 27.4 and Leonidas (*HE*) 101.1

(Meleagros [*HE*] 1.49 called him *Ἄρατος*, but Meleagros lived almost two hundred years later); poets were free to scan the first syllable of the name 'Ares' as short or long, and cf. the epic scansion ἀρά, ἀρᾶσθαι. 'Aratos' is, however, a common name on Kos throughout the Hellenistic period, in documentary contexts which do not reveal the quantity of the first α.

2. τὰν ἀγέλαν: It is not necessary to interpret this as '⟨each⟩ his herd'; Daphnis and Damoitas have been looking after different parts of the same herd, and have now combined the two parts.

3. πυρρός: The colour of an incipient beard (ctr. 11.78) in xv.130 and in Eur. *Phoen.* 32 πυρσαῖς γένυσιν ἐξανδρούμενος. **κράναν**: For this (naturally) characteristic feature of the scene cf. 1.7 f.

4. θέρεος μέσῳ ἄματι: Not 'on the day which falls in the middle of the summer' but 'in the summer, in the middle of the day'.

6 f. βάλλει τοι . . . μάλοισιν: Cf. v.88 n.

7. δυσέρωτα: Cf. 1.85 n. **τὸν αἰπόλον ἄνδρα**: If the text is right (Meineke suggested καί for τόν), the article, in accordance with a frequently attested classical idiom, suggests Galateia's own words to Polyphemos, αἰπόλε, δυσέρως εἶ, or about him, δυσέρως ὁ αἰπόλος: this is rude of her, because he is a shepherd (10), not a goatherd. Though there is no exact parallel, we may compare Aischines iii.167 καὶ τὸν καλὸν στρατιώτην ἐμὲ ὠνόμαζεν, 'and he called me ⟨sarcastically⟩ "a fine soldier" '.

8. ποθόρησθα: = προσορᾷς.

10. σκοπός: Commonly used of a sentry who watches *for* something; but the dog *looks after* the sheep, and the word can have that sense in poetry, e.g. in *Od.* xxii.395, where Eurykleia is called γυναικῶν δμῳάων σκοπός, because she 'keeps an eye on' the slave women.

11 f. τὰ δέ νιν . . . θέοισαν: It is the dog, not Galateia, that runs along the beach. **φαίνει**: 'Reflects'.

15. ἁ δέ: Galateia.

15 f. ὡς ἀπ' ἀκάνθας ... χαῖται: The simile (derived probably from the simile of *Od*. v.328 f., where tangles of dead thistles are blown hither and thither by the wind) is apt, for thistledown eludes us when we try to grasp it but sticks to us when we do not want it.

17. φεύγει ... διώκει: Both words are traditionally used of love; cf. Sappho fr. 1.21 ff. καὶ γὰρ αἰ φεύγει, ταχέως διώξει ... αἰ δὲ μὴ φιλεῖ, ταχέως φιλήσει. For the form of the line cf. xiv.62.

18. τὸν ἀπὸ γραμμᾶς κινεῖ λίθον: 'Moving the stone from the sacred line' was proverbially used of a player in a board-game who moved a piece (lit. 'stone') from a certain line as a last resort to stave off defeat. The expression is attested in Alkaios fr. 351, Epicharmos fr. 225 and later; Theokritos alters it by substituting ἀπὸ γραμμᾶς for the usual ἀφ' ἱερᾶς (*sc.* γραμμῆς). **ἔρωτι**: Perhaps '*through* love', perhaps (with the figure of speech exemplified in the English, 'Love is blind') '*to* love'.

19. τὰ μὴ καλά: Polyphemos's appearance was grotesque, as readers of the Odyssey will remember; cf. 22 n. For κᾱλὰ κᾱλά cf. Kallim. *H*. 1.55 κᾱλὰ μὲν ἤέξευ, κᾱλὰ δ' ἔτραφες.

21. εἶδον ... ἔβαλλε: 'I saw ⟨her⟩ ... when she was pelting my flock'.

22. οὐ τὸν ἐμόν ... γλυκύν: Polyphemos swears (cf. II.160 n.) by his one ⟨eye⟩ (cf. 36, XI.53), as ordinary humans swore by their two eyes; cf. Herodas 6.23 'μὰ τούτους τοὺς γλυκέας (*sc.* ὀφθαλμούς) ... no one shall hear a word ... of what you say'. **ποθορῶμι**: The manuscripts have ποθορῶμαι or ποθόρημαι, but a wish seems more likely, 'and may I see with it to the end ⟨of my days⟩'; hence the emendation.

23f. αὐτὰρ ὁ μάντις ... φυλάσσοι: In *Od*. ix.507 ff. Polyphemos, blinded by Odysseus, exclaims that the seer Telemos had foretold his blinding. Here Polyphemos's wish that the seer may 'take his hateful prophecies home and keep them for his children' owes something to the jeering words of Eurymachos to the seer Halitherses in *Od*. ii.178 f.,

'Go home and prophesy to your children, that they may come to no future harm', but it has a slightly different point: Eurymachos meant that Halitherses was a useless seer who could not expect to be believed by grown men, but Polyphemos is cursing his seer and hoping that harm may befall the seer's family. Cf. Eur. *Hec.* 1275 f., where Polymestor says to Hecuba, 'Your daughter Kassandra must die', and Hecuba, rejecting the ill-omened words with ἀπέπτυσα, 'I have averted the omen by spitting', adds, 'I give this to you to have yourself'.

25. αὐτός: He describes his own positive action, as opposed to Galateia's.

26. ἄλλαν ... ἔχεν: 'But' (*sc.* instead of looking at her) 'I say that I have another ⟨woman as⟩ wife'.

27. ὦ Παιάν: Cf. v.79 n.

28. ἄντρα: Polyphemos, as in the Odyssey, lives in a cave.

29. σίξα: The manuscripts have σίγα (which does not scan) or σῖγα; neither makes sense, and Ruhnke's σίξα is just what we want, for dogs were encouraged to attack by whistling. **ὅκ' ἤρων**: The point is: as it nuzzled her when I was in love with her, so naturally I make it hostile to her now that I am no longer in love. Polyphemos still *desires* Galateia, because she is attractive (cf. 1.97 n.), but has persuaded himself that he can get her on his own terms.

30. αὐτᾶς: The point is that whereas the dog now barks at her from a distance it used to be so fond of her that it would nuzzle her person; cf. *Il.* i.3 f., '. . . sent their souls to Hades, and gave αὐτούς' (= 'their bodies') 'to the dogs and birds'.

31. πολλάκι: With ποεῦντα in sense.

33. δέμνια: He means his own bed; in poetic language a woman who shares a man's bed is said to 'make' or 'lay' the bed; cf. Eur. *Hel.* 59 ἵνα μὴ λέκτρ' ὑποστρώσω τινί. But in *H. Hom.* 2. 143 f., spoken by Demeter in the guise of an old woman, καί κε λέχος στορέσαιμι plainly has no sexual connotation.

37. παρ' ἐμίν: παρά sometimes has the sense 'in the judgment/opinion of . . .'.

38. Παρίας: The marble of Paros, widely used in the

Aegean for buildings and sculpture, is exceptionally white and sparkling; cf. Pi. *Nem.* 4.80, 'whiter than Parian stone'. ὑπέφαινε: 'Reflected' (cf. 11); the subject can only be the sea, despite 36 f.

· **39. βασκανθῶ**: Any kind of boast or self-satisfaction may incur the malice of supernatural powers; cf. Pl. *Phd.* 95B, 'Don't boast, in case some βασκανία perverts our argument'. Euphorion (*Coll. Alex.*) fr. 175 refers to someone who brought βασκανία upon himself by looking at his reflection in water and straightway fell ill. **τρίς**: Cf. 11.43 and p. 100 **ἔπτυσα**: Spitting occurs in many magical and religious contexts (e.g. VII.127) but especially to avert an evil omen (cf. 23 f. n. above) or any kind of misfortune which may be supernaturally inflicted. The superstitious man of Theophrastos (*Char.* 16.15) shudders and spits εἰς κόλπον when he sees a madman or an epileptic.

40. γραῖα: Cf. 11.91 n., VII.126.

'41': a line identical with X.16 appears here in many manuscripts.

44 ff. The accumulated asyndeton (a phenomenon not yet adequately explored by students of Greek syntax and style) is striking; it has something in common with asyndeton at the climax of a narrative (Denniston, *Greek Prose Style* [Oxford, 1952], 119 f.) and something in common also with narratives in comedy which sum up a situation in a few key-words, e.g. Ar. *Clouds* 1076 f., Men. *Sikyonios* 8 ff.

POEM VII

No other poem of Theokritos poses problems of interpretation so numerous and interesting as this. It is a narrative in the first person singular, and the narrator's name is Simichidas (21). He and two other men were walking from the city on a hot day to the farm of some friends, when they met a goatherd, Lykidas by name, who was already acquainted with Simichidas. Lykidas and Simichidas talk

about poetry, and each of them sings a song for the appreci-
ation of the other; the two songs (52–89, 96–127) are
introduced and incorporated in the narrative very much as
the song of Thyrsis in I and the contest of the herdsmen in V
are framed within the dramatic dialogue. Lykidas's song is
based upon a prayer for the safe voyage of Ageanax, the
boy whom he loves, and Simichidas's upon a prayer that his
friend Aratos may be successful in love. At the end of their
singing their ways diverge; Simichidas and his friends arrive
at the farm, and the poem ends with a description of their
relaxation in a lush and peaceful setting.

The scene is the island of Kos. The owners of the farm are
descended (5 f.) from 'Klytia and Chalkon, who brought
into existence the spring Burina'. Burina is a spring south-
west of the city of Kos; Klytia was the wife, and Chalkon
the son ('Chalkodon' in another version of the myth,
Apollodoros ii.138), of Eurypylos, a legendary king of Kos.
Haleis (1) is attested as a place-name west of the city, and
Pyxa (130) may have some relation to the deme 'Phyxiotai'
attested epigraphically further to the south.

Lykidas is 'Kydonian' (12), and Simichidas speaks of two
pipers as ᾿Αχαρνεύς and Λυκωπίτας (71 f.). The best-known
Kydonia is in Crete, Acharnai in Attica, and Lykope in
Aitolia; but since there were other Kydoniai and the farmer-
friends of Simichidas are 'sons of Lykopeus' (4) — we may
recall the cowherd Lykopas in an Italiot context in v.62 — it
is possible that Κυδωνικός, ᾿Αχαρνεύς and Λυκωπίτας all refer to
otherwise unattested localities of Kos.

The time is the present; Daphnis and Komatas (72–89)
are treated as belonging to the legendary past. To what
extent is 'Simichidas' Theokritos himself? A poet's use of the
first person singular does not, of course, necessarily mean
that he is talking about himself. After all, poems III and XX
are written in the first person singular, but that is no reason
why we should suppose that Theokritos himself was a
goatherd (III.1) or cowherd (XX.3, 42) who suffered from
unrequited love for an Amaryllis (III.1) or Eunika (XX.1)
or anyone like them — any more than Anakreon (*PMG*)

fr. 385 (ἐκ ποταμοῦ 'πανέρχομαι πάντα φέρουσα λαμπρὰ) means that Anakreon was a washerwoman or Theognis 257 ff. (ἵππος ἐγὼ καλὴ κτλ.) that Theognis was a mare. But in the case of 'Simichidas' there are some special considerations:

(a) He is, like Theokritos, a poet (37 f.).

(b) He is not simply a poet, but an ambitious young poet of Theokritos's own time, for he says (38 ff.) that he does not *yet*, in his own judgment, 'surpass Sikelidas from Samos or Philitas'. According to Σ 40, 'Sikelidas' was an alternative name of the poet Asklepiades, who was active in the early third century B.C. (well-established by the time that Hedylos [cf. p. 120] wrote [*HE*] 6.3 f.) and was a critic of Kallimachos (cf. Σ Kallim. fr. 1.1, where Ἀσκλη[πιάδηι τῶι Σικε]λίδηι is included among τοῖς με]μφομ(έν)ο[ι]ς αὐτοῦ [*sc.* Καλλιμάχου] τὸ κάτισ[χνον τῶν ποιη]μάτων). Philitas was a famous poet and scholar who lived in the latter part of the fourth century B.C. and the first quarter of the third. He was tutor to Ptolemy Philadelphos, highly regarded by the citizens of his native Kos (Hermesianax [*Coll. Alex.*] fr. 7.75 ff.), and treated seriously, though not with unreserved admiration, by Kallimachos (fr. 1.9 f. *c. Σ*).

(c) Simichidas's statement (93) that good report has brought his poetry 'even to the throne of Zeus', although modified by a diffident που, is totally at variance with the rather precise modesty of his self-assessment in 38 ff. unless we interpret it not as mere rhetorical hyperbole but as a way of saying that he has reason to think that his poetry has come to the notice of the nearest earthly equivalent of Zeus, Ptolemy Philadelphos.

(d) Lykidas, in saying (45 ff.) that he dislikes a poet who 'seeks to build a house as high as the summit of Mt. Oromedon' and the 'cocks of the Muses' who try to rival Homer, and in contrasting Simichidas favourably (44) with such poets, participates in a controversy of Theokritos's own time. The view of poetry which he expresses was pungently defended by Kallimachos, *H.* 2.105 ff., *Aitia* fr. 1 and *Epigr.* 28. To judge from the nature of his extant work, this view was held also by Theokritos.

(e) Aratos (98, 102, 122) is a friend of Simichidas, and the same name is borne by the man to whom Theokritos addresses poem VI (cf. p. 141).

(f) In 99 ff. the compliment to a certain Aristis, which has no bearing on the theme of Simichidas's song, is most easily explicable if Aristis was a real person whom Theokritos wished to compliment.

In these circumstances it is rational to believe that Theokritos has put himself into Simichidas, and it is not altogether irrational to believe that he may have been called 'Simichidas' in real life. As we have seen, 'Sikelidas' and 'Asklepiades' were two names for the same person, and Kallimachos was sometimes called 'Battiades' (he uses the name himself in *Epigr.* 35). Derisory, laudatory or affectionate nicknames were not uncommonly attached to poets and other distinguished men at all times from the archaic period onwards. Unfortunately we do not know whether Theokritos was snub-nosed (σιμός), and the ancient theory that his father's name was not really Praxagoras (*Epigr.* 27.3) but 'Simichos' rested solely on inference from VII (Anon., *Vita Theocr.*).

Who, then, is Lykidas? There are four possible interpretations:

(i) He was a real Koan goatherd with a genius for poetry.

(ii) He was a real poet who amused himself (or 'dropped out' of urban life) by dressing and behaving as a goatherd.

(iii) He represents a real poet whom Theokritos has chosen to portray as a goatherd.

(iv) He is a wholly imaginary character.

The first interpretation is contrary to our usual idea of Koan or other goatherds, but more than that it is hard to say; stranger things have happened. As for the second interpretation, a poet who turned himself into a goatherd would have a certain affinity with Cynic 'philosophers' and Pythagorean fakirs (cf. XIV.5 f.), but his behaviour would have been regarded by most Greeks as an unseemly interpolation into everyday life of something which might be

sanctioned or enjoined in certain traditional cult obser-
vances; there will then be a humorous, ironic undertone in
Theokritos's description of him as every inch a goatherd
(13–19).

One element in the poem seems to point positively to-
wards the third and fourth interpretations: that is the fact
that Lykidas speaks to Simichidas with the relaxed, slightly
patronizing confidence of an older man speaking to a
promising youth, and also presents him with a stick as a
gift (43 f., 128 f.). This gift could not fail to remind any
Greek of the famous incident in Hesiod, *Theog.* 29 ff.:
'Thus spoke the fluent daughters of great Zeus' (*sc.* the
Muses); 'and they plucked a sprig of sturdy olive and gave
it to me as a sceptre . . . and they breathed a voice into me
. . . and bade me sing of the immortal gods . . .'. Theokritos
may mean to suggest that the relation of Lykidas to Simi-
chidas is like that of god or hero to mortal man; Lykidas
is the source, the donor, of inspiration and poetic skill. It is
interesting that they meet in the heat of the day; this was
sometimes associated in popular belief with supernatural
encounters, and Asklepiades (*HE*) 45.1 assumed, without
any justification in the text of the *Theogony*, that it was the
middle of the day when Hesiod met the Muses (on the whole
question of supernatural encounters see M. L. West's
commentary on the *Theogony* ad loc.).

This element still leaves the choice between interpreta-
tions (iii) and (iv) quite open. Theokritos may be acknow-
ledging his debt to a particular older poet who developed
the idea of bucolic poetry, or Lykidas may be the symbol of
the herdsmen's world from which Theokritos himself drew
inspiration. The chief objection to (iii) is the difficulty of
identifying the poet. B. A. van Groningen, *Mnemosyne* 1959,
50 ff., suggested Leonidas of Taras, whom he identified
with 'Astakides the Cretan' in Kallim. *Epigr.* 22 (cf. **G9**);
M. Puelma, *Mus. Helv.* xvii (1960), 144 ff., reminds us that
we cannot necessarily expect to know the name of the
person to whom Theokritos regarded himself as primarily
indebted. Yet all identifications of Lykidas with a real poet,

even with one otherwise unknown to us, seem to me un-
satisfactory when I reflect on the relation between two
data: first, the poet's insistence that Lykidas was a real
goatherd, and secondly, the great gap between the ex-
tremely tentative steps made by earlier poets towards
bucolic themes (and we must remember that the Roman
period, which possessed what we do not possess, regarded
Theokritos as the inventor of bucolic poetry) and the full-
blown development of bucolic which we encounter for the
first time in Theokritos. For these reasons I incline to
interpretation (iv), according to which Lykidas is a symbol
of the bucolic world from which Theokritos derived the
fundamental ideas for a truly original genre of poetry (cf.
J.-H. Kühn, *Hermes* lxxxvi [1958], 40 ff.). See also **G7**.

In legendary encounters between men and gods the gods
are sometimes disguised. In *Od.* x.275 ff. Hermes in the form
of a young man meets Odysseus and gives him the root which
is to protect him against Kirke's magic; and the first person
whom Odysseus meets on his return to Ithake is Athena in
the form of a noble young shepherd (*Od.* xiii.221 f.).
Similarly, the Muses who met Archilochos and turned him
into a poet appeared to him as mortal women (*Suppl. Epigr.
Gr.* xv.517.ii.28 ff.). On the other hand, the Muses who met
Hesiod were not disguised, and although Theokritos, who
knew the *Odyssey* intimately, must have had Hermes and
Athena and comparable divine appearances in mind when
he described the appearance of Lykidas, it does not follow
(as suggested by A. Cameron, *Studi Alessandrini in Memoria
di A. Rostagni* [Turin, 1963], 291 ff.) that he means us to give
precedence to this element and to see or suspect someone
quite different from a goatherd behind the disguise
humorously adopted from epic.

1. ἧς χρόνος: The expression has the same associations
as 'once upon a time', as in the myth which in Pl. *Prt.* 320c
begins ἦν γάρ ποτε χρόνος ὅτε κτλ. Cf. also an epitaph on a
doctor, *GVI* 902 (Paphos, third century B.C.) ἦν χρόνος

ἡνίκα τόνδε σοφώτατον Ἑλλὰς ἔκλειζεν / ἰατρῶν. The use of the expression here suggests that Theokritos portrays his narrator as looking back on something which has become remote to him either through lapse of time or through great changes in circumstances.

2. σὺν καὶ τρίτος: This postponement of connective καί (cf. Ap. Rh. i.74 σὺν καὶ τρίτος ἦεν Ὀϊλεύς, iii. 115 οὐκ οἷον, μετὰ καὶ Γανυμήδεα) seems modelled on the placing of adverbial (*not* connective) καί after a preposition in Pindar, e.g. Ol. 2.28 ἐν καὶ θαλάσσᾳ.

3. τᾷ Δηοῖ: Demeter (cf. 32). **ἔτευχε**: A pair or series of singular subjects is especially apt to take a singular verb when the verb precedes it; cf. Thuc. i.29.2 ἐστρατήγει ... Ἀριστεύς ... καὶ Καλλικράτης.

4 ff. εἴ τι περ ἐσθλόν ... Χάλκωνος: Lit., 'if ⟨there is⟩ anything noble of those who are illustrious from above, from Klytia and Chalkon himself', i.e. ⟨noble⟩, if anything is noble . . .', implying that the nobility of ancestry of the sons of Lykopeus is exceptional. Cf. *Epigr.* 17.3 f., 'I saw the likeness of Anakreon, τῶν πρόσθ' εἴ τι περισσὸν ᾠδοποιῶν', lit., '. . . if anything is pre-eminent of (=among) the poets of former times'. **ἐπάνωθεν**: Cf. xv.91 and *Epigr.* 22.3 πρᾶτος τῶν ἐπάνωθε ('in olden times') μουσοποιῶν.

6 f. ἐκ ποδός ... γόνυ: The attribution of a spring to the kick or stamp of a divine or heroic or divinely guided foot or hoof or stick is common (e.g. Ap. Rh. iv.1446). At Corinth there was a statue of Bellerophon mounted on Pegasos so placed that a spring issued from Pegasos's hoof (Paus. ii.3.5), and Σ here asserts that at Burina the spring came from the foot of a statue of Chalkon. 'Pushing his knee hard against the rock' (7) is an odd detail; conceivably tradition represented Chalkon as climbing out of a crevice (with superhuman strength and a touch of superhuman assistance?), opening the spring with his heel in one wall as his knee was jammed against the other, but more probably the story was that he pushed aside a tremendous rock, using the leverage of his legs in co-ordination with his arms to get it moving.

7 ff. ταὶ δέ . . . κομόωσαι: It is characteristic of Greek poetry to lead us away from the original point, the distinguished ancestry of the sons of Lykopeus, into a scene pictured in loving detail — in this case, detail imported into the mythical scene either by the poet's imagination or from the spring as he knew it in his own day. Cf. xxII.10 ff., and especially Sappho fr. 96.6 ff., where 'now she is pre-eminent among the women of Lydia, as the moon, when the sun is set, surpassing the stars . . .' continues for another five verses to describe the flowers which are refreshed by the dew of night.

12. σὺν Μοίσαισι: An event brought about by a god, or welcome to a god, can be said to happen 'with' the god; and the nature of the event may make it possible, as here, to say which god.

13. οὔνομα μέν: οὔνομα is virtually 'by name', as in (e.g.) Hdt. iv.12.1 ἔστι δὲ καὶ χώρη οὔνομα κιμμερίη.

15 f. ἐκ . . . τράγοιο . . . δέρμ': Cf. ix.10 ἐκ δαμαλᾶν . . . δέρματα.

16. ταμίσοιο ποτόσδον: Cf. v.52 n.

17. γέρων: Often used adjectivally, 'old', with reference to clothes, etc.; cf. xv.19, and *Od.* xxii.184 σάκος εὐρὺ γέρον, 'old broad shield'.

19. μ': =μοι: cf. iv.58.

21. ἕλκεις: The expression denotes the effort expended, not necessarily the speed achieved, and can thus be used indifferently of decrepit hobbling or energetic dancing; Simichidas and his friends are actually going fast (23 ff.).

22. καθεύδει: Lizards in fact (as one would expect of cold-blooded creatures) grow livelier as the heat of the day increases, and they seek the hottest places. Theokritos's idea that they retire for a rest assimilates them unthinkingly to birds and mammals. (There seems to be no limit to the extent to which zoological folklore can triumph over observation; Aelian *Vit. An.* ii.23 solemnly asserts that if a lizard is cut in half both halves will run away).

23. ἐπιτυμβίδιοι: The lark is so characterized ('⟨as it were,⟩ on tombs') because his crest reminded the Greeks of the floral motif so commonly sculptured at the top of grave-stelae. An Aesopian story, offering an explanation of the crest, told how the lark buried his father in his own head.

24. μετὰ δαῖτ' ἄκλητος: The same sequence of letters could be interpreted as μετὰ δαῖτα κλητός, but that would discard the humorous sting in the tail of the question: 'After (=to) a banquet — uninvited?' Uninvited guests had a better reception among the Greeks (e.g. Pl. *Smp.* 174B~E) than nowadays — but not necessarily a better reputation.

25. λανὸν ἔπι: But not to enjoy the vintage; it is too early in the year. **ὥς τοι ποσί:** Virtually =ποσὶ γάρ τοι. **νισσομένοιο:** Transition to the genitive of the participle after the dative τοι is made easier by the tendency of τοι to be treated more as a particle than as a dative pronoun, but is in any case not difficult; cf. II.83 n.

26. ἀείδει: Possibly he means that the stones are kicked so far and so fast that they emit a note as they fly; or, more realistically, that the stones 'ring' as Simichidas kicks against them.

29. τὸ δή: 'A thing which . . .' or 'and this . . .'.

31. ἔλπομαι: Almost 'entertain the idea'; not 'I hope that ⟨one day⟩ I *shall* . . .'.

31 f. ἑταῖροι ἀνέρες: sc. 'of mine'.

32. εὐπέπλῳ: Mention of the goddess causes Simichidas to colour his language with an epithet characteristic of elevated poetry; cf. II.147 f., 165 f.

33. ἀπαρχόμενοι: In dedicatory inscriptions an offering made to a deity in gratitude for profit or success is normally called ἀπαρχή.

34. ἁ δαίμων: Cf. II.11 n. That Demeter in person is the cause of a good barley-harvest is taken for granted. **εὔκριθον:** Cf. 32 n.

35. ξυνά: sc. 'to you and us'. For the repeated ξυνά cf. Hes. fr. 1.6, Ap. Rh. iii. 173. **ἀώς:** Clearly (21 ff.) not 'dawn'; but other passages in which ἠώς is alleged to mean 'day' seem to me to admit the translation 'dawn'. Possibly the expression was what a man actually said when he met someone setting out on the same road at dawn (the Greeks tended to get up and start journeys very early) and became stereotyped.

36. ὥτερος ἄλλον: 'One ⟨of the two⟩ . . . the other'; cf. *Il.* ix.313 ὅς χ᾽ ἕτερον μὲν κεύθῃ ἐνὶ φρεσίν ἄλλο δὲ εἴπῃ.

38. τις: Cf. 1.85 n.

39. οὐ Δᾶν: Cf. iv.50.

41. βάτραχος . . . ἐρίσδω: Cf. v.29 n.

42. ἐπίταδες: The 'purpose' may be to conciliate Lykidas by a show of modesty, on the assumption that boasting would have alienated him and he would have been reluctant to cause bad feeling by competing; but more probably it is precisely the element of boasting, especially Simichidas's claim (30 f.) that he is as good as Lykidas, which is designed to provoke Lykidas to compete.

44. Lykidas treats Simichidas as a young tree 'moulded' into the right shape by Zeus — the god of the weather, which more than anything determines the growth of a tree. He treats him also as a young man who has grown up to tell the truth. ἔρνος is a familiar metaphor (e.g. Aisch. *Ag.* 1525 ἐμὸν ἐκ τοῦδ᾽ ἔρνος ἀερθέν . . . Ἰφιγένειαν); πλάττειν can be used of training and educating the young; ἐπ᾽ ἀλαθείᾳ does not fall within the metaphorical field of ἔρνος and ἐκ Διός (the English expression 'as God made him' is alien to Greek), but perhaps we are meant to recall that σκολιός, 'crooked', can mean (as in English), 'treacherous' and 'dishonest'; cf. Hes. *Op.* 7 f. ῥεῖα δέ τ᾽ ἰθύνει σκολιόν . . . Ζεύς, 'Zeus easily punishes the dishonest man'.

45. ὥς: Cf. 35 n.; as often with γάρ, the point is '⟨I say this⟩ because . . .'.

46. Ὠρομέδοντος: Σ says that this was the name of the highest summit on Kos, and perhaps it was; but we must not forget that some geographical statements made in scholia (including those on Theokritos) are wildly erroneous inferences from the texts which the scholia are meant to expound. In *Od.* vii.58 f. *Eury*medon is king of the Giants, and no doubt Theokritos chose 'Oromedon' with this association in mind.

47. Χίον: Homer (cf. xxII.218); ancient belief in general tended to regard him as a Chian, though, of course, many other theories of his nationality existed.

48. κοκκύσδοντες: Although κόκκυξ is a cuckoo, κοκκύζειν is used of a cock's crowing (e.g. Kratinos [*CAF*] fr. 311, Plato Comicus [*CAF*] fr. 209).

50. κήγὼ μεν: Lykidas begins as if to say, 'And I composed this song . . .', but changes direction to say 'See if you like this song which I . . .'.

51. ἐξεπόνασα: Therefore not in any sense 'improvised'; contrast the couplets of poem v.

52-89. The theme of Lykidas's song is: Ageanax, whom Lykidas loves, will have a safe voyage to Mytilene if he yields to Lykidas. When he has arrived there, Lykidas will hold a celebration here; Tityros shall sing to him of Daphnis and Komatas.

Lykidas's song unfolds in the discursive manner familiar to us from Pindaric odes (and, indeed, for choral lyric in general), so that twelve out of the total of thirty-eight lines are devoted to the story of Komatas and to Lykidas's reactions to that story. The song is essentially bucolic in character, as is made plain not only by its interest in Daphnis and Komatas but by the name 'Tityros' (cf. III.2 f.); the voyage of Ageanax provides the starting-point. Prayers for someone else's safe arrival later became a common literary theme, and eventually the term προπεμπτικὸς λόγος was applied to the genre. Cf. Dioskorides (*HE*) 11, a prayer to Zephyros for the safe return of a boy.

53. ἐφ' ἑσπερίοις 'Ερίφοις: Lit., 'on the evening Kids', i.e. when the constellation Haedi rises in the evening, at the beginning of October. Cf. Aratos 1065, ἑσπερίων προπάροιθεν/ Πληϊάδων, 'before the Pleiades rise in the evening'.

54. χΩρίων: The morning setting of Orion begins in early November, so he 'has his feet on the Ocean' in the period immediately before that; Ap. Rh. i.1201 ff. treats the 'winter setting of deadly Orion' as a typical occasion for a violent storm at sea. It is not intended that 53 and 54 should both refer precisely to the same date; Ageanax is due to sail, when conditions appear favourable to the master of the ship, at a season of the year which can be described by any one or more of the astronomical phenomena which fall within it.

55. ἐξ 'Αφροδίτας: The run of the sentence seems to me to associate the phrase with ὁπτεύμενον (cf. 44, II.30), but it is not impossible that it should be taken with ῥύσηται.

56. ῥύσηται: By 'rescue me from the torments of desire' Lykidas means, of course, 'gratify my desire'. Cf. II.55 n.

57. στορεσεῦντι: Simonides (*PMG*) fr. 508 describes a period of windless calm in winter as ἱερὰν παιδοτρόφον . . . ἀλκυόνος. Lykidas's words imply a belief that halcyons could actually make the sea calm; cf. Ap. Rh. i. 1084–1102. It is a pity that no known bird has the colouring or habits ascribed to the halcyon by the Greeks (including the precise-sounding details in Arist. *Hist. An.* 616ª 14 ff.).

58. ἔσχατα: 'Furthest' or 'extreme' seems at first to suggest the highest seaweed on the beach; but this would not make a very striking thing to say of the storm-winds, for seaweed grows only where it is normally covered by a high tide. Hence the meaning must be 'deepest'; so in Soph. *Ant.* 586 a stormy sea 'rolls up dark sand from the depths' and in *Il.* ix.4 ff., when Boreas and Zephyros together disturb the sea, it throws up seaweed along the shore.

59 γλαυκαῖς . . . ἄγρα: In ταί τε, τε is the relative adjunct (as in 75, αἶτε: there is no logic in our printing conventions), but τε in 60 co-ordinates ὅσοις κτλ. with γλαυκαῖς Νηρηῖσι.

62. For the rhyme cf.xxiv.9.

63. τῆνο κατ' ἦμαρ: The day on which Lykidas learns that Ageanax has reached Mytilene safely.

64. φυλάσσων: Cf. III.22 n.

65. Πτελεατικόν: We do not know to which of several places called Ptelea (listed by Σ) this refers.

66. τις: 'Someone will roast . . .' in English sets us wondering who, but in Greek τις with an active verb often expresses what in English would be expressed passively, 'Beans will be roasted . . .'.

67. ἔστ' ἐπὶ πάχυν: ἔστε first appears combined with prepositions (εἰς, ἐπί, πρός) as early as Xenophon; in Hellenistic prose ἕως is treated similarly.

70. †αὐταῖσιν κυλίκεσσι: 'Cups and all' (cf. xxii.18; this use of αὐτός is common) would make sense only if we imagined Lykidas as eating the cup after drinking the wine in it. Cf. Ar. *Frogs* 560, where Herakles is said to have eaten cheese αὐτοῖς τοῖς ταλάροις, 'baskets and all', Ion of Chios (*TGF*) fr. 29, where Herakles eats the cooking-fire as well as the meal, and Aristophon (*CAF*) fr. 9.9, where it is said of hungry men that they'll eat their own fingers as well as the meat or fish held therein. But this strikes a note of gross fantasy at variance with Lykidas's song as a whole. Σ interpreted the words as 'in the cups themselves', and Valckenaer accordingly supposed that Theokritos wrote αὐταῖς ἐν κυλίκεσσι — as if it were remarkable to remember Ageanax at a time when one's attention should be wholly devoted to wine. But it is precisely in drinking that Lykidas would remember him; cf. ii.151 f., xiv.18 f. I do not think I know what Theokritos wrote or meant at the beginning of this line.

73. Ξενέας: Cf. p. 84. So far as it goes, this story of Daphnis could be the same as the one unfolded in 1.66 ff., but there the scene of his death seems to be the east coast of Sicily (1.68 f., 117 f.), whereas here it is the river Himeras (75), which flows into the sea on the north coast.

74 f. The idea that the scenery mourns occurs also in Moschos 3.1 ff., Bion 1.31 ff.

76. χιὼν ὥς τις κατετάκετο: i.e. εὖτε κατετάκετο ὥς τις χιὼν τάκεται. Cf. v.28 n.

76 f. μακρόν ... Καύκασον: Athos, over 2000 m. high, was a familiar enough sight to voyagers in the northern Aegean, but the other mountains named here lie outside the Greek world. The Haimos range runs eastwards across Bulgaria from north of Sofia; Rhodope runs south and south-eastwards from the same region; the vast scale of the Caucasus ranges was known to the Greeks at least by the fifth century B.C.

81. κέδρον: The chest itself.

82. χέε νέκταρ: The association between poetry and sweet liquids such as nectar and honey is traditional, as in Pi. *Ol.* 7.7 f. καὶ ἐγὼ νέκταρ χυτόν, Μοισᾶν δόσιν, ἀεθλοφόροις / ἀνδράσιν πέμπων, γλυκὺν καρπὸν φρενός / ἱλάσκομαι. Cf. also 1.146 n.

83 ff. τύ θην ... ἐξεπόνασας: τύ θην, coming immediately after the vocative expression and followed by καὶ τύ twice, is reminiscent of the way in which gods and heroes are sometimes praised in a series of general or narrative statements each beginning with σύ (σέ, etc.). Cf. Soph. *Ant.* 787 ff., addressed to Eros: 'And you (καί σ') no immortal or mortal can escape . . . you also pervert to wrong the heart of the righteous (σὺ καὶ δικαίων κτλ.) . . . you also have stirred up this quarrel (σὺ καὶ τόδε κτλ..) . . .'; Kallim. *H.* i.46 ff., 'Zeus, you (σὲ δέ) did the companions of the Kyrbantes take in their arms . . . and you (σὲ δ') did Adrasteia cradle . . . and you (σὺ δ') sucked the teat of the she-goat . . .'. Cf. E. Norden, *Agnostos Theos* (Berlin, 1923), 143 ff. But the repeated καί makes an additional point, suggesting, 'What has been said of others is true of you *too*'. Certainly others in legend had been imprisoned in a chest (Danae and the infant Perseus [Simonides (*PMG*) fr. 543]), others had been miraculously fed on honey (Iamos, the child of Euadne [Pi. *Ol.* 6.45 ff.]); according to Σ here, some such story was told (but when or by whom, we do not know) of Daphnis; and a generation before Theokritos Lykos of Rhegion (*FGrHist* 570), fr. 7, certainly told the story, as we have it here, of a Thurian shepherd (ποιμήν) devoted to the Muses. Either Theokritos has the Thurian story in mind, and intends us to understand that Komatas was preserved like the Thurian shepherd, or, more probably, he is making the point that the humble goatherd Komatas, by virtue of his skill in music and song, deserved and received supernatural help no less than the heroes and heroines renowned in earlier poetry. This point would, of course, accord well with Theokritos's attitude to poetry (**G8**).

90. Νύμφαι: The idea that one can be taught songs by

the Nymphs takes the association of Nymphs and Muses, familiar to us from 1.66 ff., 141, a stage further, and virtually identifies their function.

93. Ζηνός: One's fame can be said to 'reach the sky' (e.g. *Od.* ix.20), and in Ar. *Birds* 214 ff. the song of the nightingale reaches 'the seat of Zeus', where it stimulates Apollo to play his lyre, to which the gods sing and dance. Simichidas seems to combine the two rather different ideas in saying that favourable report has brought his poems to the throne of Zeus, and he must surely (cf. **C3**) be alluding to the court of Ptolemy Philadelphos. Meleager (*HE*) 3.3 speaks of Kos as 'having reared Zeus', and it is beyond doubt that by 'Zeus' he means Ptolemy (cf. xvii.58), who was in fact brought up on Kos. Language of this kind, in which the relation between Ptolemy and an individual subject is assimilated to the relation between Zeus and an individual mortal, does not mean that Meleager and Theokritos believed that Ptolemy was an 'incarnation' of Zeus. Cf. xiv.59 ff., xv.46 ff., 95 nn.

96–127. Simichidas's song calls upon Pan to help his (Simichidas's) friend Aratos to win over the boy whom he loves; and Simichidas calls upon the Erotes to make the boy in his turn suffer unrequited love for someone younger. Simichidas adds exhortation to Aratos to forget about the boy, who — if it is indeed Philinos with whom Aratos is in love — is losing his charm anyway. The bucolic element (103–114, twelve lines out of thirty-two) in this song is constituted essentially by Pan, who is invoked not because he has any greater power than other gods to cause a sequence of events and put ideas into people's heads, but because of his association with the countryside (**G5**) and sexual enjoyment (cf. iv.62 f. n.). Simichidas's prayer is notably irreverent; he threatens and curses the god as if Pan were a kind of djinn possessing magical powers but serving human masters. Theokritos also takes the opportunity to refer to a cult of Pan in Arkadia (106 ff.), which allows him to display both his sympathy with primitive rusticity and a characteristically Alexandrian interest in curious local cults (cf. xviii. 43 ff. n., the *Aitia* of Kallimachos, and the strong aetiological element in the *Hymns* and in Ap. Rh.).

96. Ἔρωτες: Especially from the late fifth century B.C. onwards, the Greeks often pluralized Eros, thus assimilating him to the Graces, Hours, Fates, etc. Cf. iv.63 n. **ἐπέπταρον:** Since one cannot, as a rule, choose when to sneeze, sneezing was regarded as a supernatural intervention indicating the outcome of what has just been said or done (e.g. *Od.* xvii.541). Theokritos develops from this the idea that not the human lover but the Erotes, who are necessarily present when anyone ἐρᾷ, are the vehicle of the omen. Since a sneeze seems to be a favourable omen, where the context enables us to tell (e.g. xviii.16) — though Aristotle (*Probl.* 962ᵇ 19 ff.) treats it, like the δαιμόνιον of Socrates, as a *warning* sign —, it follows that Myrto responds to the love of Simichidas and that Simichidas is contrasting himself with Aratos (after all, the spring which the goats love [97] inevitably comes). He therefore calls himself ὁ δειλός with wry humour rather than despair, for ἔρως is never fully satisfied. Cf. Catullus 45, where Love's sneezes accompany strong mutual love, but the man is still *misellus*.

98. Ὥρατος: On Aratos cf. p. 141. The μέν-element (96 f.) is essentially subordinate, equivalent to 'although . . .' or 'whereas . . .', to the δέ-element, which is now unfolded as the principal subject of the song. This treatment of finite μέν-clauses is characteristic of legal and administrative documents. **ἀνέρι τήνῳ:** Self-reference with οὗτος (ἀνήρ) and ὅδε (ἀνήρ) is common in classical poetry, but Simichidas's self-reference in '*that* man' is different; he adopts in his song the standpoint of someone who is explicitly other than Simichidas, as Telemachos calls the absent Odysseus κεῖνος ἀνήρ in *Od.* i.233.

99. ὑπὸ σπλάγχνοισι: The guts are, in Greek usage, the seat of all strong emotions. In Moschos 1.17 Eros flies from person to person ἐπὶ σπλάγχνοις δὲ κάθηται, and in Herodas 1.56 the young man who falls in love with a married woman ἐκύμηνε | τὰ σπλάγχνα. "**Ἀριστις**: Whoever he was, it is hard to see what he is doing here unless he and Aratos were both real people known to Theokritos (which is not the same as saying that 'Aristis' and 'Aratos' were their real names) and the poet wanted to bring in a compliment to Aristis.

100. μέγ' ἄριστος: No doubt the play on the name of Aristis is intentional; cf. Ar. *Frogs* 83 f. *'Ἀγάθων δέ ποῦ 'στιν;* — ἀπολιπών μ' ἀποίχεται, | ἀγαθὸς ποιητὴς καὶ ποθεινὸς τοῖς φίλοις. Play on names in Tragedy (e.g. on Πενθεύς and πένθος in Eur. *Ba.* 367) reflects a tendency to believe that the naming of a child has an ominous aspect and perhaps even that one's name can determine one's fortune.

101. Apollo (Φοῖβος) was the lyre-player among the gods, and lyre-players enjoyed his special interest and concern. The Pythian Games, held at Delphi (hence 'by ⟨his⟩ tripods'), included contests in singing to the lyre.

102. ἐκ παιδός: Cf. 1.140 n.

103. τόν: The boy. **'Ὁμόλας**: In northern Thessaly. **λέλογχας**: Every god is associated with particular places, which he loves and protects, and is said to 'have obtained by lot', λελογχέναι or εἰληχέναι, those places; cf. xvi.83 f. and Hdt. vii.53.2 ἐπευξάμενοι τοῖσι θεοῖσι οἱ Περσίδα γῆν λελόγχασι.

104. ἄκλητον: i.e. of the boy's own accord. **τήνοιο**: Aratos. **ἐρείσαις**: Cf. v.24 n.

105. εἴτε τις ἄλλος: But the possibility that the boy is anyone but Philinos is ignored in 118 ff.

106 ff. μήτι τυ . . . παρείη: Punishment of a god by beating a statue of him when he fails to do his job is a worldwide phenomenon in primitive cultures (including some parts of the modern Mediterranean). This is the first we hear of it in the Greek world; Theokritos and others of his cultural standard no doubt regarded it as a naive and thoughtless practice, but it serves to introduce a strident note of rustic simplicity. (We may compare an oracular response given to the city of Syedra in Asia Minor in the first century B.C. [*Denkschr. Oesterr. Akad. Wiss.* lxxxv.21 f.]; to secure peace the Syedrans must make an image of Ares brought in chains by Hermes to supplicate at the throne of Justice). The scarcity of 'meat' which occasions the ill-treatment of Pan may be a scarcity of deer and hares, wild creatures which fall within the dominion of Pan; but since Pan is here regarded as a herdsman (113) the idea may be that if he fails to cause fertility and health in the flocks the sacrificial victims will be few and skinny. σκίλλαις: A beating with the stalks of *scilla hyacinthoides* would not be particularly painful (especially if one is a statue), but we are concerned here with ritual; the uses of squills to avert evil (v.121 n.) include the beating of ritual scapegoats (φαρμακοί), as appears from Hipponax (D³) fr. 5 ῥαπίζοντες / κράδῃσι καὶ σκίλλῃσιν ὥσπερ φαρμακόν.

109. εἰ δ' ἄλλως νεύσαις: i.e. if you say 'no' by nodding the head backwards instead of 'yes' by nodding it forwards. Cf. *Il.* vi.311 ἀνένευε δὲ Παλλὰς 'Αθήνη, 'but Pallas Athene refused to grant her prayer'.

110. δακνόμενος: *sc.* by insects.

111 f. The Edonians lived on what is now the river Mesta, around Drama in Greek Macedonia; the river Hebros is the Maritsa, which flows through central Bulgaria and constitutes the Greek-Turkish border on the Aegean. τετραμμένος: Theokritos may have modelled τετραμμένος παρά ('placed' [or 'stationed'] 'on' [lit. 'along'] 'the Hebros') on *Il.* xix.212, where the corpse of Patroklos in the tent of Achilles κεῖται ἀνὰ πρόθυρον τετραμμένος: elsewhere τετραμμένος is followed by εἰς, ἐπί or πρός, meaning 'turned towards', 'facing', or 'occupied with' (one exception is Hes. *Op.* 727 ἀντ' ἠελίου τετραμμένος, 'facing the sun'). "Αρκτω: The constellation of the Great Bear.

113. Αἰθιόπεσσι: In *Od.* i.23 Ethiopians live both in the far west and in the far east, but in classical times the name was given to the people living on and south of the Upper Nile.

114. According to Eratosthenes (followed by Strabon 786) the Blemyes lived between the Upper Nile, north of its junction with the Atbara, and the Red Sea. Theokritos puts them very much further south; and his πέτρᾳ suggests a theory (which we find in Roman times) that the Nile rose from great rocks. Hdt. ii.46 identified Pan with the

Egyptian god Mendes, and Strabon 822 mentions Pan as one of the three deities especially worshipped at Meroe on the Upper Nile.

115. Ὑετίδος: Hyetis, according to Σ (guessing?), was at Miletos. **Βυβλίδος**: A spring at Miletos (Paus. vii.5.10), a city where there was a notable sanctuary of Aphrodite (xxviii.4).

116. Οἰκοῦντα: In Karia, founded by 'Miletos' the father of Byblis (Nikainetos *ap.* Parthenios 11.2). **Διώνας**: In Homer (*Il.* v.370 f.) Dione is the mother of Aphrodite, and so too in xvii.36 (cf. xv.106 Κύπρι Διωναία); it would seem from this passage that at Oikous she was associated with Aphrodite in cult.

118. βάλλετε: The first occurrence in Greek of the 'arrows' or 'shafts' shot by Eros is in Eur. *Hipp.* 530 ff., but βέλος had long been a common metaphor to describe the way in which one is 'struck' by desire.

120 f. μάν is connective, and καὶ δή is a 'verbal gesture' as in v.83 (v.n.). Since Philinos is 'soft' (105), 'riper than a pear' would suggest that he is becoming softer, which is not only biologically unlikely but conflicts with the point of 121: Philinos is getting *older* (πέπων and πέπειρος are used of human maturity, e.g. Ar. *Eccl.* 896, Xenarchos [*CAF*] fr. 4.9 νέᾳ, παλαιᾷ, μεσοκόπῳ, πεπαιτέρᾳ), and the point of the comparison with a pear is the speed with which pears pass from being unripe to being overripe. The vivid simile is of colloquial type, as in xi.20 f., Epicharmos fr. 154 ὑγιώτερον . . . κολοκύντας (sim. Sophron fr. 34), Theopompos (*CAF*) fr. 72 μαλθακώτερος πέπονος σικυοῦ; but cf. also xv.125. Simichidas discourages Aratos from further pursuit of Philinos by the argument that Philinos is too old to be an ἐρώμενος. It is naturally the women who draw the attention of Philinos to his fading charms, since they cannot but be jealous of male ἐρώμενοι.

122 f. μηκέτι τοι . . . τρίβωμες: Simichidas has evidently accompanied Aratos on erotic κῶμοι; cf. ii.127 f. n.

123. ἄλλον: *sc.* and not us.

124. νάρκαισιν . . . διδοίη: It is when the cock crows

that the outdoor sleeper wakes and becomes aware of his 'painful numbness'.

125. 'May Molon alone . . .'. With εἷς ἀπό cf. XVI.87, Hdt. vi.87.2 ἀπ' ἑκατὸν καὶ εἴκοσι παίδων εἷς μοῦνος ἀπέφυγε, Thuc. i.110.1 ὀλίγοι ἀπὸ πολλῶν. 'Wrestling-school' refers to the young men who, at an age when the wrestling-school is one of their main preoccupations, compete strenuously (Molon is presumably a rival of Aratos) for the favours of attractive boys, rivalling each other in this as in wrestling. ἄγχοιτο, lit. 'be throttled' but often used of any painful emotion, is within the same field of metaphor.

126. ἀσυχία: Not inactivity or lethargy, but a refusal to pursue what is difficult to attain; in Thucydides ἡσυχία and ἡσυχάζειν are frequently contrasted with aggressive war.

126 f. γραία . . . ἐρύκοι: Cf. VI.39 f. n. I do not think that Simichidas wants the old woman to spit *on* (ἐπι-) him and Aratos, but that she should spit (with the appropriate ritual or magical words) *on the occasion of* any happening which bodes ill for them.

129. ἐκ Μοισᾶν: To be taken closely with ξεινήϊον: it is to the Muses that Lykidas and Simichidas owe the ξένος-relationship expressed in the gift.

130. Πύξας: Inscriptions of a deme Φυξιῶται have been found in the central area of Kos, and this may conceivably have something to do with Πύξα.

131. ἐς Φρασιδάμω: Cf. 1.103 n.

132. Ἀμύντιχος: 'Amyntas' in 2. In Ar. *Ach.* the Theban calls his slave 'Ismenias' in 861, 'Ismenichos' in 954.

135. κατὰ κρατός: In *Od.* xi. 588 trees shed their fruit κατὰ κρῆθεν of Tantalos; since the fruit is carried away by the wind before he can grasp it, the meaning must be 'down towards his head'. Theokritos perhaps interpreted κατὰ κρῆθεν as 'above his head', for clearly κατὰ κρατός here is what we should express in English as 'above our heads'. Expressions such as Hdt. i.9.3 ἐπεὰν δέ ... κατὰ νώτου αὐτῆς γένῃ, 'when you are behind her' make this easier; and it is true that when we lie under trees whose branches stir in the wind they seem to bow down towards us, then revert, and so on.

137. κατειβόμενον κελάρυζε: A Homeric echo, *Il.* xxi.261 (-ζει).

139. ἔχον πόνον: 'Toiled'; the expression occurs at the same place in the verse in *Il.* xv.416.

141 ff. ἄειδον ... ὀπώρας: For the accumulated asyndeton cf. vi.44 ff. n.

145. ἐκέχυντο: Lit., 'had been poured', i.e. 'hung down'.

147. τετράενες: Cf. the four-year-old wine in xiv.16. Greek wine could be older, e.g. Nestor's ten-year-old wine in *Od.* iii.391. **κρατός:** sc. of ⟨each of⟩ the jars. **ἄλειφαρ:** Smeared round the lid to make the jar airtight.

148. Κασταλίδες: One might have expected Theokritos to address the local Nymphs already mentioned (137); yet Kastalia is the spring at Delphi, below Mt. Parnassos. But in 154 it becomes obvious that the Nymphs on Phrasidamos's farm *are* the 'Kastalian' Nymphs. Theokritos is treating the Nymphs not as local creatures but as true deities who can roam over the earth (cf. 1.66 n.) and have a particular association with Kastalia, just as the Muses can be called Πιερίδες (x.24) from their association with Pieria. **ἔχοισαι:** Cf. 1.68.

149. ἆρά γε πα: It comes easily to a Greek to compare the present with the legendary past; cf. (e.g.) Pindar's comparison of Hieron to Philoktetes (*Py.* 1.50 ff.) Cf. 11.15 f. iii.40–41 nn. **Φόλω:** In the version of the story given by Apollodoros ii.84 f. the centaur Pholos, entertaining Herakles, opened the centaurs' wine; the other centaurs arrived on the scene, drawn by the smell of the wine; there was a fight, in which Herakles routed the centaurs and pursued them to the cave of the great and wise centaur Chiron, whom he wounded. The entertainment of Herakles by Pholos is alluded to in a fragment ([*PMG*] 181) of Stesichoros, and was the subject of a comedy by Epicharmos. Theokritos seems to envisage a more harmonious occasion than that described by Apollodoros.

151 f. τὸν ποιμένα ... Πολύφαμον: On the Cyclops

Polyphemos as a Sicilian shepherd cf. pp. 140 f. ὤρεσι: In *Od.* ix.481 Polyphemos 'broke off the top of a high mountain' and threw it at Odysseus's ships.

155 f. ἅς ... αὖτις: We sometimes find in dedicatory inscriptions the prayer that the prosperity which has occasioned the offering may be repeated; e.g. *IG* i².650 Φαρθένε (i.e. παρθένε, Athena), ... Τελεσῖνος ἄγαλμ' ἀνέθηκε/ ... ᾧ χαίρουσα διδοίης ἄλο (i.e. ἄλλ') ἀναθεῖναι. Cf. 1.144 f. and Herodas 4.86 f. κυγίη (= καὶ ὑγιεία) πολλῇ / ἔλθοιμεν αὖτις μέζον' ἱρ' ἀγινεῦσαι. F. Lasserre, *Rhein. Mus.* cii (1959), 307 ff. suggests that Theokritos is here alluding to the early collection of epigrams called Σωρός, and he points out similarities of wording and motifs between VII and epigrams which we possess; but the manner in which our only informant on the Σωρός, Σ *Il.* xi.101, expresses himself suggests that it was a collection of epigrams all by Poseidippos, not an anthology. πάξαιμι: At the end of the winnowing.

157. ἀμφοτέραισιν: *sc. χερσί*. Plainly Theokritos envisages a cult-statue of Demeter at the farm.

POEM X

Two reapers, Milon and Boukaios, are at work (probably with other reapers [cf. 3, 44, 52]) in the morning (5 f.). Boukaios is lagging, and reveals in answer to Milon's questions that he is in love with a girl, Bombyka (15, 26). Encouraged by Milon to alleviate his desire by singing (cf. p. 173) he sings about her; and Milon, after complimenting him, sings a work-song.

The poem is dramatic in form throughout. It contains no allusions which would enable us to associate it with any region or date, but only the characteristic local and personal allusion for dramatic effect (16). The reapers are not ·slaves, but free men who earn wages (45; cf. VII.28), and Boukaios has a plot of his own (14). The status of the girl, called ἁ Πολυβώτα in 15, is, as so often, in doubt, as Σ 15 frankly admits; she plays the αὐλοί (16, 34), but in a rustic setting that is hardly enough to make her a full-time αὐλητρίς; cf. p. 95.

The dialogue is predominantly colloquial in character, full of clichés and proverbs (11, 13, 17, 41); the similes are bucolic (4, 28 ff., cf. 18), and the tone taken by Milon is one of unfeeling jocularity.

4. ποίμνας: sc. ἀπολείπεται.

5. δείλαν ... καὶ ἐκ μέσω ἄματος: '⟨During⟩ evening ... or even from mid-day'; cf. Denniston, GP 291 f.

6. ὅς: =τὺ γὰρ.

7. πέτρας: Cf. III.18 n.; the line has an epic ring to it.

8. τινὰ τῶν ἀπεόντων: But Milon takes it for granted (15) that it is a girl, not a boy. The generic participle tends always to be masculine; cf. Eur. *Andr.* 711 f. στερρὸς οὖσα μόσχος ('a barren heifer') οὐκ ἀνέξεται / τίκτοντας ἄλλους, οὐκ ἔχουσ' αὐτὴ τέκνα. Also the expression has the character of a cliché; cf. Pi. *Py.* 3.19 f. ἤρατο τῶν ἀπεόντων, οἷα καὶ πολλοὶ πάθον, and Thuc. vi.13.1, where Nikias in 415 urges the Athenians not to be δυσέρωτας τῶν ἀπόντων.

9. ἔκτοθεν: Cf. Dem. xviii.9 τοῖς ἔξωθεν λόγοις, 'by those arguments which are irrelevant' (or 'extraneous') '⟨to this case⟩'. Milon means that a working man knows better than to desire what he does not actually need; this is in the spirit of 58 (v. n.) and of Hesiod's warning (*Op.* 373 ff.) that a hard-working farmer should beware of a seductive woman. Cf. also Eur. fr. 895 ἐν πλησμονῇ τοι Κύπρις, ἐν πεινῶντι δ' οὔ.

11. μηδέ γε συμβαίη: 'No, and I hope it doesn't happen, either'; cf. Denniston, GP 156. χαλεπόν ... γεῦσαι: 'It's a bad thing' ('difficult' in the sense 'making trouble') 'to give a dog a taste of hide'. It is not true that dogs eat hide in preference to other food, or that once they have tasted it they cannot easily be prevented from trying to eat it again. The point of the proverb is sometimes (a) when a dog has got as far as tasting the hide of a carcase, it will be hard to

prevent it from going on to the flesh, and sometimes (b) when a dog has learned to gnaw through its leather lead it will not be content to stay on a lead in future. Cf. G. W. Williams, *Class. Rev.* N.S. ix (1959), 97 ff.

12. ἐνδεκαταῖος: Cf. 11.4 n.

13. ἐκ πίθω ... δῆλον: Lit., 'you draw ⟨wine⟩ from the jar, ⟨it is⟩ clear', i.e. 'Obviously you've got all you want'. **ἐγὼ δ' ... ὄξος**: i.e. there is nothing for me but the vinegary wine left at the bottom. Milon speaks as if Boukaios were happy at being in love, despite all the signs to the contrary.

14. τοιγάρ: Boukaios picks up from 12, ignoring 13; cf. v.8 n. **ἀπὸ σπόρω**: 'Since the sowing'. It is hard to believe that Theokritos's capacity to envisage the people and events which he portrayed was so deficient that he thought of Boukaios as having sown only ten days earlier (12) a crop of the same plant as that which is now being harvested; it must therefore be a different crop, e.g. lentils and peas (cf. Theophr. *Hist. Plant.* viii.1.4), which he would very naturally grow on his own plot.

16. ἁμάντεσσι: Ch. E10(e). **παρ' Ἱπποκίωνι**: 'On Hippokion's farm'.

17. εὗρε θεὸς τὸν ἀλιτρόν: Milon jocularly implies that Boukaios deserved the misfortune which has befallen him. **ἔχεις πάλαι ὧν ἐπεθύμεις**: πάλαι must belong in sense with the ὧν-clause, to give the point 'You've got what you were asking for!' If one asks why Milon says that, the answer may be that Theokritos had observed how people who talk in clichés and proverbs often apply them with extreme vagueness to particular circumstances (cf. xv.26 n.).

18. μάντις ... καλαμαία: This is explained a little further by 26 f. The praying mantis is a gawky, angular, withered-looking insect.

19. αὐτός: '*By* himself', i.e. 'alone'; cf. 11.89 n. **ὁ Πλοῦτος**: Wealth is blind because he so often bestows his favours on the wicked and leaves the virtuous to their poverty. Cf. Hipponax (D³) fr. 29 and the plot of Ar. *Wealth*.

20. Ἔρως: The god Eros is not blind, nor does he shoot at random or miss his aim, but since he does not care (hence ἀφρόντιστος) whom he strikes or what happens thereafter to the person struck, his activity can be compared to the lack of discrimination shown by Wealth. μέγα μυθεῦ: 'Talk big'; those who scoff at men in love may incur the anger of Aphrodite and be stricken themselves (cf. 1.97 f.).

21. μόνον: Like the English 'just' with an imperative.

22. κόρας: '*About* the girl'; cf. Pi. *Ol*. 3.3 Θήρωνος . . . ὕμνον.

23. ἐργαξῆ: *sc.* afterwards.

24. συναείσατε: The composer of one of the Epidaurian hymns (*IG* iv/1.131.3) commands the Muses καί μοι συναείσατε | τὰν Ματέρα τῶν θεῶν; in the earlier treatment of the Muses it is they who 'sing' or 'tell' the story, and the poet or singer who is their medium or instrument (cf. XVI.29 n.). συναείσατε brings the Muses into line with the concept of the god as συλλαμβάνων, 'taking a hand in' action initiated by humans (e.g. Ar. *Knights* 229, *Wasps* 733 f.). **Πιερίδες**: Pieria was the region, north of Mt. Olympos, where (Hes. *Theog.* 53) the Muses were born.

26. Σύραν: Presumably she is called this because she is dark, and not for some other reason which Theokritos's readers would understand; if so, it is interesting that the Greeks regarded themselves as lighter in colour than Syrians.

27. ἁλιόκαυστον: The Greeks admired a deep tan in men, a white skin in women; cf. Ar. *Eccl.* 62 ff., where a woman who is to disguise herself as a man describes how she has oiled her skin and stood in the sun. Vase-painters in the genre which uses white use it for women and goddesses. **μελίχλωρον**: Said of a man, this is an infatuated lover's euphemism for 'pale' (Pl. *Rep.* 474D); but, of course, one approaches the description of a woman's colour from the opposite end of the colour-chart. Cf. Meleagros (*HE*) 98.1, where μελίχρους is the opposite of λευκάνθης.

28. μέλαν: 'dark'; cf. III.35 n. **ἁ γραπτὰ ὑάκινθος**: The flower which Theokritos has in mind was regarded as having markings resembling the letters AI; cf. Moschos 3.6 f. νῦν ὑάκινθε λάλει τὰ σὰ γράμματα καὶ πλέον αἰαῖ | λάμβανε τοῖς πετάλοισι, and Euphorion (*Coll. Alex.*) fr. 40 calls it γεγραμμένα κωκύουσαν. Unfortunately, there is no Mediterranean flower which looks quite like that. The flowers which (to me, at any rate) most look as if marks had been made on them by pen and ink are various species of the genera *Orchis* and *Dactylorrhiza*; but those on which the markings are most striking are not as dark as violets.

29. τὰ πρᾶτα λέγονται: 'Are collected ⟨as⟩ the first ⟨things⟩', i.e. '. . . for preference'.

30. τὰν κύτισον: Cf. v.128 n.

31. ἁ γέρανος τὤροτρον: As gulls do, to eat the insects and worms turned up by the plough.

32. Κροῖσον: For the idea cf. Tyrtaios (D³) fr. 9.6, 'nor even if he were wealthier than Midas or Kinyras'; after the sixth century, the Lydian king Kroisos tended to replace legendary figures as the paradigm of wealth.

33. χρύσεοι . . . ἀνεκείμεθα: 'Statues of us, both golden, would stand dedicated to Aphrodite'. Cf. Lycurg. *Leocr.* 51 ἐν ταῖς ἀγοραῖς ἀθλητὰς ἀνακειμένους, 'statues of athletes set up in the city-centres'. Greeks often transformed their wealth into rich dedications, for these both conciliated the gods and contributed to public regard for the dedicator, during and after his lifetime.

34. αὐλώς: Cf. 16. **ῥόδον . . . μᾶλον:** Cf. II.120, XI.10 for these love-tokens. The pronoun τύ γε is not emphatic; cf. I.124 n. That the line refers to Bombyka is already made plain by the feminine ἔχοισα.

35. σχῆμα: Usually 'bearing', but here 'clothes', as in Ar. *Ach.* 64, where Dikaiopolis exclaims *Ὠκβάτανα, τοῦ σχήματος* when Athenian envoys return from Persia in oriental dress. καινόν must be understood; cf. XXII.68 χεῖρας (*sc.* ἐμάς) . . . καὶ ἐμούς . . . ἱμάντας. **ἐπ' ἀμφοτέροισιν:** *sc.* τοῖς ποσί: cf. VII. 157.

36. ἀστράγαλοι: Usually 'knuckle-bones', used as dice in games, but also the capitals of Ionic columns (*IG* i².373, the Erechtheum accounts). The odd compliment refers to the 'moulding' of Bombyka's feet. **τευς:** With πόδες: cf. *Suppl. Epigr. Gr.* xii.87.21 f. καὶ ἡ οὐσία δημοσία ἔστω αὐτοῦ, 'and let his estate become public ⟨property⟩'.

37. τρύχνος: The plant-name στρύχνος, which includes

deadly nightshade, appears also as τρύχνος: but since Anon. (*CAF*) fr. 605 says μουσικώτερος τρύχνου, it would seem that τρύχνος (-νον) must have had some other meaning. οὐκ ἔχω εἰπεῖν: Boukaios is not likely to say 'but your disposition I do not know', but rather 'and your disposition defeats my powers of description'. Cf. ἄφατος in the sense 'untold', 'indescribable', 'wonderful'.

38. Βοῦκος: It is common enough to find names which appear to be abbreviations of other names, e.g. Βοῦθος, Βουθᾶς ~ Βούθοινος, Βουθήρας; alternative forms of the same man's name are less common, but cf. VII.132 n.

39. Lit., 'how well he measured the form of the mode'. In other words, Boukaios chose a musical mode and imposed it upon the verses, which have a particular metrical form, in a way which produced a good song. ἰδέα means 'form', 'shape', 'type', 'kind'; ἁρμονία 'tuning', 'mode'; and the μέτρον, 'measure', of a verse is what we call its 'metre'.

40. A compliment to Boukaios, meaning 'although I'm older, I haven't learned to sing any better'. Cf. XIV.28, where the point is: 'I'm old enough to know better'.

41. Λιτυέρσα: Lityerses was a 'culture-hero', traditionally Phrygian; there was a work-song (or rather, a genre of work-songs; cf. XV.96 n.) which bore his name (cf. Men. fr. 230, lit., 'singing Lityerses'), and Theokritos treats him also as a legendary composer of songs (cf. G3).

42-55. The song is a mixture of prayer (42 f.), direct exhortation to the workers (44 f.), didacticism (46–51) reminiscent of Hesiod's *Works and Days* (in particular of the practical maxims 383 ff.), and jokes (52 ff.). Such glimpses as we get of real Greek work-songs (*PMG* 869, cf. 849) show much cruder stuff, metrically hard to accommodate (like some other citations from games and ritual) to the metres of literary poetry, and it may be that Theokritos strikes a false note in making Milon's song so Hesiodic in character.

42. πολύκαρπε πολύσταχυ: It was common practice, in addressing divine beings, to add a pair or string of epithets

(a practice grotesquely extended in the imperial period and in magical incantations); for the double πολυ- cf. *H. Hom.* 2.31 f., xv.109, Kallim. *H.* 3.225 πότνια πουλυμέλαθρε πολύπτολι, *H.* 4.316 'Αστερίη πολύβωμε πολύλλιτε.

44 f. μὴ παριών τις εἴπῃ: A Greek was always sensitive to shame at the contemplation of what people may say; cf. Eurymachos to Penelope in *Od.* xxi.322 ff., αἰσχυνόμενοι φάτιν ἀνδρῶν ἠδὲ γυναικῶν, μή ποτέ τις εἴπῃσι κακώτερος ἄλλος 'Αχαιῶν· 'ἦ πολὺ χείρονες ἄνδρες κτλ.'

45. χοὖτος: 'This *too* . . .', implying 'no one does a fair day's work for his wages nowadays'.

46 f. ἐς βορέαν . . . οὕτως: The crop was cut (normally at mid-stem; Xen. *Oec.* 18.2) before it was fully ripe, and then stored in a granary not exposed to the south wind.

48. Hesiod's maxims are largely expressed in the nominative and infinitive, but maxims, like laws and administrative instructions, are also commonly expressed in the accusative and infinitive; cf. Hes. *Op.* 391 f. γυμνὸν σπείρειν κτλ.

51. ἐλινῦσαι δὲ τὸ καῦμα: The normal pattern of life in the Mediterranean includes an early start to the day and a late finish, with a rest in the middle; cf. 1.15 ff.

52 f.: i.e. when the frog wants a drink, he doesn't have to call for someone to bring it to him. The article with the participle is the usual way of expressing 'someone to . . .', 'anyone who will . . .'; as for τό, the article occasionally accompanies an infinitive (without affecting the meaning in any way which translation can reflect) in constructions where more often the infinitive by itself suffices.

54. φιλάργυρε: The insinuation is that the bailiff (like the quartermaster in popular humour about armies) makes money by selling the rations. **φακόν**: Lentil-soup was a staple food of ordinary people; cf. Ar. *Wealth* 1004, 'Now that he's rich he doesn't like φακῆ any more'.

55. κατᾱπρίων τὸ κύμινον: 'Sawing the cummin-seed in half' was a proverbial reference to stingy people (first in Sophron fr. 110; cf. Ar. *Wasps* 1357). 'Boil the lentils better so that you don't cut your hand . . .' means 'Make a better job of the lentil-soup by putting in all the ingredients it ought to have'.

57. πρέπει: *sc.* 'you'. λιμηρόν: Cf. 18, 27.

58. τᾷ ματρί: Implying 'and don't bother us with it'. Boukaios, like the Cyclops (xi.67 ff.) lives with Mum while he yearns for Bombyka, and Milon unfeelingly suggests that his self-pity is childish. So in Men. *Sam.* 349 f. Demeas, trying to persuade himself to cast off Chrysis, whom he loves, tells himself to 'be a *man*, forget your desire, stop being in love.'

POEM XI

The poem is addressed, like xiii (and cf. vi, addressed to Aratos) to Theokritos's friend Nikias, to whose wife Theokritos sends a gift in xxviii. Again, as in xiii, the theme is love, its special point is 'there is no remedy for love except song', and in illustration of this (cf. **F6**) the poet portrays the Cyclops Polyphemos alleviating by song (cf. x.22 f.) his hopeless love for the Nereid Galateia. Polyphemos's song constitutes the greater part of the poem (19–79); the frame (7–78, 80 f.) is narrative.

Nikias is a doctor (5, xxviii.19 f., *Epigr.* 8), and the opening words of the poem are appropriate: 'there is no remedy (φάρμακον) for love, neither ointment nor dressing, except the Muses' (cf. 15 f., 81). He is also a poet (6, xxviii.7), and there are no grounds for denying his authorship of the epigrams ascribed to a Nikias by Meleagros (*HE*) 1.19 f. When xxviii was written, Nikias lived in Miletos (xxviii.21); we do not know when or where Theokritos came to know him, but Kos is an obvious possibility (cf. p. xix). It is a fair inference from xiii.1, 'it was not to attack us alone, as we thought, that Love was born', that they were friends in youth; and anyone who feels it reasonable also to infer that xi is veiled advice to Nikias will be inclined to date xi earlier than xxviii.

On Polyphemos in literature cf. p. 141. Theokritos is using, in both vi and xi, a myth very well established by his own time. Even the idea that Polyphemos soothed his pains by song may be derived from Philoxenos's dithyramb. It is likely that Kallimachos had Theokritos, not merely Philoxenos, in mind when he wrote (*Epigr.* 46, also addressed to a doctor) 'How excellent a charm (ἐπαοιδάν) Polyphemos discovered for the lover! I swear, the Cyclops was no fool. It is the Muses who reduce (κατισχναίνοντι) love, Philippos . . .'.

1–18. The sequence of thought in the introduction is not free from difficulty, but it seems to run thus:

(1 f.) There is no remedy for love except song.

(3 f.) Although an agreeable remedy (*sc.* unlike so many medicines, regimes and operations), it is difficult to find (*sc.* like a rare medicinal plant).

(7) At any rate, it was by singing that Polyphemos fared better than in any other way (ῥᾷστα διᾶγ'). The opinion expressed in 1–6 is supported by the particular case of Polyphemos.

(8–16) He was desperately in love, neglected his flocks, and pined away singing (ἀείδων, 13) of Galateia on the shore, horribly wounded by a shaft of love.

(17 f.) Yet he found the remedy (ἀλλὰ τὸ φάρμακον εὗρε), and sang as follows. (That is to say, by *persisting* in singing he *eventually* found a remedy which he could not have found in any other way; 17 clearly picks up 4 εὑρεῖν δ' οὐ ῥᾴδιόν ἐστι).

The sequence is summarised at the end of the poem (80 f.): thus Polyphemos fared better (ῥᾷον δὲ διᾶγ': cf. 7) than he would have done by spending money (*sc.* on doctors).

On the rhythmic peculiarity of the poem cf. **D2**(*b*) and R. Stark, *Maia* xv (1963), 373 f.

1. ποττόν: = ποτὶ τόν, i.e. πρὸς τόν.

2. οὔτ' ἔγχριστον . . . οὔτ' ἐπίπαστον: Cf. Eur. *Hipp.* 516 πότερα δὲ χριστὸν ἢ ποτὸν τὸ φάρμακον;

3. Πιερίδες: Cf. x.24 n. κοῦφον: This might mean

'giving relief' (cf. 11.92 n.), but since medicines are sometimes unpleasant or painful, 'gentle' would make sense. Cf. Pi. *Py.* 3.53, where the centaur Chiron, taught the art of medicine by Apollo, cured τοὺς μὲν μαλακαῖς ἐπαοιδαῖς ἀμφέπων ('treating'), τοὺς δὲ προσανέα ('agreeable') πίνοντας κτλ.

4. ἐπ' ἀνθρώποις: Cf. (e.g.) Bacchyl. 7.9 ἐπ' ἀνθρώποισιν εὔδοξος κέκληται.

6. ἐννέα: This does not mean that Nikias excelled in all the arts; although the idea that nine was the number cf the Muses is as old as Hes. *Theog.* 60 (cf. *Od.* xxiv.60), and Hesiod gave them individual names, strict apportionment of the different arts among them (vaguely foreshadowed in [e.g.] Pl. *Phdr.* 259c) is first found later than Theokritos.

10. μάλοις: cf. 11.120 n., x.34. **ῥόδῳ:** Cf. x.34. **κικίννοις:** It appears from this passage that a curl of hair was sometimes given as a love-token; since it could be used magically (cf. 11.53 n.), lovers would thus put themselves in each other's power — but possibly a prudent lover would take care to give the girl a bit of someone else's hair.

11. ὀρθαῖς: The sense 'real', 'outright', appears in the fourth century B.C., but ὀρθῶς, 'truly', 'correctly', is earlier. **μανίαις:** Cf. 11.136. **πάντα:** *sc.* 'else'.

12 f. πολλάκι . . . ἐκ βοτάνας: Cf. the lovesick Boukaios's neglect of his crops x.14.

14. αὐτός: Possibly '*by* himself' (cf. 11.89 n.), but there may be an antithesis between himself and his flocks.

15 f. ὑποκάρδιον . . . ἥπατι: Cf. 111.17 ἐς ὀστίον ἄχρις, VII.99 ὑπὸ σπλάγχνοισιν: there is often no great anatomical precision in descriptions of love-sickness. **Κυπρίδος:** Eros, not Aphrodite, shoots the arrow (cf. VII.118 n.), but he is her minister. **ἐκ:** Cf. 11.40 ['30'] n. **τό:** Object of πᾶξε: the antecedent is ἕλκος.

19. λευκά: Cf. x.27 n. **τὸν φιλέοντ':** Cf. VI.17, XIV.62. The point is not quite 'me, who love you', but 'one who loves you'; the article is halfway to the generalizing sense which it certainly has in 75 (v.n.).

20 f. With this effusion of rustic rhetoric cf. VII.120, x.36 f., and with the third comparison vi.45; the fourth refers to smooth, sleek skin free from wrinkles or bagginess.

22 f. Galateia emerges on to the land only when Polyphemos is asleep; cf. vi.6 ff. On the symmetrical assonance cf. **F2. αὖθ':** αὖθι here =αὐτίκα, 'at once', as in *Il.* v.296 τοῦ δ' αὖθι λύθη ψυχή. **οὕτως:** 'Without more ado' (cf. English 'just like that'), as in Plato, e.g. *Phdr.* 235C νῦν μὲν οὕτως οὐκ ἔχω εἰπεῖν. Cf. xiv.27 n.

26. **ἐμᾷ σὺν ματρί:** Cf. 67 ff. **ὑακίνθινα φύλλα:** However wide a range of genera is subsumed under ὑάκινθος (cf. x.28 n.), we can be sure that it was the flowers that Galateia wanted, not the leaves; and since the Spartan girls in xviii.39 f. go to λειμώνια φύλλα to gather flowers for sweet-smelling garlands, it seems that φύλλα can mean stem, leaves and flowers all together.

27. **ὁδὸν ἀγεμόνευον:** Cf. *Od.* vi.261 ἐγὼ δ' ὁδὸν ἡγεμονεύσω, xxiv.225 ὁδὸν ἡγεμόνευε.

28 f. **παύσασθαι δ' ... δύναμαι:** 'And, having set eyes on you, I cannot ... help ⟨loving you⟩'.

29. **οὐ μὰ Δί' οὐδέν:** The double negative reinforced by an oath has a flavour of Comedy; cf. Ar. *Clouds* 1066 ἀλλ' οὐ μὰ Δί' οὐ μάχαιραν, 'but not a knife, oh *no*!'

31 ff. **λασία μέν ... ἐπὶ χείλει:** A broad nose was thought ugly, and appears on vases as an attribute of satyrs. On the grotesque appearance of the one-eyed Cyclops cf. vi.22. **ὕπεστι:** *sc.* τῇ ὀφρύϊ.

34. **οὗτος τοιοῦτος ἐών:** Analyzable as 'being this person here, the sort of person that I am'.

34 f. **βοτά ... πίνω:** Cf. the description of the Cyclops milking his ewes and she-goats in *Od.* ix.244 ff.

37. **οὐ:** For the sequence οὔτε/οὔτε/οὐ cf. Eur. *Hipp.* 1321 f. οὔτε πίστιν οὔτε μάντεων ὄπα / ἔμεινας, οὐκ ἤλεγξας (Denniston, *GP* 510). **ἄκρω:** Not 'in the *depth* of ...' but ⟨even⟩ at the *end* of ...'; cf. Aratos 308, where ἀκρόθι νυκτός must mean not 'at dead of night' but 'just before dawn'. There should be plenty of cheese left in the depth of winter, but one expects a shortage of it at the end of the winter.

38 f. Cf. iv.30 n.

39. τίν: In this poem = σέ: cf. 5, 68. **γλυκύμαλον:** Cf. Sappho fr. 105(a).1 'as the γλυκύμαλον reddens on the end of the branch . . .'.

42. ἀφίκευσο: Σ knew of other thematic imperatives in -σο (on the analogy of athematic imperatives such as μέμνησο), e.g. στεφανοῦσο, which he regarded as Syracusan. They may indeed have been known from Epicharmos or Sophron, but not all scholiastic comments on dialect forms are responsible or even intelligent. The phenomenon is similar in character to the substitution of -ᾶσαι and -εῖσαι for -ᾳ and -εῖ in the second person middle and passive, which can be observed from the first century B.C. onwards. **ἐξεῖς οὐδὲν ἔλασσον:** 'You won't be worse off (sc. for the change)': cf. πλέον ἔχειν, 'have an advantage'.

44. τὤντρῳ: Cf. vi.28 n.

46. μέλας: Cf. iii.35 n., x.28.

47. ψυχρόν: Cf. v.33 n.

49. τῶνδε: 'In preference to this'; αἱρεῖσθαι is assimilated here to the construction of προτιθέναι (e.g. Hdt. iii. 53.4 πολλοὶ τῶν δικαίων τὰ ἐπιεικέστερα προτιθεῖσι) and προτιμᾶν (e.g. Antiphon ii.β.5 τὴν σωτηρίαν τοῦ κέρδους προτιμῶντες).

50. λασιώτερος: 'More hairy' (sc. than is right), i.e. 'too hairy'. To judge from the sparsity of body-hair on gods and heroes as depicted in vase-paintings, hair on the chest was not admired by women.

51. ὑπὸ σποδῶ: To heat the stake with which he was to put out Polyphemos's one eye, Odysseus says (Od. ix.375), ὑπὸ σποδοῦ ἤλασα πολλῆς: hence σποδῶ is more likely to be right than the variant σποδῷ (cf. R. Renehan, Harv. Stud. Class. Phil. lxvii [1963], 272 f.).

54. ὅτ': This could = ὅτε, i.e. 'because as it is', but elision of ὅτι is certain in 79.

55 f. ὡς κατέδυν . . . ἐφίλησα . . . ἔφερον: Cf. iv.49 n.

58 f. Since he has not said or implied that he would have brought her summer and winter flowers at the same time, he is not correcting himself but pedantically explaining as if to an imaginary objector (who may indeed be Galateia, better acquainted with sea than with land).

60. νεῖν: He will need more than ordinary swimming to reach Galateia, as he has already recognised (54 f.).

61. For the reader who remembers how Polyphemos fared at the hands of Odysseus there is grim irony in this line. **ὧδε:** = δεῦρο, as elsewhere (e.g. v.33) it = ἐνθάδε.

62. ὔμμιν: 'You ⟨Nereids⟩'.

66. τάμισον: Cf. vii.16.

67. μόνα: In his infatuation for Galateia he absolves *her* from blame.

68. οὐδέν ... φίλον εἶπεν: A comic assimilation of the mythological situation to one familiar in everyday life. Since the sexes were segregated in respectable society, a lover's mother had much more opportunity to speak to his girl than he could have had himself, and a well-disposed mother could act as a go-between. In Lys. i.20 it seems that a crucial stage in the adulterer's attempt to seduce Euphiletos's wife was passed when she went to the Thesmophoria (a purely female festival) with the adulterer's mother.

69. ἆμαρ ἐπ᾽ ἆμαρ: The expression defies precise analysis, although the meaning is clear; the same can be said of Soph. *Ant.* 340 ἔτος εἰς ἔτος.

72. ὦ Κύκλωψ Κύκλωψ: Cf. Eur. *Med.* 401 f. (Medeia to herself) φείδου μηδὲν ὦν ἐπίστασαι, / Μήδεια, and Men. *Sam.* 349 f. (Demeas to himself) Δημέα, νῦν ἄνδρα χρὴ / εἶναί σ᾽.

73. ἐνθών: 'Go and . . .', *sc.* from here.

75. τὰν παρεοῖσαν: *sc.* ὄιν or αἶγα. The metaphor is delightfully down-to-earth; cf. iv.39. For the sense 'available' cf. v.26 f. n. **τὸν φεύγοντα:** Despite Galateia's sex, the participle is masculine because of the generalizing nature of the utterance; cf. vi.17, x.8, xiv.62.

78. κιχλίζοντι: The girls giggle, as well they might, when Polyphemos takes their teasing approaches seriously. And he knows they are teasing, but tries (79) to tell himself otherwise.

79. ὅτ᾽: = ὅτι, the elision of which is exceedingly rare. **τις:** The usage is different from that of 1.85 and iv.30, and like the English 'I'm someone' = 'I'm important'; cf. Eur. *El.* 939 ηὔχεις τις εἶναι τοῖσι χρήμασι σθένων.

POEM XIII

This is a narrative poem addressed, like xi, to Nikias, and
(also like xi) it suggests in its opening lines that Nikias and
Theokritos have both been well acquainted with the
torments of love. The link between the opening theme and
the narrative is slender: 'We are not the only ones . . .:
Herakles loved Hylas . . .' — and the poet goes on to tell
how Hylas was kidnapped by water-nymphs when the
Argonauts had beached their ship at Kios one night and how
Herakles went looking for him in vain. For the principle of
the mythological *exemplum* cf. **F6**, and for examples of the
power of Eros cf. Soph. *Trach.* 497 ff.

Hylas disappears for ever when the Nymphs, captivated
by his beauty, drag him down into the pool in which they
live. Such a legend was told also of Bormos, who was
drowned and never seen again (Nymphis [*FGrHist* 432]
fr. 5b~Hesychios β 1394); the idea is exploited in the
'epitaph' of Kallimachos (*Epigr.* 22) on Astakides the
Cretan (not necessarily drowned; ἥρπασε Νύμφη | ἐξ ὄρεος)
and in several real epitaphs, e.g. *GVI* 952 (Rome, *c.* 100
A.D.). The motif is akin to that of boys snatched up to
Olympos by the gods — Ganymede, or Pelops in Pindar's
treatment of the myth (*Ol.* 1.37 ff.).

The story of Hylas was told, at greater length and with
many differences of detail, by Ap. Rh. *Arg.* i.1187–1357.
Hylas is there 'squire' (ὀπάων) of Herakles (i.131 f.), as
Meriones is ὀπάων or θεράπων of Idomeneus in *Il.* viii.263 f.,
xiii.246 and Patroklos θεράπων of Achilles (xvi.165), and
Herakles' fury and desperation at his ominous disappearance
reflect the shame of a hero who has failed to protect his
squire. In Theokritos, on the other hand, Herakles is the
lover of Hylas. It is hard to believe that neither poet was
acquainted with the work of the other; but which of them
wrote about Hylas first? The chronological evidence (**C4**)
might seem to tell in favour of the priority of Theokritos,
and there is one motif in Apollonios which strikes so false a

note in its context that it may result from his adaptation of a
more easily explicable motif in Theokritos. Hylas's cry, as
he falls into the pool, is heard by the hero Polyphemos, who
runs furiously in the direction of the pool 'like a wild beast
whom the bleating of sheep has reached from a distance;
burning with hunger he goes towards it, but he does not
come upon the flocks, for the herdsmen have already
driven them within the pens' (i.1243–1247). In Theokritos,
when Herakles hears the cry of Hylas, he runs to it as
'when a fawn cries in the mountains, a ravening lion speeds
from its lair to gain an easy prey' (62 f.). Both similes are
curious, since Polyphemos and Herakles alike are anxious
to save Hylas, not to destroy him; but Theokritos's simile is
explicable from the erotic relationship between Herakles
and Hylas (v.n.), and the possibility should be considered
that it gave Apollonios the idea for a similar image which
does not, in his version, have the same justification.

On the other hand, we do not find Hylas mentioned in
the lyric poets of the archaic and classical periods, and the
evidence for his appearance in tragedy is oblique and
vulnerable: an unlikely interpretation of Aisch. *Pers.* 1055
by Hesychios, a scholiast's statement that the tragic-
sounding line Ar. *Wealth* 1127 originally referred to
Herakles' search for Hylas (and 'became proverbial' — the
scholiast does not cite a specific tragedy), and a mention of
Hylas by Ovid *Tr.* ii.406 towards the end of a long list of
tragic characters. Now, Apollonios had a reason for making
something of Hylas, because the hero figured in a cult at
Kios (i.1354 ff.), and this cult was a link between the
present and the route of the Argo. Apollonios, like Kalli-
machos (frr. 108 f.) was particularly interested in links of
this kind (e.g. i.1047 f.), and once he had brought the
obscure local myth to light Theokritos could have re-
interpreted it. If, on the other hand, Theokritos wrote
before Apollonios, it would seem that he chose a very
recherché mythical example to illustrate the power of love.
However, *Σ* Ap. Rh. i.1355 mentions 'Kinaithon in his
Herakleia' as having treated the search for Hylas. Kinaithon

was a poet of the 'epic cycle'; unfortunately, *Σ* Ap. Rh. i.1165 cites 'Konon' (a late aetiological writer) 'in his *Herakleia*' in connection with another myth, and 'Kinaithon' in *Σ* i.1355 has sometimes been emended to 'Konon' to bring the two references into line. I am inclined to agree with those who reverse the remedy and emend 'Konon' to 'Kinaithon' in *Σ* i.1165; *Herakleia* sounds more like an epic than a title for any part of Konon's aetiological miscellany (it was in fact the title of an epic by Peisandros; cf. *Epigr.* 22). Thus Theokritos *could* have had a poetic source, much earlier than Apollonios, for the Hylas story. (It should be added that Hellanikos (*FGrHist.* 4) fr. 131 mentioned — under the name 'Theiomenes' — Theiodamas, who was father of Hylas; but we do not know whether he said anything about Hylas).

And yet . . . here we have Theokritos telling a story about an incident in the voyage of the Argo through the Propontis into the Euxine, and in XXII we have him telling another such story. Both stories are told by Apollonios; and stories of that region, naturally abundant in Apollonios, are notoriously rare elsewhere in Greek poetry. Confronted with this fact, arguments for the priority of Theokritos based upon individual passages and motifs speak with a faint voice; and until we have fresh evidence, I adopt the view that both XIII and XXII were written on themes drawn by Theokritos from Apollonios. Which of the two poets has handled the theme better is a matter on which readers disagree (see further Köhnken).

1. ἀμῖν: The pronoun is emphatic, and the point of the dative is, 'We are not the only ones *affected by* . . .' ἔτεχ': The subject is the unnamed god or goddess (τεκεῖν can mean 'beget' or 'bear') indicated by the whole clause ᾧτινι . . . ἔγεντο. ὡς ἐδοκεῦμες: A man seriously in love is inclined to feel that no one can ever before have been so afflicted.

2. ᾧτινι . . . ἔγεντο: There was no agreed parentage of Eros. In Hes. *Theog.* 120 he is one of the primeval beings

(cf. Pl. *Smp.* 178B), and the lyric poets invented a variety of parentages for him.

3. τὰ καλά: Since ἔρως is regarded as essentially a strong response to what is καλόν, this line makes much the same point as 1 f.

4. τὸ δ' αὔριον οὐκ ἐσορῶμες: That we mortals cannot foresee what the morrow will bring has little relevance to the theme of Eros, but it heightens the contrast between mortals and the deified Herakles.

5. 'Αμφιτρύωνος: Herakles in legend is usually the son of Alkmene by Zeus; Amphitryon was her mortal husband and therefore *in loco parentis* to Herakles, who is accordingly often called 'Αμφιτρυωνιάδης (cf. 55). Theokritos refers to the divine parentage of Herakles in XVII.33, but not in this poem. Cf. p. 251.

6. τὸν λῖν: The lion of Nemea was the most famous of the lions overcome by Herakles. The point of the reference is that Herakles could withstand a lion but could not withstand love; love, as commonly, is treated as an external force of great power against which only those of exceptional fortitude can fight, and even they with no assurance of victory. **ἤρατο παιδός**: On homosexual relations cf. II.44, v.41 f. nn. It is not clear from this poem how young Hylas was; on a famous Attic red-figure vase which depicts the pursuit of Ganymede by Zeus Ganymede is playing with a hoop and has no pubic hair. Cf. 53 f.

7. τὰν πλοκαμῖδα: The point of the article (no different in principle in a mythological and an everday allusion) is to suggest that Hylas's hair was uniquely beautiful and therefore famous.

8. ἐδίδασκε: Teaching was regarded as an important ingredient in a lasting relationship between a lover and his boy, and this is exploited for philosophical purposes by Plato in *Phdr.* and *Smp.*

9. ὅσσα: Object of μαθών. **ἀγαθός**: 'Goodness' in an adult male is above all physical courage and endurance.

10. οὔτ' εἰ ... 13. πετεύρῳ: 'Neither if ... nor when ... nor when ...' are an amplification of 'never' (οὐδέποκα).

Of the three times of day — midday, dawn and nightfall — the first is expressed plainly, the second with the grandiose personification typical of high poetry, and the third through a homely picture. ἐς Διός: Cf. 1.103 n.; here simply 'into the sky'.

14. ὡς: 'So that . . .', giving the purpose of χωρὶς δ' οὐδέποκ' ἦς. κατὰ θυμόν: Cf. καταθύμιος, 'congenial', and English 'after one's own heart'.

15. † αὐτῷ δ' εὖ ἕλκων †: 'Pulling well' is, according to Σ, a possible metaphor from oxen trained to pull the plough, but we have no parallels for it and it is hard not to suspect that Σ too had none. Moreover, αὐτῷ at the beginning of a clause cannot be the unemphatic pronoun 'for him'; if it means 'him *himself*' there is no syntactical difficulty, but the sense is unsatisfactory; possibly εὖ ἕλκων is a corruption of something meaning 'coming to resemble' or 'following the example of' (εὖ εἰκώς Sitzler) or possibly αὐτῷ is corrupt as well (οὕτω δ' εὐκλειῶς Gow).

16. ἀλλ': We would more commonly say in English, 'he was never apart from Hylas' (10) '*and*, when . . .' (an example of his not being parted), but in Greek ἀλλά contrasts positive with negative: 'he was never apart . . .; on the contrary, when . . .'.

17. Αἰσονίδας: Jason was the son of Aison of Iolkos (19 n.).

18. ὧν ὄφελός τι: Lit., 'of whom ⟨there was⟩ some use(fulness)', i.e. 'who had something of value to contribute', through their courage and skill. Cf. Xen. *Hell.* v.3.6 ὅτιπερ ὄφελος ἦν τοῦ στρατεύματος.

19. ἐς ἀφνειὸν Ἰωλκόν: Iolkos lay at the northern end of the Gulf of Pagasai in southern Thessaly, and was the traditional (e.g. Pi. *Pyth.* 4.188) launching-place of the Argo. Cf. xxii.79 n.

20. Ἀλκμήνας: Cf. 5 n. Μιδεάτιδος: Alkmena was daughter of Elektryon, king of Midea, a city of the Argolid. ἡρωίνας: She was a 'heroine' in the sense that she belonged, like the Greek 'heroes' in general, to the period when the 'half-gods' walked the Greek earth; cf. 28.

22 f. ἄτις ... διεξάιξε: Theokritos here looks ahead to what the Argo was to accomplish after the events with which the rest of this poem is concerned. The κυανεᾶν ... συνδρομάδων are the rocky outcrops at the Black Sea end of the Bosporus (Kyaneai in Hdt. iv.85.1, also 'Symplegades' and similar names). The story was that they floated free until the Argo, miraculously assisted by Athena (Ap. Rh. ii.598 ff.), sailed between them without being crushed.

23. βαθύν ... Φᾶσιν: Theokritos seems now to be looking ahead to a much later point of the voyage, the arrival at the river of Kolchis (cf. 75) at the far end of the Black Sea.

24. αἰετὸς ὡς μέγα λαῖτμα: μέγα λαῖτμα is used by Ap. Rh. iv.980, 1694 of an expanse of sea. The comparison of the Argo's arrival at the Phasis with the way in which 'an eagle ⟨runs into⟩ a great sea' strikes an odd note — if the mouth of the Phasis was so wide, there was nothing very remarkable about sailing into it — and the words which follow, ἀφ' οὖ τότε χοιράδες ἔσταν, bring us back suddenly to the clashing rocks; they also indicate that αἰετὸς ὡς μέγα λαῖτμα is a simile relating not to arrival at the Phasis but, with a powerful hyperbole, to the passage between the rocks, through which the Argo shot 'as an eagle', with unlimited space all round it, '⟨shoots across⟩ a great sea'. Thus, unless Theokritos eccentrically located the rocks not at the Bosporus but at the far end of the Black Sea (and surely he cannot have meant this; the name 'Kyaneai' was their ordinary name in his day), βαθὺν δ' εἰσέδραμε Φᾶσιν is a rather difficult parenthesis — difficult because the reader is not warned by the sense of the words that a resumption lies ahead, as he is in (e.g.) Eur. *Iph. Taur.* 1309 f. πῶς ἔλεγον αἴδε, καὶ μ' ἀπήλαυνον δόμων, ὡς ἐκτὸς εἴης; Jacobs suggested transposition:

> ἀλλὰ διεξάιξεν — ἀφ' οὖ τότε χοιράδες ἔσταν —
> αἰετὸς ὡς μέγα λαῖτμα, βαθὺν δ' εἰσέδραμε Φᾶσιν.

Here the parenthesis is easier; but if the transposition is correct, the corruption was earlier than the second century A.D., for a papyrus has the lines in the same form as the medieval text. ἀφ' οὗ . . . ἔσταν: 'And in consequence the rocks at that moment became fixed'. It was fated (Ap. Rh. ii.603 ff.) that this should happen if ever a ship succeeded in sailing between them.

26. τετραμμένου: When the spring has 'been turned', i.e. has changed, summer has begun.

27 f. θεῖος ἄωτος ἡρώων: So Pi. *Pyth.* 4.188 calls the Argonauts ναυτᾶν ἄωτος.

29. νότῳ . . . ἀέντι: Lit., 'by means of a south wind blowing a third day', i.e. 'with a south wind which had blown for three days'.

30. εἴσω: i.e. past the Hellespont and in the sea (Propontis) which separates the Hellespont from the Bosporus. **Κιανῶν**: Kios lies at the head of a deep inlet on the southern coast of the Propontis.

32. κατὰ ζυγά: Since ζυγόν is used of a bench in a ship propelled by oars (cf. 74, τριακοντάζυγον) and πολλοὶ δὲ μίαν in 33 seems to be contrasted with κατὰ ζυγά, we should refer κατὰ ζυγά not to ἐκβάντες, describing an orderly disembarkation, but to πένοντο, describing their preparation of the meal in pairs. In 37 it seems that Herakles and Telamon (v.n.) eat together, and they presumably rowed together; Ap. Rh. i.397, on the other hand, locates Herakles and Ankaios on the same ζυγόν.

36. ὁ ξανθός: Cf. 7, 11.78 nn.

37. Τελαμῶνι: Son of Aiakos (hence brother of Peleus) and father of Ajax; he is associated with Herakles in legend (e.g. Isoc. ix.16, where the two heroes fight together against Laomedon), and in Ap. Rh. i.1289 ff. it is he who reproaches Jason for leaving Herakles behind (cf. 32, 70 nn.).

40. ἡμένῳ ἐν χώρῳ: Lit., 'in a sitting (*or* seated) place'. ἥμενος can imply idleness, stillness or obscurity, and here perhaps means 'sheltered', 'hidden away'.

40. περὶ δέ . . . 42. ἄγρωστις: The wealth of botanical detail is characteristic of Theokritos and absent from Apollonios's description of the spring; cf. **G4**.

43. ὕδατι δ' ἐν μέσσῳ: Nymphs, being supernatural, can dance as well under water as on land.

44. δειναί: All supernatural beings, however beautiful, are to be feared, simply because they are more powerful than humans and can do great damage if offended. The verse is modelled on Homer's description of Kirke in *Od.* x.136 δεινή θεός αὐδήεσσα.

45. ἔαρ θ' ὁρόωσα: 'With spring in her eyes'. Cf. (e.g.) Herodas 3.17 Ἀΐδην βλέψας, 'with a murderous scowl'.

47. ἐν χερί ... ἔφυσαν: Lit., 'grew on (ἐμφῦναι) to his hand', i.e. 'clung to ...'. Cf. *Od.* xxiv.409 f. ἀμφ' Ὀδυσῆα/ δεικανόωντ' ἐπέεσσι καὶ ἐν χείρεσσι φύοντο.

48. ἀπαλάς: The word is commonly used when softness is vulnerability (as, e.g., the throat is ἀπαλός in relation to a spear-point), and the soul is ἀπαλός in relation to Eros. Cf. Archil. (D³) fr. 112.1 f. ἔρως ... κλέψας ἐκ στηθέων ἀπαλὰς φρένας. **ἐξεφόβησεν:** Lit., 'frightened ... out ⟨of its controlling seat⟩', i.e. 'routed', 'put to flight'. Eros is regarded as a victor over sanity, like panic Phobos in battle; cf. 11.137 n. Apollonios has (i.1232 f.) τῆς δὲ (*sc.* the nymph) φρένας ἐπτοίησεν ('excited', 'distracted')/Κύπρις.

49. Ἀργείῳ: We do not know what genealogy of Hylas Theokritos had in mind to justify 'Argive'; he may have meant it in the epic sense, 'Greek'. **ἐπί:** 'In their desire for ...'; cf. 11.40.

50. ἀθρόος: Lit., 'all together', suggesting that Hylas fell bunched ('like a stone', we would say) rather than with arms and legs flailing or clinging to the bank at the last moment; so too in xxv.252 the lion of Nemea 'leapt on me ἀθρόος'. We may, however, be dealing here with an early example of the late Greek sense 'sudden'. **πυρσός ... ἀστήρ:** The simile of a shooting star may have been prompted by conventional comparisons of a beautiful or distinguished person to a star.

52. παῖδες: 'Boys' in the colloquial sense common in English but not otherwise attested in Greek. **πλευστικὸς οὖρος:** An abundance of shooting stars was regarded as a sign that a wind would rise from that quarter (Aratos 926 ff.); a single shooting star (τέρας, 'portent', to sailors and landsmen alike in *Il.* iv.75) may not have had that significance, but Theokritos speaks as if he thought it had.

55. περὶ παιδί: This reversion from κοῦρος (46, 53) to παῖς is appropriate, since Herakles' agitation is that of an ἐραστής anxious for his παῖς (or, as a boy in such a relationship was called, παιδικά), and κοῦρος lacks homosexual associations. But παιδί in 49 warns us not to press the point too hard.

56. Μαιωτιστί: Lit., 'in the manner of ⟨Lake⟩ Maiotis', the Sea of Azov, in the land of the Scythians (cf. XVI.99 n.); the adverb must qualify εὐκαμπέα. The Scythian type of bow, which is gripped by the left hand at a straight 'waist' between two sweeping curves, is associated in vase-painting and literature with Herakles, and he commonly carries his club, as here (57), in the other hand.

60. παρεὼν δὲ μάλα σχεδόν: 'And although he was quite close at hand . . .'.

62-65. A simile of the form 'A; so B' instead of the more familiar 'As A, so B'; cf. XIV.39 ff. The lion and the fawn symbolise lover and boy in Theognis 949 f., though in a fragment of Kydias cited by Pl. *Charm.* 155D the lion is the power of love and the fawn the hapless lover.

66. οἱ φιλέοντες: Cf. III.28 n. **ὅσσ'**: If this = τοσαῦτα γάρ, there is a change of subject between the generalisation σχέτλιοι οἱ φιλέοντες and its exemplification in the sufferings of Herakles. It would not be quite impossible to punctuate strongly after φιλέοντες and take ὅσσ' as exclamatory.

68. γέμεν . . . τῶν παρεόντων: Lit., 'was laden with those who were present' — Herakles being an absentee. Theokritos does not explain why the Argonauts were ready to sail in the middle of the night (69 μεσονύκτιον) instead of sleeping the night ashore (cf. 33) and starting in the morning.

69. ἱστία: Although, as we have seen (32), the Argo was propelled by oars, it also (like an Athenian trireme) used sails when conditions were favourable. **ἐξεκάθαιρον**: Lit., 'cleaned'; perhaps a technical term, 'made ready' (cf. K. Latte, *Festschrift Bruno Snell* [Munich, 1956], 27 f.).

70. μένοντες: Theokritos tells us that they waited for

Herakles, but he does not tell us until 75, and then only by implication, that they sailed without him. ᾇ πόδες ἄγον: Ap. Rh. i.1263 f. says of this same chase ἐς δὲ κέλευθον | τὴν θέεν ᾗ πόδες αὐτοὶ ὑπέκφερον ἀΐσσοντα: but ch. xiv 42.

71. χαλεπός ... ἄμυσσεν: Eros; cf. ii.55 n. and xi.16.

72. μακάρων: '⟨As one⟩ of the immortals' (lit. 'blessed'). The nymphs will naturally have made him immortal, so that he can keep them company for ever.

73. Ἡρακλέην: There is a strong contrast between the felicity of Hylas and the shame of Herakles. Ap. Rh. ii.766 f. uses the rare form -κλέην in a passage alluding to the loss of Hylas: ἀφίκοντο κίον θ', ὅθι κάλλιπον ἥρω| Ἡρακλέην. λιποναύταν: sc. 'as . . .', 'calling him . . .'. λιποναύτιον was an offence under Attic law and (like λιποτάξιον) carried the stigma of cowardice; so in Aisch. Ag. 212 f. Agamemnon asks himself, when confronted with the need to sacrifice his daughter, πῶς λιπόναυς γένωμαι ξυμμαχίας ἁμαρτών;

75. πεζᾷ δ' ... Φᾶσιν: Not so in Apollonios or in earlier poets, who represented Herakles as never reaching Kolchis at all. ἄξενον: The word is appropriate to the reception which the Argonauts had from the king of Kolchis, but it has a further point in that the Black Sea (Euxine) could also be called Ἄξεινος, as in Pi. Pyth. 4.203.

POEM XIV

Two friends, Aischinas and Thyonichos meet and talk. Aischinas tells how the girl with whom he is in love, Kyniska, has shown that she is captivated by another man; this tale occupies the greater part of the poem. Aischinas contemplates going abroad to take service as a mercenary soldier, and Thyonichos encourages him to take service under Ptolemy in Egypt.

Since Egypt lies across the sea (55, 59, 68) and Aischinas knows nothing about Ptolemy, the scene is certainly not

Egypt, but there is little positive indication of where in the Greek world it might be. An Argive and a Thessalian were present at Aischinas's party (12 f., 30 f.), and Thyonichos has recently encountered an itinerant Athenian ascetic. Since nothing in the poem points to the islands or to the West, we are perhaps meant to think of the Peloponnese.

Not only does Aischinas contemplate mercenary service, and Thyonichos speak as if he had experience of it; the status of the mercenary is familiar to Aischinas (55 f.), and the fourth man at his drinking-party was 'Kleonikos the soldier' (13). If one had said of a man in the fifth century B.C. στρατιώτης ἐστίν, one would have meant, unless one specified otherwise, that he was a citizen temporarily conscripted by his own state for military or naval service. But to say the same thing of a man in Theokritos's day would normally have meant that he was a professional mercenary; the change in the predominant meaning of the word must have begun early in the fourth century, when mercenary service became increasingly common. In New Comedy we find young men who are confident of their own courage, such as Kleostratos in Menander's *Aspis*, going off to serve as mercenaries; the rewards could be splendid. Apollodoros *CAF* (iii.289) fr. 2 says that a soldier can always be sure of employment; and a soldier in Anon. (*CAF*) Nov. Com. fr. 129 lists the commanders under whom he has served.

ἐν χώρῳ (14) suggests that the scene is rural, not urban, and 24~46 that Aischines and his neighbour are widely separated. The status of the girl Kyniska is not clear. Since she is present with the men at their drinking-party (ignored, perhaps, when Aischinas says 'the four of us' [29, v.n.]) and is furiously punched by Aischinas when he is angry with her, she may be a hetaira; but the social class to which Aischinas belongs did not necessarily observe bourgeois proprieties (cf. pp. 95 f., 128).

The language of this dialogue is predominantly colloquial, full of clipped phrases (9, 31, 51), ellipses (3, 17, 18, 21, 44 f., 68) and proverbial allusions (22, 28, 43, 46, 48 f., 51). The unmethodical character of real speech is excellently captured in 12 ff., 'The Argive and I, and the Thessalian horsetrainer Agis, and Kleonikos — we were drinking — the soldier — on the farm, at my place'. Only one simile of Homeric origin (32 f.) and one of Homeric character but un-Homeric form (39 f.) conflict with the overall colloquial tone until we come to the somewhat intricate language of Thyonichos's peroration (65 ff.).

1. χαίρειν ... Θυώνιχον: Cf. Sokrates' greeting of Ion in Pl. *Ion* 530a τὸν Ἴωνα χαίρειν. It is hard to determine the colouring imported by τὸν ἄνδρα: possibly we are meant to imagine that there is a momentary delay in Aischinas's recollection of the name of the man whom he recognizes by sight. **ἄλλα τοιαῦτα**: i.e. 'and the same to you'; cf. Hdt. i.120.6 αὐτοί τε θαρσέομεν καὶ σοὶ ἕτερα τοιαῦτα παρακελευόμεθα, '... and we encourage you to be confident likewise'.

2. ὡς χρόνιος: Lit., 'how ⟨an⟩ after-a-time ⟨person you have come⟩!'; cf. 11.4 n. and xv.1.

3. ὡς λῷστα: 'As well as I could'. **ταῦτ' ἄρα**: 'So that's why ...!', a very frequent idiom in Old Comedy. **λεπτός**: *sc.* 'you are'.

5 ff. Πυθαγορίκτας ... ἀλεύρω: The portrayal of philosophers as pale (from their indoor life) and barefoot (from poverty and neglect of the good things of life) is at least as old as Ar. *Clouds* 103. In the comedy of the fourth century B.C. the Pythagoreans became a familiar butt; cf. Aristophon (*CAF*) frr. 10 and 12 (they are filthy and stink and sleep out, when they sleep at all). Like Aristophanes' Socratics, they were assumed to be ready to beg or steal what they did not earn, and, of course, always to be hungry; hence the joke in 7.

8. ἔχων: Cf. Pl. *Gorg.* 490c φλυαρεῖς ἔχων, 'You keep on talking nonsense'; the idiom is common in Old Comedy.

9. λασῶ: λανθάνειν, 'escape notice', is sometimes used in the sense 'escape one's own notice', e.g. Ar. *Wasps* 517 δουλεύων λέληθας, 'You don't realise' (*sc.* 'but I do!') 'that you're a slave'; Hdt. ii.173.4 λάθοι ἂν ἤτοι μανεὶς ἢ ὅ γε ἀπόπληκτος γενόμενος. So here: 'Some day I'll go mad before I realise what's happening'. **θρὶξ ἀνὰ μέσσον**: Lit., '⟨there is⟩ hair in the middle', i.e. 'I'm within a hairs-breadth of it'. Cf. Xen. *Symp.* 6.2, 'One couldn't insert a hair between your talking', i.e. 'You don't give me a chance to get a word in edgeways'. For ἀνὰ μέσσον cf. XXII.21.

10. ἀσυχᾷ: 'Just a bit'; cf. Men. *Heros* 20 δούλη 'στιν; — οὗτως, ἡσυχῇ, τρόπον τινά, '. . . well, you know how it is, a bit, in a way'.

11. κατὰ καιρόν: Lit., 'according to right measure' (or '. . . occasion'), i.e. 'just so', 'just right'. **εἶπον**: Imperative; in Attic εἰπέ is much commoner.

15. Βίβλινον: sc. οἶνον. In the fourth century Arches-tratos (*ap.* Ath. 29B) called Βύβλινος οἶνος Phoenician (i.e. from Byblos in Syria) and spoke of it as if he knew its taste; Epicharmos (fr. 174) knew of a Βιβλίνη grape from Thrace. Long before either of them, βίβλινος (or βύβλινος?) οἶνος was well regarded by Hesiod (*Op.* 589). Βίβλινος οἶνος takes its place in a list of wines in Philyllios (*CAF*) fr. 24, but the context of the fragment is unknown; it is missing from a list of wines in Hermippos (*CAF*) fr. 82. Whether Theokritos wrote Βύβλινον and perhaps knew what he was talking about, or Βίβλινον, simply taking the name from Hesiod, is very hard to decide.

16. If it was good that the wine should be 'almost as if ⟨straight⟩ from the wine-press', there would seem to be little point in keeping it for four years; σχεδόν κτλ. must therefore go closely with εὐώδη, which designates only one desirable quality of wine. Possibly τετόρων ἐτέων should be interpreted not as an adjectival phrase, 'four years old', but as temporal, 'in four years', i.e. 'even after four years'. Cf. Ar. *Ach.* 83 f. πόσου χρόνου . . . ; τῇ πανσελήνῳ; '*After* how long . . . ? *At* the full moon?'

17. κοχλίας: Collective singular; cf. 1.49, 53 n. **ἐξαιρέθη**: 'Was brought out'.

18. προϊόντος: With a genitive absolute participle the subject is sometimes omitted when its identity is obvious or unverifiable; cf. Pl. *Rep.* 381C οὕτως ἔχοντος, 'that being so'.

18 f. ἐπιχεῖσθαι ... εἰπεῖν: Unlike Delphis in II (cf. II.151 f. n.), Aischinas and his friends decided each to name the person loved. Cf. Kallim. *Epigr.* 29.1 f. ἔγχει καὶ πάλιν εἰπέ 'Διοκλέος'.

21. ἁ δ' οὐδέν: *sc.* 'said'.

22. λύκον εἶδες: The reference is to a superstition about wolves, presupposed by Pl. *Rep.* 336D, where Sokrates, who has earlier (336B) compared Thrasymachos to a wild beast, says, 'If I hadn't looked at him before he looked at me, I should have been struck dumb'. Logic might tempt one to emend to λύκος εἶδέ σ'; but in Theokritos's Doric the accusative of τύ is τυ, which cannot be elided. **σοφός:** This word hardly ever means 'wise' in the sense which it would bear in the English, 'How wise of you!' Here: 'That's clever of you!' — unwittingly clever, as it were, because the man who said λύκον εἶδες; hit on the name of the man with whom Kyniska is in love.

25. πολλοῖς ... ἦμεν: Nothing would induce Aischinas to admit that Lykos really is handsome.

27. οὕτως: This use of οὕτως is common in Plato, e.g. *Gorg.* 503D ἴδωμεν δὴ οὑτωσὶ ἀτρέμα σκοπούμενοι εἰ κτλ., '... just looking at it calmly ...'. Cf. also XI.22 f. n.

28. μάταν ... γενειῶν: Implying, 'What have I grown up for, if I could be such a fool?' Cf. x.40 n.

29. δ' ὤν: Resuming the narrative after a digression, as so often (δ' οὖν) in Attic; cf. Denniston, *GP* 463 f. **τοὶ τέσσαρες:** 12 f. Perhaps Kyniska does not count; but more probably she had been reluctant to drink, not only reluctant to speak.

30. χὠ Λαρισαῖος: The Thessalian of 12, as Laris(s)a is in Thessaly and the song he sings is Thessalian (31). **τὸν ἐμὸν Λύκον:** Cf. the snatch of song in IV.32. The title of a song is not necessarily intelligible by itself; cf. Ar. *Ach.* 1093 τὸ 'φίλταθ' Ἁρμόδι' οὔ' (*sc.* 'τι που τέθνηκας'), or (*sc.* 'Well may') 'The Keel Row'. **ἀπ' ἀρχᾶς:** Perhaps 'from beginning ⟨to end⟩'; but Aischinas may mean that if it had not been sung

from the beginning the fatal words τὸν ἐμὸν Λύκον would
not have been uttered.

31. κακαὶ φρένες: We are not necessarily meant to infer
that Aischinas thinks that the Thessalian acted out of
malice; κακόφρων in Soph. *Ant.* 1104 is applied by the chorus
to Kreon when it has become apparent that he has been
blinded by obstinate pride and has taken a mistaken
decision.

32 f. ἢ παρὰ ματρί . . . ἐπιθυμήσασα: The passage has
an affinity with the famous Homeric simile (*Il.* xvi.7 ff.) of
the little girl crying and begging her mother to pick her up,
but it creates a much less vivid picture of everyday life.

34. ἴσας: =οἶσθα.

35. κἄλλαν: *sc.* 'blow', as commonly; cf. Soph. *El.* 1415
παῖσον . . . διπλῆν, Ar. *Clouds* 972 τυπτόμενος πολλάς.

36. ἐμὸν κακόν: In Ar. *Birds* 931 Peisetairos refers to the
importunate dithyrambic poet as τουτὶ τὸ κακόν, and Praxinoa
in xv.10 to her husband as φθονερὸν κακόν: ἐμὸν κακόν contains
a glimmer of another idea, that Kyniska is a part of
Aischinas's evil destiny.

38. τήνῳ . . . ῥέοντι: 'It's for him that your tears are
flowing ⟨as big as⟩ apples'; cf. Moschos 4.56 θαλερώτερα
δάκρυα μήλων. Hartung suggested that Theokritos wrote
ῥεόντων, 'let . . . flow . . .'; Wilamowitz adopted this (but
as Doric -τω) and repunctuated to make τήνῳ τεὰ δάκρυα a
question, 'Are your tears for *him*?' I am not persuaded,
however, that the sentiment, 'If it's for him that you're
crying, I don't care how much you cry!' suits Aischinas
better than, 'Since it's for *him* that you're crying so much,
go and cuddle him (*sc.* because I've done with you)'.

39 f. On the type of simile cf. xiii.62 f. n.

40. βίον: Often 'livelihood', here 'food'.

42. ἀμφιθύρω καὶ δικλίδος: The ἀμφίθυρον, i.e. '⟨the
part⟩ with a door at each end', must be the part between
the inner door, which led from the courtyard, and the front
door; δικλίς will then be the front door itself.

43. αἶνος . . . ἀν' ὕλαν: A proverb or fable (αἶνος could
mean either) about a bull which has run into wild wooded

country (and will therefore be hard to catch) is presupposed by Soph. *Oed. Tyr.* 477 ff., uttered by the chorus when the search for the unknown killer of Laios has been instituted: φοιτᾷ γὰρ ὑπ' ἀγρίαν ὕλαν . . . ὁ ταῦρος.

44 f. 'Twenty, and ⟨then there were⟩ the eight, . . .'; Aischinas is going over a succession of particular events in his mind. The Greek month, although subject to the intercalation of odd days for administrative or religious convenience, was based on the moon, and therefore of 30 or 29 days (giving an average of 29½ days). Thus σάμερον ἐνδεκάτα, 'today ⟨it is the⟩ eleventh ⟨day⟩' must indicate a passage of eleven days in addition to the ten mentioned immediately before. 20 + 8 + 9 + 10 + 11 + 2 = 60.

46. Θραικιστί: We do not know exactly what was meant in Theokritos's time by a 'Thracian haircut', but there was traditionally something distinctive about it, for Thracians are ἀκρόκομοι in *Il.* iv.533 and Archil. (D³) fr. 79a.3.

49. Μεγαρῆες: The story (told by the Argive historian Deinias [*FGrHist* 306] fr. 6; cf. Kallim. *Epigr.* 25.5 f.) was that the Megarians were once told by the Delphic oracle that they were 'neither third nor fourth nor twelfth, οὔτ' ἐν λόγῳ οὔτ' ἐν ἀριθμῷ'.

50. ἐς δέον ἕρποι: Lit., 'move into what ought to be', i.e. 'turn out right'.

51. πόθεν: 'How can I?' μῦς . . . πίσσας: Lit., 'a mouse, they say, we are tasting pitch', i.e. 'I'm like — as they say — a mouse that's tasting pitch'; cf. Theognis 347 κύων ἐπέρησα χαράδρην, 'I'm like a dog which has got across a torrent'. It appears from the use of the proverb in Dem. l.26 ἄρτι μῦς πίττης γεύεται, that it means 'in trouble which is only just beginning'; presumably mice sample pitch and then cannot free themselves from it. There is no other instance of the assimilation of the thematic verb γενέσθαι to epic athematic forms such as στεῦται, λῦτο, etc.; and it may be that since ε + ο contract to ευ in very many Greek dialects what has happened is assimilation to the words in which -εύμεθα is a contradiction of -εόμεθα. Cf. Attic λούμενος (for λουόμενος) on the analogy of -ούμενος = -εόμενος or -οόμενος.

52. φάρμακον: Cf. p. 173.

53. πλάν: 'Except that . . .'. **ἐπιχάλκω**: *Σ* recognises a variant *ὑποχάλκω*, and interprets both alike as denoting the soldier's shield. This sense of ἡ ἐπίχαλκος is attested in Ameipsias (*CAF*) fr. 17 τὸ μὲν δόρυ / μετὰ τῆς ἐπιχάλκου ... ἀπέβαλεν: but in the present context, where Simos is cited as a man who recovered from a love-affair by going abroad, τᾶς ἐπιχάλκω must obviously refer to a girl. Either 'Epichalkos' (or 'Hypochalkos') is a man's name, and the girl was his daughter or slave (cf. 11.66, x.15) or ἐπίχαλκος (or ὑπόχαλκος) has a metaphorical meaning not attested elsewhere. No one can assert that 'Epichalkos' or 'Hypochalkos' is an impossible Greek name, but it happens not to occur among the many thousands of Greek names known to us, and since Greek did not distinguish proper names by capital letters (or by any other graphic convention) it is hard to see how Theokritos could have expected his readers to recognise a proper name here (unless we assume an esoteric joke about a man actually known to the poet and his friends). ἐπίχαλκος, lit. 'with bronze over it', might possibly be a slang term for 'sunburnt', but since the price one pays for something is often denoted by ἐπί with the dative, another possible meaning is 'whom you could get for a bronze coin' (modern parallels: 'Half-crown Maggie', 'Dol for a dollar'); bronze was used for the smallest denominations (the Athenian χαλκοῦς was 1/24 of a drachma). χαλκός and its derivatives are not used metaphorically in the sense of English 'brazen'.

56. ὁ στρατιώτας: The article is generic.

57. Lit., 'would that what you desired had moved according to your mind', i.e. 'I wish that what you wanted had gone according to your liking'. Cf. Ar. *Peace* 939 f. ὡς πάνθ' ... χωρεῖ κατὰ νοῦν.

58. οὕτως . . . ἀποδαμεῖν: Although a simple infinitive normally depends upon δοκεῖν, it can be reinforced (like infinitives depending on a wide variety of verbs) by ὥστε, and οὕτως here looks forward to that ὥστε (and there would be no objection to οὕτω σοι δοκεῖ without any following infinitive; cf. Pl. *Crito* 49D οἷς οὕτω δέδοκται).

59. οἷος ἄριστος: '⟨Is such a man⟩ as ⟨the⟩ best ⟨is⟩'.

60. At the end of the line the medieval manuscripts repeat the last three words of 59; all that is legible of the ancient text is τοισινάρ.

61. φιλόμουσος: A suitable (and true) compliment from Theokritos, but less suitable from Thyonichos. **ἐρωτικός**: According to the historical work written by Ptolemy VIII ([*FGrHist* 235] fr. 4; cf. Polyb. xiv.11.2), Ptolemy Philadelphos was far from secretive about his own love-affairs; no doubt he was proud of his lovers' beauty, and the man in the street thought better of a warm ruler than of a cold one. **εἰς ἄκρον**: Lit., 'to topmost', i.e. 'as . . . as you can imagine'. **ἁδύς**: Italian *simpatico*, modern English 'nice'.

62. Cf. VI.17; if the line is modelled on utterances which resemble it except that they lack a definite article, this would explain the negative οὐ, abnormal with the generic article and participle.

63. οὐκ ἀνανεύων: Cf. VII. 109 n.

64. οἷα χρὴ βασιλῆ': Well-judged generosity was always a quality admired in rulers; cf. Pindar's advice to Hieron in *Py.* 1.90 ff. and praise of him in *Py.* 2.56 ff. **ἐπὶ παντί**: 'On every occasion'.

65 f. κατὰ δεξιόν . . . περονᾶσθαι: The standard type of military cloak in the third century B.C. was fastened with a brooch on the right shoulder.

66. ἐπ' ἀμφοτέροις δὲ βεβακώς: *sc. τοῖς ποσί*: cf. VII.157 n., X.35. The ability to stand firm without flinching — and without looking, by a wavering of one foot, as if one were ready to flinch — is obviously the first requisite of a soldier in hand-to-hand fighting. Archilochos respected a general who was ἀσφαλέως βεβηκὼς/ποσσί ([D³] fr. 60.3 f.), and Tyrtaios exhorted the Spartan soldiers ([D³] fr. 6/7.31 f.) ἀλλά τις εὖ διαβὰς μενέτω ποσὶν ἀμφοτέροισι / στηριχθεὶς ἐπὶ γῆς.

68. ᾷ τάχος: Lit., 'the way in which ⟨there is⟩ speed', i.e. 'with all speed', as in Pi. *Ol.* 6.23. **ἀπὸ κροτάφων**: Because the whitening of the hair usually begins at the temples.

POEM XV

The poem portrays a few hours in the life of two women,
Gorgo and Praxinoa, who are of Syracusan birth or
parentage (90) and live with their husbands at Alexandria
during the reign of Ptolemy Philadelphos (22 ff., 46 f.,
106 ff.); the occasion portrayed can be dated within a year
or two either side of 274 (cf. C4). The form of the poem is
dramatic throughout, and from 44 to 78 there is a continuous
progressive change of scene (much more elaborate than the
change in III.6) which has to be understood from the dialogue.

Gorgo calls on Praxinoa, who welcomes her. After they
have enjoyed some gossip, in which complaints about their
husbands play a conspicuous part, they decide to go to the
royal palace to see the festival of Adonis. They struggle
through the crowd in the streets, briefly encountering an
old woman and a man (who have 'speaking parts') and
eventually get into the palace grounds. After they have
admired the tapestries (and incurred the anger of another
man by their incessant chatter) they listen to the solo sung
by a professional woman singer in honour of Adonis. This
song is incorporated (100–144) into the poem (cf. the song of
Thyrsis in I and the songs of Lykidas and Simichidas in
VII); after it, Gorgo and Praxinoa leave for home (145 ff.).
Gorgo's husband will be waiting for his midday meal (from
which it is clear that Gorgo must have left home to call on
Praxinoa first thing in the morning).

The two families are of respectable status; nothing is said
to indicate what the husbands do for a living. The clichés
of which the women's conversation is composed, and the
attitudes and values which underlie everything they say,
give them an extraordinary resemblance to their modern
counterparts, but the spiteful element in their characters is
sharpened for comic effect, just as in some of Herodas's
portrayals of women (cf. II.19 f. n.).

The style of the dialogue is largely colloquial, as in XIV,

with many ellipses and proverbial tags; this element is naturally absent from the hymn to Adonis.

A dramatic dialogue of Sophron portrayed women spectators at the Isthmian festival, but we do not know whether Theokritos's debt to Sophron extends into details. On the passages in which the women (80–86) and the singer (112–130) admire and describe works of art cf. 1.29–63 n.

1. χρόνῳ: Cf. Eur. *El.* 578 ὦ χρόνῳ φανείς and χρόνιος in xiv.2.

2. θαῦμ': '⟨It's a⟩ wonder that . . .'. The reason why Praxinoa thinks this appears in 7 ff. **ὄρη**: 'See to', i.e. 'get'; cf. *Od.* viii.443 αὐτὸς νῦν ἴδε πῶμα, 'Now you must provide yourself with a cover'. **Εὐνόα**: In so far as one believes in *nomen omen* (cf. vii.100 n.), there is good reason to name a slave Eunoa, 'loyal'.

3. ἔχει κάλλιστα: 'It's fine!', i.e. 'Please don't bother!' Cf. Ar. *Frogs* 507 ff. 'Do come in!' — κάλλιστ', ἐπαινῶ. — 'No, I won't let you go away . . . Do please come in with me!' — καλῶς ἔχει. — 'What nonsense! I won't let you go . . .'.

4. τᾶς: i.e. 'my'. **ἐσώθην**: 'Got through alive'. For σωθῆναι followed by a genitive in the sense 'from' cf. Eur. *Or.* 779 σωθῆναι κακῶν.

5. τεθρίππων: For racing, not warfare; cf. Ar. *Clouds* 1407, where Strepsiades' 'maintaining a four-horse team' refers to his son's passion for racing.

7. ἑκαστέρω αἰέν: 'Further and further' may imply that Praxinoa has made at least one move during the time that Gorgo has known her; but a modern Gorgo sometimes says 'It's further every time' meaning 'It *seems* further . . .'.

8. ταῦθ' ὁ πάραρος τῆνος: Praxinoa is speaking of her husband. For the expression cf. our idiom, 'That's my husband', which sometimes means 'That's my husband's doing' and sometimes 'My husband's just like that'.

10. ποτ' ἔριν: ποτί (πρός) can sometimes be analysed as 'taking . . . as a standard', and in different adverbial phrases it needs widely different translations; so here '*out of spite*'; πρὸς βίαν, '*by* force'; πρὸς ἡδονήν, '*for* pleasure'. φθονερὸν κακόν: A comment on her husband, not on ἔριν: cf. xiv.36 n.

11 ff. μὴ λέγε ... ἀπφῦς: Expressing fear that Praxinoa's baby may understand the reference of ὁ πάραρος τῆνος Gorgo clumsily makes it much more likely (11, 13 f.) that he will indeed understand. **αἰσθάνεται**: As people say of their dogs, 'I do believe he understands!', except that it is much more likely to be true of a baby. **ναὶ τὰν πότνιαν**: Probably Persephone (so Σ). Cf. 94; and the old woman in Herodas 1.32 swears μὰ τὴν Ἀιδεω κούρην. **καλὸς ἀπφῦς**: To the baby: 'Nice Daddy!'

15. λέγομες δέ: The narrative present λέγει is Herodotean (e.g. iii.134.5) and φημί and φησί are commonly so used in New Comedy in reporting a conversation (e.g. Men. *Dysk.* 107, 109). δέ is not easily explained, and may be subliterate; cf. the equally curious δέ in Ar. *Ach.* 2 ἤσθην δὲ βαιά, πάνυ δὲ βαιά, τέτταρα.

16. πάππα: The transmitted text is πάντα; Wilamowitz's suggestion πάππα was derived from a statement in the *Etymologicum Magnum* that it is a Syracusan word for 'father'. One difficulty, however, is that a Greek wife does not seem to have called her husband 'father'; hence Stark's emendation ἀφρόνιτρον, a Koine word for a form of soda called in Attic ἀφρὸς λίτρου. **ἀγοράσδειν**: Shopping was a man's job, as appears from Ar. *Wasps* 439 ff., *Eccl.* 817 ff. The infinitive (here an emendation; the transmitted participle makes no sense) is used as an imperative not only in laws, military orders, etc., but in a wide range of contexts (including comic dialogue) in which we cannot honestly say why it should be more appropriate than the imperative. With Stark's emendation (v. supr.) the infinitive will be dependent on λέγομες and no quotation marks should be printed.

17. ἴκτο φέρων: Cf. Hes. *Theog.* 481 ἔνθα μὲν ἴκτο φέρουσα κτλ. **τρισκαιδεκάπαχυς**: Praxinoa speaks hyperbolically in her indignation; a big man is only τετράπηχυς in Ar. *Wasps* 553. For the colloquial use of 'thirteen' (as we might say 'a man a mile high') cf. Ar. *Wealth* 846, where a poor man says of his old clothes, 'I shivered in them for thirteen years'.

19 f. ἑπταδράχμως . . . πόκως: Lit., 'he got costing-seven-drachmai five fleeces ⟨which were⟩ κυνάδας, etc.'. The elasticity of Greek word-order (cf. XIV.13) facilitates the rhetorical effect of bringing the indignant word (ἑπταδράχμως) describing the high price of the fleeces next to the equally indignant word (κυνάδας) describing their quality. Data from documents of the third century B.C. indicate that seven drachmai would be a fair price for five fleeces of normal quality. **γραιᾶν . . . πηρᾶν:** γραία (=γραῦς) can be used as an adjective of things, just as γέρων can (cf. VII.17 n.), and Gorgo may mean 'hair plucked off old skin bags'. Since, however, Greek women commonly depilated themselves (τίλλειν: in Ar. *Lys.* 578 ἀποτίλλειν is used of plucking out hairs), it is possible that πήρα is a slang term for the pubic region.

20. ἔργον ἐπ' ἔργῳ: 'Work upon work', as in Hes. *Op.* 382; and perhaps the expression was proverbial. Gorgo means that because of the poor quality of the wool spinning took her an unconscionable time.

22. ἐς: Cf. VII.131 n.

23. θασόμεναι τὸν "Αδωνιν: There is no strong reason why we should not translate, 'To see Adonis', given 84 ff., but θεᾶσθαι is used of the audiences of plays, etc., and in such circumstances includes hearing as well as seeing. **χρῆμα καλόν τι:** Object of κοσμεῖν. For the (predominantly colloquial) use of χρῆμα cf. 83, 145.

24. ἐν ὀλβίῳ: Cf. 22, VII.131 n. It seems from what follows that Praxinoa needs persuading; so the point of her proverb-like utterance must be 'Well, of course she's putting on a good show, you'd expect her to'.

25. ὦν ἴδες: The aorist is used from the viewpoint of the hypothetical situation in which 'you could tell . . .'. ὦν εἴπαις κεν: On ὦν cf. II.82 n., IV.39.

26. ὥρα κ' εἴη: As we might say, 'It'*ll be* time . . .' or 'it *must be* time . . .' **ἀεργοῖς αἰὲν ἑορτά:** It sounds as if

Praxinoa is being rude to Gorgo, implying that she herself
is more industrious, but she is probably doing no more than
utter the nearest available cliché about work and leisure
without thinking of its precise application; cf. x.17 n.

27 f. καὶ ἐς μέσον ... πάλιν: ἐς μέσον means 'available',
'exposed', 'lying around' (*sc.* for anyone to take or use); so
the point of the command is a suppressed 'if you dare!' or
' — and when you do, I'll punish you!' δρύπτειν is used of
scratching the face (e.g. in mourning and grief), and αἰνο-
means 'with deadly or painful consequences'. Hence
αἰνόδρυπτος = αἰνοδρυφής, used by Antimachos (Wyss) fr.
156 of a mourner with lacerated cheeks; for Praxinoa's use
of the vocative to Eunoa cf. κέντρων and μαστιγίας in Comedy.

28. γαλέαι: Greeks kept weasels as domestic animals;
and weasels, like cats, would be delighted to find a soft bed
in a heap of wool on the floor. (In Alexandria, however, the
domestic γαλῆ may have been a mongoose; cf. A. S. F. Gow,
(*CQ* N.S. xvii [1967], 195 f.)

29 f. ὕδατος ... φέρει: Praxinoa addresses this despair-
ing comment on Eunoa's incompetence to Gorgo.

30. λᾳστρί: The transmitted text ἄπληστε does not scan,
since πολύ cannot be elided. Schwartz's emendation λᾳστρί
is supported by Herodas 6.10, where a woman calls her lazy
slave-girl λῃστρί. It is a less recherché term of abuse than it
might seem, for λῃσταί, whether 'free-lance' pirates or
raiders from a state at war, were one of the disagreeable
facts of life in the Aegean (relevant to the plot of Menander's
Sikyonios; cf. 357).

32. οἷα ... νένιμμαι: Presumably it was a common joke
to say that one had done a thing 'as far as the gods allowed'
(as if offering an excuse) when in fact the decision to stop
was one's own. We can hardly tell from the context how
much of herself Praxinoa has washed.

33. Praxinoa evidently keeps her clothes locked in a chest,
the Greek equivalent of a wardrobe (cf. Ar. *Wasps* 1056 ff.).
Between 33 and 34 we are to imagine her as receiving the
key, opening the chest, taking out the περονατρίς, taking
off her χιτώνιον, and putting on the περονατρίς.

34 f. μάλα τοι . . . πρέπει: Gorgo's compliment to Praxinoa, her interest in the price, and Praxinoa's outburst about the high cost and her own hard work, can be heard in other ages and other languages, except that the British are shyer than Mediterranean peoples of asking directly, 'What did it cost you?' **ἐμπερόναμα**: This must be the περονατρίς of which Gorgo spoke in 21; the ἀμπέχονον of 21 appears in 39.

35. πόσσω . . . ἀφ' ἰστῶ: Lit., 'of how much did it come down to you from the loom?', i.e. 'What did it cost you as it came off the loom (*sc.* before being made up into a dress and embroidered)?'

37 f. πλέον . . . ἢ δύο: 2 mnai = 200 drachmai, a very high price; data from the period suggest that even 50 drachmai would be high. Perhaps we are meant to see that Praxinoa is exaggerating for ostentation. **καθαρῶ**: She is not contrasting 'pure' silver money with 'impure' in any serious sense; καθαρῶ is emotive, as in our idiom 'good money' or 'hard cash'.

37. ἔργοις: Dressmaking as we know it did not exist among the Greeks, whose clothes were of very simple and uniform design; the work lay in embroidery of ornamental patterns. **ψυχάν**: 'I put my soul into it', as we might say 'It cost me my life-blood' or 'It took years off my life'. Cf. Bion fr. 8.11 f. ψυχὰν . . . ποτὶ κέρδεα . . . βάλλομες.

38. τοῦτό κεν εἴπαις: If Praxinoa says these words, they are grudging (and therefore modest) rather than complacent; if Gorgo says them, they are comforting.

39. θολίαν: A 'sun-hat', with a very wide brim and pointed crown. We see it in some sculpture of the period, perched so high that it seems to be balanced rather than worn; but presumably it was kept in place by hatpins.

40. οὐκ ἀξῶ τυ: The baby sees that his mother is going out without him, and begins to cry (an interesting indication that even in a family which owned female slaves it is the mother, not the nursemaid, who is the focus of the baby's emotional interest). **Μορμώ**: 'Mormo' (and generically, μορμών) is the name of an ubiquitous demon feared by

children; Praxinoa means, 'I'm going out to see something
nasty that would only frighten you'. Perhaps Greeks said
'(it) bites!', as some adults nowadays say 'hot!', when they
wanted a small child to keep away from something.

42 f. Φρυγία . . . ἀπόκλαξον: Eunoa goes with her
mistress, as we see from 66 f. The protection afforded by
locking the front door when Phrygia is alone was hardly
needed when Praxinoa and Eunoa were at home too, be-
cause at least one of them could have run out for help if an
intruder had come in.

44–77. *The journey to the palace.*

44 f. πῶς . . . χρή: As often, not 'how must we . . .?' or
'how ought we to . . .?', but 'how are we to . . .?', tending
towards 'how can we . . .?'

46. The apostrophe to Ptolemy, complimenting him on
his suppression of violent crime, sounds stilted and ornate
in the mouth of Praxinoa and betrays the desire of the poet
to capture royal favour by flattery. **τοι**: Functioning here
fully as a pronoun, 'achieved . . . *by you*'.

47. ἐξ ὦ . . . ὁ τεκών: Lit., 'from when your father ⟨has
been⟩ among the immortals', i.e. 'since your father'
(Ptolemy Soter) 'died'. The idea that a great and virtuous
man should be separated after death from the ordinary run
of ghosts and acquire superior status as a hero, even as a
god, gained ground in the Hellenistic period, but had much
older roots. If people chose to sacrifice and pray to him as
to an immortal god, that, for practical purposes, is what he
was; cf. 107 n., xviii.48 n.

48. τὸν ἰόντα: 'Anyone who goes', i.e. 'the passer-by' or
'the traveller'. **Αἰγυπτιστί**: The Macedonians and Greeks
brought with them to Egypt a deeply implanted belief that
the Egyptians were a dishonest and violent people; in
Kratinos (*CAF*) fr. 378 αἰγυπτιάζειν is used in the sense 'play
dirty tricks'. Cf. 50.

49. 'The sort of games . . . they got up to'. παίζειν
nowhere else covers crimes of violence (indeed, the speaker
of Dem. liv.14 suggests that what he regards as crime his

opponents will laugh off as part of what young men do παίζοντες), and Praxinoa seems to imply that robbing a traveller is something which Egyptians would do 'for fun'. ἄγρια παίζειν, used in xx.6 of a brutish lover and in Moschos i.11 of Eros himself, exploits the amatory associations of παίζειν and is intended as an oxymoron. **ἐξ ἀπάτας κεκροτημένοι**: 'Deceit' is the material of which they are 'forged' or 'struck' (as we speak of 'striking' coins and medals); for the literal sense cf. Lykophron 888 χρυσῷ πλατὺν κρατῆρα κεκροτημένον, and for ἐξ cf. XVII.21 τετυγμένα ἐξ ἀδάμαντος, 'wrought of adamant'.

50. κακὰ παίχνια: Rather as Hera addresses the Greeks in *Il.* v.787 as κάκ' ἐλέγχεα. Although παίχνιον (Attic παίγνιον) is cognate with παίζειν, users of a language (as distinct from those who study it) often overlook such relationships, so that each member of a group of cognates has associations not shared by the other members; and the point of παίχνια here is that the Egyptians fall short of being 'real' or 'serious' people.

51. πολεμισταί: Since the term was used of a type of racehorse (attested in an inscription from Delphi in the second century B.C.), the reference here is probably to such horses, not to a detachment of cavalry.

52. μή με πατήσῃς: We are to imagine that the people nearest the line of horses try to keep clear of them, so that the surging crowd is suddenly compressed.

53. κυνοθαρσής: Eunoa is less of a coward than her mistress (58 f.), but, human nature being what it is, she can hardly expect to be complimented on that. On κυνο- cf. II.12, v.38 nn.

**55. Cf. 40 f.

58. τὸν ψυχρὸν ὄφιν: The point of the article is not to distinguish cold snakes from warm snakes but to characterize snakes in general.

60. ἐξ αὐλᾶς: The old woman is evidently walking against the flow of the crowd.

63. χρησμώς: Gorgo calls the old woman's utterance 'oracles' because it was a pompous and allusive generalization which evaded a direct answer to the question asked.

64. καὶ ὡς Ζεὺς ἀγάγεθ' "Ηραν: The point is: 'a woman would even talk about the wedding of Zeus and Hera as if it had been a neighbour's wedding and she'd been there'. ἄγεσθαι, 'take to oneself', 'bring home', is not a euphemism for seduction or sexual intercourse.

67. Εὐτυχίδος: Gorgo's slave.

69. θερίστριον: This must be the ἀμπέχονον of 21, 39, 71.

70 f. εἴ τι γένοιτο εὐδαίμων: Lit., 'if you were to become fortunate' is (like 'so may you become fortunate!') a formula of entreaty; cf. Herodas 3.56, where a schoolboy's mother begins her entreaty, lit., 'if . . . you were to meet with good fortune . . .', and the schoolmaster interrupts to assure her that entreaty is unnecessary.

72. ἐπ' ἐμίν: 'In my power'. ὄχλος: The word denotes not simply a crowd but the inconveniences, distractions and fatigue which one experiences in a crowd, and also 'bother', 'nuisance' of all kinds; hence Praxinoa is not saying just 'What a lot of people!' but expressing a qualitative judgment on the crowd — reinforced by ἀλαθέως and amplified in the words which follow.

73. ἐν καλῷ: 'In a good ⟨place, situation, etc.⟩'. Cf. Ar. *Thesm.* 292 ποῦ ποῦ καθίζωμ' ἐν καλῷ, 'Where's a good place for me to sit?'

74. κῆς ὥρας: 'In ⟨future⟩ seasons', i.e. 'for all time'; the addition of κἤπειτα is as comic as it would be to say 'For ever, and after that too.'

76. Eunoa is not pitied for being squashed, but blamed for not pushing harder. Cf. 53 n.

77. The Greek form, ' "...", said the man who ...' corresponds to our, ' "...", *as* the man said when he ...' Cf. xiv.51 n. When ἀποκλείειν (Doric ἀποκλᾴειν) has a personal object it denotes preventing a person (e.g. by locking a door) from going where he or she wants to go (whether in or out, makes no difference). Thus, lit., 'he who shut off the daughter-in-law', must be either (*a*) someone who kept a bride (cf. xviii.15 τεὰ νυός = 'your bride') from her bridegroom, or (*b*) if ἔνδοι πᾶσαι functions as an imperative (cf. 'All aboard!') a husband who insisted on locking his new wife and her female slaves into the house every time he left it. On interpretation (a), the man could be the bridegroom's friend, whose role on the wedding night was to guard the door and ensure that the couple were left alone, or the bridegroom himself. Praxinoa has no option but to say ἔνδοι πᾶσαι, speaking as a woman and for women, but the traditional joke may have been ἔνδοι πάντες, referring to a bridegroom who was not interested in his bride but (e.g.) preferred to drink with his friends. If so, Theokritos is satirizing the unthinking use of clichés; cf. 26 n.

78–99. *In the palace precinct.*

78. ποικίλα: The word means 'patterned', 'complicated', and we see only from the following lines that Gorgo must be speaking of hanging tapestries. This does not mean that the women have gone into the palace building itself; tapestries could be hung out of doors in temporary structures, and the rarity of rain at Alexandria would make this particularly easy.

79. ὡς: Exclamatory. **θεῶν περονάματα**: 'Clothes of the gods', i.e. fit to be worn by gods. Cf. 1.32. **φασεῖς**: Cf. 1.150.

80 f. ποῖαι . . . ποῖοι: Virtually (though not formally) an exclamation, as (e.g.) *Il.* xiii.824 ποῖον ἔειπες, lit., 'What kind of thing did you say?' and vii.455 οἷον ἔειπες, lit., 'What a kind of thing you said!' amount to the same.

81. γράμματ': Not writing, but the 'lines' of the embroidered pictures.

83 σοφόν τι χρῆμ' ἄνθρωπος: The modern equivalent would be 'Isn't it marvellous what they can do nowadays?' — which, however, rests on familiarity with continuous technological progress, whereas the Greeks were more struck by the achievements of man in a natural environment not of his designing, as in Sophokles' famous ode (*Ant.* 332 ff.) on the δεινότης of man. On χρῆμ' cf. 23 n.

84. αὐτὸς δ': *sc.* Adonis, represented on one of the tapestries; the detail shows that the reference is not to the tableau described in 123 ff.

85. καταβάλλων: The person on whom a beard grows can be said to καταβάλλειν or καθιέναι the beard. Cf. 130.

86. τριφίλητος: τρι- is intensive here (cf. Moschos 3.51 ὦ τριπόθητε, addressed to the dead Bion) and has no literal reference to three occasions or three lovers. **κἦν Ἀχέροντι**: i.e. even after death; cf. III.46 ff. n., but there may also be a reference to the story that Adonis in the underworld was the lover of Persephone (Apollodoros ii.14.4, citing the epic poet Panyassis, and *Orph. H.* 56.9).

88. ἐκκναισεῦντι: Having addressed the women, the unnamed man grumbles indignantly to himself or to a neighbour. If he thought that they would be abashed, he was badly mistaken. Theokritos could have made him speak Ionic, or at any rate a different dialect from the Syracusan women, but — unless there has been interference with the transmitted text on a large scale — chose not to, preferring consistency to realism; or is satire intended?

89. μᾶ: This exclamation (of pleasure, surprise or indignation) is often on the lips of the female characters of Herodas.

90. πασάμενος ἐπίτασσε: Lit., 'having acquired give orders', i.e. 'don't give orders to people you don't own as slaves'; cf. Soph. *Ajax* 1107 (Teukros to Menelaos, angrily) ἀλλ' ὧνπερ ἄρχεις ἄρχε.

91. Κορίνθιαι: Syracuse was founded by Corinth in the eighth century B.C., and very proud of the fact; cf. XXVIII.17 n. **ἄνωθεν**: Cf. VII.5.

92. Βελλεροφῶν: When the story of Bellerophon (-phontes) is told in Homer (*Il.* vi.152 ff.) he is son of Glaukos and grandson of Sisyphos, kind of 'Ephyre', which in classical times was regarded as the original name of Corinth.

92 f. Πελοποννασιστί . . . τοῖς Δωριέεσσι: 'Peloponnesian' and above all 'Dorian' were emotive words in Dorian colonies throughout the Greek world; cf. Hermokrates' boast at Kamarina (Thuc. vi.77.1), '. . . show them that this isn't Ionia . . . but Dorians who came from the Peloponnese, which is under no master, and dwell as free men in Sicily'.

94. φύη: This is the optative of the aorist φῦναι (φύ-η < *φυ-ίη); cf. *Od.* ix.377 μή τις . . . ἀναδύη (~ἀναδῦναι).

Μελιτῶδες: According to *Σ*, this is a cult-title of Persephone; cf. 14 n.

95. πλὰν ἐνός: We may doubt whether an indignant Syracusan housewife at Alexandria, reproving an impertinent stranger, would remember this humble compliment to Ptolemy; cf. 46 n. **οὐκ ἀλέγω**: *sc.* 'about you'; cf. Eumaios to Antinoos, *Od.* xvii.389 f., αὐτὰρ ἐγώ γε | οὐκ ἀλέγω. **μή μοι κενεὰν ἀπομάξῃς**: 'Don't level an empty ⟨vessel⟩', i.e. 'don't waste your time by giving orders to me'.

96. τὸν "Αδωνιν ἀείδειν: Neither 'sing about Adonis' nor 'sing that song which is called *Adonis*', but something which cannot be expressed in English without expansion: 'sing this year's Adonis-song'; the text might differ completely from occasion to occasion, but the part played in the festival by the hymn to Adonis was a constant.

97. ἀ τᾶς 'Αργείας θυγάτηρ: We cannot be sure why the singer is referred to in this way, or why her mother is called 'the Argive woman', unless for dramatic realism; Gorgo, like most of us, forgets names. So we might say, 'It's the Irish girl who was at the Palladium last year'. **πολύϊδρις**: *Σ* speaks of the singer as a poet — presumably, therefore, as composer of the song which she sings — and πολύϊδρις, with ὅσσα ἴσατι in 146, may justify this. I am not sure, however; the singer's 'knowledge' could be her musical expertise, to which she adds a good voice (146 γλυκὺ φωνεῖ).

98. τὸν ἰάλεμον: Cf. Kallim. fr. 193.37 f. "Αδωνιν ... ἰηλεμίζειν. Gorgo is probably referring to the lament (accompanying the bearing of Adonis to the sea; cf. 135) at last year's Adonia. Bion's 'Επιτάφιος 'Αδώνιδος, with its dirge-like refrains, gives us some idea of its nature.

99. διαχρέμπτεται: 'She's clearing her throat' — not with a polite 'ahem!', but with the noisy and violent hawking and spitting which in Greece (by contrast with the West) is enjoyed as uninhibitedly by women as by men. (The variant διαθρύπτεται is probably a reminiscence of vi.15, iii.36.) Old Comedy rarely extracts from spitting the humour which it is so fond of extracting from defecation, but cf. Ar. *Thesm.* 381 f., 'Quiet, pay attention! She's clearing her throat now, as the speakers do; it looks as if she's going to make a long speech!'

100–144. *The Adonis song.* At the classical Athenian Adonia, a women's festival, but not one hidden from the eyes and ears of men (for details see L. Deubner, *Attische Feste* [Berlin, 1932], 220 ff.) the death of Adonis was lamented and his funeral enacted like a human funeral; plants which had been grown as offerings to him in pots or seed-boxes (which through this association came to be called 'gardens of Adonis', as in Pl. *Phdr.* 276B) were thrown into the sea. The Alexandrian ritual portrayed by Theokritos plainly has some of the same features: 'gardens' in baskets (113 f.); it is predominantly for women, Arsinoa's responsibility rather than Ptolemy's (23 f., 109 ff.), — cf. εὐθυμεύσαις in 143 — but men are not excluded (87 ff.); and 'tomorrow morning we will carry him to the sea . . .' (132 ff.). But it seems to be less funereal than the Athenian festival, and to make more of the welcome to Adonis, in company with Aphrodite, on his annual return from the underworld; cf. W. Atallah, *Adonis dans la littérature et l'art grecs* (Paris, 1966), especially 105 ff.

To judge from the inscribed hymns which we have from Epidauros, Delphi and other sites, it is likely that the actual Adonis-song at the Alexandrian festival would have been in lyric metres, not in dactylic hexameters; Theokritos has assimilated it to the metrical form of his poem as a whole. It would be wrong not to ask whether he has written a hymn which satisfied him and which he would have admired if he had heard it sung at an actual festival, or one intended as a sly parody of the songs characteristic of these occasions and applauded by audiences whose thoughts and tastes, like those of Gorgo and Praxinoa, existed only as strings of clichés. Occasional preciosities of language (101, 103, 112, 142) are not cogent evidence, for similar preciosities are found elsewhere in passages where there is no reason to suspect parody (e.g. xxiv.15, and note 125 μαλακώτεροι ὕπνω ~v.51 ὕπνω μαλακώτερα). But the hyperbolical effusion of 123 does raise such a suspicion, and it is reinforced by the clumsy rampage through mythology in 137 ff., which compares unfavourably with the *exempla* sung by the goatherd in III.40 ff. I should have expected Theokritos to take the opportunity of showing how well he could write a hymn, not the opportunity of showing how badly most people wrote them; but this expectation founders on the hymn we have before us.

100 f. δέσποιν'... "Ερυκα: The invocation of the goddess names her favourite places; cf. Chryses' prayer to Apollo (*Il.* i.37 f.) as ruler of Chryse, Killa and Tenedos, and the women's prayer to Asklepios in Herodas 4.1 ff., 'Lord Paieon, who rule Trikka and dwell on sweet Kos and Epidauros' (Norden, *Agnostos Theos*, 168 ff.). Golgoi and Idalion are both in Cyprus, with which Aphrodite ('Kypris') is most often associated (especially with Paphos, as in *Od.* viii.362 f.); cf. Lykophron 589, where she is called 'Queen of Golgoi'. Eryx is the mountain in northwest Sicily on which lay a famous temple of Aphrodite. **ἐφίλησας**: The aorist φιλῆσαι means 'demonstrate love for', hence often 'kiss' (cf. XI.55), but also 'welcome', 'show approval of', 'choose with delight'.

101. χρυσῷ παίσδοισ': Gold is naturally associated with deities (cf. Kallim. *H.* 6.126 f. on the worship of Demeter). Aphrodite in particular is often 'golden', as in *Il.* xxii.470, and in Mimnermos (D³) fr. 1, 'What life is there, what pleasure, without golden Aphrodite?' She also παίζει because the enjoyment of sex belongs to παιδιά, that side of life which occupies us from choice and not from necessity (cf. XI.77). Hence I would interpret this phrase as meaning 'whose sport is golden'; the relation of the dative to the verb is like that which we find in XI.10 f.

102. οἷον: Exclamatory.

103. μαλακαὶ πόδας: A person is μαλακός if he lacks courage, aggression or energy; hence sometimes 'dilatory' or 'unenthusiastic', as (e.g.) Archidamos was suspected in 431 of ἐν τῇ ξυναγωγῇ τοῦ πολέμου μαλακὸς εἶναι (Thuc. ii.18.3). Nothing can hurry the Seasons.

104. φίλαι: The words which follow explain the affection; cf. 1.150. There is nothing unusual in calling gods φίλος: cf. Aisch. *Sept.* 159 ὦ φίλ' "Απολλον, Ar. *Clouds* 1478 ὦ φίλ' Ἑρμῆ.

106. Διωναία: Cf. vii.116 n. τὺ μέν: Cf. vii.83 ff. n. ἀθανάταν: Cf. 47 n.

107. ἀνθρώπων ὡς μῦθος: To our way of thinking, these words suggest doubt about the proposition that Berenike had become immortal, but not so to a Greek. For one thing, most people's concepts of evidence were still rudimentary, so that the fact that 'it is told among men' was regarded as strengthening a story, not as weakening it; ὡς φάτις ἀνδρῶν in Soph. *Ant.* 829 is treated as testimony to the truth of the story of Niobe. Secondly, Greek religion was not dogmatic in character, and was concerned rather with the establishment of the right forms of human intercourse with the supernatural. Among these forms, the dissemination of a story which increases the κλέος of a deity or hero is important.

108. ἀμβροσίαν: So in Pi. *Py.* 9.62 f. the Seasons confer immortality on the infant Aristaios by feeding him on nectar and ambrosia; Demeter with similar intentions anointed with ambrosia the skin of the infant Demophoon (*H. Hom.* 2.237); ἐς στῆθος suggests that Aphrodite dabbed it on the breast of Berenike like a perfume.

109. χαριζομένα: The proper word (frequent in dedications) for pleasing a deity by an offering. πολυώνυμε καὶ πολύναε: Cf. x.42 n.

110. ἁ Βερενικεία: In some parts of the Greek world an adjective formed from the parent's name was normally used instead of the genitive of that name, and this usage is sporadic in all genres of poetry, e.g. *Il.* ii.20 f. Νηληίῳ υἱι ... /Νέστορι, and cf. xxviii.9. Ἑλένᾳ εἰκυῖα: Strong language. It is to be hoped that Arsinoe was at any rate attractive enough to prevent the comparison from sounding absurd. For the facile comparison with heroes and heroines cf. ii.15 f., vii.148 ff. nn.

112. πὰρ μέν οἱ: The dative singular pronoun οἱ is almost always treated by poets as if its original initial digamma were still present: for this exception cf. *Od.*

xiii.430 κάρψε μέν οἱ (– ◡ ◡ –). δρυὸς ἄκρα: Lit., 'tops of an oak', but it is in fact a dismantling of ἀκρόδρυα, 'fruit' (as in XXIV.15 [v. n.] σταθμὰ κοῖλα might be a dismantling of κοιλόσταθμα). καλεῖται: 'Are named', i.e. every kind of fruit that is known; cf. Pl. *Phd.* 103c θερμόν τι καλεῖς καὶ ψυχρόν; 'Do you use the terms "hot" and "cold"?'

113. πεφυλαγμένοι: Cf. III.22 n.

114. Συρίω: Perfumes are 'Syrian' as early as Aisch. *Ag.* 1312, where the reference is plainly to incense.

116. ἄνθεα: Probably 'colours', a not uncommon meaning of ἄνθος in Hellenistic literature.

117. Lit., 'and as many things as ⟨they make⟩ from sweet honey, and the ⟨things which are made⟩ in smooth oil'.

118. If this line referred to cakes of different shapes, there would be no reference to meat. πετεηνὰ καὶ ἑρπετά means 'everything ⟨edible⟩ that goes in the air or on the ground'; although ἑρπετά commonly denotes things which are especially low on the ground, e.g. snakes and beetles, Xen. *Mem.* i.4.11 uses it of all creatures except man, since he alone goes upright.

119. σκιάδες: Adonis on his couch may have been in one of these 'bowers'; Dioskorides (*HE*) 3.1 f. refers to the καλύβη of Adonis at the festival.

120. Ἔρωτες: Cf. VII.96 n.

122. ὄζον ἀπ' ὄζω: Cf. 20 and γῆν πρὸ γῆς (Aisch., Ar.).

123. There is a formal resemblance (not extending beyond mere form) to the opening words of Antigone's farewell to life, Soph. *Ant.* 891 f. ὦ τύμβος, ὦ νυμφεῖον, ὦ κατασκαφὴς / οἴκησις αἰείφρουρος.

124. The boy whom the eagles are carrying to Zeus is the Trojan Ganymede, 'most beautiful of all mankind' (*Il.* xx.232 ff.; cf.265 f.), seized by the gods as a present for Zeus. The legend was highly acceptable to the homosexual enthusiasm of the late archaic and classical poets and vase-painters, who represent Zeus as personally carrying off Ganymede and as requiring more services of him than pouring out wine. The notion that one or more eagles carried Ganymede up to Olympos appears in the visual arts in the fourth century B.C., so that it was a familiar motif by the time that Theokritos wrote here of its use in the ivory on Adonis's couch (presumably on the legs of the couch, the eagle's wings merging into the horizontal member of the couch and the body of Ganymede moulded on the leg).

125. ἄνω: 'On it', and so above the mouldings just described.

126. 'Miletos and he who pastures the Samian ⟨land⟩' = 'Milesians and Samians'. This is a roundabout way of saying that the couch or coverlets or both are of Milesian and Samian workmanship. κλίνη Μιλησιουργής is known from the fifth century B.C. (Kritias [DK] fr. 35) — Alkibiades had one (*Suppl. Epigr. Gr.* xiii.12.233) — but the issue is complicated by the fact that Miletos also produced very good wool (cf. Ar. *Frogs* 542 ff., where to recline ἐν στρώμασιν Μιλησίοις is luxurious), and we are not sure whether Samos was known in Theokritos's time for wool or dyes or woodwork.

127. ἄλλα: Implying pride that the magnificent object is produced year after year. It is, however, possible — as Ahrens suggested — that Theokritos wrote ἀμά (= ἡμετέρα), i.e. 'the couch which has been spread . . . ⟨is⟩ our ⟨work⟩'; confusion between ΛΛ and M was easy in ancient texts, since the mid-point of M was lower than in a modern M.

128. τὸν μέν . . . τὰν δέ: The transmitted text is τὰν μέν . . . τὰν δέ, implying that Aphrodite and Adonis have two different couches. But it is hard to believe that they have, and that we should be so casually informed that Aphrodite has a couch of her own, when the previous lines have concentrated our interest on the couch of Adonis. Hence Rossbach's emendation, giving 'Him (*sc.* Adonis) . . . and her (*sc.* Aphrodite) . . .'. The corruption may well have been engendered by misinterpretation of ἄλλα in 127.

129. ἐννεακαίδεχ': The treatment of a compound adjective as equivalent to an adjective plus a noun (in this case ἐτῶν) is particularly common when the compound is numerical; cf. *GVI* 683.1 (Crete, first century A.D.) πέντε με καὶ δεχέτιν κτλ.

130. περὶ χείλεα πυρρά: If πυρρά (cf. vi.3) is feminine singular, the noun understood (cf. v.61 n.) must be θρίξ, collective as in (e.g.) Aisch. *Ag.* 562. Since the Greeks did not shave (or, to be more precise, since the habit of shaving had only begun to spread in Theokritos's lifetime), the growth of the beard in adolescence was slow, and youthful heroes (Jason was twenty when the voyage of the Argo began [Pi. *Py.* 4.104]) are shown on vase-paintings as beardless. Cf. 85 and 1.109 n.

131. χαιρέτω: 'Farewell'; the song is, as it were, over the summit and now begins the downhill journey. Cf. the transition from the ἄρχετε-refrain to the λήγετε-refrain in 1.127.

132. ἅμα δρόσῳ: Σ thought that dew 'fell' at daybreak, but it is hard to believe that Theokritos had never been out at night late enough to learn better; by ἅμα δρόσῳ he means something like 'at the dewy hour', i.e. when the dew is most abundant.

133. πτύοντα: Not an entirely felicitous adaptation of *Il.* iv.426, where an angry swell breaking on the shore 'spits' (ἀποπτύει), i.e. 'hurls' brine.

134. ἐπὶ σφυρά: In lamentation women sometimes dropped the top part of their clothes to expose their breasts (cf. *Il.* xxii.80). Thus the κόλπος (cf. ii.120 n.) fell over the lower part of the clothes; and although the belt was worn high, the loose folds customary above the belt would hang out straight to not far short of the ankles.

137. ὡς φαντί: Cf. 107 n. **μονώτατος:** It is strictly true that Adonis is the only 'half-god' i.e. 'hero'; (cf. xiii.69) who revists earth regularly.

138. βαρυμάνιος: Ajax is traditionally 'wrathful' (cf. xvi.74) against Odysseus and his Greek colleagues because the arms of the dead Achilles were not awarded to him; hence the implacable refusal of his ghost to speak to Odysseus in *Od.* xi.543 ff.

139. εἴκατι: Priam claims in *Il.* xxiv.496 nineteen sons by Hecuba.

140. Πατροκλῆς: His name in Homer is Πάτροκλος, but with a vocative Πατρόκλεες (e.g. *Il.* i.337) and an alternative genitive Πατροκλῆος (*Il.* xxiii.65). **Πύρρος**:=Neoptolemos, Achilles' son.

141. Λαπίθαι: We first meet the heroic leaders of the Lapithai in *Il.* i.262 ff. (cf. XII.127 ff., 181 f.), where Nestor compares them, much to their advantage, to the Greeks at Troy. **Δευκαλίωνες**: Deukalion and his wife Pyrrha were the survivors of a flood which destroyed the rest of mankind (*Pl. Ti.* 22A). Theokritos treats 'Deukaliones' as if it were the generic name of an earlier race of men; the idea of successive species was familiar from Hes. *Op.* 109 ff.

142. Πελοπηϊάδαι: The descendants of Pelops include Agamemnon, already mentioned in 137. **Ἄργεος ἄκρα Πελασγοί**: A curious muddle (not Theokritos's fault) lies behind this expression. In the Homeric catalogue Πελασγικὸν Ἄργος is in Thessaly (*Il.* ii.681), but Ἄργος is also used by Homer to mean (*a*) Agamemnon's kingdom, and (*b*) part of Diomede's kingdom, the historical city of Argos in the Peloponnese. Since in the fifth century B.C. the Pelasgians were regarded as a widely distributed pre-Greek people, the city of Argos was regarded as 'Pelasgian' by the tragedians (e.g. Eur. *Or.* 692). ἄκρα is lit., 'highest', i.e. 'the rulers', 'the leading men'. Cf. Aisch. *Eum.* 487 ἀστῶν τῶν ἐμῶν τὰ βέλτατα.

143. ἵλαος: Cf. v.18 n.

144. ἀφίκη: 'Return' (as often implied by 'come' and 'arrive' in Greek).

145. ἁ θήλεια: Lit., 'the thing is very skilled ⟨I mean⟩ that woman.' The reference is to the singer, not to the female sex, which would be τὸ θῆλυ. Cf. Eur. *Phoen.* 198 φιλόψογον δὲ χρῆμα θηλειῶν ἔφυ, lit., '⟨the⟩ thing of female persons is by nature fond of criticizing', i.e. 'women are by nature given to carping'.

146: For the rhythm cf. XXIV.9. ὄλβιος, as first word of an utterance, is common in congratulatory or envious exclamations, e.g. *H. Hom.* 2.480 ὄλβιος ὃς κτλ., 'Blessed is he who . . .'. **ὄσσα**:=ὅτι τοσαῦτα. **ἴσατι**:=οἶδε: cf. v.119.

147. ὥρα: *sc.* ἀπιέναι.

148. ὄξος ἄπαν: Cf. III.18 τὸ πᾶν λίθος, and ὀξίνης=

'sour', 'bitter', 'angry', in Ar. *Knights* 1304. **μηδὲ ποτένθης**: 'Don't go near him', i.e. 'You can't . . .'.

149. χαῖρε "Αδων: Cf. Nossis (*HE*) 5.4 καλὸν "Αδωνα χρίει (– ∪ ∪ – ∪ ∪ –). The hiatus may be modelled on that familiar in χαῖρε ἄναξ (e.g. *H. Hom.* 15.9), where it is due to an original digamma, rather as, perhaps, in epitaphs χαίρετε οἱ παριόντες (*GVI* 1209.1) was modelled on an original χαίρετε τοὶ παριόντες (*GVI* 1210.1). **καὶ ἐς χαίροντας ἀφικνεῦ**: A prayer that when he returns next year he will find that all is well with them; cf. 1.144 f. n.

POEM XVI

Theokritos seeks a patron (68 f. δίζημαι δ' . . . σὺν Μοίσαις is the keystone of the poem), someone who will be to him what the Skopadai of Thessaly were in earlier days to Simonides (36–47). In Theokritos's time the belief that good men are rewarded in the afterlife was almost universal among ordinary people, as is clear from the epitaphs of the period, but it had by no means ousted the older belief that the afterlife is a pale reflection of life on earth. The Greek felt that he would be to some extent compensated for death if his memory were honoured by posterity; hence his appetite for 'fame' (κλέος) and his distaste for the possibility that he might be forgotten (cf. especially Pl. *Laws* 721BC). Theokritos adopts this conservative sentiment giving no hint of any other: men are remembered for ever after death, he says, if their achievements are celebrated by a good poet (29–33, 58 f.; cf. XXII.217–220). In claiming that Odysseus 'would not have obtained enduring fame' but for Homer, Theokritos is saying what Pindar (*Nem.* 7.21) said more succinctly; to Pindar (e.g. *Ol.* 10.91 ff.) it was self-evident that κλέος is conferred above all by the Muses.

One of the greatest patrons of Pindar and Bacchylides was Hieron I of Syracuse, and it is not surprising that

Theokritos's poem contains many echoes of the Classical lyric poets. They, like Theokritos, had every reason to urge wealthy patrons not to keep their wealth in too tight a fist (cf. Pi. *Nem.* 1.31 f., *Isthm.* 1.67 f., and *Pyth.* 1.90 εἴπερ τι φιλεῖς ἀκοὰν ἀδεῖαν αἰεὶ κλύειν μὴ κάμνε λίαν δαπάναις). Theokritos's own self-advertisement is aimed unashamedly at Hieron II, whom he compliments (76–103) by a flattering comparison (80 f.) and extravagant prayers for his success and prosperity (82–100). On the date of the poem, cf. C4; whether or not Hieron responded by inviting Theokritos to his court, we do not know. Modern readers are commonly repelled by an ancient poet's flattery of a patron or potential patron, and Aristophanes' satirical presentation of an impoverished and mercenary lyric poet in *Birds* 904–957 suggests that modern sentiment was shared by the Athenians of the late fifth century B.C. There are, however, pleas in mitigation. Theokritos was himself a Syracusan, and it would be surprising if his prayer for the victory of Hieron over the Carthaginians was not heartfelt. His world was a world of monarchies, and he would have been proud to be its Pindar; he is frank enough in declaring what he wants and what he can offer in return.

He imagines his 'Graces' (Χάριτες) as going from house to house, seeking a welcome and a gift — but in vain; they come back to him (5–12) barefoot and empty handed (cf. Leonidas [*HE*] 37 on his own poverty). In the end (104–109) he declares that he will stay at home until someone invites him; to that man he will go, and take the Graces with him (108 f.). The Graces (conspicuous in Pindar; *Ol.* 14 is the *locus classicus*) are a personification of those attributes of persons and events which compel admiration and affection and pleasurable recollection; translated out of the traditional poetic language of personification, Theokritos's meaning is that he can make a man admired by writing admirable poetry about him. Pindar, too, comes to the subject of one of his poems σὺν χάρισιν (*Isthm.* 5.21), and Bacchylides (5.9) 'weaves a song σὺν χαρίτεσσι' for Hieron I.

By portraying his Graces as begging from door to door Theokritos hints at a well-known phenomenon of Greek society and, as in his bucolic poems, builds a sophisticated construction on a popular foundation. It was customary for bands of children, on the occasion of certain festivals, to go round the houses in disguise, singing and asking for gifts (cf. the Scottish 'guysers' and the American 'trick or treat'). A Samian boys' song of this kind, traditionally ascribed to Homer, appears in the 'Herodotean' *Life of Homer*; it includes extravagant wishes for the prosperity of the house from which the gift is demanded, just as beggars or gypsies invoke blessings on those whom they importune. Athenaios 360B preserves a Rhodian song which is blunter (*PMG* 848): '... you'd better give us something; if not, we shan't leave you alone ...'. This Rhodian song is formally uncouth; Phoinix of Kolophon, a contemporary of Theokritos, used the idea for an elegant choliambic poem (*Coll. Alex.*, p. 233) in which prayers for the prosperity of the house again play a large part. R. Merkelbach, *Rheinisches Museum* xcv (1952), 312 ff., discusses these aspects of the poem and suggests that Theokritos's immediate model is not the begging-songs of his own time but a poem addressed by Simonides to Hieron I. It is, however, possible that the symmetry of lines 3 f. of Theokritos's poem is deliberately 'folkloristic' (cf. **G8**[*a*]):

> Μοῖσαι μὲν θεαί ἐντι· θεοὺς θεαὶ ἀείδοντι.
> ἡμεῖς δὲ βροτοὶ οἵδε· βροτοὺς βροτοὶ ἀείδωμεν.

Cf. the opening of the Rhodian song: ἦλθ' ἦλθε χελιδών,/ καλὰς ὥρας ἄγουσα,/καλοὺς ἐνιαυτούς,/ἐπὶ γαστέρα λευκά,/ἐπὶ νῶτα μέλαινα, κτλ.

1. **τοῦτο**: Amplified in ὑμνεῖν κτλ. **Διὸς κούραις**: The Muses, daughters of Zeus in Hes. *Theog.* 25.

2. The line seems to say that both the Muses (cf. *H. Hom.* 3.189 ff.) and the mortal poets whom they inspire like to sing of both gods and men. Lines 3 f., however, say that the Muses sing of gods, and imply that they do not sing of men. But the distinction is not as sharp, nor is the contradiction

so outright, as might at first sight appear; and, of course, the implication that men do not sing of gods would be absurd. In so far as the Muses inspire poets, it is true to say that 'singing about gods and men' μέλει to the Muses; and when Theokritos introduces his own subject by saying 'let us sing of mortals', it is natural for him to lead into it by recalling how the Muses in Hes. *Theog.* 43 ff. sing *first* of the gods. ἀγαθῶν κλέα ἀνδρῶν: The expression is adopted from *Il.* ix.189, where Achilles passes his time in singing κλέα ἀνδρῶν. On ἀγαθός cf. XIII.9 n.

3 f. Cf. F2. θεοὺς θεαί . . . βροτοὺς βροτοί: Cf. *H. Hom.* iv.154 μητέρα δ' οὐκ ἄρ' ἔληθε θεὰν θεός, Ar. *Th.* 538 f. ἵνα διδαχθῇ / γυνὴ γυναῖκας οὖσα μὴ κακῶς λέγειν. οἴδε: Virtually 'we *here*'; cf. I.120.

5. τίς γάρ: 'Now, who . . . ?' Cf. *Od.* xvi.222 ποίῃ γὰρ νῦν δεῦρο . . . νηΐ σε . . . ἤγαγον κτλ., where 'Why, who . . . ?' would not be appropriate to the context. But it is hard to find an absolutely exact parallel for this γάρ even among the examples collected by Denniston, *GP* 82. τῶν ὁπόσοι: 'Of all those who . . .'. γλαυκάν . . . ὑπ' ἀῶ: a modification, 'beneath the blue dawn' (i.e. beneath the blue sky which reaches from horizon to horizon when day breaks), of the conventional 'all that is under the dawn and the sun' (*Il.* v.267) or 'all men who are under the sun' (Dem. xviii.270).

6. πετάσας: Cf. 'open' and 'open up' in English, with the object unspecified.

7. αὖθις: 'Back again'. ἀποπέμψει: Not quite 'send away', but 'send on their way', which one can do nicely to a guest laden with gifts; cf. 28, and (προ)πέμπειν in the sense 'escort'.

8. αἱ δέ: 'And ⟨when they are sent back again without a gift⟩ they . . .'. 8–12 expand the picture begun in the second half of 7.

9. ὅτ': Probably = ὅτι (cf. XI.54 n.) rather than ὅτε in the sense τότε γάρ.

10. κενεᾶς . . . χηλοῦ: In 8–12 as a whole the poet represents his Graces in terms appropriate to ordinary

persons, but this phrase gives them the character of fairies or
djinns. It was probably suggested to him by an anecdote
about the notoriously hard-headed Simonides (Stob. iii.10.
38), who said that he had one chest for gratitude (χάριτες)
and another for money, and that when he opened the
former he found nothing in it that was any use to him. But
by employing the image with a different sense of χάριτες
Theokritos makes an additional point (cf. vii.44 n.): the
chest contains *his* χάριτες, i.e. the poems which he writes
but cannot sell.

11. On the word-order, cf. **F9**(*b*). The grief-stricken
posture, head bowed to the knees (and hands round the
knees) is described also in Ap. Rh. iii.706 f. The knees of the
Graces are 'cold' as the poor are cold, through lack of fuel.

13. τοιόσδε: i.e. who will receive them (55 ff.) and not
send them away (7). τίς εὖ εἰπόντα φιλήσει: 'Who will
show affection for one who has praised ⟨him⟩?'

14. ὡς πάρος: With the sentence as a whole, not with
ἐσθλοῖς: '. . . no longer . . . are zealous, as they were of
old . . .'.

16. ὑπὸ κόλπου: Cf. ii.120 n. If the hand is concealed
inside the κόλπος, it is not only not stretched out in the act
of giving, but nervously protecting the money.

16 f. πόθεν . . . ἄργυρον: 'Looks to see whence . . .'. Cf.
F9(*b*).

17. ἰὸν ἀποτρίψας: Hoarded money rusts, and this is
relevant to the admonition to spend generously, implying
'hoarding is actually bad for money' and 'if you hoard
money so long that it rusts, that shows you didn't need it all
that time'.

18. εὐθύς: 'Without more ado'; cf. Xen. *Hieron* 2.8,
'Ordinary citizens' (as opposed to tyrants) 'can go εὐθύς
wherever they like'. ἀπωτέρω ἢ γόνυ κνάμα: Cited as a
proverb in the form 'the knee is nearer than the shin' by
Arist. *Eth. Nic.* 1168[b]8. The equivalent modern excuses for
parsimony are 'Charity begins at home' and 'Blood is
thicker than water'.

19. αὐτῷ μοί τι γένοιτο: 'I wish I had something

myself', implying, 'I've nothing to give away'. **θεοί**: Implying, 'so men need not'; cf. 'You'll get your reward in heaven'. Another anecdote (Cic. *De Or.* ii.352) about Simonides is relevant: Skopas cheated Simonides of half the reward which he had promised him, and told him to pray to the Dioskouroi for the other half.

20. ἄλλου: *sc.* than Homer. **ἅλις πάντεσσιν "Ομηρος**: And dead too, so that he needs no patrons.

21: 'The best ... is the one who is not going to ...', a cynical rejection of any claim on one's own generosity; the utterance is of the same type as 'The only good X is a dead X'.

22. δαιμόνιοι: This vocative expression, most often courteous or conciliatory, has here an undertone of expostulation. **δέ**: A connective which would logically be placed after a vocative is normally placed instead after the word which follows the vocative.

23. φρονέουσιν: Dative plural participle, 'in the eyes of thinking people'; cf. Eur. *Rhes.* 973 σεμνὸς τοῖσιν εἰδόσιν θεός.

24. ἀλλά: *sc.* ὄνασίς ἐστι. **ψυχᾷ**: Essentially 'self'; cf. Aisch. *Pers.* 841 ψυχῇ διδόντες ἡδονήν. **που**: As often, the diffident tone associated with που does not imply that the speaker doubts the rightness of what he is saying, but softens its expression.

25. ἄλλων: Greek morality recognised that one's own family and friends have first claim, but a wider generosity was esteemed; in Lys. xiv.59 the speaker praises his father for contributing to the dowries of the daughters and sisters of poor citizens and to funerals and the ransoming of prisoners.

28. ἀποπέμψαι: *sc.* 'them'. The emphasis lies on the participle μειλίξαντ': 'to treat them kindly ... and ⟨only then⟩ to ...'. Cf. 7 n.

29. ὑποφήτας: As in XVII.115, the word implies that the poet sings what the Muses put into his head; cf. Ap. Rh. iv.1381, where the poet is ὑπακουός ... Πιερίδων. Pi. fr. 150 uses προφᾱτεύειν of the poet in the same relationship. For a different sense, cf. XXII.116 n.

30. ὄφρα: Here = ὅπως ἄν. **ἐσθλὸς ἀκούσῃς**: 'Be called good', i.e. 'be well spoken of'; cf. (e.g.) Soph. *Oed. Col.* 988 οὐ γάρ . . . ἀκούσομαι κακός.

31. ἐπί: 'Beside', 'on the banks of'.

32 f.: The poor man, who cannot afford to pay a poet to sing his praise, and who has achieved nothing which the poet could praise, must necessarily be ἀκλεής after death as in life. **ἔνδοθι**: i.e. on the palms. **ἐκ πατέρων**: Cf. xxiv.108 ἐκ πατέρων . . . ἀφνειός.

34–57: The generalisation of the preceding section is now amplified by examples; cf. **F6** and iii.40 ff. 34–47 refer to the Thessalian nobles who patronised Simonides, 48–50 to epic poetry in general, and 51–57 to Odysseus and other characters of the *Odyssey*. Pindar on several occasions illustrates the fame conferred by poetry by reference to the *Iliad* and the *Odyssey*: *Pyth.* 3.112 ff., Nestor and Sarpedon; *Nem.* 7.20 f., Odysseus; *Isthm.* 3/4.55, Ajax; 8.49 f., Achilles.

34. Ἀντιόχοιο: The genealogy of this Thessalian ruler was apparently mentioned (so *Σ*) by Simonides (*PMG*) 528. The line seems modelled on *Il.* xi.132 πολλὰ δ' ἐν Ἀντιμάχοιο δόμοις κειμήλια κεῖται. **Ἀλεύα**: The Aleuadai (Hdt. vii.6.2) or 'sons of Aleuas' (ibid. 130.1) are praised in Pindar's earliest extant ode (*Pyth.* 10.5, of 498); they were powerful in Thessaly at the time of Xerxes' invasion and 'medised' without delay.

35. ἔμμηνον: Hes. *Op.* 766 f. advises the farmer to distribute rations to his slaves on the last day of each month.

36. Σκοπάδαισιν: The sons of Skopas — a patron of Simonides, to whom he addressed the poem discussed by Pl. *Prt.* 339A ff. (*PMG* 542) — were killed in an accident for which Simonides wrote a lament (*PMG* 521). By the late fifth century the Skopadai were a traditional example of wealth, as we see from Kritias (D³) fr. 6.

38. Κραννώνιον: Krannon was a city in the centre of Thessaly, associated with the Skopadai by Hdt. vi.127.4 and Kallim. fr. 64.13 f.

39. Κρεώνδαις: Skopas's father was named Kreon

(Pl. *Prt.* 339A), and we should expect his sons and descendants to be called Κρεοντίδαι; but Theokritos has modelled Κρεῶνδαι on northern Greek names in -ώνδᾱς (particularly common in Boeotia). The effect of the layout of 34–39 is to suggest that the Kreondai and the Skopadai were distinct families, and perhaps Theokritos thought they were; but the evidence cited above suggests that he was wrong.

40. τῶν: The demonstrative ὁ is here embodied in a phrase closely modelled on epic, *Il.* xviii.80 ἀλλὰ τί μοι τῶν ἦδος;

40 f. γλυκύν ... θυμόν: Lit., 'emptied out the sweet spirit', i.e. 'underwent the emptying-out of ...'; one's soul is 'sweet' because life is sweet, and the body is alive only when the soul is in it. **στυγνοῦ 'Αχέροντος:** Hemsterhuis may well have been right in suspecting that Theokritos wrote στυγνοῖο γέροντος, i.e. Charon, the ferryman of the dead.

43. ἔκειντο: 'Would have been lying'. Imperfects such as ἔμελλον and ἐγιγνόμην are commonly used without ἄν in the sense 'were in danger of being ...', and so too ἦν; this usage is much rarer with other verbs and with the aorist. Perhaps Theokritos's words can be analysed as: 'they had been put ... ⟨apparently⟩ unremembered — *but ...*'; cf. Agamemnon's words in Eur. *Hec.* 1111 ff., 'If we had not known (ᾖσμεν) that Troy had fallen, the noise would have created (παρέσχεν) a panic', i.e. 'Except that we knew ..., it created ...' (*sc.* but not for long).

44. ὁ Κήϊος: Simonides was a native of the island of Keos.

44 f. αἰόλα ... πολύχορδον: Lit., 'uttered varied ⟨utterances⟩ into a many-stringed barbitos', i.e. singing poems, musically modulated, to the accompaniment of the type of lyre called barbitos; cf. Eur. *Ion* 498 ff. συρίγγων ὑπ' αἰόλας ἰαχᾶς ὕμνων, Soph. *Ichn.* 319 αἰόλισμα τῆς λύρας.

46 f. τιμᾶς δέ ... ἀγώνων: The association of horse-racing with commemoration in song is a natural one for a Greek, since victories in racing were the subject of encomiastic odes (e.g. Pindar on the Sicilian tyrants, Hieron and Theron).

224   COMMENTARY

48. ἀριστῆας Λυκίων: The Lykians appear on the Trojan side in the *Iliad* (ii.876 f.).

48 f. κομόωντας Πριαμίδας: This may seem an error of memory or a pointless perversity on the part of Theokritos, for the epithet is most commonly applied by Homer to the Greeks, especially in the formula κάρη κομόωντες Ἀχαιοί, and never to the Trojans; but in other epics it may have been applied to the Trojans, and Theokritos is not restricting himself to Homer at the moment (cf. 49, 50 nn.).

49. θῆλυν ... Κύκνον: Kyknos, the first eminent Trojan victim of the war (according to Proclus's summary of the *Kypria*), is not mentioned by Homer. He is called white-haired by Hes. fr. 237, but white-*skinned* by Hellanikos (*FGrHist* 4) fr. 148, and the latter is the usual version. ἀπὸ χροιᾶς implies, 'To judge from his skin, you would take him for a woman'.

50. προτέρων: 'The men of old'. **ἀοιδοί:** Theokritos has in mind both Homer and the poet(s) of the *Kypria*.

52. ἔσχατον: Odysseus did not go to the furthest point of Hades from the earth, but to the border of Hades at the furthest point of the earth (*Od.* xi.13–22).

54. ἔσχεν: 'Would have had'; for the omission of ἄν, cf. 43 n. ἐσιγάθη δ' ἄν is a completely fresh clause, separable from ἔσχεν by quite strong punctuation.

55. βουσί ... ἀμφ' ἀγελαίαις: Cf. Bacchylides 10.44 ἀμφὶ βοῶν ἀγέλας.

56. περίσπλαγχνος: Homer calls Laertes μεγαλήτωρ (*Od.* xxiv.365), and περίσπλαγχνος (cf. iii.45 περίφρων, a Homeric epithet of Penelope) seems to be a rather contrived synonym.

57. Ἰάονος: Homer's birthplace was disputed, but there was at least a wide measure of agreement that he was Ionian; cf. vii.47 Χῖον ἀοιδόν.

58–109: Theokritos returns to his original theme, and comes round to praise of Hieron (76–103), ending with an invocation of the Graces.

60 ff. ἀλλ' ἴσος γὰρ κτλ.: Lit., 'but' (cf. v.44) 'the toil is equal ... to measure ... or to wash ... *and* to persuade

...', i.e., 'It is as hard to persuade ... as to measure ...'. The uncountable number of waves on the sea is a banal image; cf. Ap. Rh. iv.214 ff. on the host of the Kolchians: ὅσσα τε πόντου κύματα ... κορύσσεται ... ἢ ὅσα φύλλα ... πέσεν ... (τίς ἂν τάδε τεκμήραιτο;). κύματα μετρεῖν is recorded later as a proverb.

62. ἢ ὕδατι νίζειν: On the prosody cf. *Il.* vii.425 ὕδατι νίζοντες (⌣⌣ 2̱ _ 3̱⌣) and **D4**.

63. βεβλαμμένον: 'Corrupted', 'misled'; cf. Pi. *Nem.* 7.17 f. σοφοί ... οὐδ' ὑπὸ κέρδει βλάβεν. **παρελθεῖν**: The word suggests some degree of deceit (cf. English 'get past'), but Theokritos seems to regard it as meaning 'persuade', 'prevail upon'; perhaps he took *Il.* i.132 οὐ παρελεύσεαι οὐδέ με πείσεις as the same kind of tautology as ἀγορήσατο καὶ μετέειπεν, etc.

64. χαιρέτω: Lit., 'let ... rejoice', i.e. 'I say "good-bye" to ...', 'I wash my hands of ...'. **τοῖος**: *sc. ἐστί*. **εἴη**: *sc.* 'for all I care'.

65. αἰεί ... αὐτόν: The second member of the complex wish is a malediction founded on the commonplace observation (e.g. Solon [D³] fr. 1.71 ff.) that avarice increases continually in strength.

66 f. αὐτάρ ... ἑλοίμαν: If Theokritos is thinking of himself *as poet*, his wish is a little out of place in a poem which is basically a request for money; but he seems, at least in part, to be putting himself into the position of the rich man (who might acquire honour and friends if only he would spend his money) while in part remaining a poet content that the rich should be rich (Pindar's patrons were notably rich in 'mules and horses') so long as he is loved and honoured for his poetry. Cf. the sentiment of Pi. *Nem.* 8.37 ff., 'Some pray for gold, others for boundless land; but I ...'.

68 f. ὅτινι ... σὺν Μοίσαις: A poet who comes 'with the Muses' is a good poet, inspired by them with skill in his craft, and Theokritos is confident of his own skill. θνατῶν is an appropriate substitute for ἀνθρώπων in that the poet has the opportunity to convey to mortal men the blessings of the divine Muses.

73. ἔσσεται οὗτος ἀνήρ: The confidence with which Theokritos prophesies is explained in 76 ff. His language is a shade oracular; cf: *Il.* iv.164 'the day will come (ἔσσεται ἦμαρ) when Troy shall perish' and the prophecy interpolated in xxiv.86 f. ἔσται δὴ τοῦτ᾽ ἆμαρ κτλ.: but the same expression admits of colloquial adaptation, e.g. Herodas 4.50 ἔσσετ᾽ ἡμέρη κείνη κτλ., where a mistress is threatening a slave-girl.

74: i.e. ῥέξας ὅσσον ἔρρεξεν ἢ ᾿Αχιλλεύς . . . ἢ . . . Αἴας. In so far as μέγας is a stock epithet of Ajax (cf. xv.138 n.), not of Achilles, Theokritos is avoiding too close adherence to Homeric tags. On βαρύς cf. xv.138 βαρυμάνιος ἥρως.

75. ὅθι . . . ῎Ιλου: The 'tomb of Ilos son of Dardanos' is mentioned in the *Iliad* (e.g. xi.371 f.) as a landmark close to Troy.

76. Φοίνικες: i.e. the Carthaginians, dominant in western Sicily since the fourth century and periodically at war with Syracuse since the early fifth century.

76 f. ὑπ᾽ ἠελίῳ . . . σφυρόν: Carthage lies on the same latitude as Syracuse, but some 260 miles further west; Tunisia, the Carthaginian heartland, lies as a whole south-west of Sicily, and the coast thence westwards to the strait of Gibraltar was regarded as a Carthaginian preserve. By 'the extreme edge of Africa' Theokritos may mean either 'the African coast' or '⟨even⟩ the furthest part of the African coast'.

78. βαστάζουσι . . . δοῦρα: '. . . grasp their spears by the middle'.

80. προτέροις: Cf. 50.

82: For the form of the prayer cf. that of Agamemnon in *Il.* ii.371 αἲ γὰρ Ζεῦ τε πάτερ καὶ ᾿Αθηναίη καὶ ῎Απολλον κτλ., and for its content cf. Pi. *Pyth.* 1.71 ff., a prayer to Zeus that the Carthaginians and Etruscans may remain cowed by the naval victory of Hieron I at Cumae.

83. κούρη: Persephone; she and her mother Demeter are associated with Sicily, and not least with Syracuse. Cf. Bacchyl. 3.1 f. Σικελίας κρέουσαν Δάματρα ἰοστέφανόν τε Κούραν ὕμνει, Pi. *Ol.* 6.94 f., and xv.14, 94 nn. ᾿Εφυραίων: The Corinthians, founders of Syracuse; cf. xv.91

84. εἴληχας: Cf. vii.103 n. **Λυσιμελείας**: A marsh, mentioned by Thuc. vii. 53.2, which seems to have lain along the shore of the great harbour of Syracuse north of the river-mouth.

86. Σαρδόνιον: If the Carthaginians are to depart via the 'Sardinian sea', Theokritos must envisage them as defeated on the north coast of Sicily; and possibly he is influenced by Pindar's mention (82 n. above) of the battle off Cumae.

86 f. φίλων . . . ἀλόχοισιν: Probably 'taking news, to children and wives, of the death of ⟨the children's and wives'⟩ dear ones', rather than 'taking news of the death of ⟨their own⟩ friends to the children and wives ⟨of those friends⟩'. It is not nowadays customary to express a hope of victory in terms of the grief to be inflicted on the families of the enemy, but the Greeks had no such inhibition. **ἀπὸ πολλῶν**: Cf. Thuc. i.110.1 ὀλίγοι ἀπὸ πολλῶν . . . ἐσώθησαν.

88 f. Over a long period many Sicilian cities had suffered destruction and enslavement, and Syracuse herself had played no small part in this process; but Theokritos is (prudently) not looking too far back into the past, but only to a re-establishment of Sicilian Greeks on recently devastated sites when Carthaginian power has been eradicated by Hieron.

92 f. βόες . . . ὁδίταν: The simple wish 'may cattle be abundant' is converted into a particular scene, in which the movement of the cows reminds a traveller that the hour is late.

94. νειοί: It is the summer ploughing (Hes. *Op.* 462 f.) which Theokritos pictures.

94 f. ἀνίκα τέττιξ . . . ἐν ἀκρεμόνεσσιν: Cf. v.110 f.; and as in xiii.40 ff., details characteristic of bucolic appear in a non-bucolic context.

96. ἀράχνια: The spinning of cobwebs over arms and armour is a symbol of the blessings of peace in a paean of Bacchylides (4.31 ff.); so is the creeping of rust.

97. διαστήσαιντο: Lit., 'set up wide apart', 'set up across gaps'; middle, because it is their own webs that they spin for their own use. **μηδ' ὄνομ'**: So Chalkiope in Ap. Rh.

iii.680 wishes that she were living 'at the ends of the earth, ἵνα μηδέ περ οὔνομα Κόλχων': cf. Anon. (*HE*) 32 καὶ χαρίτων λοιπὸν ἔτ' οὐδ' ὄνομα.

99. πόντου Σκυθικοῖο: The sea which a Greek would most naturally think of as 'Scythian' is the Sea of Azov, Μαιῶτις (Hdt. Μαιῆτις) λίμνη. Pi. *Isthm.* 6.23 speaks of the fame of the Aiakidai as travelling 'beyond the sources of the Nile and through the Hyperboreans', the latter a people regarded by the Greeks (e.g. Hdt. iv.13.1 f.) as beyond the Scythians.

99 f. πλατύ . . . ἐμβασίλευεν: The bricks of the walls of Babylon, known in tradition to have been of extraordinary size and strength, were bound with bitumen (Hdt. i.179). Semiramis, mentioned by Hdt. i.184 as a queen of Babylon, was later represented by Ktesias (*ap.* Diod. ii.7 ff.) as builder of the city.

101. εἷς μὲν ἐγώ: 'I am ⟨only⟩ one', as the sequel shows.

102. Σικελήν: Cf. 1.125 n. **'Αρέθοισαν**: Cf. 1.117 n.

103. αἰχμητήν: Cf. 80 f.

104f. At Orchomenos in Boeotia there was a cult of the Graces (cf. Pi. *Ol.* 14.3 f.) believed to have been created by Eteokles in the days of the people called Minyai (*Il.* ii.511, Pi. loc. cit., Strabo 414; this Eteokles is not the son of Oidipous). The manner of mentioning the ancient enmity between Orchomenos and Thebes — revived in the fourth century, when Orchomenos rebelled against the domination of the Boeotian federation by Thebes, and suffered harsh treatment — leaves us with the impression that the Graces are enemies of Thebes. Theokritos's reason for saying this is that in the end Orchomenos — thanks, he implies, to the divine protection of the Graces — triumphed; for Thebes was utterly destroyed by Alexander in 335, and Orchomenos lent a vengeful hand.

106. ἄκλητος . . . μένοιμί κεν: 'If I am not invited I will stay ⟨at home⟩'; the potential optative with ἄν or κε is sometimes best translatable by the English future, as in (e.g.) Eur. *Hec.* 1132 λέγοιμ' ἄν, 'I will tell you, then'. ἐς δὲ καλεύντων: Cf. 1.103 n.

107. ἀμετέραισιν: The first person plural pronoun can be used in the sense of the singular even in the closest possible association (as here) with a singular verb.

108. οὐδ' ὔμμε: 'Not . . . you, either'.

108f. τί γάρ . . . ἀπάνευθεν: Pi. *Ol.* 14.5 ff. speaks of the indispensability of the Graces for all τά τε τερπνὰ καὶ τὰ γλυκέα: and cf. Mimnermos (D³) tr. 1.1 τίς δὲ βίος, τί δὲ τερπνὸν ἄτερ χρυσῆς 'Αφροδίτης;

109. εἴην: Cf. the pious wishes of vii.155 ff., xxvi. 30.

POEM XVIII

At a Greek wedding, after the feast was over and the bride had been brought to her husband's bedroom, the un-married girls of her own age sang an 'epithalamion' outside the room. Cf. Pi. *Pyth.* 3.17 ff., '. . . the sound of wedding-songs proclaimed in chorus, such as it is the custom for her companions, the girls of her age, to sing as evening falls, addressing her fondly'. Theokritos here presents an epi-thalamion as if for the marriage of Helen, daughter of Zeus and Leda (whose mortal husband was Tyndareos), to Menelaos, son of Atreus.

1–8: *Narrative Introduction.*

1. ἄρα: In Hes. *Op.* 11 ἄρα introduces an exposition, 'Well, now, . . . ', which follows an introductory passage, and Theokritos uses it similarly in xxii.27; it would seem that he felt it also appropriate at the beginning of a narra-tive which has had no introduction. In prose a speech some-times has ἀλλά as its first word or δέ as its second, but this is a response to a previous speech, to an implied question (cf. connecting particles at the beginning of oracular utterances which answer explicit questions) or to an attitude which is part of a situation. The opening of [Xen]. *Resp. Ath.*, περὶ δὲ τῆς 'Αθηναίων πολιτείας, conveys the impression that the writer has selected for exposition one item from the store of his reflections, and similarly ἔν ποκ' ἄρα Σπάρτᾳ suggests that the poet has selected one brief chapter from the mass of narrative legend available to him. ξανθότριχι: ξανθός is a regular epithet of Menelaos in Homer (e.g. *Il.* iii.284); cf. also II.78 n.

2. κόμαις: 'In their hair'; cf. VII.16 ὤμοισι, 'on their shoulders'.

3. νεογράπτω: In *Il.* xvii.36 it is said of Menelaos, who has killed the young Euphorbos, that he has 'left Euphorbos's wife a widow within the new thalamos'; Odysseus built his own θάλαμος, when he married (*Od.* xxiii.192); and cf. *GVI* 585 (Diodoros [*GPh*] 6.1), which speaks of the ἡμιτελὴς θάλαμος of a man who died before his wedding. ἐστάσαντο: ἱστάναι can = 'create', 'do', 'bring into being', when the object is something upright or a set of uprights (e.g. χορός, a collection of dancers), and the middle χορὸν ἵστασθαι is appropriate when the subject of the verb is the dancers themselves.

4. πρᾶται: 'Foremost', i.e. the highest in status. μέγα χρῆμα Λακαινᾶν: The idiom is especially used to imply great size or numbers, e.g. Hdt. i.36.1 ὑὸς χρῆμα . . . μέγα, 'a monstrous boar', and Teleklentides (*CAF*) fr. 1, 'men in those days were . . . μέγα χρῆμα γιγάντων'. It is hard not to suspect in Theokritos's phraseology an allusion to the massive, muscular build of Spartan women, which was regarded as unusual in the Greek world, though not necessarily as repellent; cf. Ar. *Lys.* 79 'you could strangle a bull;' ~ 81 οἷον τὸ κάλλος.

5. Τυνδαρίδα: Τυνδαρίς = 'daughter of Tyndareos', as often in Euripides (e.g. *Hec.* 269). On the scansion of -δα cf. D4.

7. εἰς ἓν μέλος: 'In time to one' (i.e. 'the same') 'song'.

9 ff. *The Song.* The elements which may be distinguished in this song can be paralleled from scattered citations of the epithalamia of Sappho (cf. Page, *Sappho and Alcaeus*, 119 ff.), from the wedding-songs at the end of Ar. *Peace* and *Birds*, and from Catullus 61 and 62.

(i) 9–15. Ribald jocularity, pretending that Menelaos

is a cold bridegroom who has gone to sleep, and reproaching him accordingly. Of course, the chorus has no actual grounds for supposing any such thing. Sappho fr. 110 is jocular; fr. 111 is probably obscene (cf. G. S. Kirk, *CQ* N. S. xiii [1963], 51 f.), and cf. the *procax Fescennina iocatio* of Catullus 61.119 f. The straightforward obscenity of Ar. *Peace* 1337 ff., 1352 ff. does not involve mockery of the bridegroom.

(ii) 16–18. Congratulations to the bridegroom. Cf. Sappho frr. 112, 115.

(iii) 19–37. Praise of Helen. This can be subdivided:

(*a*) 19. The fact that she is the daughter of Zeus.

(*b*) 20–31. Her beauty, expressed mostly in similes. Cf. Sappho fr. 105, where the bride is compared to fruit at the top of a tree, and fr. 113, 'there is no girl like her'.

(*c*) 32–37. Her accomplishments, ending with a final compliment to her beauty.

The classification and sequence — family, beauty, accomplishments — remind us of what we find in Classical enkomia, notably Agathon's enkomion on Eros in Pl. *Smp.* 194E ff.: birth, beauty, virtues, effects. Xenophon's *Agesilaos* begins with the king's family, recounts his achievements, and goes on to his virtues.

(iv) 38–48. A promise always to remember Helen.

(v) 49–55. Prayers for the happiness and prosperity of the couple. With 49 χαίροις κτλ. cf. Sappho frr. 116 f.

(vi) 56 f. Promise to return at dawn. This indicates that the chorus has begun singing at nightfall; cf. Pindar's reference (*Pyth.* 3.19) to 'songs at evening', Sappho's invocation (fr. 104) of the Evening Star, and the importance of Vesper/Hesperus in Catullus. Aischylos (M) fr. 124 mentions singing by youths and girls together in honour of the couple at dawn, and Sappho fr. 30 speaks unmistakably of youths, the bridegroom's friends, as joining the girls to sing the whole night long; but Theokritos does not indicate whether he envisages other choruses as filling the gap between the departure and the return of his chorus of girls.

10. τις: Cf. iv.30 n.

11. πολύν τιν': sc. οἶνον: cf. Eur. Cycl. 569 ὅστις ἂν πίνῃ πολύν. τιν' reinforces πολύν on the analogy of πολύ τι, μέγα τι, etc. **ἔπινες . . . κατεβάλλευ**: The sequence of tenses suggests, 'Were you engaged in drinking . . . when you began to be put down . . .?' (sc. by your companions, if you were incapably drunk), but it is hardly possible to bring this out in translation without cumbrousness.

12. σπεύδοντα: 'If you were eager . . .'. **καθ' ὥραν**: Lit., 'at ⟨the right⟩ time', sc. for sleep, i.e. comparatively early. **αὐτόν**: Cf. 11.89 n.; sc. εὕδειν.

13. παῖδα: '⟨Her⟩ (sc. Helen) ⟨as a⟩ girl'.

14. παίσδειν ἐς βαθὺν ὄρθρον: If Helen had been left with the girls, she would not have played games 'until the last hour of the night'; she would have played (sc. and gone to bed early) instead of making love — as she should now be doing — until the last hour of the night. Cf. Anon. (HE) 41, where a certain Timareta on the eve of her wedding dedicates her toys to Artemis.

14 f. ἐπεί . . . ἅδε: The point of 'since . . .' is: if you had wanted to go to sleep early tonight, you could have put off the wedding; you would not have lost your bride by doing so. **καὶ ἐς ἀῶ**: 'And on the day after that'. **κἠς ἔτος ἐξ ἔτεος**: Cf. xi.69 n.

15. Μενέλαε: $\stackrel{4}{\smile}|\smile$ has no parallel in Theokritos; cf. D2(b).

16. ἀγαθός τις ἐπέπταρεν: On the sneeze as an omen cf. vii.96 n. We do not meet elsewhere the idea that a good man's sneeze is an omen more likely to be fulfilled than a bad man's. The emendation ἀγαθόν is tempting: 'someone gave a sneeze of good omen'; but it is possible that Theokritos wrote ἀγαθός and meant by it (cf. Σ) 'someone whose sneeze constituted a good omen sneezed', for ἀγαθὴ τύχη and ἀγαθὸς δαίμων are established expressions, and cf. Kallim. H. 5.124 καὶ ποίων οὐκ ἀγαθαὶ πτέρυγες, 'and of which ⟨birds⟩ the flight is not a favourable omen'.

16 f. ἐρχομένῳ τοι . . . ὡς ἀνύσαιο: (i) The meaning is probably, '. . . going to Sparta in order to accomplish that which the other princes ⟨were going to Sparta to accomplish⟩', i.e. to win Helen. (ii) Alternatively, ὡς ἀνύσαιο could depend on ἐπέπταρεν. The sneeze which serves as the omen does not *cause* a favourable event, but a sequence of events which is fated can be expressed as if one event had been intended to cause the next: cf. *Il.* xxii.328 f., 'but the spear did not sever his windpipe, *in order that* (ὄφρα) he might address Achilles . . .' (we would say: '*and so he was able to* address Achilles'). All the heroes of the time came to woo Helen; Hesiod (frr. 196–204, cf. *Scut.* 1–56) told the story and listed them in what seems to have been a peculiarly monotonous catalogue. Menelaos won her because he gave the most numerous and most valuable presents (Hes. frr. 198.5 f., 204.41, 85 ff.).

18. When Menelaos and Helen were in Egypt on their way back from Troy, Proteus assured Menelaos that he would not die as other mortals die but would be taken by the gods to Elysion, 'because you have Helen and they look on you as the son-in-law of Zeus' (*Od.* iv.561 ff.). ἡμιθέοις: Men called the heroes in retrospect 'half-gods' (e.g. *Il.* xii.23, and especially Hes. *Op.* 159 f.); Theokritos's Spartan girls are prophesying with the assurance of his own erudition that there will be no other hero who can claim Zeus as father-in-law.

19. τὰν μίαν: 'One and the same'. χλαῖναν: 'Cloak' in its function as bedcover.

20. Modelled on *Od.* xxi.107, a compliment to Penelope: οἴη νῦν οὐκ ἔστι γυνὴ κατ' 'Αχαιΐδα γαῖαν.

21. That parents should produce children like themselves is regarded as a blessing (in Hes. *Op.* 235 it is one of the god-given rewards to the just), and XVII.63 f. says of Ptolemy Philadelphos that he was born πατρὶ ἐοικώς. μέγα suggests great size in mother and child. Size was certainly an aspect of physical beauty in Greek eyes (*Od.* xv.418 καλή τε μεγάλη τε, xi.309 f. μηκίστους . . . καὶ πολὺ καλλίστους, Hdt. iii.1.3 θυγάτηρ κάρτα μεγάλη τε καὶ εὐειδής), and there may be the same allusion to the women of Sparta as in line 4; but the neuter μέγα . . . τι suggests equally 'important', 'mighty', 'famous'.

22. ἄμμες δ' ... 25. παρισωθῇ: The sense seems to be: 'We, the whole company of her coevals, for whom . . . , four times sixty girls, the female youth (*sc.* of Sparta) — of *them* (τᾶν) not one . . .'; not only does the sentence change direction, but when it does so the first person with which it began is forgotten and the demonstrative (cf. xvi.40 ἀλλ' οὔ σφιν τῶν ἧδος) is used with reference only to the appositional phrases. Alternatively, the sense might be: 'We, . . . , ⟨are⟩ four times sixty girls . . . , *of whom* (= but of us) . . .'.

23. ἀνδριστί: That Spartan girls anointed themselves and took violent physical exercise, like men, made them remarkable in the Greek world; in Ar. *Lys.* 82 the Spartan woman replies γυμνάδδομαι γάρ to compliments on her physique.

24. τετράκις ἑξήκοντα: The 12 'leading' girls who are singing (4) speak on behalf of the entire age-group which they represent. If any demographic speculation about Sparta in the heroic age underlay Theokritos's figure — and I do not seriously imagine that it did — he may have imagined a city of some 10,000 adult male citizens.

25. οὐδ' ἄτις: '⟨There is⟩ not even ⟨one⟩ who . . .', but perhaps it is wrong to analyse the expression at all; it seems clear from (e.g.) Xen. *Hell.* i.5.9 ὅπως τῶν Ἑλλήνων μηδὲ οἵτινες ἰσχυροὶ ὦσιν, 'that *no nation* among the Greeks should be strong', that οὐδ' ὅστις and μηδ' ὅστις had come to mean 'no one at all'.

26–31. Two similes express the beauty of Helen in extravagant terms, the first in the form 'A and B; so C' (cf. xiii.62 n.), the second in the form 'as A or B, so C'. In both, the generalising aorist (26, 29) is used of the point of comparison, but the imperfect in 28 refers to Helen's days (now over) among the girls.

26. καλόν: The emphasis lies here: 'Beautiful is the face which . . .'. The aorist is an emendation (Ahrens) of the imperfect διέφαινε, to bring the simile into line with the generalising aorist of the second simile (29). The imperfect could not be used in a generalisation equally applicable to past and present.

27. πότνια Νύξ: The reverent vocative is slightly apologetic; they wish to avert any possible offence to Night (who is with them at present) by their praise of Dawn. **τό τε**: If ἄτε (the transmitted text) were right, we should have the oddity of a simile within one member of another simile: 'Beautiful is the face of Dawn . . . , like the spring . . .; so Helen . . .'. This is a good reason for adopting Kaibel's emendation τό τε, 'and ⟨so is⟩ the . . .', understanding καλόν ἐστι.

28. διεφαίνετ': The imperfect here is right, as the reference is purely to the past.

29. ἄτ': 'As'; translate as if ἄτε preceded πιείρα. **κόσμος**: Part of the predicate; κυπάρισσος (30) is the subject.

30. ἢ ἅρματι Θεσσαλὸς ἵππος: sc. κόσμος ἐστί. The simile is curious, to our taste; a horse's relation to the chariot which it draws is quite different from that of a tree to a landscape or Helen's to Sparta.

32. ἔργα: ἔργον is not 'work' in the abstract, but a product of work, e.g. a tilled field, a statue or a cloak.

34. ἔταμ': The freedom with which the aorist can be used in generalising statements is strikingly apparent from the sequence πανίσδεται – ἔταμε – ἐπίσταται.

35. κροτῆσαι: The verb is appropriate, since stringed instruments were normally played with a plectrum.

36. εὐρύστερνον: The epithet is not elsewhere attached to an Olympian goddess, however warlike (in Hes. *Theog.* 117 it is an epithet of Earth); but cf. 4, 31 nn.

37. τᾶς . . . ἐντί: The Greeks commonly regarded a force located in a woman's eyes and emanating from them (e.g. Soph. *Ant.* 795) as the stimulus activating the desire for her felt by a man who looks at her; hence, 'on whose eyes are all desires' means 'whose eyes kindle a desire surpassing all others'. Pl. *Phdr.* 251B seems to have discarded this view in favour of a 'stream' which enters the eye of the beholder from the beautiful person as a whole.

39. δρόμον: This may be a proper name (ctr. 22), since there was an area so called at Sparta, used for young men's races and gymnastics (Paus. iii.14.6). φύλλα: Cf. xi.26 n.

41 f. ὡς γαλαθηναί . . . ποθέοισαι: The simile would be appropriate if they were speaking of a woman of their mother's age or of a goddess who had protected them; used of Helen, it is a very odd simile indeed. Possibly (if this is not one of Theokritos's earliest poems) bucolic imagery (cf. xi.30 f.) is trespassing here on heroic legend; and possibly Theokritos allowed it to trespass because he had in mind (or at the back of his mind) the legendary beauty of Helen's breasts — Menelaos discarded all thought of vengeance when he saw them (Eur. *Andr.* 627 ff., Ar. *Lys.* 155 f.) — and the size and beauty of the breasts of Spartan women generally (cf. Ar. *Lys.* 83).

43. πρᾶται: 'We shall be the first to . . .' (cf. 45) makes it plain that 43–48 give the origin of a Spartan cult; on Hellenistic poets' fondness for aetiology cf. **F7** and p. 180. We know no more about this cult, but we hear of a sanctuary of Helen Dendritis at Rhodes (Paus. iii.19.10) and of a plane-tree called Menelais in Arkadia (id., viii.23.4).

46. ὑπὸ σκιερὰν πλατάνιστον: Cf. **F2**.

48. Δωριστί: Since the tree is in Lakonia, most passers-by will be Doric-speakers and will therefore read the inscription (aloud, as they decipher the letters) with a Doric accent. As for the inscription itself, neither σέβευ nor Ἑλένας is exclusively Doric, though both forms are alien to the Attic Koine, but that is not the point. σέβευ: People and things do not become sacred necessarily because the gods decree that they are so, but because men decide to *treat* them as sacred; so in Hellenistic times the only practicable definition of ἥρως is 'one who is worshipped by his family or compatriots with the rites customarily given to ἥρωες'.

50–52. On the repetition of the names cf. **F1**(*a*); the prayer gives the impression of expanding the type of exclamation ὦ Ζεῦ Ζεῦ. εὐτεκνία is not normally regarded as the special gift of Leto, but as the mother of Apollo and Artemis she is the divine paradigm of the bearing and rearing of noble children; that was the point of Niobe's intemperate boast (*Il.* xxiv.602 ff.) that her own εὐτεκνία was superior to Leto's. The other divinities, Aphrodite and Zeus, are associated with their traditional gifts, sexual pleasure and wealth respectively.

53. 'That it' (*sc.* the ὄλβος of the family) 'may pass again' (*sc.* as from Atreus to Menelaos) . . .

54. φιλότητα: This is Homer's normal word for love in bed, and I have (with diffidence) retained -τη- (as in the ancient and medieval texts) rather than emend to Doric -τᾱ-.

55. ἐγρέσθαι . . . μὴ 'πιλάθησθε: From xxiv.7, where Alkmena bids her babies εὕδετ' . . . ἐγέρσιμον ὕπνον, there seems little doubt that it was ill-omened to say 'sleep!' without adding a reference to waking; 'sleep' is a metaphor of death. There is, however, the further point that the chorus will return before dawn precisely in order to wake up the couple, who will no doubt make love again; this song is called διεγερτικός in later Greek.

56. νεύμεθα: 'We shall return'; cf. *Il.* xviii.101 (Achilles speaking) οὐ νέομαί γε φίλην ἐς πατρίδα γαῖαν.

57. ἀοιδός: i.e. cock.

58. χαρείης: Unlike χαίροις in 49, χαρῆναι (cf., in the same kind of context, χαριείς and κεχαρισμένος) is specially associated with dedications, sacrifices and festivals, in which the god is asked to approve of what men do.

POEM XXII

This poem is a hymn to the Dioskouroi, Kastor and Polydeukes; and, in the manner of Greek hymns, it encloses detailed narratives within a conventional frame.

The Dioskouroi were twin sons of Leda, and therefore brothers of Helen and Klytaimestra. One strand of legend (Hes. fr. 24) represented them as sons of Zeus; another (Pi. *Nem.* 10.79 ff.) represented only Polydeukes as begotten by Zeus, Kastor being begotten by Leda's mortal husband Tyndareos (cf. p. 251, on Herakles). Tyndareos was king

of Sparta, and the Dioskouroi are therefore associated
primarily with Sparta (Hes. fr. 198.7 f.); hence (5)
Λακεδαιμονίους δύ' ἀδελφούς. Amyklai, just south of Sparta,
is sometimes treated by poets as the chief city of Lakonia
in the heroic age (e.g. Pi. *Pyth.* 1.65 ff.); hence Polydeukes
is called in 122 'Ἀμυκλαίων βασιλῆα. In legend and cult the
Dioskouroi were associated with athletics: both (24, cf.
Alkman [*PMG*] fr. 2) with horse-racing, but especially
Kastor (34, 136; cf. *H. Hom.* 33.3 Κάστορα θ' ἱππόδαμον),
and Polydeukes with boxing (2 f.). They were also invoked
as protectors of ships at sea (8 ff.; cf. *H. Hom.* 33.7 ff., Eur.
El. 1347 ff.) and, to a less conspicuous extent, as protectors
against disasters on land (6 f.; cf. *H. Hom.* 33.6).

1–26. Prooemium.

2. πὺξ ἐρεθίζειν: The phrase depends on φοβερόν: cf.
Eur. *Phoen.* 127 φοβερὸς εἰσιδεῖν.

3. μέσας: The boxer's thongs were wrapped around the
hand in such a way as to leave the fingers free; see also
80 f.

4. καὶ δὶς καὶ τὸ τρίτον: In line 1, ὑμνέομεν amounts
to, 'This poem is a hymn to the Dioskouroi'. If we give
ὑμνέομεν the same sense in 4, the poet appears to be
saying, 'This poem is a second, even a third hymn . . .'. In
the absence of any apparent reason for his presenting the
poem as if it were the third of three occasions, we must look
for another interpretation, either (*a*) 'we ⟨constantly⟩
hymn . . . twice, and even for a third time . . .', or (*b*) 'we
⟨utter the word⟩ "ὑμνέομεν" . . . twice, and even for a
third time . . .', or (*c*) 'we hymn . . . in two ways, and in a
third way too'. (*a*) does not seem to make much sense.
(*b*) is not impossible, and would represent an assimilation of
the announcement ὑμνέομεν to the address χαῖρε, which is
sometimes uttered three times, e.g. Pi. *Pyth.* 4.61 χαίρειν
ἐστρὶς αὐδήσαισα, Ar. *Frogs* 184 χαῖρ' ὦ Χάρων χαῖρ' ὦ Χάρων
χαῖρ' ὦ Χάρων. (*c*) will refer to the threefold predication
which follows, ἀνθρώπων σωτῆρας . . . ἵππων θ' (*sc.* σωτῆρας)

. . . νηῶν θ' (sc. σωτῆρας); a little clumsy and obscure, because (i) at first sight it looks as if ἵππων κτλ. is a genitive absolute and as if ἵππων θ' and νηῶν θ' specify two notable ways in which the Dioskouroi are 'saviours of men', but in 8 f. we have to think back and realise that 7 was not a genitive absolute; (ii) 'saviours of ships' could be subsumed under 'saviours of men', since it is the saving of the men in a ship that matters. But in 6 Theokritos must be thinking of occasions which differ from those of 7 and 8.

5. Θεστιάδος: Leda was daughter of Thestios; cf. Eur. *Iph. Aul.* 49 Λήδα Θεστιάδι.

6 ff. ἀνθρώπων κτλ.: As in *H. Hom.* 33:6 ff., it is the rescue of storm-tossed sailors which figures largest in the account of the Dioskouroi as saviours. The full and vivid pictorial detail of the passage tends to put the Dioskouroi themselves out of our minds, rather as similes in Homer and archaic poetry take charge, as it were, and are built up into scenes in their own right.

9. βιαζόμεναι: Ships can 'force' the stars in the sense that they can put to sea when the sky warns them not to.

10. οἱ δέ σφεων: οἱ refers to the winds, σφεων (dependent on κατὰ πρύμναν) to the ships.

11. ἑκάστου: sc. 'wind'. The winds are personified, from Homer onwards.

12. εἰς κοίλην: κοίλη ναῦς is the usual expression for a ship's hold. **ἔρριψαν**: The 'great wave' is the object of the verb, as of ἀείραντες.

14. πολὺς δ': sc. ἐστι.

18. αὐτοῖς ναύτῃσιν: 'Sailors and all', 'with their sailors'; cf. *Il.* xxiii.8 αὐτοῖς ἵπποισι καὶ ἅρμασιν ἄσσον ἰόντες . . . Πάτροκλον κλαίωμεν, Thuc. iv.14.1 ἔλαβον καὶ μίαν (sc. ναῦν) τούτων αὐτοῖς ἀνδράσι, Ap. Rh. i.501 f. ποταμοὶ κελάδοντες / αὐτῆσιν Νύμφῃσι.

19. ἀπολλήγουσ': Often in epic, when λ is the initial letter of a word or of the second component of a compound, the syllable preceding it is long, e.g. *Od.* xii. 224 ἀπολλήξειαν, Ap. Rh. i.1154: probably λλ should be written, as in *GVI* 1251.4 (Rhamnous, fourth century B.C.) ΥΠΟΛΛΙΠΑΡΩΙ =

ὑπὸ λιπαρῶι. **λιπαρή**: Cf. Kallim. *Epigr.* 5.5, where a calm is λιπαρὴ θεός.

20. διέδραμον: On the aorist cf. XVIII.34 n.

21. Ἄρκτοι: The Great Bear and the Little Bear.

21 f. Ὄνων . . . Φάτνη: Described in Aratos 892 ff., where it is a sign of bad weather if the 'Manger' between the 'Asses' (both in the region of the Crab) suddenly becomes invisible.

24. ἱππῆες κτλ.: The description of the Dioskouroi as 'lyre-players . . . singers' is a novelty; cf. **F7**.

25 f. Cf. **F2**.

27–134. The Victory of Polydeukes over Amykos.

Amykos (like the Cyclops) was a large, brutal and inhospitable son of Poseidon (97) and ruler of the Bebrykes at the entrance to the Black Sea (28 f.), in whose territory the Argonauts stopped for a night on their way to Kolchis.

Theokritos departs from traditional form in presenting this story partly (54–74) as a dramatic dialogue in strict stichomythia. The story of the famous boxing-match between Polydeukes and Amykos, provoked when Amykos refused to give Polydeukes water, was told by the epic poet Peisandros and was the subject of a dramatic poem, *Amykos*, by Epicharmos (frr. 6–8); there was also a satyr-play *Amykos* by Sophocles. Ap. Rh. ii.1–97 also narrates it; the question of priority between Apollonios and Theokritos is even harder to determine on internal grounds in this case than in the case of XIII (cf. Köhnken, 84–121). There are some significant differences of detail: Apollonios locates the scene in the Propontis, before the Argonauts come to the Symplegades, but for Theokritos the scene is beyond the Propontis (27 f.); in Apollonios Amykos's challenge, which he represents as the custom of his country, is uttered to the Argonauts as a whole and taken up by Polydeukes, who eventually — after an evenly-balanced first round — kills Amykos with a blow above the ear, and in the general mêlée which follows the Bebrykes are routed by the

Argonauts. The progress of the fight is described in quite different terms by the two poets, and there is little or no verbal coincidence anywhere; on 65 εἰs ἐνὶ χεῖραs ἄειρον ~Ap. Rh. ii.14 ἐὰs ἀνὰ χεῖραs ἀεῖραι cf. Ar. *Birds* 759 αἶρε πλῆκτρον, εἰ μαχεῖ. Equally, neither poet draws to any extent on the brief but decisive boxing-matches described in *Il.* xxiii.664 ff. (Epeios and Euryalos) and *Od.* xviii.89 ff. (Odysseus and Iros); note, however, in Theokritos 98 f. αἷμα φοίνιον~*Od.* xviii.97 φοίνιον αἷμα and 129 ἀλλοφρονέων~ *Il.* xxiii.698 ἀλλοφρονέοντα. The characterisation of Polydeukes in Theokritos as courteous and unaggressive is attractive; one feels that Apollonios's Polydeukes is highly conscious of his divine ancestry and confident that he will kill his adversary. In Peisandros and in Epicharmos, as in Theokritos, Amykos was not actually killed. On Greek boxing cf. E. N. Gardiner, *Athletics of the Ancient World* (Oxford, 1930), 197 ff., and H. A. Harris, *Greek Athletes and Athletics* (London, 1964), 97 ff.

(a) 27–53. *Narrative.*

27. προφυγοῦσα . . . ξυνιούσας: Cf. XIII.22 n. Ap. Rh. ii.321 f. says of the Symplegades ξυνίασιν . . . εἰs ἕν.

29. θεῶν φίλα τέκνα: The Argonauts were not only 'heroes' (i.e. treated in later times as superhuman) but also 'half-gods' in that most of them had one divine parent or (like Jason himself, in some versions of the legend) ancestor.

30. μιᾶς: In XIII.33 πολλοὶ δὲ μίαν στορέσαντο χαμεύναν has a point, because in the preceding words we were told that they prepared their meal κατὰ ζυγά. In the present passage the point of saying that they all disembarked by one ladder must be the contrast with the separation of the Dioskouroi from the rest in 34 f.; in which case we have to keep 30 in mind while reading 32 f. ἀμφοτέρων: There was one set of rowers' benches down the port side and another down the starboard side.

32 f. Cf. XIII.32 f.

33. πυρεῖα: It is important to remember that kindling fire was not easy for the Greeks. The use of the burning-

glass was known by the late fifth century (Ar. *Clouds* 766 ff.),
but it was commonly easiest to relight a lamp from a neigh-
bour's (Lys. i.14).

34. οἰνωπός: Cf. xi.19 n.

37 ff. Cf. xiii.39 ff.

45. οὔατα: Cauliflower ears are (naturally enough)
associated with boxing, e.g. in Pl. *Prt.* 342B ὠτά τε κατάγνυνται
... καὶ ἱμάντας περιελίττονται.

48. ἄκρον ὑπ' ὦμον: i.e. the upper arm immediately
below the shoulder-point.

52. The wearing of a lionskin is more commonly
associated with Herakles than with any other legendary
figure.

(b) 54–74. *Dialogue*

55. χαίρω πῶς: It is always possible to take the greeting-
formula χαῖρε in its literal sense; so in Ar. *Ach.* 832 the
despondent and starving Megarian, returning to his un-
fortunate homeland, replies to Dikaiopolis's χαῖρε πολλά
(a hearty 'Goodbye!') with ἀλλ' ἁμὶν οὐκ ἐπιχώριον, 'It' (*sc.*
χαίρειν) 'is not the way of my country'.

56. Polydeukes politely assumes that Amykos's churlish
reply is occasioned by apprehension. **φάθι**: Cf. ii.130 n. and
Soph. *El.* 8 f. οἱ δ' ἱκάνομεν, / φάσκειν Μυκήνας ... ὁρᾶν.

58. Polydeukes is asking a question, as the form of the
answer shows; he does not at any point descend to abuse.

59. 'But *I'm* not trespassing on *your* ⟨land⟩', implying,
'You can't complain if I'm the sort of man I am'.

61. μήτε σύ με ξείνιζε: Implying, 'I wouldn't expect
presents from you'; the main weight lies on the next words.
ἐν ἑτοίμῳ: 'Available'; cf. 212.

62. δαιμόνι': Cf. xvi.22 n.

63. γνώσεαι: 'You'll find out ⟨that I won't⟩'. **εἰ**: Cf.
Aisch. *Eum.* 597 ἀλλ' εἴ σε μάρψει ψῆφος ('if the vote condemns
you'; the speaker is confident that it will), ἀλλ' ἐρεῖς τάχα.

66. ὄμμα τ' ὀρύσσων: The manuscripts have ὄμματα δ'
ὀρθά, which makes no sense; the emendation (Platt) is
founded on the fact that according to Philostratos *Imag.*

ii.6 the Spartan form of the pankration permitted eye-gouging (ὀρύττειν).

68. καὶ ἐμούς: Cf. x.35 n.

69. κεκλήσεθ' ὁ πύκτης: i.e., 'You don't need to know his name; he will be called' (*sc.* by those who will tell the awe-inspiring story of the fight) ' "the Boxer" '.

70. ἄεθλον: Polydeukes has already been told that the match is the price of drinking from the spring, but as a true Greek he naturally associates prizes with sporting events; cf. the careful specification of the prizes before each event in the funeral games of Patroklos, *Il.* xxiii.262 ff., 700 ff., 740 ff.

71. σὸς μὲν ἐγώ: *sc.* κεκλήσομαι, αἴ κε κρατήσῃς: cf. Thuc. vi.79.1 ὅταν ὑπ' ἄλλων καὶ μὴ αὐτοί . . . ἀδικῶσιν 'when ⟨they are wronged⟩ by others and do not . . .'.

72. Polydeukes is shocked at the barbarous and uncompromising demand; he speaks as a Greek familiar with cock-fighting, to which there are abundant references in Comedy.

73. Cf. (e.g.) *Il.* iii.151 τεττίγεσσιν ἐοικότες.

(c) 75–134. *Narrative: the Fight.*

76. συνάγερθεν: = συνηγέρθησαν.

77. ἀεὶ . . . κομόωντες: i.e. who never cut their hair. On the word order cf. **F9**(*b*).

79. Μαγνήσσης: Magnetis is the coastal region of Thessaly which includes Iolkos, whence the Argo sailed (Pi. *Pyth.* 4.188 f.), and Pagasai, where it was built. **ἐν δαΐ**: Closely with ὑπείροχος.

81. γυῖα: Here the forearms, round which boxers commonly wound thongs almost to the elbow.

82. σύναγον: Cf. Poseidippos (*HE*) 7.2 μηκέτι μοι πρόσαγε, and Polyb. xi.18.4 συναγαγὼν ἐκ μεταβολῆς . . . αὐτῷ, 'turning and coming to grips with him'; intransitive usage of the compounds of ἄγειν became increasingly common in Hellen-istic Greek (e.g. ὑπάγειν, 'go' in the New Testament).

84. ὁππότερος: '⟨To decide⟩ which of them . . .'. **λάβοι**: For the optative cf. *Il.* iii.316 f., 'they drew lots to decide who was to throw first' (ὁππότερος . . . ἀφείη). **φάος**:

The Argonauts have landed for the night (30 ff.), so the sun is very low in the west.

85. μέγαν ἄνδρα: 'The big man', i.e. Amykos.

90 f. νενευκὼς ἐς γαῖαν: i.e. 'with his head down'.

94. χώρῳ ἐνὶ στεινῷ: 'Since they were in a confined space' — confined, presumably, by the crowd around them — the Argonauts are afraid that Polydeukes may not be able to dodge Amykos. **Τιτυῷ**: The gigantic Tityos, who attempted to rape Leto, was seen by Odysseus in the underworld undergoing eternal punishment (*Od.* xi.576 ff.).

96. ἀμφοτέρῃσιν: Cf. vii.157 n.

98. ἔστη: *sc.* Amykos.

100. ἕλκεα λυγρά: The phrase is epic: *Il.* xix.49.

102. ἄναξ: Although often used in poetry of mortal rulers (e.g. vii.79), the word is particularly associated with the invocation of praise of gods and heroes. In several regions the Dioskouroi had the title ἄνακε or Ϝάνακοι and their sanctuary was called ἀνάκειον. **ἐτώσια χερσὶ προδεικνύς**: In 1.38 ἐτώσια μοχθίζοντι means that the men's efforts do not achieve what they want; but here the point is that Polydeukes' blows are not what Amykos expects them to be, i.e. they are feints. Xen. *Hipp.* 8.24 uses προδεικνύναι of making a cavalry movement which is swiftly reversed.

104. The blow is facilitated if Amykos is still attacking with his head down (90 f.).

109 f. ἔξω . . . αὐχένος: i.e. below the neck.

112–114. What Theokritos says of Polydeukes is a rhetorical exaggeration which accords with a common subjective impression (cf. xv.7 n.), but what he says of Amykos reflects his indifference to boxing as it really is.

112. ᾧ μέν: The manuscripts have αἱ μέν, which gives a contorted antithesis ('the one ⟨lot of flesh⟩', *sc.* Amykos's ∼ ὁ δ', *sc.* Polydeukes), and Reiske's ᾧ μέν is probably right. The use of ὅς μέν = ὁ μέν is very rare until the late fourth century but common thereafter.

113. πάσσονα: The epic comparative of παχύς is always complimentary, implying not fat but swelling muscles and the absence of aged wrinkles.

114. ἁπτομένου: If this is right, it must mean something like 'as the labour warmed up', but there is no parallel for this application of ἅπτειν to labour or effort. Meineke's αὐξομένου is not as bold an emendation as it seems, for in late Greek ἁπτ was pronounced [aft] and αὐξ [afks].

115 ff. The rhetorical question and the appeal to the Muse originate in epic motifs (e.g. *Il.* i.8 f., 'Which of the gods made them quarrel? The son of Leto and Zeus . . .') but are used also in Classical and Hellenistic poetry, e.g. Bacchyl. 15.47 ff. Μοῦσα, τίς πρῶτος λόγων ἆρχεν δικαίων; Πλεισθενίδας . . . φθέγξατ' κτλ., Kallim. *H.* 3.183 ff. 'Which of the islands . . . pleased Artemis? . . . Tell me (εἰπέ), goddess, and I will sing of it to others', Ap. Rh. ii.851 τίς γὰρ δὴ θάνεν ἄλλος . . .; Ἀγνιάδην Τῖφυν θανέειν φάτις (note there the same non-inferential γὰρ δή as in Theokritos).

115. ἀδηφάγον: Cf. IV.10, 34 nn.

116. ἑτέρων ὑποφήτης: We should expect ὑποφήτης with a genitive to mean 'interpreter of . . .' or 'speaker for . . .' (cf. XVI.29 n.); but here the meaning must be 'interpreter ⟨of others⟩ at the service of . . .'. Cf. the ambiguity of 'their interpreter' in English.

120. ἀπὸ προβολῆς: i.e. from the 'guard' position, in which both adversaries would have had their left arms somewhat extended towards each other. ἑτέρῳ: sc. ποδί: emendation of the manuscripts' ἑτέρῃ is obvious. ἐπιβαίνων: Stepping forward, close in to his opponent, with his right foot.

121. λαγόνος: sc. his own. γυῖον: Cf. 81.

124. ἐπέμπεσεν ὤμῳ: Lit., 'fell on ⟨him⟩ *with* his shoulder', i.e. he put his weight behind the punch.

125. λαιῇ: As a result of 123 ff., Polydeukes' left hand is no longer gripped by Amykos.

129. ἀνέσχεθε: ἀμφοτέρας . . . χεῖρας is the object.

131. ἀτάσθαλον: The word characterises not only action which is reckless and foolish, inasmuch as it brings disaster subsequently on the agent, but also action which repels the observer because it is arrogant and 'goes too far'; cf. *Od.* iv.693, where Odysseus is praised as a just king who never acted unfairly and 'never did anything ἀτάσθαλον to any man'.

132. πύκτη: After Amykos's boast (69), it is appropriate that Polydeukes should now be hailed as πύκτης.

133. Cf. 97.

135–211. Kastor's Victory over Lynkeus.

Turning to praise of Kastor, Theokritos chooses as his theme the fight between the Dioskouroi and Lynkeus and Idas, the sons of Aphareus. The legend was told in the *Kypria* (and possibly also by Alkman; cf. [*PMG*] frr. 7 f.), and we find it in Pindar *Nem.* 10.55–90. The Dioskouroi carried off Hilaeira and Phoibe, the daughters of Leukippos (or of Apollo, according to the *Kypria*), who were betrothed to the sons of Aphareus; Pindar says nothing of the girls, adopts an alternative version (an early one, as can be shown from its representations in painting and sculpture) in which the quarrel was about cattle, and characteristically avoids indicating who was in the right. Theokritos fills in some details about which we have no other information: that the Dioskouroi had persuaded Leukippos by lavish presents to renege on his promises to Lynkeus and Idas (149 ff.), and that there had been a long period of argument (152 ff.) before the Dioskouroi carried the girls off. Theokritos seems to accept the lawless brutality of the Dioskouroi as a datum, and even to heighten our awareness of it by putting dignified and reasonable reproof into the mouth of Lynkeus (note φίλοι in 154, 165). It is necessary to say 'seems', because a portion of the poem is missing after the speech of Lynkeus, and we next find Kastor challenging him to single combat, to avoid superfluous bloodshed (175–180). Kastor wins the fight; Lynkeus's death is described in bloody detail; his brother Idas is slain by a thunderbolt from Zeus. (In Pindar's version Kastor is mortally wounded, and it is Polydeukes who kills Lynkeus). Theokritos was as well aware as Pindar two centuries before him (to say nothing of men of greater intellectual stature in the intervening period) that the data of mythology pose disagreeable problems to those who wish to believe both that knowledge of the gods is attainable through mythology and that the gods are the ultimate sanction of morality. Instead of rewriting the story or choosing a different story altogether, he has accepted the fact that stories of the execution of divine purposes often put the gods at a moral disadvantage by comparison with mortal men; it was easy for him to do that if, as is probable, he regarded mythology solely as the material of poetry and not as authentic tradition about the gods (cf. H2).

136. On the multiplication of epithets cf. 24.

143. βαρυνόμενοι: Cf. xvi.79.

145. δαιμόνιοι: Cf. xvi.22 n.

146. χαλεποί: *sc. ἐστε*. We might say in English, 'Why are you being so difficult?', but χαλεπός in fact suggests 'angry', 'fierce'. γυμναί: Cf. 191 n. A reasonable answer to the question would be, 'Because you are pursuing us, fully armed!'.

148. ἐν ὅρκῳ: i.e. settled by an oath.

157. 'Αχαιῶν: Since all the other places named in 156–158 are Peloponnesian, it is probable that 'Achaeans' here means not (as in epic) 'Greeks' but (as in historical times) the people living between Sikyon and Elis along the south coast of the Corinthian Gulf.

158. Σισυφὶς ἀκτή: Sisyphos was the legendary ruler of Corinth; cf. *Il*. vi.152 ff.

162. ὡς: 'Since . . .', 'for . . .'.

164. καί: 'And ⟨so are⟩ . . .'. πατέρες: This would be a patronising utterance if Lynkeus regarded Polydeukes as son of Zeus (as Theokritos himself does [213]), and he must mean, 'your father Tyndareos and Tyndareos's father'; then πατρώϊον αἷμα refers to more remote forbears. Since Lynkeus and Idas are paternal cousins of the Dioskouroi (170), Lynkeus is boasting as well as complimenting. ἄνωθεν: Cf. vii.5, xv.91.

166. ἄλλον: *sc. γάμον*.

167 f. τὰ δ' . . . ἀνέμοιο: Cf. *Od*. viii.408 f., 'And if any word has been spoken in anger, may the winds straightway catch it up and bear it away'. Soph. *Trach*. 467 f. ταῦτα μέν / ῥείτω κατ' οὖρον; Ap. Rh. i.1334 ἀλλ' ἀνέμοισιν / δώομεν ἀμπλακίην. χάρις: Cf. p. 217.

169 f. ἀλλ' ... πείθεσθ': Cf. Thuc. vi. 39.2, where ἀλλ' ἔτι καὶ νῦν introduces an indignant plea.

170. ἀνεψιώ: Apollodoros (i.9.5 and iii.10.3.3 ff.) represents Tyndareos, Leukippos and Aphareus all as sons of Perieres; he cites Stesichoros as his authority for the marriage of Perieres, but it is not clear whether Stesichoros also listed the sons.

171. However appropriately 171 f. follow 169 f., it is plain that Kastor is speaking now, for in 173 we have 'Idas and my brother, Polydeukes', and in 175, 'I and Lynkeus' (where there is a variant reading, 'I and Kastor', irreconcilable with 173). Therefore some verses are missing between 169 and 170, and we do not know how Kastor justified the Dioskouroi's action in reply to Lynkeus's arguments. It is characteristic of such occasions that each side accuses the other (170 ∼ 145) of wanting a fight. **αἵματι:** With ἔγχεα λοῦσαι (172).

172. ὁμοίιον: In *Il.* iv. 444 Strife νεῖκος ὁμοίιον ἔμβαλε μέσσῳ, which suggests the meaning 'affecting' (or 'involving') 'all alike', and Homer also applies the word to death and old age; hence perhaps here 'on equal terms', 'with equal risk to both'.

177 f. ἐξ ἑνὸς οἴκου εἷς: If only Lynkeus and Kastor fight, neither house can lose more than one son.

179. ὑμεναιώσουσι ... τάσδ': Whoever wins the fight, there will remain the victor plus Idas and Polydeukes, and three men cannot marry two girls. Yet it is curious how often one can read the passage without realising that. The reason is, I think, that Kastor has spoken rhetorically as if both he and Lynkeus were going to die in the fight, magnanimously sacrificing themselves for their brothers, and this rhetoric is realistic; it is just how people speak under the compulsion of self-deception.

180. ὀλίγῳ ... κακῷ: Presumably each side would regard it as a greater κακόν to give up the girls to the other side so that everyone might stay alive.

181. τὰ δ': 'And his words ...'. **θεός:** The idea is Homeric (cf. *Il.* iv. 363 [a wish] τὰ δὲ πάντα θεοὶ μεταμώνια θεῖεν);

POEM XXII 249

we could express it by saying 'his words *were destined* to be fulfilled'. θεός or ὁ θεός, 'whatever god is concerned', can always be substituted for θεοί in such expressions, for men may perceive the effects of divine intervention without knowing the identity of the divine agent.

184. πρώτην: So in *Il.* xx.275 Achilles' spear strikes the shield of Aineias ἄντυγ' ὑπὸ πρώτην, i.e. at the very edge.

185. δούρατος ἀκμάς: Cf. Sarpedon in *Il.* xii.298, δύο δοῦρε τινάσσων. One spear was poised in the right hand; the left forearm went through the grips of the shield, and the left hand held the second spear. Cf. A. M. Snodgrass, *Early Greek Armour and Weapons* (Edinburgh, 1964), 137 f., 198 f.

189. πάρος: As in epic, πάρος here = πρίν and governs an infinitive.

191. ἄορ ... ἐρυσσαμένω: One cannot be sure that Theokritos remembered that he had made Lynkeus say (146), 'and your swords are naked in your hands'. If he did, he must have supposed that the swords were sheathed before the spear-fight began.

193. πολλὰ μέν: sc. 'struck', given ἔνυξεν in 194.

194. ἀκριβὴς ὄμμασι: A mythological point underlies this: Lynkeus had the sharpest eyesight of all mankind (Pi. *Nem.* 10.62 f., where the story as told in the *Kypria* fr. xi [Allen] is followed). Cf. Ap. Rh. i.153 ff.

195. ὅσον: 'Only', 'merely', as in *Il.* ix.354 ὅσον ἐς Σκαιάς τε πύλας ... ἵκανεν, 'he only got as far as ...'.

196 f.: = τοῦ μέν (sc. Lynkeus) φάσγανον ὀξὺ φέροντος ἐπὶ σκαιὸν γόνυ (sc. Kastor's), ὑπεξαναβὰς ποδὶ σκαιῷ Κάστωρ ἄκρην χεῖρα (sc. Lynkeus's) ἐκόλουσεν. Cf. F9(b).

199. ποτὶ σῆμα πατρός: Cf. 141.

201 f. διαπρό ... ὀμφαλοῦ: In through the side, below the ribs, and out through the navel.

203. νενευκώς: Collapsing on the ground, head down; ctr. 90 f.

204. ὕπνος: Cf. xviii.55 n.

206. παίδων: With τὸν ἄλλον (205). **Λαοκόωσα:** Elsewhere the mother's name is Arene (Pherekydes [*FGrHist* 3] fr. 127) or Polydora (Peisandros [*FGrHist* 16] fr. 2).

210. ἀλλὰ Ζεὺς ἐπάμυνε: For the gods of mythology help to their own kin takes precedence over both justice and compassion.

212–223. Conclusion.

The farewell to the Dioskouroi is characteristic of hymns. Cf. *H. Hom.* 1.20 f., 3.545 f., 4.579 f., 5.292 f.; Kallim. *H.* 1.91 ff., 2.113, 3.259 ff., 4.325 f., 5.140 ff., 6.134 ff. Two of Kallimachos's hymns (1 and 3) resemble Theokritos's in going beyond the bare formulae of farewell to pronounce generalisations or admonitions. Theokritos strikes an original note in speaking of poets in general and their relation to the divine and heroic world. Just as in xvi he expresses at length his thoughts about writing in honour of contemporary patrons, so here his excursion into the archaic genre of hymns prompts him to express himself on the subject of the whole genre.

212. So Pindar *Nem.* 10.71 f., after recounting how Idas was killed by Zeus, says χαλεπὰ δ' ἔρις ἀνθρώποις ὁμιλεῖν κρεσσόνων.

214. κλέος . . . πέμποιτε: Cf. 24 n. Whether or not Theokritos regards the Dioskouroi as having a special function as protectors of poets, any god may be asked to influence the course of events in any way that his worshippers desire; cf. vii.103 ff.

216: Helen, as sister of the Dioskouroi, is the only link by which the poet can connect them with the Trojan War.

218. ὑμῖν: The reference here and in 221 ὑμῖν must be the same. Since ἄνακτες is specially appropriate to the Dioskouroi (cf. 102 n.) and θεοῖς in 223 strongly suggests that ὑμῖν αὖ are gods, it would seem at first sight that Theokritos must be addressing the Dioskouroi. But he knew his Homer intimately, and cannot have been unaware that so far from honouring the Dioskouroi the *Iliad* only alludes to them once in passing. That is in the passage (iii.236 ff.) where Helen wonders why they are not to be seen among the Greek leaders; Homer adds that she did not know that they were dead and buried at Sparta. Evidently Homer did not regard them as gods and chose not to adopt (if he knew of it at all) the story that they returned from the dead to a divine existence alternately. Therefore ὑμῖν and ὑμῖν αὖ refer to the gods and heroes of legend as a whole, and θεοῖς in 223 has a similarly wide reference.

222. ὡς ἐμὸς οἶκος ὑπάρχει: Lit., 'as my estate is available', i.e. 'as well as my resources ⟨of poetic skill⟩ allow'. Cf. Aisch. *Ag.* 961 f., where οἶκος ὑπάρχει τῶνδε . . . ἔχειν is contrasted with πένεσθαι.

POEM XXIV

Herakles and Iphikles were the twin sons of Alkmena, the wife of the Theban hero Amphitryon. According to the story told by Hesiod *Scutum* 27 ff., Herakles was begotten by Zeus, but Iphikles by Amphitryon on the same night (cf. Pi. *Nem.* 10.80 ff.; the biology of Greek myths is not always sound). Hera, through jealousy of Alkmena, was the enemy of Herakles, and sent two monstrous snakes to kill him; but Herakles, even as an infant, had supernatural strength, and throttled the snakes (cf. Pherekydes [*FGrHist* 3] fr. 3 and Eur. *Herc. Fur.* 1263 ff.).

In essentials Theokritos follows the story told by Pindar in *Nem.* 1.33–72, thus:

	Theokritos	Pindar
Herakles and his twin are put to bed.	1–10	35–38
Hera sends the snakes to the infants' room.	11–19	39–43
Panic of Iphikles.	20–26	—
Herakles throttles the snakes.	26–33	43–47
Alkmena awakes, and rouses Amphitryon	34–40	—
Panic in the household; Alkmena rushes from her bed.	—	48–50
Amphitryon arouses the slaves	41–53	—

The chieftains of Thebes come armed	—	51
All rush in.	54	—
Amphitryon comes sword in hand.	—	52–54
Astonishment and delight of Amphitryon at his son's prowess.	55–59	55–59
Alkmena comforts Iphikles	60 f.	—
Herakles is put back to bed.	62 f.	—
Teiresias is summoned by Alkmena (Th.) or by Amphitryon (Pi.).	64–72	60 f.
Teiresias foretells the achievements and deification of Herakles.	72–102	62–72

It will be observed that Pindar includes one heroic element (51) irreconcilable with the domesticity with which Theokritos (cf. 50 n.) has invested the scene (though in a recently published fragment of Pindar, *Pap. Oxy.* 2442 fr. 32, it is the slaves, not Theban nobles, who come running). Furthermore, Theokritos's Herakles is ten months old, but Pindar's surmounts his ordeal in the first day of his life (so too in *Pap. Oxy.* 2442 Alkmena jumps up naked while still recovering from childbirth). Theokritos has perhaps attempted a compromise with realism, ultimately under the influence of Pherekydes, in whose version (fr. 69) Amphitryon himself set the snakes on the twins when they were a year old, to discover which of them was son of Zeus.

The archaic and classical poets were capable of blending accurate and tender observation of babies as they really are with fantasy about the valour and intelligence displayed by heroic or divine babies. The theft of Apollo's cattle by the newly-born infant Hermes, the theme of the Homeric Hymn to Hermes (*H. Hom.* 4), was the subject also of Sophokles' satyr-play *Ichneutai*, and among the titles of his lost plays we find *Dionysiskos* and *Herakleiskos*. The motif of the newborn prodigy is a familiar one in the folklore of all parts of the world. (On the general question of the portrayal of children by the Greeks cf. R. Kassel, *Quomodo . . . apud veteres scriptores Graecos infantes . . . commemorentur* [Diss. Würzburg, 1954]).

The poem as we have it in the medieval tradition appears to be simply a literary narrative, like xxv (which, however, is somewhat more complex), the *Hekale* of Kallimachos and the *Europa* of Moschos. The immediate ancestor of this popular Hellenistic genre was Philitas (cf. p. lxxii), who wrote a *Demeter* (in elegiacs) and a *Hermes* (in hexameters); cf. *Coll. Alex.* 90–92. (It has become common practice to call narrative poems on this scale 'epyllia', though in Athenaios 65A, the only passage of ancient literature in which the word ἐπύλλιον denotes a genre of poetry, it probably refers to something smaller and more frivolous). However, we have a papyrus which plainly continued xxiv for more than thirty lines beyond the point at which the medieval text stops, and although the text of the papyrus is too fragmentary to be legible there is a marginal note implying that the poet ended with a prayer to Herakles for victory in a poetic contest. It seems, therefore, that Theokritos adopted the form of (e.g.) *H. Hom.* 6.19 ff. either for an actual competitive occasion or as if for such an occasion.

1. **Μιδεᾶτις**: Cf. xiii.20 n.

3. **γάλακτος**: Cf. 31 n.

4. **Πτερελάου**: The little-known myth is to be found in Apollodoros ii.4.7.3 f.: Pterelaos was ruler of Taphos and neighbouring islands off the west coast of Greece. A hero's possessions often had a bloody history; cf. *Il.* xxiii.568 ff., where Achilles gives Antilochos as a consolation prize the breastplate of which he had despoiled Asteropaios.

7. **εὕδετ'** . . . 9. **ἵκοισθε**: On the formal characteristics of this lullaby cf. F2. **ψυχά**: A natural enough term of endearment, since one's own ψυχή is dearest of all things to oneself; cf. Eur. *Andr.* 418 f., 'Their children are ψυχή to

all men', and Meleagros (*HE*) 48.2 calls Heliodora ψυχὴ τῆς ψυχῆς. ἐγέρσιμον: Cf. xviii.55 n.

11 f. The Bear and Orion are naturally mentioned together in *Il.* xviii.486 ff. (= *Od.* v.273 ff.), where the Bear αὐτοῦ στρέφεται (αὐτοῦ, 'on the spot', because it never sets) and 'watches' (δοκεύει) Orion. If Theokritos had written no more than ἆμος δὲ στρέφεται μεσονύκτιον "Αρκτος | 'Ωρίωνα κατ' αὐτόν, he would have given us a picture of the sky in the middle of a typical night, for every constellation στρέφεται, 'moves on a curved course' (cf. Soph. *Trach.* 130 f. κυκλοῦσιν οἷον ἄρκτου στροφάδες κέλευθοι), and the position of the Bear and Orion relative to each other is constant. By adding ἐς δύσιν and ὁ δ' ἀμφαίνει μέγαν ὦμον he has given us (whether he meant to or not) an indication of the time of year: for the Aegean in the early third century B.C., the middle of February, whether ἐς δύσιν means 'westwards' or 'downwards'. In Aratos 322 αὐτός with 'Ωρίων seems to be magniloquent, as if one were to say 'the mighty Orion'.

14. φρίσσοντας ὑπὸ σπείραισι: The picture seems to be one of snakes progressing like caterpillars, arching themselves upwards and so moving 'under' their coils, rather than moving by the sideways coiling motion of real snakes.

15. σταθμὰ κοῖλα: The 'doorposts' are 'hollow' because a door is recessed; the adjective and noun κοιλόσταθμος occur in Hellenistic Greek in architectural senses which have something to do (but exactly what, is uncertain) with panels, shutters or lattices. In Pi. *Nem.* 1.41 the snakes enter οἰχθεισᾶν πυλᾶν: a miraculous opening at their approach, or had the door been left open by domestic chance? (Cf. H. Herter, *Rhein Mus.* lxxxiii [1940], 152 ff. and K. J. McKay, *CQ* N.S. xvii [1967], 187 f.).

16. φαγεῖν: As a snake swallows a frog; these supernatural snakes are bigger than any of which the ordinary Greek had any experience.

19. βαρὺν δ' ἐξέπτυον ἰόν: Possibly Theokritos thought that a snake's flickering tongue was envenomed; or possibly these supernatural snakes drool venom as they approach. Cf. 28 f. n. Nikandros *Ther.* 185, 232 speaks of snakes as

'belching' (ἐρεύγεσθαι) venom from their fangs, the physio-
logical oddity of which can be reduced by translating in
such a way as to make the venom 'erupt' from the fangs.

21 f. It seems that the unnatural blaze of light (cf. 35 f.)
is not a concomitant of the snakes, despite its extinction (46)
with their death, but a counter-measure on the part of
Zeus. When Demeter enters the palace of Keleus (*H. Hom.*
2.188 ff.) she fills the doorway with 'divine light', and
Metaneira is struck with awe; cf. Eur. *Bacch.* 1083. *Od.*
xix.36 ff. is not really a parallel, for Athena there is carrying
a golden lamp.

26. φευγέμεν: A baby ten months old could not 'flee'
far, even if we interpret φευγέμεν as 'escape' (by twisting
himself away) the picture is not entirely realistic (cf. 57);
a baby would be more likely to duck under the bedclothes.

28 f. τόθι ... ὀφίεσσι: Nikandros (*Ther.* 110 f.) also
thought that the venom was produced in the vertebrae,
though he knew (182 ff.) the function of the fangs. For the
relative τόθι cf. xxii.199.

31. γαλαθηνὸν ὑπὸ τροφῷ: This may merely designate his
age-category rather than making a statement to the effect
that his mother did not suckle him herself; line 3 suggests
that she did. **αἰὲν ἄδακρυν**: He showed as a baby the
fortitude which distinguished him as an adult.

33. ἀναγκαίου: Almost 'inescapable'.

35 f. ἄνσταθ' ... ἄνστα: Cf. 73 f. and **Fi**(*a*). The abrupt-
ness of Alkmena's words, which are not introduced by
(e.g.) 'and then she spoke ... ', suits the occasion admirably.

36. μηδέ ... θείης: So the chorus in Aisch. *Prom.* 135
says that it 'sped unshod' when it heard the fettering of
Prometheus.

38. που: The force of the particle is close to 'it must
surely be ...' or ' — isn't it?'

39. καθαρᾶς ἄτερ ἠριγενείας: Lit., 'without clear dawn',
i.e. 'and it is not caused by the clear light of dawn', if the
text is right. But ἅπερ (Briggs), 'as' (cf. ἅτε), is attractive;
for the genitive cf. the expressions in xi.37 and xiv.47.

40. ἔστι ... ἔστι: Cf. 1.15 and **Fi**(*a*). **νεώτερον**: The word often has sinister associations; cf. Thuc. ii.6.2., where μηδὲν νεώτερον ποιεῖν περὶ τῶν ἀνδρῶν implies 'not to execute the men'. φίλ' ἀνδρῶν: It is a possible inference from xv.74 (though it does not by any means follow necessarily) that this expression belongs to the spoken language.

42. ὃ οἱ ὕπερθεν: – ◡ ◡ – ⌒: cf. *Il.* xxii.307 τό οἱ ὑπό 1̱ ◡ ◡ 2̱) and **D4**.

47. ὕπνον βαρὺν ἐκφυσῶντας: The expression probably describes the deep breathing of sound sleep, not an attempt to wake up, to which 'breathe out' or 'blow out' is physiologically inappropriate.

48. οἴσετε: Not a future in an imperatival sense, but an epic aorist imperative, as the existence of the singular οἶσε proves. **ὅτι θᾶσσον**: A unique blend (metrically protected) of θᾶσσον, in which the comparative intensifies 'quickly' (e.g. xv.29) and ὅτι τάχιστα, 'as quickly as possible'. **ἀπ' ἐσχαρεῶνος**: Cf. xxii.33 n.

49. στιβαρούς ... ὀχῆας: The door of the children's bedroom would naturally be held shut from the outside.

50. αὐτός: A common slave's way of referring to the master of the house. Cf. Men. *Samia* 255 f., ' "Sh! Don't talk so loud", she says, "The master's in!" ' (ἔνδον ἐστὶν αὐτός).

51. ἦ ῥα: Cf. *Il.* vi.390 ἦ ῥα γυνὴ ταμίη, 'so spoke the housekeeper'. **Φοίνισσα**: Such as appears, πατρὸς ἐμοῖο ... ἐν οἴκῳ ... ἀγλαὰ ἔργ' εἰδυῖα, in Eumaios's story of his own kidnapping, *Od.* xv.417 f. **μύλαις ... ἔχουσα**: In Odysseus's palace a dozen women sleep at the mill where they grind the corn (*Od.* xx.105 ff.).

57. ἐπάλλετο δ' ὑψόθι: Cf. 25 f. n.

61. ξηρὸν ὑπαὶ δείους: There is deliberate variation here on the epic phrase χλωρὸς ὑπαὶ δείους, 'pale with fear' (e.g. *Il.* x.376), but the point of ξηρός, 'dry', is not entirely clear: 'dry-mouthed' and dumb, or 'stiff' and so not relaxed? **ἀκράχολον**: χολή, 'bile', was regarded as the physical ingredient of all powerful emotional states, most often of rage and insanity, but evidently also of fear, since ἀκρηχολίαι in Hippocr. *Epid.* vii.11 must refer to panics.

63. ἐμνάσατο κοίτου: An epic expression for 'went to

bed' (*Od.* xvi.481), which does not suggest in Greek, as its literal translation does in English, that Hera's snakes could be shrugged off as all part of the night's work.

64. : 'The birds' (= 'cocks') 'were just celebrating in song ⟨for the⟩ third ⟨time⟩ the last ⟨moment⟩ before dawn'.

65. Τειρεσίαν: The blind seer is prominent in many of the Theban legends (e.g. the Oidipous legend). **τόκα**: Almost certainly to be interpreted as a relative, like τόθι in 28.

66. χρέος: The word is sometimes equivalent to χρῆμα, e.g. Eur. *Herc. Fur.* 570 τί καινὸν ἦλθε δώμασιν χρέος; ~*Med.* 867 f. ἀκούσομαι / τί χρῆμα βούλῃ καινὸν ἐξ ἐμοῦ. The variant τέρας is an example of substitution, by an ancient reader, of a more intelligible word.

67. ὅπως τελέεσθαι ἔμελλεν: Cf. (e.g.) *Od.* ii.156 ἅπερ τελέεσθαι ἔμελλον.

68. μηδ' εἰ κτλ.: 'Even if . . ., do not . . .'.

69. καὶ ὥς: 'Even so', i.e. even if a seer conceals evil, it will happen none the less.

70. ὅτι . . . ἐπείγει: Lit., 'that which Fate makes to hasten down a thread'. κατά with the genitive of a noun denoting a period of time means 'for', e.g. *DGE*³ 62.1.50 (Herakleia, S. Italy) αὖτα ἐμισθώθη ἁ γᾶ κατὰ βίω, 'this land was leased for life'; and see LSJ κατά A.II.6. Since a person's life has the duration of his 'thread' spun by Fate (cf. 1.139 f. n.), Alkmena is speaking of the possibility that Herakles is destined to a premature death.

71. Εὐηρείδα: Teiresias is addressed by this patronymic also in Kallim. *H.* 5.86, 101, and the name of his father Eueres is given by Dikaiarchos (Wehrli) fr. 37. **μάλα . . . διδάσκω**: 'I am teaching one who is most wise', sc. and therefore needs no instruction from me; the point of τοι is to compliment Teiresias by reminding him of his wisdom.

73. Περσήϊον αἷμα: Alkmena was grandchild of Perseus.

74. Lit., 'put in your mind the better ⟨part⟩ of future things', i.e. '. . . the good which the future holds'. The infinitive is very commonly used in an imperatival sense; cf. 98 f., xv.16 n.

75. Kallim. *H.* 5 tells one story (it is not the only story) of how Teiresias lost his sight: he accidentally glimpsed Athena bathing, and was automatically blinded, but Athena gave him the power of prophecy in compensation.

76. Ἀχαιϊάδων: 'Greek women', as in Homer.

77. κατατρίψουσιν ... ἀείδουσαι: We would normally distribute the emphasis differently: '... will sing ... as they rub ...'.

78. σέβας: Commonly used of a person towards whom σέβας, 'awe', 'respect', is felt. Ἀργείαισι: Cf. 76 n. and xxvi.36 n.

79 f. ἐς οὐρανόν ... ἀμβαίνειν: Not a metaphorical description of Herakles' fame, but a reference to his eventual deification (cf. 82).

80. ἀπὸ στέρνων: Hardly '⟨beginning⟩ from the chest' (cf. xiv.68 f. ἀπὸ κροτάφων ... γηραλέοι), for Herakles' shoulders would also have been very broad. Probably the point is that his chest is the part of him from which the observer receives the most striking impression of his breadth; cf. Theophr. Char. 28.4, 'for he is an ugly sort of man ἀπὸ τοῦ προσώπου'.

81. οὗ ... ἥσσονες: Lit., 'than whom ...⟨will be⟩ less ...', i.e., 'who will be mightier than ...'.

82 f. i.e. πεπρωμένον ἐστί οἱ δώδεκα μόχθους τελέσαντι ἐν Διὸς οἰκεῖν: cf. 79 f. n., and on the interlaced clauses cf. F9(b). The canonical number twelve for the labours of Herakles (cf. Eur. Herc. Fur. 359 ff.) seems to have become established at least by the second quarter of the fifth century, when the twelve metopes of the temple of Zeus at Olympia were scupltured.

83. θνητὰ δὲ πάντα: 'All ⟨of him that is⟩ mortal'. πυρὰ Τραχίνιος: The pyre of Mt. Oita, above Trachis, to which the dying body of Herakles is taken at the end of Sophokles' Trachiniai.

84. γαμβρὸς δ' ἀθανάτων: Herakles, once he had become immortal, married Hebe, daughter of Zeus and Hera (Hes. Theog. 950 ff.). The plural οἱ κτλ. avoids specification of Hera (cf. 13) by implying that the snakes were sent by the divine will in general.

86 f.: There is a high probability (ctr. Stark, *Maia* xv [1963] 365 f.) that these two verses were interpolated by someone whose understanding of mythology and sense of relevance were inferior to Theokritos's. A prophecy that the wolf will spare the fawn *from* the day of Herakles' deification is demonstrably false, for Herakles was deified long ago, but wolves still eat fawns. The idea that the order of nature will temporarily undergo an idyllic reversal (cf. 1.132 ff.) *on* the day of Herakles' deification and reconciliation with Hera is either a hyperbolic and unparalleled treatment of the feud between Herakles and Hera or an equally hyperbolic extension of Herakles' role as destroyer of animals harmful to man, representing him as frightening animals away from their natural prey.

89. ἐτοιμάσατ': The plural, here and in 96 and 100, is addressed to the whole household, not exclusively to Alkmena.

91. ἀγρίαισιν ἐπὶ σχίζαισιν: There are some very late references to the burning of monstrosities on the wood of wild plants.

92. νυκτὶ μέσᾳ: Just as malevolent powers have to be attracted in the dark (cf. p. 100), so rites designed to control them have to be performed in the dark.

94. ἧρι ... ἄστρεπτος: To cast something 'beyond the bounds' is an obvious ritual practice (the Athenians, for example, did it to inanimate objects which had caused a person's death [Aischines III.244]), and in dealing with dangerous or malevolent powers one does not turn round and risk the danger of seeing them. So in Aisch. *Cho.* 96 ff. Elektra, wondering how to make Klytaimestra's offering at the grave of Agamemnon, says, 'Shall I pour it out and go back καθάρμαθ' ὥς τις ἐκπέμψας, throwing away the vessel with averted eyes?' Jason, too, is told not to turn round (Ap. Rh. iii.1038 ff.) after sacrificing to Hekate.

96. καθαρῷ ... θεείῳ: After the killing of the suitors Odysseus purified his palace by burning sulphur (*Od.* xxii. 481 f.). In such contexts καθαρός should perhaps be interpreted as 'cleansing' rather than 'pure' (cf. II.92 n.). Since human beings suffer from paroxysmal coughing if they breathe the fumes of burning sulphur, it may have been felt that it would drive evil spirits too out of every corner of the house.

97 f. ἄλεσσι . . . ὕδωρ: Salt water was used in purification rites, and purification by the sprinkling of water was customary (e.g.) after a funeral. On the branch garlanded (presumably) with wool cf. p. 98.

99. καθυπερτέρῳ: Cf. ὕπατος as an epithet of Zeus in .ᴄxᴠɪ.34. **χοῖρον:** The sacrifice of a pig was part of the purification of Orestes at Delphi (Aisch. *Eum.* 283), and cf. Aisch. (M) fr. 648.

100. The nature of the wish determines which god should receive the offering, and under which title.

102. πολλοῖσι . . . ἐνιαυτοῖς: The point is that he was able to walk briskly despite his great age.

103 f. φυτόν . . . ἐτρέφετ': So Thetis says of Achilles (*Il.* xviii.56) ὁ δ' ἀνέδραμεν ἔρνεϊ ἶσος· τὸν μὲν ἐγὼ θρέψασα, φυτὸν ὡς γουνῷ ἀλωῆς, κτλ.: cf. vii.44 n., xxvii.7.

104. Ἀργείου: Literally 'Argive', as Amphitryon is called also in Eur. *Herc. Fur.* 2; he was son of a king of Tiryns, and when Argos swallowed up Tiryns in the fifth century it seems to have taken over Tirynthian legend also (as e.g. in Pi. *Nem.* 10.13 θρέψε δ' [*sc.* Argos] αἰχμὰν Ἀμφιτρύωνος). Amphitryon's settlement at Thebes was exile.

105. γράμματα: The first subject of a Greek boy's education, as we see from Pl. *Prt.* 325ᴇ. **Λίνος:** The story that Linos taught Herakles to read can be traced back into the fourth century, with Alexis's comedy *Linos* ([*CAF*] fr. 135), and there was also a story (Diod. iii.67.1) that it was Linos who adapted Phoenician script to Greek (an event which actually occurred in the eighth century ʙ.ᴄ.). Alternative myths, in keeping with the legendary role of Linos as lyre-player (Hes. fr. 306), represented him as attempting to teach Herakles the lyre and as being killed by his violent and wilful pupil (Apollodoros ii.4.9., Diod. iii.67.2).

106. υἱὸς Ἀπόλλωνος: There were alternative gene-alogies of Linos.

108. Εὔρυτος: The legendary archer of Oichalia who unwisely challenged Apollo (*Od.* viii.223 ff.). Cf. XIII.56 n. We do not know why Theokritos describes Eurytos as wealthy in inherited land.

110. Φιλαμμονίδας Εὔμολπος: Philammon was a son of Apollo (Pherekydes [*FGrHist* 3] frr. 26, 120) and a musician; he belongs to the borderland between myth and history (Plu. *De Mus.* 3). Eumolpos appears as the father of Mousaios (Diog. Laert. i.3).

111. ἀπὸ σκελέων: ἀπό here seems to mean 'by means of'; the phrase goes with σφάλλοντι. **ἑδροστρόφοι**: ἕδραν στρέφειν is associated by Theophr. *Char.* 27.14 with wrestling. **'Αργόθεν**: An 'Argive wrestler' is a wrestler *par excellence* in Aristophon (*CAF*) fr. 4.4.

113. προπεσόντες: In the pankration (to which πάμμαχοι refers) fighting on the ground could continue when one of the contestants had fallen. **τέχνᾳ**: With σύμφορα, 'furthering their skill'.

116. 'Αρπαλύκῳ Πανοπῆϊ: 'Autolykos' is named by Apollodoros ii.4.9. as the hero who taught Herakles wrestling, and Pherekydes (*FGrHist* 3) fr. 120 makes Autolykos a son of Hermes. On this kind of variation in heroic names cf. II.16 n.

117. ἔμεινεν: i.e. no one would have awaited his onset with confidence.

119 f. καὶ περὶ νύσσαν . . . φυλάξαι: A sharp turn round the post and a quick getaway on the return course were vital in chariot-racing (cf. Nestor's advice to Antilochos, *Il.* xxiii.338 ff.), and striking the post on the turn could lead to a fatal accident, as described in Soph. *El.* 743 ff.

122 f. ἐπεί . . . κειμήλια: The point is that Amphitryon (διφρηλάτας in Pi. *Pyth.* 9.81a) was, as a prize-winner, the best qualified to teach Herakles chariot-racing.

123 f. καὶ οἱ ἀαγεῖς . . . ἱμάντας: All the emphasis lies on χρόνῳ: thanks to Amphitryon's skill, the chariots never came to grief, but lasted so long that it was not until the leather straps (cf. *Il.* v. 727 f.) perished that they had to be discarded.

125. ὦμον: The transmitted text has νῶτον, 'keeping his *back* under his shield', which is nonsese; Herakles must have been taught how to protect the front of his body while wielding a spear in his right hand.

127. ἀναμετρήσασθαι: A commander must estimate the extent of the enemy's line, to know whether or not it will overlap his own, and must gauge its depth and strength; cf. the last-minute manoeuvres of Agis at the battle of Mantineia in 418 (Thuc. v.71.2 f.).

129. Κάστωρ: Ἱππαλίδας and the further details show that Theokritos does not mean Kastor the brother of Polydeukes; whom he does mean, is not known. **Ἄργεος**: '*From* Argos'; the simple genitive in this sense is abnormal, but φυγάς makes it easier (cf. Soph. *Phil.* 1044 τῆς νόσου πεφευγέναι).

130 f. Tydeus, according to *Il.* xiv.120 ff., married the daughter of Adrastos and possessed great wealth in land at Argos. ὧ or οὗ can hardly mean 'where', given the sequence Ἄργεος . . . οὗ . . . ναῖε . . . Ἄργος: the participial and finite clauses are intertwined (cf. F9[*b*]), and the meaning must be: 'having received whose estate . . . from Adrastos Tydeus dwelt in Argos'.

132. ἡμιθέοις: Cf. XXII.29 n.

138. Δωρικός: How Dorian bread differed from other bread, either in size of loaf or in quality, is not known for sure, but there is evidence that the Spartans (Dorians *par excellence*) used a coarse and inferior bread (Herakleides Ponticus [Müller] fr. II.8). **ἀσφαλέως**: 'Without fail'. **φυτοσκάφον**: Cf. IV.10 ∼ IV.34 nn.

139. ἐπ' ἄματι: 'By day', i.e. up to the time of the evening δεῖπνον: cf. Hes. *Op.* 102, where ἐφ' ἡμέρῃ and ἐπὶ νυκτί are contrasted. **ἄνευ πυρός**: i.e. uncooked.

149. οὐκ ἀσκητά: Perhaps 'of coarse weave', but possibly 'undecorated'. **μέσας . . . κνάμας**: The suggestion is that a himation so skimpy that it did not reach the ankles was a mark of fortitude.

POEM XXVI

This poem describes the fate of Pentheus at the hands of his mother Agaue, her sisters Ino and Autonoe, and the Bacchanals. The story was (and has remained) a famous one, thanks especially to Euripides' *Bacchae*, which from the fourth century B.C. onwards overshadowed the earlier treatment of the legend by Aischylos. There are, however, certain differences between Euripides' narrative and Theokritos's, and the relation between the two is set out in the following table:

Theokritos		Euripides
1 f.	The three sisters and their three thiasoi.	680 ff.
2	εἰς ὄρος.	116 εἰς ὄρος εἰς ὄρος.
3–9	The construction of the altars.	—
10	Pentheus spies on the Bacchanals from a steep rock.	1063 ff. (from a pinetree).
12	Autonoe sees him first.	1078 ff. (a voice from the sky).
13 f.	The ὄργια which the profane must not see; Autonoe upsets them.	471 f., 1080
16 f.	Pentheus flees, the Bacchanals in pursuit.	—
		731 ὦ δρομάδες ἐμαὶ κύνες (Agaue to the Bacchanals); 1090 f., their great speed; 1103 ff., they uproot his tree.
18 f.	Pentheus cries, 'What do you want?'; Agaue replies threateningly.	1118 ff., Pentheus cries to Agaue, but she does not reply; 1106 ff., 1123 ff., 1141 f., she thinks he is an animal.

20	Agaue seizes Pentheus's head.	1125 ff., Agaue tears off his arm; 1139 ff., she brings home his head.
21	Agaue roars like a lioness	1141 f., 1173 f., 1196, Agaue thinks Pentheus's head is a lion's.
22	Ino tears Pentheus on one side, Autonoe tears him on the other.	1129 ff.
24	The other women distribute the pieces.	1133 ff.
25	The Bacchanals return to Thebes, spattered with blood.	742 ἀναπεφυρμέν' αἵματι, referring to the cattle torn to pieces; 1135.
26	πένθημα/Πενθεύς	367 Πενθεὺς δ' ὅπως μὴ πένθος εἰσοίσει δόμοις (cf. 507 f.).
27–32	Moral conclusion.	1148 ff.

The poem plunges straight into the story, 'Ino, Autonoe and Agaue . . . had led three companies to the mountains . . .', in the manner of xxiv, 'Once, when Herakles was ten months old, . . . '; and we are reminded of the opening of vii (despite the totally different nature of the poem), 'There was a time when Eukritos and I were going to the Haleis . . .'. After the swift narrative Theokritos dissociates himself, sanctimoniously and without compassion, from the impiety of Pentheus. So too Kallimachos in *H.* 6.116 f. exclaims, after relating the fate of Erysichthon, 'Demeter, never may the man who is hateful to you be a friend or neighbour of mine!' A Greek poet commonly extracted from a narrative or description a moral or religious generalisation (e.g. Alkman [*PMG*] fr. 1.34 ff., ' . . . unforgettable was their suffering for the evil which they had plotted.

There is such thing as punishment by the gods; and fortunate is he . . .'). Commonly, too, he declared his own attitude, linked the narrative to his patron, or uttered a prayer; cf. Pi. *Pyth.* 1.29, where the prayer, 'May it be granted, Zeus, may it be granted to please you!' arises out of his description of the eruption of Mt. Etna, under which lies the hundred-headed Typhos, enemy of Zeus; or Bacchylides 3, where the poet draws personal conclusions (66–76, 91–96) from the stories of Kroisos and Admetos. We may compare the concluding lines of messenger-speeches in tragedy, e.g. Eur. *Med.* 1224–1230, 'This is not the first time that I have counted the fortunes of mortal men a mere shadow . . .', and the reactions of choruses to narrative speeches.

Theokritos adds a second traditional element when he concludes (33–38) with a farewell (χαίροι) to Dionysos and Semele, whose power the poem honours by relating its most impressive vindication; on this element, characteristic of hymns, cf. p. 250. The poem differs from hymns, however, in the abruptness of its narrative opening; in hymns the subject is announced more elaborately ('I will tell of . . .' or 'Sing, Muse, of . . .'); cf. XXII.1–25 and Kallimachos's general practice. It is thus doubtful whether Theokritos conceived the poem as a hymn and wrote it as if for a festival; he may have conceived it rather as a narrative poem on a mythical subject, in which he felt free to incorporate a hymn-like ending. The poem contains no allusion to singer, chorus or ritual act (contrast Kallim. *H.* 2.1–8, 3.266, 5.1–58, 137–142, 6.1–7, 118–138), and in this respect it may have differed (cf. p. 253) from XXIV. Reference to 'Drakanon' in 33 (v. n.) is not a good reason for believing that Theokritos had a Koan cult in mind.

The title of the poem, λῆναι ἢ βάκχαι (so too the Antinoe papyrus), strikes a note unfamiliar to us because λῆναι is not an Attic word, despite the Attic sanctuary 'Lenaion' and festival 'Lenaia'. But Herakleitos (DK) B14 (cf. B15) associates λῆναι with βάκχοι; Hesychios calls λῆναι an Arkadian term for βάκχαι: Dionysos had the title Ληναγέτας at Halikarnassos in Theokritos's time; and the month 'Lenaion' occurred in many Greek calendars.

1. μαλοπάραυος: καλλιπάρηος is an epithet of Agaue in Hes. *Theog.* 976. -ραυ- may be what Theokritos wrote, but παραυᾱ, 'cheek', is Aeolic; ctr. Pi. *Pyth.* 12.16 εὐπαράου. μᾱλός = 'white'.

3. χαὶ μέν: If one is to regard μέν as introducing the first member of an antithesis, the second member is ἱερὰ δὲ κτλ. in 7.

4. ζώοντα: Perhaps 'which continued ⟨miraculously⟩ to live' and did not droop or shrivel in spite of being cut. τὸν ὑπέρ γᾱς: Perhaps 'which was carpeting the ground'.

5. καθαρῷ: Given the religious context, this is likely to mean more than simply 'clear' or 'clean', and it may be meant to suggest a meadow apparently unsullied by man. We are reminded of the garland offered by Hippolytos to Artemis ἐξ ἀκηράτου λειμῶνος (Eur. *Hipp.* 73 f.) and of the general Greek practice of leaving land which was sacred to a deity uncultivated and ungrazed. βωμώς: It appears from νεοδρέπτων (8) and from Theokritos's silence on any other ingredients that these 'altars' were constructed entirely of heaps of foliage and plants.

6. τώς: The article is normally used with numerals which form part of a larger numeral; cf. *Il.* v.270 ff. ἐξ ἐγένοντο . . .· τοὺς μὲν τέσσαρας . . . ἀτίταλλ' . . . , τὼ δὲ δύ' Αἰνείᾳ δῶκεν, and it is normal Attic prose usage (e.g. Thuc. vii.22.2).

7 f. ἱερά . . . πεπονάμενα: It is not surprising that we never have precise details of sacred objects, for description would itself be a profanation; in Dionysiac and other mystery-cults they were kept in a κίστη.

13. σὺν δ' ἐτάραξε ποσί: Not by accident, as she jumped up, but to conceal them as quickly as possible from profane eyes.

14. βέβαλοι: Cf. III.51 n.

18 f. Cf. F2 and Heine's *Knabe sprach: 'Ich breche dich,|Röslein auf der Heide'.|Röslein sprach: 'Ich steche dich| . . .'*, etc.

23. καὶ Αὐτονόας ῥυθμὸς ωὑτός: Lit., 'and of Autonoe the way of working was the same'. Cf. Eur. *El.* 772 f., 'In what way καὶ τίνι ῥυθμῷ φόνου has he killed Aigisthos?'

27. οὐκ ἀλέγω: *sc.* about the sufferings of Pentheus.

27 f. μηδ' ἄλλος . . . φροντίζοι: 'And let not anyone else' (*sc.* other than I) 'concern himself about one who is an enemy of Dionysos.' The ancient text, μηδ' ὅστις ἀπεχθόμενος κτλ., 'And may whoever is an enemy of Dionysos not concern himself', makes no sense in the context.

28. μηδ' εἰ κτλ.: 'Not even if he (*sc.* the enemy of Dionysos) . . .'.

29. The point seems to be that one should feel no pity even for a child who suffers something (what?) worse than being torn to pieces by his mother and aunts, if he is an enemy of Dionysos. But ἐνναετής suffices to make that point, and the addition of 'or were even embarking on his tenth ⟨year⟩' does not strengthen it; the sufferings of a child of ten years and one month are not more pitiable than those of a child three months younger. The difficulty of interpretation is increased by textual uncertainty; the ancient text has ἐπιβαίην, and no one has explained satisfactorily why the poet should express a wish to be nine or just ten, or, if he did so, why he should continue with αὐτὸς δέ, with reference to himself, as if he were drawing a contrast. If the medieval text is right, it is possible that Theokritos refers to an actual case, unknown to us, of a boy just ten years old who perished horribly and was held up as an object-lesson because he was believed to have committed some outrage against Dionysos. In that case, χαλεπώτερα τῶνδε would be hyperbole, and the over-precise statement of age would be designed in the manner of an epitaph; cf. *GVI* 745.3 ἔνδεκ' ἔτη πλήσας δωδεκάτου δ' ἐπιβάς.

31. οὕτως: By being εὐαγής. Servius on *Aen.* i.394 refers to a story that Zeus's eagle was a transformation of a loyal childhood companion. If Theokritos does not mean that, I do not know what he means.

32. The sentiment is similar to that of Hes. *Op.* 280 ff.: Zeus gives prosperity to the man who bears true witness, and his descendants flourish, but the descendants of the perjurer sink into poverty.

33. Δρακάνῳ: One of the five legendary birthplaces of Dionysos listed in *H. Hom.* 1.1 ff. It is the name of a promontory on the island of Ikaros, and this may be what Theokritos intended, but since *H. Hom.* cites Ikaros as well as Drakanon the reference may be to the promontory of Kos called 'Drekanon' in Strabo 657. In either case 'snowy' is an inappropriate epithet.

33. ἐπιγουνίδα: The story was (Eur. *Bacch.* 6 ff., 286 ff.) that Hera encompassed the death of Semele before Dionysos was born; Zeus rescued the foetus and brought it to parturition inside his own thigh.

36. πολλαῖς μεμελημέναι ἡρωῖναις: On heroes and heroines cf. xiii.38 n. Theokritos's description of Semele and her sisters as 'women of Thebes admired' (or 'spoken about with interest'; cf. xvi.1) 'by many heroines' must mean: their fame extended beyond Thebes and they were talked of by women in other cities in the 'heroic' age (cf. xxiv.76 ff.).

38. μηδείς τὰ θεῶν ὀνόσαιτο: The sentiment accords with the fatalistic acceptance of divine cruelties implicit in much that is said in the *Bacchae*.

POEM XXVIII

For this poem, as for xxix, xxx and almost certainly for one further poem originally contained in the Antinoe papyrus, Theokritos imitates the Lesbian poets of the early sixth century B.C., Sappho and Alkaios, in dialect and metre.

The numerous papyrus fragments (nearly all much later in date than Theokritos) of those poets present a fairly consistent form of Aeolic dialect, which is confirmed in essentials by some extensive Lesbian inscriptions of the fourth century B.C. The features conspicuous in Theokritos's imitation are:

1. No rough breathing: hence 4 ὑπ' ἀπάλω = ὑφ' ἀπαλοῦ.

2. Recessive accent, except on prepositions: hence 5 Δίος, not Διός, and 24 ἴδων σ', not ἰδών σ', but 16 ἀπύ = ἀπό.

3. Doubled consonants representing what were originally combinations of consonants: hence 6 ξέννον = ξένον, from an original ξένϝον (which in fact survived in some dialects in the Classical period), 9 χέρρας = χεῖρας, from an original *χέρσας, and 15 ἐβολλόμαν = ἐβουλόμην, probably from an original *ἐβολσόμαν. So too 13 ἔννεκ', 16 ἀμμετέρας, 21 ἐραννάν, all attested in one or both of the Lesbian poets. The doubled π of ὄππα (4) and ὄππως (6), universal in the Lesbians (ὄππότα, ὄπποι, etc.) and sometimes used by Homer (e.g. ὁππότε, etc.), is of different phonological origin.

4. Accusative plural of the first and second declensions in -αις and -οις, dative plural in -αισι and -οισι (-αισ' and -οισ' before vowels); hence 12 μαλάκοις . . . πόκοις and 20 νόσοις . . . λύγραις are accusatives. The dative plural of the definite article in Lesbian, however, does not always follow this rule, and the texts of Sappho and Alkaios present us with a few other exceptions. Theokritos uses -οις for the dative in 10 ἀνδρείοις πέπλοις without risk of serious ambiguity.

5. Athematic conjugation of verbs with vowel-stems: hence 3 θέρσεισ' = θαρσοῦσα and 5 αἰτήμεθα = αἰτούμεθα. Cf. Ε10(e) and 1.36 n.

6. In many respects, e.g. in the preservation of original ᾱ and in the second declension genitive singular in -ω, Lesbian resembles Theokritos's Doric; in other respects, e.g. σύ (not τύ) it resembles Attic and Ionic. Some special peculiarities will be explained in the notes and given in the vocabulary.

The metrical form of the poem is

$$\text{o o} \; -\cup\cup- \; -\cup\cup- \; -\cup\cup-\cup \cap$$

This, which it is customary to call the 'greater asclepiad', was the metre of most of the poems which in Hellenistic times were put together in 'Book III' of Sappho, of some well-known poems of Alkaios, e.g. fr. 346 πώνωμεν· τί τὰ λύχν' ὀμμένομεν; δάκτυλος ἀμέρα (imitated in elegiacs by Asklepiades [HE] 16.5 f. πίνωμεν Βάκχου ζωρὸν πόμα δάκτυλος ἀώς·/ἦ πάλι κοιμιστὰν λύχνον ἰδεῖν μένομεν;) and of Kallim. fr. 400. In Sappho the 'base', i.e. the first two morae, should be symbolised not as o o (i.e. – –, – ᴗ or ᴗ –, excluding ᴗ ᴗ) but as × × (i.e. any of the four possible combinations of long and short), and Theokritos uses that freedom in xxix (of which the metre is that of Book II of Sappho) and in xxx. All Sappho's poems in the greater asclepiad had an even number of lines, which creates the presupposition that she thought of it in distichs (Hephaistion, 63.16 ff.). Theokritos xxix and xxx have an even number, but xxviii has 25. The metricians' term 'asclepiad' and the imitation of Alkaios fr. 346 noted above suggest that Asklepiades (cf. vii.39 f. n.) may have inspired Theokritos's interest in the early Lesbian poets.

The occasion of the poem is Theokritos's gift of a distaff to Theugenis (13, 22), the wife (9) of his friend Nikias (7), on whom cf. pp. xix and 173. For poems ostensibly accompanying gifts cf. Antipatros (GPh) 31, 41 ff., Antiphilos (GPh) 1, Krinagoras (GPh) 3 ff.

1. γλαύκας: Athena is γλαυκῶπις in epic, but γλαυκή in Eur. Hcld. 754. 'Αθανάας: (ᴗ – ᴗ –) Cf. Alkaios fr. 325.1 ἄνασσ' 'Αθανάα (ᴗ – ᴗ – × –); 'Αθηνάα<'Αθηναία is also Attic.

3. θέρσεισ' ... ὑμάρτη: =θαρσοῦσ' ... ὁμάρτει. Νείλεος: Ne(i)leus, son of Kodros, was the legendary founder of Miletos (Hdt. ix. 97).

4. Cf. vii.115 n. It sounds as if reeds grew within the boundaries of the sanctuary, so that the ἱρον (whether this means the temple or the sanctuary-precinct as a whole) could be described as χλῶρον. The metre requires ἀπάλω or ἀππάλω: it is possible (M. L. West, CQ n.s. xvii [1967], 82 f.) that Theokritos misinterpreted ἀπάλαν at the beginning of Sappho fr. 94 as – ᴗ –, not realising (though he learned better before writing xxix and xxx) that the Sapphic form of the verse could begin with ᴗ ᴗ.

6. κἀντιφιληθέω: The Attic aorist passive subjunctive -θῶ is a contraction of -θέ-ω, which most dialects preserved.

7. χαρίτων ... φύτον: Ibykos (PMG) fr. 288 addresses a

certain Euryalos as χαρίτων θάλος: and cf. VII.44 n., XXIV.103 f.

9. Νικιάας: (– ◡ ◡ –) For the adjective in the sense 'Nikias's' (a common phenomenon throughout the Aeolic area) cf. Alkaios fr. 129.13 τὸν Ὕρραον (– ◡ –) δὲ παῖδα, 'but the son of Hyrrhas . . .'.

10. τᾷ: Relative; cf. (e.g.) III.22. **ἐκτελέσεις**: It was Hellenistic practice to write -ηις, not -εις, in the second person singular in texts of Sappho and Alkaios; but I am not convinced that this practice was already established by Theokritos's time, let alone that it was right.

13. ἔννεκ': (= ἔνεκ'). 'As far as . . . is concerned', i.e. even if they were shorn twice a year, she would still cope with all the spinning which that would entail.

14. σαόφρονες: σώφρων is the conventional compliment to the dutiful and industrious wife and mother; cf. Lys. i.10 (a disillusioned husband is speaking), 'I was so foolish as to think that my wife was πασῶν σωφρονεστάτη', and Xen. Oec. 9.19, where it comes naturally τῇ σώφρονι to look after her children and the family property.

15 f. εἰς ἀκίρας . . . δόμοις: The wide separation of δόμοις (accus.) from εἰς and the treatment of the genitives ἀκίρας and ἀέργω as if they were adjectives are undoubtedly facilitated by the existence of the idiom εἰς +genitive.

16. ἔσσαν: =Koine οὖσαν: the form is fairly widespread in the Doric areas, though not yet attested in any Aeolic inscription.

17. ἄν: =ἆν. **Ἐφύρας**: Cf. xv.91, xvi.83 nn. **Ἀρχίας**: So too Thuc. vi.3.2; there is no variation in the tradition which made Archias the founder of Syracuse.

18. Τρινακρίας: Thuc. vi.2.2 is the first extant source to mention this name for Sicily, but he treats it as an old name. **μύελον**: The unusual metaphor may be derived from Od. ii.290, where ἄλφιτα is described as μυελὸν ἀνδρῶν, because men depend on it for their growth and strength.

19 f. πόλλ' . . . ἀπαλαλκέμεν: Cf. xxiv.26. The infinitive ending -μεν is not otherwise attested in Sappho or Alkaios, but they use epic elements in certain poems, and no doubt Theokritos felt free to do likewise.

21. Μίλλατον: We have no other instance of the Aeolic name for Miletos, but *Μίλλᾱτος* may have been it, even if some philologically 'false' analogy underlies λλ.

22. εὐαλάκατος: This is part of the predicate, not of the subject.

23. τῶ φιλαοίδω . . .ξένω: i.e. Theokritos.

24. κῆνο . . . ἴδων σ': Cf. *Il.* iv.176 ff. καί κε τις ὧδ' ἐρέει ...· 'αἶθ' οὕτως κτλ.' and Theognis 22 ὧδε δὲ πᾶς τις ἐρεῖ· 'Θεύγνιδός ἐστιν ἔπη κτλ.' **χάρις**: Cf. p. 217.

25. σύν: Here σῦν (σύνν?) in accordance with Sappho fr. 68.10 ἐνν 'Αχέρ[οντ-, Alkaios fr. 3.4 συ]ννέχει (?), fr. 130.27 ὀννέλην = ἀνελεῖν.

EPIGRAMS

(Numbered as in Gow's edition of Theokritos)

EPIGRAM 4
= (*HE*) 20, *Anth. Pal.* ix.437

This elegiac (**D5**) poem is included in the Palatine Anthology, but it differs both in scale and in character from the majority of epigrams. An unidentified speaker asks a goatherd to utter a prayer on his behalf to Priapos; the occasion of the prayer is erotic, the 'newly-carved' statue of Priapos is described, and so are the plants and birds around the spring in the sanctuary of the god; all these elements have many parallels in the epigrams of other poets, particularly in those which purport to be dedications of statues and springs, and the third element is one already familiar to us in Theokritos.

On Priapos cf. **G5**; he is a common subject of Hellenistic epigrams (e.g. Hedylos [*HE*] 1, Leonidas [*HE*] 83 f., Nikarchos [*HE*] 1), which are often jocular in tone, for a statue of Priapos was distinguished by its erect penis, of abnormal size, and (as protector of gardens and orchards) he was regarded as threatening thieves and intruders with painful penetration.

The speaker's prayer, which the goatherd is to deliver, has something of the ambivalence of the song of Simichidas in vii: either to fall out of love, or to satisfy his love; cf. ii.55 n. The object of the speaker's love is Daphnis — a role for Daphnis which is hinted at in vi, more than hinted at in the spurious poem viii, and conspicuous in Epigram iii (where Pan and Priapos themselves pursue him, intent on rape), but absent from i and vii.73 ff.

3. τρισχελές: The word reminds us of modern jokes about the 'third leg', appropriate to an ithyphallic statue, but it does not suit a description of a statue so rough that the bark is still on the wood and the head is not carved with sufficient refinement to include the ears; more plausibly, the penis on such a statue would be represented by a natural branching of the wood, and the emendation ἀσκελές, 'legless' may be justified; the corruption must then be the deliberate introduction of a joke.

4. Κυπρίδος: Garden-thieves being mostly male, the activities of Priapos are predominantly homosexual, but Aphrodite is associated as much with homosexual (e.g. Xen. *Hieron* 1.29) as with heterosexual intercourse.

11. ξουθαί: The word is used of birds and insects in contexts to which their swift movement or noise is appropriate; Empedokles (DK) fr. 128.7 uses it of honey or honeycombs, which make no noise; and Chairemon (*TGF*) fr. 1.7 uses it of winds, which have no colour. There seems little doubt that it meant different things to different poets; here probably 'tuneful'.

15. ἐπιρρέξειν: The construction of εὖχε' ἀποστέρξαι . . . με carries over to this infinitive, but in translation one must change from 'pray that I may . . .' to 'vow that I will . . .'.

16. τοῦδε: *sc.* Daphnis. τυχών: The sacrifice promised for satisfaction of his passion is much greater than that

promised for its remission, which is not surprising. Priapos is regarded as having the power to determine Daphnis's emotions, as is Pan in VII.104, and note the coincidence of ἦν δ' ἀνανεύσῃ ~VII.109 εἰ δ' ἄλλως νεύσαις.

EPIGRAM 17

= (HE) 15, Anth. Pal. ix.599

The poem is written as if for the base of a statue of Anakreon set up in his native city, Teos. Anakreon, a lyric poet, was patronised by the tyrant Polykrates of Samos in the third quarter of the sixth century B.C.; Teos, an Ionian city, lies on the coast of Asia Minor some 90 km north-west of Ephesos and 40 km by sea from Samos.

The poem is composed of three distichs; the first verse of each distich is an iambic trimeter, the second verse a 'phalaecian', more familiar to the student of Classics as the Catullan 'hendecasyllable':

$$0\ 0 - \cup \cup - \cup - \cup - \cap$$

Epigram 22 is composed entirely in phalaecians; the use of a distich composed of an iambic trimeter followed by a verse of different metrical form goes back to the epodes of Archilochos.

1. ὦ ξένε: The same form of address to a hypothetical passer-by who stops to read the inscription is common in actual epitaphs.

4. Lit., 'pre-eminent, if anything ⟨is⟩, among the poets of former days'; cf. VII.4 f.

5. τοῖς νέοισιν ἄδετο: Anakreon had a reputation (consistent with such fragments and citations of his poetry as we have) for the single-minded pursuit of pretty girls and handsome boys, and for the eloquent expression of erotic emotions. Cf. C. M. Bowra, Greek Lyric Poetry (ed. 2, Oxford, 1961), chapter VII.

EPIGRAM 18

= (*HE*) 17, *Anth. Pal.* ix.600

This too is ostensibly an inscription for a statue-base; the statue is of Epicharmos, in bronze, and erected in his native city, Syracuse. He was active in the period 485–475, but the upper and lower limits of his career cannot, on present evidence, be determined; by the end of the fourth century he was commonly regarded as the first person to compose and circulate comedies in writing — hence the claim made in the first two lines of the epigram that he 'invented comedy'. Cf. Sir Arthur Pickard-Cambridge, *Dithyramb, Tragedy and Comedy* (ed. 2, Oxford, 1962), chapter IV.

The metrical scheme is:

1, 5, 9: trochaic tetrameter:

$$-\cup-\times \quad -\cup-\times \quad -\cup-\times \quad -\cup\cap$$

3, 7: iambic trimeter
2, 4, 6, 8: reizianum:

$$\times-\cup\cup-\cap$$

10: $\cup\cup-\cup\cup--$, which in other metrical contexts would commonly require interpretation as a familiar form of ionic dimeter, but in this context is obviously regarded by Theokritos as a variant on the reizianum, with $\cup\cup$ in place of $\times$ at the beginning of the verse.

1. φωνά: *sc.* of the epigram. **Δώριος**: Certain adjectives in -ιος, although not compounds, are sporadically treated as two-termination adjectives, and the fact that Δώριος (*sc. ἐστί*) here has a second subject which is masculine (χωνήρ) is relevant to the poet's choice.

3 f. χαλκέον . . . ἀνέθηκαν: Cf. x.33 χρύσεοι ἀμφότεροί κ' ἀνεκείμεθα. **ἀντ' ἀλαθινοῦ**: Cf. the paean of Hermokles to Demetrios Poliorketes (Diehl, *Anth. Lyr. Gr.* ii, p. 249), 18 f. σὲ δὲ παρόνθ' ὁρῶμεν οὐ ξύλινον οὐδὲ λίθινον, ἀλλ' ἀληθινόν ('flesh and blood').

5. τοί: Relative, 'they who . . .'. **πελωρίστᾳ**: 'Monstrous' (~πέλωρον, πελώριος: cf. XXIV.13) seems a surprising word for a man to use of his native city, but a word does not have the same nuances in all dialects, and what is derogatory in one may be complimentary in another; and cf. XXII.46. Mimnermos (D³) fr. 12.4 refers to his forefathers, the founders of Kolophon, as ὕβριος ἡγεμόνες, and he may be simply boasting of their superiority to their enemies in the field.

6. οἵ: 'As being . . .', 'for he was . . .'. **πολίταν**: '⟨Fellow-⟩ citizen', 'citizen ⟨of their city⟩'.

7 f. The manuscripts have σωρὸν γὰρ εἶχε, and then ῥημάτων and χρημάτων are variants. 'Have a heap of . . .' is a possible Greek expression (cf. Ar. *Wealth* 269 f.), and it is conceivable that Epicharmos, to whom many quasi-philosophical utterances were attributed (cf. 9), could be said to have 'had a heap of ῥήματα' (not, I think, to have had a heap of χρήματα, for no tradition associated Epicharmos with wealth). But in order to make sense of the words which follow it is necessary to introduce an impersonal verb, and something on the lines of Kaibel's σοφῶν ἔοικε ῥημάτων is indicated; possibly σοφῶν γὰρ οἶκε (οἶκε = ἔοικε is normal in Hdt. and οἶκας = ἔοικας is cited from Alkman [*PMG*] fr. 110), but Theokritos may have intended 7 f. to have at least half the character of a generalisation, returning to Epicharmos specifically in 9 f., thus: 'it is fitting that men should remember . . . and . . .; for he . . .'.

9. παισίν: Cf. Theognis 27 f., 'I will give you such guidance, Kyrnos, as I learned from good men when I was still a boy'.

EPIGRAM 19

= (*HE*) 13, *Anth. Pal.* xiii.3

Like a number of early Hellenistic epigrams, this poem is composed as if for inscription on the tomb of an archaic

poet; cf. Mnasalkes (*HE*) 18, on Hesiod, and Leonidas
(*HE*) 58, on Hipponax. Hipponax of Ephesos lived in the
late sixth century B.C. and wrote ἴαμβοι (cf. Epigr. 21.2 n.)
in the spirit of Archilochos, infused with an obscenity and
violence which gave him (as it did Archilochos, too) the
reputation of a blunt and outspoken critic of human vices.

Hipponax made great use of the metre called σκάζων,
identical with the iambic trimeter except that the third
metron is × – – ◠, and that is the metre of this epigram.

3. κρήγυος: 'Good' in *Il.* i.106, and several times in
Hellenistic poetry, notably in Herodas, who imitated the
metre and dialect of Hipponax; little doubt, therefore, that
Hipponax used the word, and it may have belonged to the
spoken language of some Ionian areas. παρὰ χρηστῶν: Not
'⟨descended⟩ from . . .', but '⟨coming⟩ from . . .', with
reference to the community from which the hypothetical
wayfarer has come.

EPIGRAM 21

= (*HE*) 14, *Anth. Pal.* vii.664

This is ostensibly for the base of a statue of Archilochos
of Paros, the prolific and versatile poet active in the mid-
seventh century B.C. and the first Greek to put into circula-
tion poems in elegiac, iambic, trochaic and related metres.

The epigram consists of two stanzas, each of which is
composed thus:

(1) – ◡◡ – – – ◡◡ – ◡◡   – ◡ – ◡ – ◠

i.e. dactylic tetrameter plus 'ithyphallic'.

(2) iambic trimeter.

(3) × – ◡ –   × – ◡ –   ◡ – ◠

i.e. an iambic trimeter 'catalectic', the third metron being
abbreviated. Distichs composed of (1) and (3) are found in
citations from Archilochos himself, e.g. (D³) fr. 112, and

many of his epodes were written in distichs combining an iambic trimeter either with an iambic dimeter or with a dactylic hemiepes.

1. i.e. 'stop and look upon Archilochos . . .'; the command is of a kind common in epitaphs, e.g. *GVI* 1224.1 (Attica, *c.* 540). The phraseology, Object₂ Verb₁ + Verb₂ (one could not say Ἀρχίλοχον στᾶθι by itself) is very unusual; Verb₁ + Verb₂ Object₁ is well attested.

2. ἰάμβων: In ordinary Greek usage, as opposed to the technical terminology of metricians, ἴαμβος means a *poem* wholly or partly in any kind of iambic or trochaic rhythm; Aristotle *Rhet.* 1418ᵇ28 applies it to a poem in trochaic tetrameters, and it is possible that to Archilochos himself ([D³] fr. 20) it covered elegiacs also.

3. κἠπὶ νύκτα: 'to the sunset', i.e. 'to the West'.

4. Δάλιος: The biographical tradition asserted that Apollo debarred from the temple at Delphi the man who killed Archilochos, declaring that he had killed 'the servant of the Muses'; 'Delian' is evidently considered by Theokritos a more appropriate epithet than 'Pythian', for Delos was the centre of the worship of Apollo in the Aegean islands, and Archilochos may plausibly be imagined as having excelled in the festivals of Apollo on Delos.

6. ἔπεα: 'Verses', simply; the specific meaning 'hexameter' was slow to attach itself to ἔπος.

EPIGRAM 22

= (*HE*) 16, *Anth. Pal.* ix.598

Ostensibly for the base of a bronze statue of Peisandros in his native city, Kameiros on Rhodes. Peisandros was an epic poet of uncertain date (but note πρᾶτος in line 3), author of an epic *Herakleia*. See G. L. Huxley, *Greek Epic Poetry from Eumelos to Panyassis* (London, 1969), 99ff.

The metre is phalaecian; cf. Epigr. 17 n.

1. τόν ... υἱόν: F9(a).

2. λεοντομάχαν: Cf. xiii.6 n.

3. ἐπάνωθε: Cf. vii.5 n.

5. i.e. καὶ εἶπε (sc. Peisandros) ὅσους ἐξεπόνησεν (sc. Herakles) ἄθλους.

6. αὐτόν: 'Himself' as opposed to his works, which have already been described. **ὡς σάφ' εἰδῆς:** Cf. xv.91, where ὡς εἰδῆς καὶ τοῦτο introduces a proud boast, 'And let me tell you, too'. Here, however, it is not clear what exactly the reader of the epigram is being told; possibly a blend of 'Let me tell you, the people . . .' and 'The people . . ., in order that you' (i.e. 'everyone') 'might know ⟨about him⟩'.

8. μησίν: The point underlying 'months', when the interval of time is so great, is obscure, but it is presumably that the erection of a commemorative statue might commonly be expected in a matter of months after the death of the person so honoured, whereas Peisandros has had to wait for centuries.

Vocabulary

THE vocabulary includes the majority of the words used in the poems printed in this book, but it excludes the commonest words (e.g. κακός), compounds of obvious meaning (e.g. ἐκβαίνειν) and words which can easily be guessed (e.g. γυμνάσιον). The English meanings given are those appropriate to the relevant passages of Theokritos, and in many cases would be quite inappropriate in other contexts.

The spelling ζ is used throughout, whether or not the manuscripts in a given passage have σδ. First declension nouns are listed indifferently as forms in -ᾱς or -ης and in -ᾱ or -η. The Attic infinitive endings -ᾱν, -ᾱσθαι and -ναι are given in preference to the Doric -ῆν, -ῆσθαι and -μεν. With these exceptions, words are given in the form in which they occur in Theokritos, and the Attic Koine (and occasionally epic) equivalents are added in brackets.

ἀᾱγής, *unbroken*
ἅβᾱ (ἥβη), *youth, manhood*
ἀβλαβής, *harmless*
ἀγάλλεσθαι, *exult*
ἀγανός, *affectionate*
ἀγαπᾶν, *love*
ἀγαπᾱτός (-πη-), *beloved*
ἀγαυός, *illustrious*
ἄγγος (neut.), *vessel*
ἀγείρειν, *collect*
ἀγεῖσθαι (ἡ-), *think, regard*
ἀγέλᾱ, *herd, flock*
ἀγελαῖος, adj. ~ ἀγέλᾱ
ἀγεληδόν, *in herds*
ἀγεμονεύειν (ἡ-), *lead*

ἀγητός, *admired*
ἀγκλέπτειν (ἀνα-), *steal*
ἀγκρούεσθαι (ἀνα-), *strike up*
ἄγλαος (ἀγλαός), *splendid*
ἀγνο(ι)εῖν, *fail to know*
ἀγοράζειν, *buy*
ἀγορεύειν, *speak*
ἄγρᾱ, *hunt*
ἀγριέλαιος, *wild olive*
ἄγριος, *wild, fierce*
ἀγροιώτης, *countryman*
ἀγρός, *field*
ἀγρυπνεῖν, *lie awake*
ἄγρυπνος, *sleepless*
ἄγρωστις, *a kind of grass*

281

ἄγχειν, *strangle, get by the throat*

ἀγχίθυρος, *next door*

ἀγχόθι, *near*

ἄδακρυς, *not crying*

ἀδαμάντινος, adj. ⁓ ἀδάμας

ἀδάμας, *adamant*

ἄδεσθαι (ἥ-), *take pleasure in . . .*

ἀδηφάγος, *greedy, gluttonous*

ἀδίαντον, *maidenhair*

ἄδικος, *dishonest, lawless*

ἀδονίς = ἀηδών

ἀδώρητος, *without a gift*

ἀεθλεύειν (ἀθ-), *compete (in games)*

ἀεθλητήρ (ἀθ-), *athlete*

ἄεθλον (ἀθ-), *prize*

ἀεθλοφόρος (ἀθ-), *prize-winner*

ἀείδειν (ἄδειν), *sing*

ἀεικής, *disfiguring*

ἀέναος, *ever-flowing*

ἀεργός (ἀρ-), *idle*

ἀηδονιδεύς, *nightingale fledgling*

ἀηδών, *nightingale*

ἀῆναι, *flow*

ἀήτης, *wind*

ἀθρεῖν, *see, look at . . .*

ἀθρόος, *all together*; see XIII. 50 n.

αἰ = εἰ

αἴγειρος, *black poplar*

αἰγιαλός, *shore*

αἴγιλος, *an unidentified plant*

αἰγίοχος, *bearer of the aegis*

αἰγίπυρος, *restharrow*

αἰετός, *eagle*

αἰθαλίων, αἰθαλόεις, *sooty, black*

αἴθε = εἴθε

αἴθειν, *burn*

αἴθριος, *clear (sky)*

αἱμασιά, (dry) *stonewall*

αἱματόεις, *bloodstained*

αἱμοβόρος, *blood-drinking*

αἰνεῖν, *praise*

αἰνόδρυπτος, *painfully lashed*

αἶνος, *saying, proverb*

αἰνός, *terrible*

αἴνυσθαι, *take*

αἴξ, (nanny-)goat

αἰολόπωλος, *riding swift horses*

αἰόλος, *modulated*

αἰπεινός, *lofty*

αἰπολικός, adj. ⁓ αἰπόλος

αἰπόλος, *goatherd*

αἶπος (neut.), *summit*

αἰχμητής, *warrior*

αἶφα, *quickly*

ἀΐειν, *hear*

ἀϊών (ἡ-), *shore*

αἰών, *time, age*

αἰωρεῖν, *hang*

ἀκάματος, *undying*

ἄκανθα, *thorny plant*

ἀκανθίς, a species of songbird

ἄκανθος, *acanthus*

ἀκήλητος, *impervious*

ἀκήρατος, *pure*

ἄκιρος, probably *sluggish*

ἀκλεής, *inglorious*

ἄκλητος, *uninvited*

ἀκμά, *point*; see IV.60 n.
ἀκοίμητος, *never-resting*
(ἄκρᾱ): κατ' ἄκρᾱς, *utterly*
ἀκράτιστος: see I.50 n.
ἄκρᾱτος, *unmixed*
ἀκράχολος, *pallid*
ἀκρεμών, *frond*
ἀκρέσπερος, *at nightfall*
ἀκρῑβής, *exact, accurate*
ἀκριδοθήκᾱ, *grasshopper-cage*
ἀκρίς, *grasshopper, locust*
ἀκρόκομος, *with leafy top*
ἀκτή, *shore*
ἀκτήμων, *without possessions*
ἄκτιος, adj. ∼ ἀκτή
ἀκτίς, *ray*
ἄκυλος, a species of acorn
ἀκωκή, *point*
ἄκων, *javelin*
ἀλάβαστρον, *scent-bottle*
ἀλάθινος (-λή-), *true*
ἀλακάτᾱ (ἠλακάτη), *distaff*
ἀλᾶσθαι, *wander*
ἀλγεῖν, *be in pain*
ἄλγος (neut.), *pain, sorrow*
ἀλέγειν, *care*
ἄλειφαρ, *oil; pitch*
ἀλέκτωρ, *cock*
ἀλέματος (ἠ-), *helpless*
ἄλευρον, *wheat-flour*
ἀλίβατος (ἠ-), *steep*
ἀλίθιος (ἠ), *pointless, silly*
ἀλικιώτᾱς (ἡλικιώτης), *of
  … own age*
ἀλίκος (ἠ-), *how great*
ἀλιόκαυστος (ἠ-), *sunburnt*
ἀλιτρός, *sinner*
ἀλίτρυτος, *worn down by the sea*

ἀλκυών: see VII.57 n.
ἄλλεσθαι, *jump, leap*
ἄλλοκα = ἄλλοτε
ἀλλότριος, *belonging to others*
ἀλλοφρονεῖν, *be bewildered*
ἄλλυδις, *another way*
ἀλοιᾶν, *thresh*
ἄλσος (neut.), *wood, copse*
ἀλύσκειν, *avoid*
ἄλφιτα (pl.), *barley-flour*
ἀλωά, *vineyard, orchard;
  threshing-floor*
ἀλώπηξ, *fox*
ἄμ (before labial) = ἀνά
ἀμᾷ = ἅμα
ἀμαθύνειν, *shrivel*
ἀμαλδύνειν, *consume*
ἀμαλλοδέτᾱς, *binder* (of
  sheaves)
ἀμᾶν, *reap, cut*
ἀμαξιτός, *main road*
ἀμαυρός, *hard to discern*
ἀμβαίνειν (ἀνα-), *go up*
ἀμβάλλεσθαι (ἀνα-), *strike
  up*
ἀμβροσίᾱ, a mythical food
  and unguent of the gods
ἀμβρόσιος, *divine*
ἀμέλγειν, *milk*
ἀμέργεσθαι, *pick*
ἄμετρος, *measureless*
ἀμητήρ, *reaper*
ἀμηχανεῖν, *be at a loss*
ἀμήχανος, *helpless*
ἄμναστος (-μνη-), *unremem-
  bered*
ἀμνεῖος, adj. ∼ ἀμνός
ἀμνίς, fem. of ἀμνός

ἀμνός, *lamb*
ἀμοιβαδίς, *by turns*
ἄμος (ἦ-), *when*
ἀμπαύεσθαι (ἀνα-), *take a rest*
ἄμπελος, *vine*
ἀμπέχονον, *wrap*
ἀμπλέκειν (ἀνα-), *tie*
ἄμπυξ, *headband*
ἀμύκλαι, a kind of shoes
ἀμύσσειν, *strike, hurt*
ἀμυχμός, *slashing*
ἀμφαίνειν (ἀνα-), *reveal*
ἀμφίθυρον, *vestibule*
ἀμφιλαφής, *spacious*
ἀμφιπολεῖν, *go about on* . . .
ἀμφίπολος, *servant*
ἀμφιστέλλεσθαι, *put on*
ἀμφιτιθέναι, *put round*
ἀμφώης, *with two handles*
ἄμωμος, *without blemish*
ἄν sometimes = ἀνά
ἄνᾱβος (-νη-), *adolescent*
ἀναγιγνώσκειν, *catch sight of*
ἀναδραμεῖν, aor. ⁓ ἀνατρέχειν
ἀναιδής, *pitiless*
ἀναιρεῖν, *remove*
ἀνακεῖσθαι, *be dedicated*
ἀνακόπτειν, *knock back*
ἀνακράζειν, *cry out*
ἀναμετρεῖσθαι, *take the measure of*
ἀνανεύειν (lit. *nod up*), *refuse*
ἀνάνυτος (-νη-), *endless*
ἀναπληροῦν, *fill*
ἀνάριθμος (-νη-), *countless*
ἀνάριστος, *without lunch*

ἀναρπάζειν, *seize*
ἀναρρηγνύναι, *smash; let loose*
ἀνάρσιος, *hateful*
ἀνατιθέναι, *dedicate*
ἀνατρέχειν (lit. *run up*), *rise up*
ἀναΰειν, *cry out*
ἀναφύειν, *grow*
ἄνδηρον, *flower-bed*
ἀνδρέϊος (ἀνδρεῖος), adj. ⁓ ἀνήρ
ἀνδριάς, *statue*
ἀνδρίον, dim. ⁓ ἀνήρ
ἀνδριστί, advb. ⁓ ἀνήρ
ἀνέλπιστος, *without hope*
ἄνεμος, *wind*
ἀνεμώνᾱ (-νη), *anemone*
ἀνερύειν, *draw up*
ἀνερωτᾶν, *ask*
ἀνεψιός, *cousin*
ἄνηθον, *dill*
ἀνήσσᾱτος (-σση-), *unconquered*
ἀνήτινος, adj. ⁓ ἄνηθον
ἀνθεῖν, *flower*
ἀνθέριχος, *asphodel stem*
ἄνθος (neut.), *flower*
ἀνίᾱ, *pain, grief*
ἀνῑᾱρός, adj. ⁓ ἀνίᾱ
ἀνιᾶν, *suffer*
ἀνῑέναι, *let go*
ἀνίκητος, *unconquered*
ἀννεῖμαι (ἀνα-), aor. ⁓ ἀνανέμειν, *read*
ἀνοίγειν, *open*
ἀνορθοῦν, *raise up*
ἀνούατος, *without ears*

ἀνστᾶμεν (ἀναστῆναι), aor.
~ ἀνίστασθαι
ἀνταμείβεσθαι, reply
ἀντᾱχεῖν (-τη-), sing in reply
ἀντέλλειν (ἀνα-), rise up
ἀντίος, opposing, rival
ἀντιφιλεῖν, greet in response
ἀντλεῖν, draw (drink)
ἀντολᾱ́ (ἀνατολή), rising
ἄντρον, cave
ἄντυξ, chariot-rail
ἀνύειν, make, complete
ἀνυπόδητος, barefoot
ἄνυσιεργός, industrious
ἀνωγέναι (pf.), command
ἄξενος, inhospitable
ἀοίδιμος, celebrated
ἀοιδός, singer, poet
ἄορ, sword
ἀπάγχεσθαι, hang oneself
ἀπαλαλκέμεν (aor.), defend
ἀπαλός, supple, soft
ἀπάνευθε, without
ἀπάρθενος, no longer a virgin
ἀπάρχεσθαι, offer first-fruits
ἀπάτᾱ, deceit
ἀπαυδᾶν, forbid
ἀπειλεῖν, threaten
ἀπειπεῖν (aor.), give up
ἀπεχθάνεσθαι, ἀπέχθεσθαι,
   be hateful
ἀπεχθής, hateful
ἀπέχεσθαι, abstain
ἀπηνής, hard, cruel
ἄπιον, pear
ἀποβαίνειν, turn out (intr.)
ἀποβάλλεσθαι, reject
ἀποβρίζειν, take a nap

ἀποδᾱμεῖν (-δη-), be away
   from home
ἀποδύειν, take off
ἀποικεῖν, live at a distance
ἀποίχεσθαι, go away
ἀποκλᾱ́ειν (-κλει-), shut off
ἀποκλᾶν, break off
ἀποκλῑ́νειν, turn aside
ἀποκλῑ́νεσθαι, lean
ἀπόκομμα, chip
ἀπολείπειν, leave behind
ἀπολήγειν, cease
ἀπολύειν, remove
ἀπομάσσειν, level off
ἀποπαύεσθαι, stop
ἀποπέμπειν, send away, let . . .
   go away
ἀπόπροθι, far-off
ἀπορρεῖν, dwindle
ἀποσβεννύναι, extinguish
ἀποσκῡλεύειν, remove (as
   spoils)
ἀποσπένδειν, pour a libation
ἀποστάζειν, drop, pour
ἀποστε(ι)νοῦν, narrow
ἀποστέργειν, cease to love
ἀποσύρειν, tear away
ἀπότιλμα, plucking
ἀποτρίβειν, crush
ἀποτρώγειν, eat away, eat into
ἀποφέρεσθαι, carry off (prize)
ἀποφθίνεσθαι, die
ἀπρεπής, uncouth, repulsive
ἄπρᾱκτος, unsuccessful
ἀπρίξ, with a tight grip
ἅπτειν, light
ἅπτεσθαι, touch, take hold of
ἀπφῦς, daddy

ἄπωθεν, *at a distance*
ἀπωτέρω, *further away*
ἀραβεῖν, *clash*
ἀραῖος, *accursed*
ἀραιός, *thin*
ἀράσσειν, *knock*
ἀράχνᾱ, *spider*
ἀράχνιον, *cobweb*
ἀρβυλίς, *boot*
ἀργαλέος, *disagreeable*
ἀργύρεος, adj. ~ ἄργυρος
ἀργύριον, *money*
ἄργυρος, *silver*
ἄρδειν, *wet, water*
ἀρείων, *better*
ἀρέσκειν, *please*
ἀρέσκεσθαι, *gratify*
ἀρήγειν, *help*
ἀρίθμητος, *easily counted*
ἀριστερός, *left*
ἀριστεύειν, *excel*
ἀριστεύς, *champion*
ἀριστοτόκεια, *mother of noble children*
ἀριφραδής, *plainly seen*
ἀρκεῖν, *be enough*
ἄρκευθος, *juniper*
ἄρκτος, *bear; the Great Bear*
ἀρμαλιά, *ration*
ἄρμενα (pl.), *tackle*
ἀρμοῖ, *just now*
ἁρμονίᾱ: see x.39 n.
ἀρν- (nom. sing. not in literature), *lamb*
ἀρνᾶ (-νέᾱ), *lambskin*
ἄροτρον, *plough*
ἄρουρα, *field*
ἄρρηκτος, *hard*

ἄρσην, *male*
ἀρτιγλυφής, *newly carved*
ἀρτίζεσθαι, *array*
ἄρτος, *loaf*
ἀρχηγός, *leader*
ἅς = ἕως
ᾆσαι (aor.), ᾀσεῖσθαι (fut.) ~ ἀείδειν
ἄσκαλος, *not hoed*
ἀσκητός, *adorned, dressed*
ἀσπάλαθος, a species of thorny bush
ἀσπασίως, *gladly*
ἀσπιδιώτᾱς, *soldier* (~ ἀσπίς)
ἀσπίς, *shield*
ἀστεμφής, *steadfast*
ἀστήρ, *star*
ἄστοργος, *loveless*
ἀστράγαλος, *knucklebone*
ἄστρεπτος, *without turning back*
ἄστρον, *star*
ἀσυχᾶ (ἡσυχῇ), *quietly*
ἀσυχίᾱ (ἡ-), *quiet, peace*
ἄσφαλτος, *bitumen*
ἀσφόδελος, *asphodel*
ἀτάρτηρος, *harsh*
ἀτασθαλίᾱ, n. ~ -λος
ἀτάσθαλος, *brutal, reckless*
ἄτερ, *without*
ἀτέραμνος, *hard, stony*
ἄτῑμος, *not honoured*
ἀτιτάλλειν, *show affection for . . .*
ἀτρακτυλλίς, a species of thistle
ἀτρεκής, *exact, truthful*
ἀτρέμας, *gently*

ἄτριον (ἤ-), *fabric, weft*
ἄτριπτος, *untrodden*
ἄτρῡτος, *endless*
ἀτύζειν, *amaze*
αὐγά, *brightness*
ἀῦειν, *cry*
αὖλαξ, *furrow*
αὐλείᾱ (sc. θύρᾱ), *front door*
αὐλεῖν, *play a pipe*
αὐλητρίς (fem.), *piper*
αὐλίον, *sheep-pen*
αὖλις, *byre*
αὐλός, (musical) *pipe*
αὖος, *dry, withered*
ἀῦσταλέος, *dried-up*
ἀῦτεῖν, *cry*
ἀῦτή, *cry*
αὐτοενεί, *in the same year*
αὐτόθε, *from where one is*
αὐχήν, *neck*
ἄφαντος, *disappeared*
ἀφάπτειν, *hang*
ἄφαρ, *quickly, straightway*
ἀφέρπειν, *go off*
ἄφθιτος, *everlasting*
ἄφθονος, *abundant*
ἀφνειός, *wealthy*
ἀφρόντιστος, *reckless*
ἀφύσσειν, *draw* (wine)
ἄχερδος, *wild pear*
ἀχεῖν (ἤ-), *sing, make a noise*
ἀχήν, *pauper*
ἄχθεσθαι, *be weighed down*
ἄχραντος, *uncontaminated*
ἄχρις, *all the way*
ἄχυρον, *grain and chaff*
ἄψ, ἄψορρον, *back*
ἀῶθεν (ἤ-), *in the morning*

ἀωρί, *at an unseasonable hour*
ἀώς (ἕως), *dawn*
ἄωτος, *fine wool; fine flower*

βάθος (neut.), *depth*
βαθύς, *deep*
βαθύσκιος, *densely shaded*
βαίτᾱ, (herdsman's) *coat*
βάπτειν, *dip; fill by dipping*
βάρβιτος, a type of lyre
βάρδιστος = βραδύτατος,
    sup. ~ βραδύς, *slow*
βαρυγούνατος, *heavy-limbed*
βαρυμάνιος (-μή-), *formid-*
    able in anger
βαρύνειν, *weigh down*
βασίλεια, βασίλισσα, *queen*
βασκαίνειν, *look evilly upon...*
βαστάζειν, *carry*
βατεῖν, *mount* (sexually)
βάτος, *bramble*
βάτραχος, *frog*
βαΰζειν, *bark*
βδέλλα, *leech*
βέβᾱλος (-βη-), *profane,*
    uninitiated
βέλεμνον, *shaft, weapon*
βέντιστος = βέλτιστος
βιάζεσθαι, *force*
βλέφαρον, *eye* (lid)
βληχᾶσθαι, *bleat*
βλοσυρός, *frightening, grim*
βόειος, *oxhide* (adj.)
βοηθόος (-θός), *helper*
βολβός, (edible) *bulb*
βόλος, *throw*
βομβεῖν, *buzz*
βόσκειν, *feed, tend*

βόσκεσθαι, *graze*
βοτάνᾱ, *pasture*
βοτόν, *animal*
βοτρύπαις, *growing grapes*
βουκολεῖν, *look after* (herds)
βουκολιάζεσθαι, βουκολι-
 άστᾱς, βουκολικός : see
 p. liv
βουκόλος, βούτᾱς, *cowherd*
βούτομον, *sedge*
βράβιλον, *sloe*
βραγχία (pl.), *gills*
βρᾱϊδίως = ῥᾳδίως
βράκος (ῥάκος), *fabric, gar-*
 ment
βρίθειν, *be laden*
βρόχθος, *throat*
βυθός, *depth*
βύσσος, *linen*
βωστρεῖν, *call*

γα = γε
γᾱθεῖν (γη-), *rejoice*
γάλα, *milk*
γαλαθηνός, *feeding at the*
 breast
γαλᾱνᾱ (-λήνη), *calm*
γαλέᾱ (γαλῆ), *weasel*
γαμβρός, *bridegroom, son-in-*
 law
γᾱρύεσθαι, *call, sing*
γαστήρ, *belly*
γαυλός, *pail*
γαῦρος, *wilful, arrogant*
γείτων, *neighbour*
γελᾶν, *laugh, smile*
γέλως, *laughter, smile*
γέμειν, *be laden*

γενεά, *age, generation*
γενειάζειν, *begin to grow a*
 beard
γενειᾶν, *have a beard*
γενειάς, *down* (on chin)
γένειον, *chin*
γένυς, *jaw; cheek*
γεραίρειν, *honour, reward*
γεραίτατος, *eldest*
γέρανος, *crane*
γερόντιον, dim. ∼ γέρων
γέρας, *privilege, prize*
γεώλοφον, *knoll*
γηραλέος, *old*
γλάχων (βλήχων), *penny-*
 royal
γλυκερός = γλυκύς
γλυκύκαρπος, *bearing sweet*
 fruit
γλυκύμᾱλον, (lit. *sweet-*
 apple), a term of endear-
 ment
γλυκύς, *sweet*
γλύφανος, *knife* (for carving
 wood)
γναθμός = γένυς
γονεύς, *parent*
γραῖᾱ, *old woman*
γράμμα, *letter; drawing*
γραμμᾱ́, *line*
γραπτός, *marked*
γρῑπεύς, *fisherman*
γυῖον, *limb; arm*
γυμνός, *naked*
γυμνοῦν, *bare*
γύννις, *womanish*

δᾱγύς, *doll*

δαῆναι (aor.), *be taught*
δαιδάλεος, an epithet of outstanding works of art
δαίδαλμα, *work of art*
δαίειν, *burn*
δαιμόνιος : see XVI.22 n.
δαίνυσθαι, *feast*
δάϊς, *fighting*
δακρυόεις, *tearful*
δακρύειν, *weep*
δᾱλεῖσθαι (δη-), *hurt*
δαμάλᾱ, *heifer*
δαμάζειν, *subdue*
δᾶμος (δῆ-), *deme, village*
δᾱμότᾱς (δημότης), *member of deme*
δᾱμότις (δη-), *woman of the same community*
δασπλῆτις, an epithet of frightening supernatural beings
δασύθριξ, *hairy*
δασύκερκος, *with a bushy tail*
δάφνᾱ, *bay(-leaves)*
δαψιλέως, *abundantly*
δέδαεν = ἐδίδαξεν
δεδμῆσθαι, pass. pf. ~ δέμειν, *build*
δειδιότες, part. ~ δεδοικέναι
δειελινός, *evening* (adj.)
δεικανᾶν, *show*
δείλαιος, δειλός, *miserable, worthless*
δεῖν, *bind together*
δεῖπνον, *evening meal*
δειρά, *neck*
δεκάμηνος, *ten months old*
δέμνιον, *bed*

δένδρον, *tree*
δεξιός, δεξιτερός, *right (-hand)*
δέος (neut.), *fear*
δέπας, *cup*
δέρκεσθαι, *look*
δέρμα, *skin*
δεσμός, *grip*
δέσποινα, *mistress*
δεσπότᾱς, *master*
δηθά, *for a long time*
δήλεσθαι, *wish, want*
δῆλος, *clear, obvious*
δηναιός, *long-lasting*
δηρίεσθαι, *contend*
διάγειν, *spend* (time)
διαδηλεῖσθαι, *tear to pieces*
διαδραμεῖν, aor. ~ διατρέχειν, *run in different directions*
διαδύεσθαι, aor. -δῦναι, *slip through*
διαειδής, *clear*
διαείδειν (-άδ-), *go on singing*
διαθρύπτεσθαι, *preen oneself*
διακρᾱνᾶν (-κρη-), *make . . . with spring-water*
διακρίνεσθαι, *settle one's quarrel*
διάκριτος, *pre-eminent*
διαλακτίζειν, *kick aside*
διαλύειν, *relax*
διαπιαίνειν, *fatten*
διαπόντιος, *crossing the sea*
διαπρό, *right through*
διατείνεσθαι, *exert oneself*
διαφαίνειν *reveal*
διαχεῖν (lit. *pour different ways*), *cut to pieces*

διαχρέμπτεσθαι, *clear one's throat*
διαχρῆσθαι, *do away with*
διδυμᾱτόκος, *which has borne twins*
δίζησθαι, *seek*
διϊέναι, *spread* (intr.)
διΐστασθαι, *set up this way and that*
δίκη, *way, mode*
δικλίς, (*outer*) *door*
δίκτυον, *net*
δῑνᾱ, *eddying current*
δῑνεῖν, *revolve; rock*
δίς, *twice*
δίφραξ, δίφρος, *chair*
δίχα, *in two*
δίψος (neut.), *thirst*
δμώς, *slave*
δοιώ (dual), *two*
δόκιμος, *of high repute, admirable*
δόλος, *guile*
δονεῖν, *shake*
δορυσσόος (lit. *spear-brandishing*), *warrior*
δοχμός, *sideways*
δράγμα, *sheaf*
δράκων, *snake*
δράσσεσθαι, *grasp*
δρέπεσθαι, *pick*
δρῑμύς, *bitter*
δρόμος, *course*
δρόσος, *dew*
δρῡμός, *wood*
δρῦς, *oak*: see also xv.112 n.
δρυτόμος, *woodcutter*
δυνατός, *able*

δύνειν, *set* (intr.)
δύσερως, *unfortunate in love*
δύσις, *setting*
δυσμενής, *hostile*
δύσμορος, *accursed*
δυσσεβής, *impious*
δύσσοος, *hopeless, accursed*
δύστᾱνος (-τη-), *wretched*
δωδεκαταῖος, *on the twelfth day* (adj.)
δῶλος = δοῦλος
δωρεῖσθαι, *give*
δῶρον, *gift*
δωρύττεσθαι = δωρεῖσθαι

ἐάγη, 3rd. s. pass. aor. ~ ἀγνύναι, *break*
ἔαρ, *spring*
ἔβενος, *ebony*
ἐγείρειν, *awaken*
ἐγέρσιμος : see xxiv.7 n.
ἐγκεῖσθαι, *be wholly taken up with . . .*
ἐγκροτεῖν, *stamp*
ἐγκύρειν, *encounter*
ἔγματα, *guts*
ἐγρέσθαι, aor. ~ ἐγείρεσθαι
ἐγχεῖν, *pour in*
ἔγχος (neut.), *spear*
ἔγχριστος, *put on as ointment*
ἐγών = ἐγώ
ἔδειν, fut. ἔδεσθαι, *eat*
ἐδνοῦν, *betroth*
ἕδος (neut.), *dwelling*
ἕδρᾱ, *seat*
ἑδροστρόφος, *twisting the loins*
ἐέρση, *dew*
ἕζεσθαι, *sit*

ἔθειρα, *hair*
ἐθειράζειν, *wear long hair*
εἶα, an exclamation of encouragement
εἴδατα (pl.), *food*
εἴδεσθαι, *seem*
εἶδος (neut.), *appearance*
εἴκατι = εἴκοσι
εἰκῇ, *in disorder*
εἰκών, *likeness*
εἰλεῖν, *wind, twist*
εἰλιτενής, *spreading over marshy ground*
εἵματα (pl.), *clothes*
εἰν = ἐν
εἴρια = ἔρια
εἰσαΐειν, *hear*
εἰσανϊέναι, *go up into* . . .
εἰσαφικάνειν, *arrive*
εἰσκαλεῖν, *invite*
εἰστρέχειν, *run in*
εἴσω, *inside*
ἑκαστέρω, *further*
ἐκγελᾶν, *laugh aloud*
ἐκκαθαίρειν : see XIII.69 n.
ἐκκενοῦν, *empty out*
ἐκκναίειν, *wear out*
ἔκκριτος, *pre-eminent*
ἐκλελάθειν, *make* . . . *to forget*
ἔκλυσις, *release*
ἐκμαίνειν, *drive mad*
ἐκμαραίνεσθαι, *shrivel away*
ἐκπίνειν, *suck out*
ἐκπλεῖν, *sail out*
ἐκπονεῖν, *complete*
ἐκποτᾶσθαι, *fly out*
ἐκπτύειν, *spit out*
ἐκρηγνύναι, *break off*

ἐκσαλάσσειν, *shake violently*
ἐκτανύειν, *stretch out*
ἐκτελεῖν, *accomplish*
ἔκτοθεν, ἔκτοσθε, *outside*
ἐκφοβεῖν : see XIII.48 n.
ἐκφῡσᾶν, *breathe out*
ἐκχυθῆναι, pass. aor. ∼
    ἐκχεῖν, *pour out*
ἐλαίᾱ, *olive-tree*
ἔλαιον, (*olive-*)*oil*
ἐλαύνειν, *drive ; strike*
ἔλαφος, *deer*
ἐλαφρός, *agile, easy*: and see
    II.92 n.
ἐλεεῖν, *pity*
ἐλεφάντινος, adj. ∼ ἐλέφας
ἐλέφας, *ivory*
ἑλικτός : see I.129 n.
ἐλῑνύειν, *cease*
ἕλιξ, *tendril*
ἑλίσσειν, *wind, coil*
ἑλίχρῡσος, *helichryse ; ivy-flower*
ἕλκειν, *pull, draw*
ἕλκος (neut.), *wound*
ἑλλοπιεύειν, *fish*
ἔλπεσθαι, *expect, believe*
ἐλπίς, *hope*
ἐμβάλλειν, *put in*
ἐμβασιλεύειν, *reign in* . . .
ἐμμελής, *musical*
ἔμμηνος, *monthly*
ἐμπλῆσαι, aor., ἐμπλησθῆναι pass. aor. ∼ ἐμπιμπλάναι, *fill*
ἐμφύλιος, *among kindred* (adj.)
ἐμφύεσθαι, *cling to*

add: ἐκπλήγδην, *in amazement*

ἔμψῡχος, *living*
ἐναλίγκιος, *like*
ἔναλλος, *reversed*
ἐναρίθμιος, *numbered among* . . .
ἔνας (ἔνης), *on the day after tomorrow* (adj.)
ἐνδεῖσθαι, *tie in* . . .
ἐνδιαθρύπτεσθαι, *behave conceitedly towards* . . .
ἐνδιᾶν, *be in the open air*
ἐνδῑνεῖν, *move about in* . . .
ἔνδῑος, *in the heat of the day* (adj.)
ἔνδοθι, ἔνδοι (ἔνδον), *inside*
ἐνεργεῖν, *be on the job*
ἐνερείδεσθαι, *press against* . . .
ἐνεύδειν, *sleep in* . . .
ἐνῆσθαι, *sit in* . . .
ἐνθεῖν = ἐλθεῖν
ἐνί = ἐν
ἐνιαυτός, *year*
ἐνίδρυσθαι, *dwell in* . . .
ἐνῑέναι, *put in*
ἔννυσθαι, *put on*
ἐνόρχᾱς (-χης, -χος), *not castrated*
ἐντανύειν, *draw* (bow)
ἔντοσθεν, *within*
ἐνυφαντός, *woven in*
ἐνώπιος, *face to face*
ἐξαετής, (ἐξέτης), *six years old*
ἐξαίρεσθαι, *win*
ἐξανέχειν, *rise up*
ἐξαπίνᾱς (-νης), *suddenly*
ἐξεγρέσθαι, aor. ∼ ἐξεγείρεσθαι, *wake up*

ἐξειλύεσθαι, *uncoil*
ἐξελαύνεσθαι, *drive out*
ἐξετάζειν, *inquire into* . . .
ἐξευρίσκεσθαι, *invent*
ἔξοχος, *outstanding, supreme* (advb. -χα)
ἐοικέναι, *be like* . . ., *be fitting*
ἑορτά, *holiday*
ἑός, *his, her*
ἐπάβολος (-πή-), *knowledge-able in* . . .
ἐπᾴδειν, *recite a spell*
ἐπαμύνειν, *bring help*
ἐπανθεῖν, *flower on* . . .
ἐπανιέναι, *return*
ἐπάνωθεν (lit. *above*), *in ancestry*
ἐπαῡτεῖν, *acclaim*
ἐπείγειν, *hasten, urge*
ἐπείγεσθαι, *hasten* (intr.)
ἐπεμπίπτειν, *put one's weight behind* (a blow)
ἐπέχειν, *put down into* . . .
ἐπήν = ἐπεί + ἄν
ἐπιβαίνειν, *step in, step on to* . . .
ἐπιβρίθειν, *press heavily*
ἐπιβρύειν, *teem*
ἐπιβώμια (pl.), *sacrifices*
ἐπιγουνίς, *thigh*
ἐπιδέξιος, *elegant, skilful*
ἐπιδευής, *lacking*
ἐπιδόρπιος, *for the meal* (adj.)
ἐπιέναι, *attack*
ἐπιζευγνύναι, *bind in* . . .
ἐπιθῡμεῖν, *want*
ἐπικεῖσθαι, *be above* . . .; *attack*

ἐπιλαμβάνειν, *go over* . . .
ἐπιλανθάνεσθαι, *forget*
ἐπιμελητής, *overseer*
ἐπιμέμφεσθαι, *find fault*
ἐπιμωμᾱτός (-μωμη-),
   blameworthy
ἐπινεύειν, *nod above*
ἐπιπάσσειν, *sprinkle on, paste
   on*
ἐπίπαστος, *sprinkled on, pasted
   on*
ἐπιπταρεῖν, aor. ~ ἐπιπταί-
   ρειν, *sneeze* (as omen)
ἐπιρραίνειν, *sprinkle*
ἐπιρρέζειν, *sacrifice*
ἐπιρρεῖν, *swamp*
ἐπισκύνιον, *brow*
ἐπισπεύδειν, *hasten*
ἐπισχερώ, *step by step*
ἐπίτᾱδες (-τη-), *on purpose*
ἐπιτάσσειν, *impose*
ἐπιτυμβίδιος : see VII.23 n.
ἐπιφθύζειν, *spit*
ἐπιφράζεσθαι, *think of, con-
   trive*
ἐπίχαρμα, *object of ridicule*
ἐπίχειρα (pl.), *reward*
ἐπιχεῖσθαι, *tell* . . . *to pour in*
ἐπιχώριος, *native*
ἕπεσθαι, *follow*
ἔπλεο, ἔπλετο, 2nd & 3rd
   sing. aor. ~ πέλειν,
   πέλεσθαι
ἐπορνύναι, *send* (against . . .)
ἔπος, *word, verse, utterance*
ἔποψ, *hoopoe*
ἑπτάδραχμος, *at seven
   drachmai*

ἔραζε, *to the ground*
ἐρᾶν, ἔρασθαι, *be in love*
   (with . . .)
ἔραννος (ἐραννός), ἐρατός,
   lovely
ἐργάζεσθαι, *work*
ἐργάτᾱς, ἐργατίνᾱς,
   labourer
ἔρδειν, aor. ἔρξαι, *do, make*
ἐρεθίζειν, *irritate, rouse*
ἐρείδειν, *push, press*
ἐρεῖκαι (pl.), *heather*
ἐρεύθεσθαι, *be red*
ἐρευνᾶν, *seek*
ἐρημάζειν, *be alone*
ἔρια (pl.), *wool*
ἐρίζειν, *contend, compete*
ἔρῑθος, *spinning-* or *weaving-
   woman*
ἐριπεῖν, aor. ~ ἐρείπεσθαι,
   fall
ἔρις, *quarrel, contest*
ἔριφος, *kid*
ἔρνος (neut.), *plant*
ἑρπετόν, *reptile, insect*
ἕρπειν, *go*
ἐρρῑγέναι, pf. ~ ῥῑγεῖν,
   bristle
ἐρυγεῖν, aor. ~ ἐρεύγεσθαι,
   roar
ἐρύ-ειν, εσθαι, *draw, pull*
ἐρυθρός, *red*
ἐρύκειν, *ward off*
ἐρωεῖν, *push away*
ἐρωή, *respite*
ἔρως, *love*
ἐρωτᾶν, *ask*
ἐρωτικός, adj. ~ ἔρως

ἑσπέριος, *western*
ἐσσυμένως, *furiously*
ἔστε = ἕως
ἑστίᾱ, *hearth*
ἐστρῶσθαι, pass. pf. ⁓ στορεννύναι
ἐσχαρεών = ἑστίᾱ
ἐσχατιά, *marginal land*
ἔσχατος, ἐσχατόων, *furthest, last*
ἑτοιμάζειν, *get ready*
ἑτοῖμος, *ready, available*
ἔτος (neut.), *year*
ἔτυμος, *real*
ἐτώσιος, *useless; deceptive*
εὐαγεῖν, *be innocent, be pious*
εὐαγής, *innocent, pious*
εὐᾱλάκατος (-η-), *possessing a notable distaff*
εὐάνεμος (-η-), *enjoying a favourable wind*
εὔβοτος, *fat, well pastured*
εὐγνώμων, *considerate*
εὕδειν, *sleep*
εὔδιος, *fair, calm*
εὔεδρος, *with strong benches*
εὐειδής, *beautiful*
εὔεργος, *easy to work at*
εὐθύ, *straightway*
εὐθῡμεῖν, *be glad*
εὐίερος = ἱερός
εὐκαμπής, *curved*
εὔκᾱλος (-κη-), *quiet*
εὔκρῑθος, *full of good barley*
εὐκτός, *ideal* (adj.)
εὐμάκης (-μή-), *tall*
εὐμαρής, *easy*
εὐμενής, *friendly*

εὔμηλος, *with good flocks*
εὐνά, *bed*
εὐνάζεσθαι, *sleep in bed*
εὔοδμος, *sweet-smelling*
εὐπατρίδᾱς, *of noble lineage*
εὐπένθερος, *married to the daughter of a noble father*
εὔπεπλος, *wearing beautiful robes*
ἐϋπλόκαμος, *having beautiful hair*
εὔπλοος, *enjoying a safe voyage*
εὐρύνειν, *make broad*
εὐρύς, *broad*
εὐρύστερνος, *with broad breast*
εὐρώς, *mould*
εὐσεβής, *pious*
ἐΰσκιος, *pleasantly shady*
εὔσοος, *safe*
ἐΰσφυρος, *with beautiful ankles*
εὔτε = ὅτε
εὐτεκνία, *enjoyment of good children*
ἐΰτριχα, acc. ⁓ εὔθριξ, *with handsome feathers*
εὔτυκος, *ready*
εὐφάμως (-φη-), *with no inauspicious words*
εὐφραίνειν, *gladden*
εὔχεσθαι, *pray, declare*
εὐώδης, *sweet-smelling*
ἐφάπτεσθαι, *take hold of . . .*
ἐφαρμόζειν, *fit together*
ἐφέρπειν, *come on*
ἐφίμερος, *delightful*
ἐφίζειν, *roost*
ἐχθαίρειν, *hate*

ἐχθές, *yesterday*
ἕψειν, *boil*

ζᾱλοῦν (ζη-), *envy*
ζᾱλωτός (ζη-), *enviable*
ζᾱτεῖν (ζη-), *seek*
ζόᾱ (ζωή), *life*
ζοός = ζωός
ζυγόν, *pair*
ζώννυσθαι, *put on armour*
ζωογράφος, *painter*
ζωός, *alive*
ζωστήρ, *belt*
ζώστρᾱ, *headband*
ζώειν = ζῆν

ἠέ = ἤ
ἠδέ = καί
ἦδος (neut.), *pleasure*
ἠέλιος = ἥλιος
ἠΐθεος, (*unmarried*) *young man*
ἠλαίνειν, *fly about*
ἤμενος, part. ~ ἧσθαι
ἡμιγένειος, *with beard half grown*
ἡμίθεος, *demigod*
ἡμίφλεκτος, *half consumed*
ἠνίδε, *see!*
ἧπαρ, *liver*
ἦρι, *in the morning*
ἠρίον, *tomb*
ἡρωΐνη, *heroine*
ἥρως, *hero*
ἧσθαι, *sit*
ἤτοι, *and, then*
ἠϋγένειος, *full-bearded*
ἠΰτε, *like*

θάημα (θέᾱμα), *sight*
θᾱητός (Epic θηη-), *wonderful to see*
θάλαμος, *bedroom*
θαλερός, *big, abundant*
θάλλειν, *flourish*
θαλλός, *green shoot*
θάλπειν, *warm, comfort*
θαλυσιάς (fem. adj.), *for a harvest festival*
θάπτειν, *bury*
θαρσαλέως, *confidently*
θαρσεῖν, *be confident, take courage*
θαρσύνειν, *encourage*
θάσασθαι (θεᾱ-), aor. ~ θᾱεῖσθαι (Epic θη-)
θαῦμα, *wonder*
θάψος, *a yellowish wood*
θέειον (θεῖον), *sulphur*
θείνειν, *strike*
θέμις (noun), *permitted* (by the gods)
θεμιτός, adj. ~ θέμις
θερίστριον, *summer dress*
θερμός, *hot, warm*
θέρος (neut.), *summer*
θεσπέσιος, *enormous*
θεσπίζειν, *speak like an oracle*
θεῖν, *run*
θεωρεῖν, *look at . . .*
θηεῖσθαι (θεᾶσθαι), *look (at . . .), admire*
θηλάζειν, *suck, be suckled*
θῆλυς, *female*
θην, a particle which appears in different contexts akin to δή, που or τοι

θήρ, θηρίον, *animal*
θίασος, *band* (of worshippers)
θίς, *shore*
θνᾱτός (θνη-), *mortal*
θολερός, *muddy*
θολίᾱ, *sun-hat*
θοός, *swift*
θρασύς, *bold*
θρηνεῖν, *lament*
θρίξ, *hair*
θρόνα (pl.), *herbs*
θρόνος, *seat*
θρῡλεῖν, *talk at length*
θρύον, *a kind of reed*
θρώσκειν, *hurry*
θύειν, *sacrifice*
θῡμαλγής, *painful*
θῡμᾰρεῖν, *find acceptable*
θύννος, *tunny*
θύος (neut.), *sacrifice, spell*
θύρᾱ, *door*
θῶκος, *seat*
θώς, *jackal*

ἰαίνειν, *gladden*
ἰάλεμος, *dirge*
ἴαμβος : see *Epigr.* 21.2 n.
ἰάπτειν, *wound*
ἰᾱτρός, *doctor*
ἰαύειν, *sleep*
ἰαχεῖν, *cry, shout*
ἰγνύᾱ (-η), (back of) *thigh*
ἰδέᾱ, *form*
ἰδρείη, *skill*
ἰδρώς, *sweat*
ἰητήρ (ἰᾱ-), *doctor*
ἰθύς, *straight*
ἰκάνειν, *come*

ἴκελος, *like*
ἵλᾱος (ἵλεως), *gracious*
ἰλεός, *hovel*
ἵλαθι (imp.), *be gracious*
ἱμάς, *rope, rein, thong*
ἱμείρειν, *desire*
ἱμερόεις, *desirable*
ἵμερος, *desire*
ἱμερόφωνος, (ῐ-), *with lovely voice*
ἰνδάλλεσθαι, *be like*
ἰξύς, *waist*
ἴον, *violet*
ἰός, *venom; rust*
ἴουλος, *down*
ἵππειος, adj. ~ ἵππος
ἱππεύς, *horseman*
ἱππήλατος, *where horses are ridden*
ἱππόβοτος, *where horses are grazed*
ἱπποδιώκτᾱς, *horseman*
ἱππόκομος, *adorned with horsehair*
ἱππομανές : see 11.48 n.
ἴς, *muscle*
ἴσκειν, *say*
ἰσοπαλής, *equal as a stake*
ἰσοφαρίζειν, *be a match (for . . .)*
ἱστίον, *sail*
ἱστός, *loom*
ἰσχάς, *dried fig*
ἴσχειν, *hold, have*
ἰσχίον, *thigh*
ἰσχνός, *shrivelled*
ἰτέϊνος, *of willow wood*
ἴυγξ, *wryneck*

ἰχθύς, *fish*

κᾱ = ἄν
κάγκανος, *dry*
καθαίρειν, *dust, clean up*
καθαιρεῖν, *pull down, over-throw*
καθαρός, *pure*
καθέζεσθαι, *sit*
καθεύδειν, *sleep*
κάθησθαι, *sit*
καθίζ-ειν, -εσθαι, *sit*: see also 1.51 n.
καθυπέρτερος, *supreme (over . . .)*
καίειν, *burn*
κακοεργός (-ουρ-), *criminal*
κακόκνᾱμος (-κνη-), *with ugly legs*
κακοχράσμων, *nasty to deal with*
κάκτος, *cactus*
καλάμᾱ, *stalk*
καλαμαῖος, adj. ~ καλάμᾱ
καλαμευτής, *hunter* (with limed reeds)
κάλαμος, *reed, pipe*
καλλιερεῖν, *sacrifice with good omen*
κάλπις, *pitcher*
κάλυξ, *bud*
κάμνειν, *exert oneself*
κάμπτειν, *follow round*
κάνεον (κανοῦν), *basket*
καναφόρος (-νη-), *basket-bearer* (in procession)
κανεῖν, aor. ~ καίνειν, *kill*
κάνθαρος, *beetle*

κᾶπος (κῆ-) *garden*
καππυρίζειν (καταπυ-), *catch fire*
καπυρός, *clear-sounding*
καροῦν, *stupefy*
καρπάλιμος, *swift*
κάρπιμος, *fruitful*
καρπός, *fruit*
κάρτα, *very*
καρτερός, *strong, violent*
κάρτος (neut.), *strength*
καρτύνεσθαι, *strengthen*
καρχαρόδων, *with jagged teeth*
κασίγνητος, *brother*
καταβληχᾶσθαι, *bleat in derision*
καταβρίθειν, *be weighed down*
καταδαίσασθαι, aor. ~ -δαίνυ-, *make a meal off . . .*
καταδεῖν, *bind down*
καταδύεσθαι, *go down, be submerged*
καταίθειν, *burn*
κατακλάεσθαι (-κλει-), *lock in*
κατακλίνεσθαι, *lie down*
κατακόπτειν, *slaughter, cut up*
καταλαμβάνειν, *catch, come upon*
καταλέγειν, *tell fully*
καταλείβεσθαι, *pour down (intr.)*
καταμύσσειν, *scratch, rend*
καταπρίειν, *saw in half*
καταπτυχής, *full, billowing*
κατάντης, *sloping down*
καταρρεῖν (lit. *flow down*), *come down*

κατασμύχειν, *consume*
κατατάκεσθαι (-τη-),
    waste away
κατατρίβειν, *rub*
κατατρύχειν, *torment*
κατατρώγειν, *devour*
καταφρύγειν, *burn up*
κατᾱχής (-τη-), *sounding*
κατέδραθες, 2nd. sing.
    aor. ~ καταδαρθάνειν,
    go to sleep
κατείβεσθαι, *trickle down*
κατελαύνειν (lit. *drive down*),
    slang word for sexual
    penetration
κατεριπεῖν (aor.), *fall down*
κατεύχεσθαι, *boast; adjure*
κατηρεφής, *roofing over*
κατοικεῖν, *inhabit*
καῦμα, *heat*
καυχεῖσθαι (-χᾱ-), *boast*
καχάζειν, *guffaw*
καχλάζειν, *splash*
κε(ν) = ἄν
κέδρινος, adj. ~ κέδρος
κέδρος, *cedar*
κειμήλια (pl.), *treasures*
κεκμᾱκώς (-κμη-), pf.
    part. ~ κάμνειν
κεκαρμένος, pass. pf.
    part. ~ κείρειν, *cut* (hair)
κελαδεῖν, *make a noise*
κελαρύζειν, *murmur*
κελέοντες, *beams* (of loom)
κελέβᾱ, a kind of large pot
κέλεσθαι = κελεύειν
κενεός (κενός), *empty*
κεντεῖν, *prick*

κεραός, *horned*
κεραυνός, *thunderbolt*
κέρδος (neut.), *gain, profit*
κερκίς, *shuttle*
κερουχίς = κεραός
κερτομεῖν, *make fun of* . . .
κηρίον, *honeycomb*
κηρός, *wax*
κιθαριστής, *lyre-player*
κίκιννος, *curl* (of hair)
κικλήσκειν, *call*
κίναδος, *trickster*
κίσθος, *rock-rose*
κίσσα, *magpie*
κισσός, *ivy*
κισσύβιον: see p. 78
κίστᾱ, *box*
κιχλίζειν, *giggle*
κλάειν (κλείειν), *shut*
κλάξ (κλείς), *key*
κλᾶρος (κλῆ-), *inheritance*
    (of land)
κλέος, *fame*
κλέπτειν, *steal*
κλῖμαξ, *ladder*
κλίνᾱ, *bed, couch*
κλίνειν, *draw down*
κλίνεσθαι, *lie down; lean*
κλιντήρ, κλισμός = κλίνᾱ
κλύζειν, *wash, splash*
κλύμενος, *famous*
κλωστήρ, *thread*
κνᾱκός (κνη-), *tawny*
κνάκων (κνη-), *tawny*
    (goat)
κνάμᾱ (κνήμη), *shin*
κνᾶσθαι, *scratch* (intr.)
κνίδη, *nettle*

κνίζειν, *sting*
κνύζα, *fleabune*
κνυζεῖσθαι, *whimper*
κνώδαλον, *monster*
κοῖλος, *hollow, deep*
κοῖτος, *bed*
κοκκύζειν, *crow*
κολεόν, *sheath*
κολοσσός, *statue*
κολούειν, *cut off*
κόλπος, *lap; folds*
κόμᾱ, *hair*
κομᾶν, *wear long hair; be leafy*
κόμαρος, *arbutus*
κονίειν, *sprinkle*
κόνις, *dust*
κόπτειν, *strike, cut*
κορεννύναι, *satisfy*
κόρθυς, *swathe*
κόριον, dim. ~ κόρη, *girl*
κόρρᾱ, *temple* (of head)
κορυδαλλ-ίς, -ός, κόρυδος, *lark*
κορύνᾱ, *stick*
κορύπτιλος, *given to butting*
κορύπτειν, *butt*
κόρυς, *helmet*
κορυφᾱ́, *peak*
κοσκινόμαντις, *diviner by sieving*
κοσμεῖν, *array*
κόσμος, *order, beauty*
κόσσυφος, *jackdaw*
κότινος, *wild olive*
κοῦρος (κόρος), *boy*
κουροσύνᾱ, *boyishness*
κουροτρόφος, *bringing up boys*

κουφίζειν, *lift*
κοῦφος, *light* (adj.)
κοχλίᾱς, *snail*
κοχυδεῖν, *bubble*
κραδίη = καρδία, *heart*
κράνᾱ (κρήνη), κρᾱνίς (κρη-), *spring*
κράσπεδον, *bit of cloth*
κρᾱτ- ~ κάρᾱ, *head*
κρατερός = καρτερός
κρᾱτήρ, *mixing-bowl* (for wine and water)
κράτιστος = ἄριστος
κρεᾱνομεῖσθαι, *divide up meat*
κρέας, *meat*
κρέμασθαι, *hang* (intr.)
κρήγυος = ἀγαθός
κρηπίς, (military) *boot*
κρίνον, *lily*
κρῑός, *ram*
κροκόεις, *saffron-coloured*
κρόταφος, *temple* (of head)
κροτεῖν, *strike*
κρύβδᾱν (-δην), *secretly*
κρύσταλλος, *crystal*
κρωσσός, *pitcher*
κτέατα (pl.), *possessions*
κτίζειν, *found*
κύαμος, *bean*
κῡάνεος, *blue*
κυανόφρυς, *with dark eyebrows*
κύδιστος, *glorious*
κυδοιμός, *battle*
κῦδος (neut.), *glory*
κυκλάμῑνος, *cyclamen*
κύκνος, *swan*

κυλίειν, *twist*
κυλίνδειν, *roll*
κύλιξ, *cup*
κυλοιδιᾶν, *be hollow-eyed*
κύμῑνον, *cummin*
κυνάς, *dogskin*
κυνοθαρσής, *bold as a bitch*
κυνόσβατος, *briar rose*
κυπαρίσσινος, adj. ~ κυπά-
    ρισσος
κυπάρισσος, *cypress*
κύπειρος, *galingale*
κυρεῖν, *attain*
κύτισος, *medicago*
κῶας, *fleece*
κωμάζειν, *go on a* κῶμος:
    see p. 109
κώμῡς, *bundle*
κῶνος, *cone*
κώρᾱ (κόρη), *girl*
κῶρος = κοῦρος
κωτίλλειν, *chatter*
κωτίλος, *talkative*

λαγωβόλον, *stick*
λαγών, *side (of body)*
λάζ-εσθαι, -υσθαι, *take*
λάθᾱ (λήθη), *forgetfulness*
λάθρη, *unperceived*
λαιμός, *throat*
λᾱΐνος, *stone* (adj.)
λαῖτμα, *gulf, expanse*
λᾱκεῖν (λη-), *crackle*
λαλαγεῖν, *chatter*
λαλεῖν, *talk*
λάλος, *talkative*
λάλλαι, *pebbles*
λαμπάς, *torch*

λάμπειν, *shine*
λᾱνός (λη-), *winepress*
λάξ, *with the heel*
λᾶον (λήϊον), *harvest*
λᾳοτομεῖν (λη-), *reap*
λάρναξ, *chest, box*
λάσιος, *hairy*
λαύρᾱ, *lane*
λάψεσθαι (λη-), fut. ~
    λαμβάνειν
λέαινα, *lioness*
λειμών, *meadow*
λειμώνιος, adj. ~ λειμών
λεῖος, *smooth, amenable*
λέκτρον, *bed*
λεοντομάχᾱς, *fighter against
    lions*
λεόντειος, adj. ~ λέων
λέπαργος, *white*
λεπράς (fem. adj.), *rough*
λεπτός, *thin, fine, small*
λεπτύνειν, *grow thin*
λεπύριον, *rind*
λεύκᾱ, *white poplar*
λευκαίνειν, *whiten*
λεύκιππος, *drawn by white
    horses*
λευκόϊον, (wild) *stock*
λεύσσειν, *see*
λέχος (neut.), *bed*
λήγειν, *end, cease*
λῆν = ἐθέλειν
λιγυρός, λιγύς, *shrill, clear*
λιγύφθογγος, *with clear voice*
λιλαίεσθαι, *desire*
λῑμηρός, *starved*
λίμνᾱ, *lake, marsh*
λιμνᾶτις, fem. adj. ~ λίμνᾱ

λίνον, *thread*

λιπαρός, λιπαρόχροος, *shining*

λῖς (acc. λῖν) = λέων

λισσάς (fem. adj.), *smooth*

λιτανεύειν, *entreat*

λιχμᾶσθαι, *flick the tongue*

λοετρά (λουτρά), pl., *washing-place*

λοιπός, λοίσθιος, *remaining*

λούειν, *wash*

λόφος, *crest*

λόχος, *troop*

λυγίζειν, *throw down*

λυγρός, *deadly*

λυκιδεύς, *wolf-cub*

λύκος, *wolf*

λῡμαίνεσθαι, *maltreat*

λῡπεῖν, *hurt*

λῡπρός, *bitter*

λύσσα, *madness*

λυσσᾶν, *run mad*

λύχνος, *lamp*

λωβᾶσθαι, *damage*

λῶπος (neut.), *cloak*

λώτινος, *a type of wood*

λωτός, *trefoil*

λώων = ἀμείνων

μᾶζα, *loaf* (of barley-flour)

μαζός, *breast, teat*

μαίνεσθαι, *be mad*

μάκαρες (pl.), *blessed*

μακαριστός, *fortunate*

μακαρῖτις (fem.), *dead, 'departed'*

μακέλᾱ, *mattock*

μάκων (μη-), *poppy*

μαλακός, *soft*

μάλευρον, *wheat-flour*

μαλθακός, *soft, effeminate*

μᾶλον (μῆ-), *apple, quince*

μᾱλοπάραυος : see xxvi. 1 n.

μᾱλοφορεῖν (μη-), *carry fruit*

μάνδρᾱ, *byre*

μανίᾱ, *madness*

μανιώδης, *frenzied*

μαννοφόρος, *with markings round the neck*

μάντις, *seer; mantis* (insect)

μᾱρύεσθαι (μη-), *wind* (intr.)

μάσσειν, *knead*

μάσταξ, *morsel*

μαστίζειν, *flog*

μαστός, *udder*

μάτᾱν (-την), *for nothing*

μάχαιρα, *blade*

μᾶχος (μῆ-), *remedy*

μεγαίρειν, *begrudge*

μεγάλοιτος, *doomed*

μεθύειν, *be drunk*

μειδιᾶν, *smile*

μείλιγμα, *affectionate offering*

μειλίζειν, *treat with kindness*

μέλαθρον, *house*

μελάμφυλλος, *with dark leaves*

μελανόχρως, *dark-skinned*

μελεδαίνειν, *care about*

μελεδωνεύς, *guardian*

μέλεσθαι (impers.) = μέλειν, *be of concern to ...*

μέλημα, *concern*

μέλι, *honey*
μελίγᾱρυς(-γη-), *sweet of utterance*
μελίζ-ειν, -εσθαι, *sing, make music*
μελίκτᾱς, *singer*
μελίπνους, *breathing sweet music*
μέλισμα, *song*
μέλισσα, *bee*
μελίτεια, *balm*
μελίχλωρος, *honey-coloured*
μελιχρός, *honey-sweet*
μελλόγαμος, *on the eve of one's wedding*
μέλος (neut.), (1) *limb*; (2) *song*
μέλπ-ειν, -εσθαι, *sing*
μελύδριον, dim. ∼ μέλος (2)
μεμῖχθαι, pass. pf. ∼ μίσγειν
μέμφεσθαι, *criticise*
μεσᾱμβρινός (-ση-), μεσᾱμέριος (-ση-), *mid-day* (adj.)
μέσατος, *halfway*
μεσονύκτιον, *midnight*
μέσσος = μέσος
μέσφα, *until*
μετᾱΐσσειν, *rush after*
μεταμώνιος, *unfulfilled*
μετάρσιος, *up in the air*
μετρεῖν, *measure, count*
μέτρον, *measure, quantity*
μέτωπον, *forehead*
μήσασθαι, aor. ∼ μήδεσθαι, *devise*

μηκάς, *she-goat*
μῆλα (pl.), *flocks*
μήν, *month*
μικκός = μῑκρός
μίμνειν = μένειν
μινύρισμα, *bird-song*
μινυρός, *piping* (adj.)
μίσγειν, *mix*
μῑσεῖν, *hate*
μισθοδότᾱς, *paymaster*
μισθός, *pay*
μνᾶ, *mina* (100 drachmai)
μνᾱστεύειν (μνη-), *woo*
μνᾶστις (μνῆ-), *recollection*
μογεῖν, *labour, suffer*
μοῖρα, *fate*
μόλις, *with difficulty*
μολύνειν, *mess up*
μοῦνος = μόνος
μόρος, *death*
μοσχίον, dim. ∼ μόσχος
μόσχος, *calf*
μουσίζειν, *make music, sing*
μουσικός, *musical*
μουσοποιός, *poet*
μοχθεῖν, μοχθίζειν, *toil*
μόχθος, *toil*
μοχλός, *bar*
μύελος (-λός), *marrow*
μῡθεῖσθαι, μῡθίζειν, *tell*
μῡκᾶσθαι, *low, roar*
μύκημα, *roar*
μύλη, *mill*
μύλλειν, *grind* (slang)
μύρεσθαι, *lament*
μυρίκη, *tamarisk*
μύρμᾱξ (-μηξ), *ant*
μύρον, *perfume*

μύρτος, *myrtle*
μῦς, (1) *mouse, rat;* (2) *muscle*
μυσαρός, *criminal, vile*
μύσταξ, *moustache*
μωμᾶσθαι = μέμφεσθαι
μῶνος = μόνος

ναίειν, *dwell* (*in* . . .)
νάκος (neut.), *goatskin*
νᾶμα, *stream*
νάρκη, *numbness*
νάρκισσος, *daffodil* (and related species)
νᾶσος (νῆ-), *island*
ναύτης, *sailor*
ναυτιλίᾱ, *seafaring*
νεβρίς, *fawnskin*
νεβρός, *fawn*
νεικείειν, *quarrel, contend*
νεῖκος (neut.), *quarrel, contest*
νειοί, *fallow land*
νεῖσθαι, *go, come, return*
νεκρός, νέκυς, *dead body*
νεμεσσᾱτός (-σση-), *hateful*
νέμεσθαι, *graze*
νεόγραπτος, *newly painted*
νεόκλωστος, *newly spun*
νεολαίᾱ, *young people*
νεοσσός, *young chicken*
νεοτευχής, *newly made*
νεότης, *youth*
νεότμᾱτος (-τμη-), *newly cut off*
νεοχμός, *new, strange*
νεύειν, *nod, assent; put the head down, let the head fall*
νεφέλη, *cloud*
νεῖν, *swim*

νέωτα, *next year*
νήλιπος, *barefoot*
νῆμα, *yarn, spinning*
νίζειν, νίπτειν, *wash*
νίσσεσθαι, *go*
νίτρον, *soda*
νιφόεις, *snowy*
νοεῖν, *perceive; have in mind*
νομεύς, *herdsman*
νομεύειν, *pasture*
νόσος, *sickness*
νόσφιν, *away, apart*
νότιος, *damp*
νύμφα, *bride, girl*
νύμφιος, *bridegroom*
νυός, *bride*
νύσσα, *turning-post*
νύσσειν, *stab*
νωμᾶν, *use, move*
νῶς = νόος
νῶτον, *back*

ξανθόθριξ, *yellow-haired*
ξανθός, *yellow*
ξεινήϊον (ξένιον), *gift*
ξε(ι)νίζειν, *entertain*
ξε(ι)νοδόκος, *host*
ξένια (pl.), *hospitality*
ξηρός, *dry*
ξίφος, *sword*
ξόανον, (wooden) *image*
ξουθός, *tuneful*
ξύλον, *wood*
ξυλοχίζεσθαι, *cut* (trees, bushes etc.)
ξῦνός (κοινός), *shared*
ξυρόν, *razor, razor's edge*
ξυστίς, (long) *dress*

ὄγμος, swathe
ὁδίτᾱς, traveller
ὀδούς, tooth
ὀδύρεσθαι, lament
ὄζειν, smell (intr.)
ὄζος, branch
ὀθνεῖος, alien
οἰδεῖν, swell
οἰΐς = ὄϊς
οἰκεῖν, dwell
οἰκέτις, housewife
οἴκησις, house
οἰκτίρμων, compassionate
οἰκωφελίᾱ, housekeeping
οἰναρέον, vine-leaf
οἰνόπεδον, vineyard
οἰνοχόος, cupbearer
οἰνωπός, dark (of face)
ὄϊς, sheep
ὀϊστός, arrow
οἰστρεῖν, be frantic
οἴχεσθαι, be gone
ὄκα = ὅτε
ὀκνηρός, cowering
ὄλβιος, prosperous, fortunate
ὄλβος, wealth, prosperity
ὀλέκειν, destroy
ὀλοίτροχος, smooth, round
ὀλολῡγών, tree-frog
ὀλοός, terrible
ὄλπᾱ, ὄλπις, oil-flask
ὄμαιμος, of the same blood
ὀμαλός, ordinary; alike
ὄμβρος, rain
ὅμῑλος, crowd, throng
ὀμόσ(σ)αι, aor. ∼ ὀμνύναι,
    swear
ὁμοῦ, together

ὀμφαλός, navel
ὄμφαξ, unripe grape
ὅμως, all the same, none the
    less
ὄνᾱσις, enjoyment, profit
ὀνᾱσεῖν fut., ὀνᾶσαι aor. ∼
    ὀνινάναι, bring good to . . .
ὄνειαρ, store, abundance
ὀνομαστί, by name
ὀνομαστός, famous
ὄνυξ, nail
ὄξος (neut.), vinegar
ὀξύς, sharp, keen
ὀξύχειρ, prompt to act
ὀπ-, voice
ὄπᾳ, ὄππη = ὄπη
ὀπᾱδεῖν (-πη-), accompany
ὀπᾱδός, attendant
ὀπαζειν, give
ὄπισθε(ν), behind; later
ὁπλά, hoof
ὅπλα (pl.), tackle; arms
ὁπλότερος, younger
ὁππόκα = ὁπότε
ὀπτᾶν, roast
ὀπτός, roasted
ὀπυίειν, wed
ὀπώρᾱ, autumn; fruit harvest
ὁρᾱτός, visible
ὀρέγειν, give
ὀρέγεσθαι, aim at . . .
ὀρέσθαι, aor. ∼ ὄρνυσθαι,
    come
ὀρεχθεῖν, beat noisily
ὀρθοῦσθαι, get up
ὄρθρος, time just before dawn
ὀριγνᾶσθαι, reach for . . .
ὀρίνειν, anger

ὅρκος, oath
ὁρμαίνειν, try, seek
ὁρμ-ᾶν, -ᾶσθαι, move quickly
ὁρμή, attack
ὅρμος, anchorage
ὁροδαμνίς, bough
ὀρομᾱλίς, wild apple
ὀρούειν, rush
ὄρπᾱξ (-πηξ), branch
ὄρσαι, aor. ~ ὀρνύναι, send
ὀρτάλιχος, chick
ὀρύσσειν, dig up
ὄρφνᾱ, darkness
ὀρχεῖσθαι, dance
ὄρχος, row (of vines)
ὄσσε, eyes
ὁσσίχος, how small
ὀστέον, ὀστίον, bone
οὔατα (ὦτα), ears
οὐδάλλος, neither
οὐδαμά, never
οὐδέποκα = οὐδέποτε
οὐδός, threshold
οὖλος, woolly
οὔνομα = ὄνομα
οὖρος, (favourable) wind
οὖρος (neut.) = ὄρος
ὀφείλειν, owe
ὄφελος, advantage
ὄφις, snake
ὄφρα = ἵνα
ὀφρῦς, eyebrow
ὀχεύς, bolt
ὀχεύειν, mount, cover
  (sexually)
ὄχθη, bank
ὄχλος, crowd
ὄχνᾱ, pear

ὀψᾱμάτᾱς (-μήτης), reaping
  until late
ὀψίγονος, young

πᾷ = ποῖ, ποῦ
πᾳ (πη) = που
πᾱγά (πηγή), spring
παγῆναι, pass. aor ~
  πηγνύναι,
πᾱγνύμεν (πηγνύναι), fix,
  stiffen
παιδεύεσθαι, have ... educated
παιδίον, dim. ~ παῖς
παιδογόνος, begetting children
παίζειν, play; joke
παίχνιον (παιγν-), game,
  trick
πᾱκτά (πηκτή), cream-cheese
παλαίστρᾱ, wrestling-school
παλίγκοτος, spiteful
παλίουρος, a species of
  thorn
πάλλεσθαι, jump, skip
πάμμαχος, all-in wrestler and
  boxer
πᾱνίζεσθαι (πη-), wind
  (thread)
πανόλβιος, blessed
παντᾷ (πάντη), everywhere,
  every way
πάντοθε(ν), on every side,
  from everywhere
παντοῖος, of every kind
πάντοσε, everywhere
πάντως, come what may
παπταίνειν, peer, spy
πάρ = παρά
παραισθάνεσθαι, notice

παρακεκλίσθαι (pf.), *lie beside* . . .

πάρᾱρος (παράορος), *madman*

παρατρέπεσθαι, *divert from purpose*

παραψύχεσθαι, *console*

παρελᾶν (-ελαύνειν), *drive past*

πάρεργος, *of little importance*

παρέρπειν, *creep up on* . . .

παρήϊον, *cheek*

παρθενική, παρθένος, *girl, virgin*

παρισοῦν, *compare*

παρκύπτειν (παρακ-), *peep*

πάσασθαι, aor. ∼ πεπᾶσθαι

πάσσαλος, *peg*

πάσσειν, *sprinkle*

πάσσων, comp. ∼ παχύς, *sturdy*

παστάς, (bed-)*room*

παταγεῖν, *roar*

πατάσσειν, *hit, strike*

πατεῖν, *tread, trample*

πατρίς, *native land*

πατρῷος, πατρώϊος, adj. ∼ πατήρ

πᾶχυς (πῆ-), *forearm*

πεδά = μετά

πεδίον, πέδον, *plain*

πεζᾷ (-ζῇ), *on foot*

πεῖ = ποῦ

πεινᾶν, *be hungry*

πεῖρα, *attempt*

πειρᾶσθαι, *attempt*

πέκειν, *shear*

πέλαγος, *sea*

πέλ-ειν, -εσθαι, *be*

πέλεκυς, *axe*

πέλλᾱ, *pail*

πέλλος, *black*

πελώριος, *enormous*

πελώριστος : see *Ep.* 18.5 n.

πέλωρον, *monster*

πένεσθαι, *prepare*

πενέσται, *serfs*

πενθερός, *father-in-law*

πένθημα, πένθος (neut.), *grief*

πενίᾱ, *poverty*

πεπαίνειν, *warm*

πεπαίτερος, *riper, softer*

πεπᾶσθαι (κεκτῆσθαι, pf.), *possess*

πέπλος, *dress, robe*

πεπρωμένος, *fated*

πέρᾱν, *beyond*

περᾶν, *go in ; go through*

περιδεδρομέναι, pf. ∼ περιτρέχειν, *surround*

πέριξ, *around*

περιξεῖν, *roll smooth*

περιπεπτάσθαι (pf.), *be spread around*

περίπλεκτος, *weaving* (metaph.) *this way and that*

περίσπλαγχνος, *wise*

περισσός, (1) *exceptional*, (2) *remaining*

περισταδόν, *around*

περιστέλλειν, *protect*

περίφρων, *wise*

περκνός, *dusky*

περονᾶσθαι, *pin*

περονᾱτρίς (-νη-), *dress*

πέρυσιν, *last year*
πέταλον, *leaf*
πεταννύναι, *spread open*
πετεηνός (-την-), *winged*
πέτεσθαι, *fly*
πέτευρον, *perch*
πέτρᾱ, *rock*
πέτρος, *stone*
πεύθεσθαι, *learn of* ...
πεύκη, *pine-tree*
πηοί, *kinsmen*
πήποκα = πώποτε
πήρᾱ, *bag*; and see xv. 19 n.
πιάζειν (πιέ-), *grasp*
πῑαίνεσθαιι, (*grow and*) *ripen*
πῑδαξ, *spring*
πίθος, *jar*
πικραίνεσθαι, *lose one's temper*
πικρός, *short-tempered*
πίσσα, *pitch*
πιστεύειν, *believe*
πίτυλος, *rain of blows*
πίτυς, *pine-tree*
πίειρα, fem. ~ πίων
πίων, *rich, fertile*
πλάθανον, *kneading-tray*
πλακερός, *broad*
πλάν = πλήν
πλανᾶσθαι, *stray*
πλάσσειν, *mould, train*
πλατάγημα, *smack*
πλαταγώνιον, *petal*
πλατάνιστος, πλάτανος, *plane-tree*
πλατειάζειν, *talk with a broad accent*
πλᾱτίον = πλησίον
πλατύς, *broad*

πλέγμα, *plaiting*
πλεῖν, *sail*
πλεῖος (πλέως), *full*
πλέκειν, *plait*
πλέος = πλεῖος
πλευρά, *side*
πλευστικός, *for sailing*
πληγή, *blow*
πληγῆναι, pass. aor. ~ πλήσσειν
πλήθειν, *be full*
πλήρης, *full*
πληροῦν, *fill*
πλήσσειν, *strike*
πλίνθος, *brick*
πλοκαμίς, *curly hair*
πλόος (πλοῦς), *voyage*
πλοῦτος, *wealth*
πλύνειν, *wash*
πνεῖν, *breathe; smell of* ...
πνο(ι)ή, *breath; breeze*
ποδεών, *end* (of animal-skin)
ποθεῖν, *desire*
ποθεινός, *longed-for, welcome*
ποθέρπειν (προσ-), *come*
ποθέσπερος (προσ-), *towards evening* (adj.)
ποθίκειν = προσιέναι
ποθορῆν = προσορᾶν
πόθος, *desire*
ποίᾱ, *grass*
ποικίλος, *coloured, patterned*
ποικιλότραυλος, *warbling*
ποιμαίνειν, *look after*
ποιμενικός, adj. ~ ποιμήν
ποιμήν, *shepherd*
ποίμνᾱ, *flock*
ποίμνιον, dim. ~ ποίμνᾱ

ποιολογεῖν, *cut grass*
πόκα, ποκα = πότε, ποτε
ποκίζεσθαι, *shear*
πόκος, *fleece*
πολεμίζειν, *war against* . . .
πολεμιστής, *warrior*
πολιός, *grey*
πολύγναμπτος, *curly*
πολυδένδρεος (-δρος), *with many trees*
πολύϊδρις, *skilled*
πολύκαρπος, *with abundant fruit*
πολύκληρος, *wealthy*
πολυμήχανος, *resourceful*
πολύμοχθος, *wrought with great labour*
πολύμῡθος, *loquacious*
πολύνᾱος, *worshipped in many temples*
πολύσταχυς, *giver of abundant grain*
πολυχανδής, *capacious*
πολύχορδος, *of many strings*
πολυώνυμος, *called by many names*
πομπά, *procession*
πομπεύειν, *go in a procession*
πον-εῖν, -εῖσθαι, *make, labour at* . . .
πονηρός, *bad*
πόνος, *toil*
πόντος, *sea*
ποππύζειν, ποππυλιάζειν, *make a noise with the lips*
πορθμεύς, *ferryman*
πόρρω, *far*
πόρτις, *calf*

πορφύρεος (-ροῦς), *red, purple*
πορφύρειν, *become red*
πόσις, *drinking*
πόσσος = πόσος
ποτί, πότ = πρός
ποτάγειν = προσάγειν
ποταείδειν (προσάδειν), *sing to* . . .
ποταμείβεσθαι (προσ-), *reply*
ποταμέλγειν (προσ-), *milk in addition*
ποταυλεῖν (προσ-), *pipe to* . . .
ποτᾱῷος (προση-), *towards the east*
ποτερίζειν (προσ-), *contend against* . . .
ποτέχειν (προσ-), *pay attention*
ποτιβλέπειν (προσ-), *look at* . . .
ποτιδέρκεσθαι (προσ-), *look at* . . .
ποτιδεύεσθαι (προσδεῖσθαι), *need*
ποτίζειν, *water* (animals)
ποτιθιγγάνειν (προσ-), *touch*
ποτικιγκλίζεσθαι (προσ-), *move the tail in unison*
ποτίκρᾱνον (προσ-), *cushion*
ποτιλέγεσθαι (προσ-), *speak to* . . .
ποτιτιθέμεν = προστιθέναι
πότν(ι)α, *mistress, queen*
ποτόζειν (προσ-), *smell* (intr.)

ποτόν, *drink*
πότορθρος (προσ-), *towards dawn* (adj.)
πότος, *drinking-party*
πρᾶν (πρώην), *the other day*
πρᾶτος = πρῶτος
πρᾱτοτόκος (πρω-), *which has borne young for the first time*
πρέπειν, *suit* (impers.), *be fitting*
πρέσβυς, *old man*
πρεσβῦτις, *old woman*
πρῖνος, *ilex*
πρόᾱν = πρᾶν
προβόλαιος, *held in front*
προβολή, *guard* (in boxing)
προγένειος, *with projecting beard*
προγίγνεσθαι, *come forth*
προδεικνύναι, *show as a feint*
πρόθυρον, *street door*
προϊέναι, *put forth*
προλέγειν, *choose, pick*
προσπτύσσεσθαι, *embrace*
πρόσσω = πόρρω
προστιθέναι, *add*
πρόσωπον, *face*
προφέρειν, *excel*
πρόφρων, *glad*
πρύμνα, *poop*
πρωϊζός, *early*
πρῶξ, *dewdrop*
πρώρᾱθεν, *from the prow*
πταίειν, *strike* (intr.), *collide*
πτελέᾱ, *elm*
πτέρις, *fern*
πτέρυξ, *wing*

πτολίεθρον, *town*
πτόλις = πόλις
πτύειν, *spit*
πτύον, *winnowing-fan*
πτώξ, *hare*
πῡγίζειν, *bugger*
πύγισμα, (act of) *buggery*
πυγμάχος, *boxer*
πυγμή, *fist*
πυθμήν, *bottom*
πυκάζειν, *cover*
πυκ(ι)νός, *dense*
πύκτᾱς, *boxer*
πύματος, *furthest*
πύξ, *with the fist*
πύξινος, *boxwood* (adj.)
πυρά, *pyre*
πύργος, *tower*
πυρεῖα (pl.), *firesticks*
πυροῦν, *fumigate*
πυρρίχος, πυρρός, πυρσός, *reddish, fiery*
πώγων, *beard*
πῶλος, *colt*
πῶμα, *drink*
πωτᾶσθαι, *fly*

ῥᾱγίζειν, *despoil*
ῥαδινός, *slim*
ῥάμνος, *thorn*
ῥέζειν, *perform; sacrifice*
ῥεῖθρον, *stream*
ῥεῖν, *flow*
ῥῆμα, *utterance, word*
ῥιπτεῖν = ῥίπτειν, *throw*
ῥίς, *nose, nostril*
ῥοδόεις, adj. ~ ῥόδον

ῥόδον, *rose*
ῥοδόπᾱχυς (-πη-), *with rosy arms*
ῥοδόχρως, *rose-coloured*
ῥοικός, *curved*
ῥόμβος, *bull-roarer*
ῥόος (ῥοῦς), *stream*
ῥόπαλον, *club*
ῥύεσθαι, *rescue*
ῥυθμός, *manner, behaviour*
ῥύπον, *muck*
ῥωγάς (fem. adj.), *jagged*

σᾱκίτᾱς (σηκίτης), *stall-fed animal*
σάκος (neut.), *shield*
σᾱκός (ση-), *stall; precinct*
σᾶμα (σῆ-), *tomb*
σάμερον (σή-, τή-), *today*
σαόφρων (σωφ-), *dutiful*
σάρξ, *flesh*
σαύρᾱ, σαῦρος, *lizard*
σέβας, *veneration*
σέβεσθαι, *venerate*
σεί-ειν, -εσθαι, *shake, brandish*
σέλας, *flame*
σέλῑνον, *parsley or wild celery*
σεσᾱρέναι (-ση-),
   pf. ~ σαίρειν, *grin*
σημαίνειν, *signify*
σθένος (neut.), *strength*
σία (pl.), *a kind of reed*
σῑγά, *silence*
σιγᾶν, *be silent*
σιδήρε(ι)ος (σιδηροῦς), *iron (adj.)*
σίζειν, *whistle*

σῑμός, *snub-nosed*
σίνεσθαι, *plunder*
σῑτίζεσθαι, *feed on . . .*
σῖτος, *grain*
σίττα, *a cry to scare sheep or goats*
σκαιός, *left*
σκαίρειν, *gambol*
σκᾱνά (σκηνή), *shop*
σκαπάνᾱ, *spade*
σκαφίς, *cup*
σκέλος (neut.), *leg*
σκιά, *shade*
σκιᾶν, *overshadow*
σκιαρός (-ιε-), *shady*
σκιάς, *bower*
σκίλλα, *squill*
σκιρτᾶν, *ship about*
σκληρός, *hard*
σκνῑφαῖος, *in the evening*
σκοπιά, *peak, crag*
σκοπός, *guard; target*
σκύζεσθαι, *be angry, be gloomy*
σκύλαξ, *dog*
σκύμνος, *cub*
σκύφος (neut.), *bowl*
σκώψ, *a species of owl*
σμᾶμα (σμῆ-), *soap*
σμᾶνος (σμῆ-), (neut.), *swarm, hive*
σοβεῖν, *drive away*
σόφισμα, *trick*
σπεῖρα, *coil*
σπένδειν, *pour a libation*
σπέσθαι, aor. ~ ἕπεσθαι
σπεύδειν, *hasten; exert oneself*
σπῆλυγξ, *cave*
σπιλάς, *rock*

σπλάγχνα (pl.), *vitals*
σποδός, *ash*
σπόρος, *sowing*
σπουδᾷ (-δῇ), *carefully, seriously*
στάζειν, *pour, drop*
σταθμά (pl.), *doorposts*
σταφυλή, *cluster* (of grapes)
στάχυς, *ear* (of grain)
στέγος (neut.), *roof, house*
στε(ι)νός, *confined, restricted*
στείχειν, *go*
στένειν, *moan*
στερεός, *firm*
στέρνον, *breast*
στεφανηφόρος, *crowned*
στέφανος, *wreath, crown*
στέφειν, *wreath, crown*
στῆθος (neut.), *breast*
στήλη, *(grave)stone*
στιβαρός, *stout, strong*
στιβάς, *bed* (of leaves, etc.)
στίλβειν, *shine*
στόμα, *mouth*
στορ(εν)νύναι, *spread*
στρέφειν, *turn, twist*
στυγνός, *gloomy*
στωμύλος, *talkative*
σύκινος, *of fig-wood*
σῦκον, *fig*
συλλέγειν, *collect*
συμβαίνειν, *happen*
συμβλητός, *comparable*
συμπαίζειν, *sport with . . .*
συμπλέκειν, *weave together*
συμπλήγδην, *crashing together*
συμφλέγειν, *burn up*

σύμφορος, *useful*
συμφύρειν, *crush into a mess*
συναγείρειν, *assemble*
συναγείρεσθαι, *pull oneself together*
συνάγειν, *drive together; run together* (intr.)
συναείδειν (-νᾴ-), *join in singing*
συναλοιᾶν, *pound to pieces*
συνδρομάδες (fem. pl. adj.), *moving together*
συνέπεσθαι, *accompany*
συνερείδειν, *strike together*
συνιζάνειν, *collapse, shrink*
συνομᾶλιξ (-μῆ-), *of the same age*
συνταράσσειν, *throw into turmoil*
σύρειν, *trail*
σῦριγξ, *pan-pipes*
σῦρίζειν, *play pan-pipes*
σῦρικτᾶς, *player of pan-pipes*
σφαιροῦν, *swell firmly*
σφάλλειν, *trip, throw*
σφάξ (σφήξ), *wasp*
σφίγγειν, *tie*
σφῦρήλατος, *made with a hammer*
σφυρόν, *ankle*
σφύζειν, *throb*
σχαδών, *honeycomb*
σχεδίᾱ, *raft*
σχεδόν, *near, nearly*
σχέτλιος, *unhappy*
σχῆμα, *dress*
σχίζαι (pl.), *firewood*
σχίζειν, *split, tear*

σχῖνος, *mastic*
σχοῖνος, *reed*
σῴζειν, *keep safe*
σωρός, *heap*
σωτήρ, *saviour*

τᾷδε = τῇδε = δεῦρο
τάκειν (τή-), *melt, consume*
ταλαεργός, *enduring, hardy*
ταλαρίσκος, dim. ∼
    τάλαρος
τάλαρος, *basket*
ταλασίφρων, *strong, hard-working*
ταμ-εῖν, -έσθαι, aor. ∼
    τέμν-ειν, -εσθαι, *cut*
τάμισος, *rennet*
τᾶμος = τῆμος = τότε
τᾶνίκα = τότε
τάπης, *coverlet, blanket*
ταράσσειν, *disturb, throw into confusion*
ταρσός, *cheese-rack*
ταῦρος, *bull*
ταχινός, *quick, flighty*
τάχος (neut.), *speed*
ταχυπειθής, *credulous*
ταχύπωλος, *rider*
τεθᾱλώς (-θη-), pf. ∼
    θάλλειν
τέθριππον, *team of four horses*
τεῖδε = ἐνθάδε, δεῦρο
τέκος (neut.), *child*
τέκτων, *joiner, builder*
τελαμών, *sword-belt*
τελέθειν = εἶναι
τεθλασμένος, pf. part ∼
    θλᾶν, *crush*

τέμπεα (-πη, pl.), *woods*
τεός = σός
τέρας, *portent, miracle*
τέρπειν, *delight*
τερπνός, *delightful*
τέρψις, *delight*
τέτορες = τέσσαρες
τετράκις, *four times*
τέττιξ, *cicada*
τεύχεα (-χη pl.), *arms, weapons*
τεύχειν, *make, construct*
τετύχθαι, pass. pf. ∼
    τεύχειν
τηλεθᾶν, *flourish*
τηλέφιλον : see III.29 n.
τηλόθεν, *from far away*
τηλόθι, *far away*
τημόσδε = τότε
τηνεῖ = ἐκεῖ, ἐκεῖσε
τῆνος = ἐκεῖνος
τηνῶ(θε) = ἐκεῖθεν
τηρεῖν, *watch*
τίειν, *honour*
τίλλειν, aor. τῖλαι, *pluck to pieces*
τιμᾱτός (-μη-), *valued*
τίν = σοί (and = σέ in XI)
τινάσσ-ειν, -εσθαι, *brandish*
τιτύσκεσθαι, *aim*
τόθι = οὗ, *where*
τοῖχος, *wall; side* (of ship)
τόκα = τότε
τοκάς (fem. adj.), *which has borne cubs*
τοκεύς, *parent*
τολμᾶν, *venture*
τομά, *cut end*

τοσσῆνος = τοσοῦτος
τουτεῖ = ἐνθάδε
τουτόθε, τουτῶθεν = ἐνθένδε
τραγείᾱ, *goatskin*
τραγίσκος, dim. ~ τράγος
τράγος, (*billy-*)*goat*
τράπεζα, *table*
τράφειν (τρέ-), *bring up, look after*
τριᾱκοντάζυγος, *having thirty benches*
τρίβειν, *crush, rub, wear out*
τρίοδος, *road junction*
τρίπους, *tripod*
τρισκαιδεκάπηχυς, *thirteen cubits high*
τρισκελής, *three-legged*
τρισσοί, *three*
τριφίλητος, *dearly loved*
τρίχες, pl. ~ θρίξ
τρομεῖν, *tremble at . . .*
τροφός, *nurse*
τροχός, *wheel*
τρῡγών, *dove*
τρύζειν, *murmur*
τρύξ, *lees*
τρῡπᾶν, *trip*
τρυφάλεια, *helmet*
τρύχνος : see x.37 n.
τρώγειν, *eat, nibble*
τρώξιμος, *eatable*
τύ = σύ
τυ = σε
τυίδε = ἐκεῖσε
τυκτός, *worked*
τυλοῦν, *harden*
τυτθός, *little*

τυχθῆναι, pass. aor. ~ τεύχειν

ὑακίνθινος, adj. ~ ὑάκινθος
ὑάκινθος : see x.28 n.
ὑβός, *bent over, hump-backed*
ὑγιής, *sound, healthy*
ὑγρός, *liquid, watery, supple*
ὑδάτινος (ὑ-), *translucent*
ὕειν, *rain*
ὕλᾱ, *wood, forest*
ὑλακτεῖν, *bark*
ὑμεναιοῦν, *marry*
ὑπακούειν, *listen; respond*
ὑπᾱνέμιος (-πη-), (*borne*) *on the wind*
ὑπαντᾶν, *meet*
ὑπάρχειν, *provide*
ὑπείροχος, *pre-eminent*
ὑπένερθεν, *below*
ὑπεξαναβαίνειν, *step back*
ὑπεραχθής, *heavy-laden*
ὕπερθε, *above*
ὑπέροπλος, *mighty*
ὑπερόπτης, *contemptuous*
ὑπερούριος, *beyond the boundaries*
ὑπερπᾱδᾶν (-πη-), *jump over*
ὑπερπωτᾶσθαι, *fly above*
ὑπέρτερος, *superior*
ὑπερφίαλος, *confident*
ὑπήνεμος, *sheltered from the wind*
ὑπῑάχειν, *resound*
ὑποδέχεσθαι, *welcome, receive*
ὑποκάρδιος, *beneath the heart*
ὑποκόλπιος, *held in embrace*
ὑποκρίνεσθαι, *explain*

ὑπομάσσειν, smear
ὑπομένειν, withstand
ὑποτιθέναι, put on
ὑποτίτθιος, nursling
ὑποφαίνειν, reflect
ὑποφήτης, interpreter
ὕπτιος, on one's back
ὑπωρόφιος, under the roof
ὗς, pig
ὑσμίνη, battle
ὑφᾱγεῖσθαι (-φη-), lead
    unobtrusively
ὑφῑέναι, put under
ὑφορβός, swineherd
ὑψηλός, high
ὑψόθε(ν), from a height
ὑψόθι, high, at the top

φαγεῖν (aor.), eat
φακός, lentils
φάλης, phallus
φᾱμᾱ (φήμη), report, fame
φάρυγξ, throat
φάσγανον, sword
φάσσα, dove
φάτνη, manger
φέγγος (neut.), light
φείδεσθαι, spare
φέρβειν, feed
φέρτερος, superior
φθάνειν, anticipate
φθέγγεσθαι, utter, cry, sing
φθίμενος, dead
φθονερός, malevolent
φθόρος, waste, plague
φιλάοιδος, lover of song
φιλάργυρος, avaricious
φιλέρῑθος, devoted to spinning

φιλεχθής, quarrelsome
φίλημα, kiss
φιλικός, lover's
φιλοίφᾱς, randy
φιλοκέρδεια, avarice
φιλοκέρτομος, malicious
φιλόμουσος, lover of the arts
φιλόξε(ι)νος, hospitable
φιλοποίμνιος, friend of the
    flocks
φιλόστοργος, loving
φιλότης, love, affection
φίλτρον, (magic) herb
φίλυπνος, fond of sleep
φλᾶν (lit. crush), castrate
φλέγεσθαι, blaze, blush
φλιᾱ, lintel
φλίβειν (θλ-), squeeze, squash
φλόγεος, flaming
φλογερός, burning hot
φλοιός, bark
φοβερός, formidable
φοινῑκεος (-κοῦς), red
φοινικόλοφος, with red crest
φοῖνιξ, red
φοίνιος, (blood-)red
φοιτᾶν, go (frequently)
φονεύς, killer
φόρμιγξ, lyre
φραγμός, fence
φρῑμάσσεσθαι, snort
φρίσσειν, ripple
φρουρεῖν, guard
φρύγειν, roast
φυγάς, fugitive
φυή, beauty (of body)
φῡκιόεις, covered with seaweed
φῡκίον, seaweed

φῦκος, (red or purple) *dye*
φυλάσσειν, *guard*
φυλάσσεσθαι, *beware of . . .,*
  be careful of. . .
φύλλον, *leaf*
φύλοπις, *battle*
φῦσᾶν, *blow*
φυτόν, *plant*
φυτοσκάφος, *digger*
φωλάς (fem. adj.), *lurking*
φωλεύειν, *lurk*
φωνεῖν, *speak, utter*

χανεῖν, aor. ∼ χάσκειν, *gape*
χαῖται, *hair*
χάλαζα, *hail*
χάλκε(ι)ος, adj. ∼χαλκός
χαλκεοθώρηξ, *wearing a*
  brazen breastplate
χαλκεοκάρδιος, *having a*
  heart of bronze
χαλκέον, (bronze) *gong*
χαλκός, *bronze*
χαμαί, *on the ground*
χαμεύνᾱ (-να, -νη), χαμευ-
  νίς, *bed (on the ground)*
χανδάνειν, *grasp*
χᾱός, *noble*
χαρίεις, *attractive, beautiful,*
  handsome
χαρίζεσθαι, *be generous to . . .,*
  show affection for . . .
χασμᾶσθαι, *gape*
χεῖλος (neut.), *lip, rim*
χεῖμα, *winter*
χειμάρρους, *swollen* (of a
  river)
χειμών, *winter*

χελῑδόνιον, dim. ∼ χελῑδών
χελῑδών, *swallow*
χερείων (χείρων), *inferior*
χέρσος, *dry land*
χεῖν, *pour*
χηλός, *chest, box*
χθόνιος, adj. ∼ χθών
χῑλιάς, *thousand*
χίμαιρα, (nanny-) *goat*
χίμαρος, *kid*
χιτών, *tunic*
χιτώνιον, dim. ∼ χιτών
χιών, *snow*
χλαῖνα, *cloak, blanket*
χλαμυδηφόρος, *wearing a*
  (military) cloak
χλωρός, *fresh, green, young*
χοιράς, *rock*
χοῖρος, *pig*
χολᾱ, *bile, anger*
χορεύειν, *dance*
χορίον, *hide*
χόρτος, *hay*
χρήζειν, *want*
χρήσιμος, *useful*
χρησμός, *oracle*
χρίεσθαι, *anoint oneself*
χροιά, *colour*
χροΐζεσθαι, *cuddle up to . . .*
χρόνιος, *after a long time*
  (adj.)
χρύσε(ι)ος, *golden*
χωλός, *lame*
χῶρος, *place*

ψε = σφε = αὐτούς
ψιθυρίζειν, *whisper*
ψιθύρισμα, *whispering*

ψῦχρός, *cold*
ψύχεσθαι, *become cold*

ᾠδοποιός, *poet*
ᾠζῡρέ, a term of commiseration
ὠθεῖν, aor. ὦσαι, *push, drive*
ὠκύς, *swift*
ὠμοπλάτᾱ, *shoulder-blade*
ὦμος, *shoulder*
ὠμός, *unripe*

ὠμοφάγος, *eater of raw meat*
ὦν = οὖν
ὦνος, *price*
ὡραῖος, *beautiful*
ὥριος, *favourable*
ὥριος, *at the right season* (adj.)
ὦρος (neut.) = ὄρος
ὠρύεσθαι, *howl*
ὡς sometimes = οὗ, *where*
ὧς = οὖς, *ear*
ὤφελ-, *if only . . . had . . .*

Indexes

I GREEK

317

II ENGLISH

◆ **Beginning** ◆ **Intermediate** ◆ **Advanced**
Textbooks and Audiotapes
from Bolchazy-Carducci Publishers

Beginning Text

The Wars of Greece and Persia
by Herodotus
Edited by W. D. Lowe

SELECTIONS IN ATTIC GREEK FROM
HERODOTUS

THE WARS OF GREECE
AND PERSIA

"In Lowe's selections the student is able to begin an easy and enter-
taining entry into Attic Greek... the passages from Greek history
complement the ancient history studies and add a certain element of
prestige to a student who is reading the `original'."
— Frank P. Raispis
St. Ignatius College Prep

The writings of the "father of history" are brought to life vividly in this
excellent introduction to Herodotus. The tales of this master storyteller
are presented in simplified language that moves the reader along at a com-
fortable, yet progressively more demanding, pace. The book features stu-
dent notes, vocabulary and illustrations.
Paperback, ISBN#: 0-86516-054-6; Order #: 054-6; Price: $10.00

Beginning Text

Vera Historia
by Lucian
Edited by G. S. Jerram

LUCIANI
VERA HISTORIA

"Ideal for a second-year course in classical Greek. Lucian's prose style
and use of Attic Greek parallel that of early Plato, so teachers may
consider this text as a substitute or counterpoise to Socratic dialogues."
— Casey Fredericks
The Classical Journal

A reprint of the second edition of a Victorian English-
annotated edition of *Vera Historia*, this is the only English-language com-
mentary on that work in print. The notes are helpful in explicating the
language and Lucian's references. Includes an introduction, vocabulary
and illustrations.
Paperback, ISBN#: 0-86516-240-9; Order #: 240-9; Price: $6.00

Intermediate Text
Apology
by Plato
Edited by James J. Helm

"The commentary is splendid and excellently meets the needs of students." —F. Carter Philips, Vanderbilt University

"[the] notes are lucid, helpful and almost always to the point: in most cases they avoid the sort of artificial erudition that characterizes many other commentaries." —Brent W. Sinclair, University of Manitoba

Extensive notes and enlightening commentary make this an ideal text to aid students in their appreciation and understanding of Plato's *Apology*.
Paperback, ISBN#: 0-86516-005-8; Order #: 005-8; Price: $10.00

Intermediate Text
Iphigenia in Tauris
by Euripides
Edited by M. Platnauer

"This artful and lively drama provides an excellent introduction to Euripides. It is full of his characteristic dramaturgy... and great Euripidean themes like illusion vs. reality, the nature of Hellenism and the irrationalities of mythology." —Richard Moorton, Connecticut College

A complex and thoughtful work that further illustrates Euripides' mastery of the drama, this reprint of a 1938 Oxford edition is the only English-language edition in print with full commentary. It includes a brief introduction, 120 pages of commentary and a clear, line-by-line metrical schema for the play.
Paperback, ISBN#: 0-86516-060-0; Order #: 060-0; Price: $13.00

Intermediate Text
Civil Wars, Book I
by Appian
Edited by J. L. Strachan-Davidson

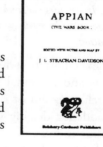

Appian's writings offer the only account of events during the epoch between Polybius and Cicero, and *Civil Wars* covers the period from the reign of Tiberius Gracchus to the first consulship of Pompey and Crassus. This reprint of the Oxford edition features Greek text and notes.
Paperback, ISBN#: 0-86516-021-X; Order #: 021-X; Price: $9.00

Intermediate Text
Meleager: The Poems
Edited by Jerry Clack

As a poet and an editor of an anthology that conveyed the poetry of many Hellenistic epigrammatists to modern times, Meleager is an important literary figure, and this text provides an excellent introduction to his poetry. The total of 132 epigrams are encompassed in a little more than 800 lines, allowing a complete reading within a reasonable time. The volume includes notes, vocabulary, and proper name and epigram source indices.

Paperback, ISBN#: 0-86516-254-9; Order #: 254-9; Price: $18.00

Advanced Text
Thucydides, Book II
Edited by E. C. Marchant and Thomas Wiedemann

This edition includes Greek text and apparatus criticus, an extensive introduction that offers historical information about Thucydides and his time, a list of essential dates and bibliography.

Paperback, ISBN#: 0-86516-041-4; Order #: 041-4; Price: $16.00

Advanced Text
Life of Pericles
by Plutarch
Edited by Hubert Ashton Holden

"This commentary can be used with profit by the advanced student of Greek. It provides vocabulary assistance with some of the glosses in Latin; parallel Greek passages are cited throughout; cruxes receive critical elucidation." —Gail Smith, *The Classical Outlook*

This excellent text features an extensive apparatus criticus and marginal notes that enhance the student's understanding of Plutarch's account of Pericles' life. The introduction concludes with a valuable addenda dealing with textual matters. The book includes vocabulary and four indices.

Paperback, ISBN#: 0-86516-026-0; Order #: 026-0; Price: $12.00

The Living Voice of Greek Literature

Dramatic Readings by Stephen G. Daitz

Pronunciation and Reading of Ancient Greek: A Practical Guide

Two cassettes contain explanations of the pronunciation of the vowels and consonants and the pitch accents of ancient Greek and also present a method for reading Greek poetry that integrates the pitch accents with the rhythm based upon syllabic quantity. An accompanying booklet offers additional pronunciation guidance.
Order #:23660; Price: $29.95

Recital of Ancient Greek Poetry

These four cassettes contain selections from the *Iliad*, the *Odyssey*, the lyric poets and Greek tragedies and comedies. Each is read first in English and then in the original Greek. An accompanying booklet contains an introduction and complete Greek text.
Order #: 28600; Price: $48.00

The Iliad

The Greek text and English translation is covered in six cassettes and one booklet for each part.
Part I, Books 1-6, Order #: S23810; Price: $59.50
Part II, Books 7-12, Order #: S23817; Price: $59.50
Part III, Books 13-18, Order #: S23821; Price: $59.50
Part IV, Books 19-24, Order #: S23830; Price: $59.50

Each of the following programs includes two cassette recordings of the text read in ancient Greek and an accompanying booklet with complete Greek text and facing English translations.

Selections from the Greek Orators

Speeches of Gorgias, Pericles, Lysias, Isokrates and Demosthenes are read on the cassette.
Order #: 23690; Price: $29.95

Euripides' Hekabe

Order #: 23650; Price: $29.95

Aristophanes' Birds

Order #: 23670; Price: $29.95

Plato's Portrait of Sokrates

Includes excerpts from Plato's *Apology*, *Krito* and *Phaedo*.
Order #: 23695; Price: $29.95